NEWMAN THE ORATORIAN

In Memoriam

Gerard Tracey
(1954–2003)
For many years Archivist and Librarian
of the Birmingham Oratory and
Editor of the *Letters and Diaries of John Henry Newman.*
His scholarly expertise and knowledge of Newman and his age
were legendary.
He never hesitated to share his extraordinary learning with all
who consulted him.
His untimely death was a great loss to friends and scholars alike
from around the world.

Newman The Oratorian

His unpublished Oratory Papers

edited
with an Introductory Study on
the Continuity between his
Anglican and his Catholic Ministry

by
PLACID MURRAY, O.S.B., D.D.
Monk of Glenstal

GRACEWING

First published in 1968 by Fowler Wright Books Ltd

This edition published in 2004
by
Gracewing
2 Southern Avenue, Leominster
Herefordshire HR6 0QF

De approbanda dissertatione, ad ordinem theologorum retulerunt:

Augustinus Mayer, O.S.B.
Raphael Schulte, O.S.B.

Roma, die 14 Februarii 1968

Imprimi potest: ✠ Augustine O'Sullivan, O.S.B.
Abbas
Glenstal, die 23 Novembris 1968

Nihil obstat: John Hackett
Censor Deputatus

Imprimatur: ✠ Thomas Morris
Archiepiscopus Cassiliensis
et Imolacensis
die 2 Decembris 1968

ISBN 0 85244 632 2

SANCTI PHILIPPI
APVD BIRMINGHAM
DOMVI
HOC DE PATREFAMILIAS OPVS
PER IV IAM LVSTRA FREQVENS HOSPES
GRATO ANIMO DEDICAT
SCRIPTOR

CONTENTS

NEWMAN THE PRIEST

Being a Study of the Continuity between his Anglican and his Catholic Ministry.

The Oratory a central, not a peripheral feature in Newman's vocation as a priest—Newman and Faber in the Oratory—(*a*) The scope and location of the first Oratory in England—(*b*) The Oratorian idea of 'The House'—(*c*) Birmingham, London and the 'Ordo honestior'—(*d*) Newman's estrangement from Faber and the London Oratory—The relatively restricted growth of the Oratory in England—The Oratory as Newman's priestly vocation.

'Preservation of Type' as a test of true development—Newman did not 'newmanize' St Philip Neri—St Philip, 'Forma Senectutis' and 'Vir Prisci Temporis'—Newman's Oratory true to the Italian, not to the French type, even in its intellectual work.

The central theme of Newman's Oratorian spirituality: Perfection through 'unvowed' obedience in community life—A critical assessment of Newman's view that only Oratorians practise community life, willingly, and as the great means of perfection—'Santa Comunità' the second basic principle of the Oratory—Is Newman's idea of perfection theologically adequate?

The Anglican elements in Newman's priestly spirituality—(*a*) Newman and the care of souls—(*b*) Newman the preacher—(*c*) Newman and the ministry of the Eucharist—(*d*) Newman and prayer—Were these elements specifically Anglican?—Newman's vocation to the Oratory—Newman's Oratorian spirituality a true development—Newman a 'Father of Souls'.

NEWMAN'S ORATORY PAPERS

PREFACE

THE following complete collection of Newman's Oratory Papers, transcribed directly from the autographs, may be said to offer a threefold message. First of all, in providing for the first time ever, a full documentation of Newman as an Oratorian, it enables the reader to gain a sense of identity and continuity in Newman's life as a priest. From first to last we follow Newman here pursuing his vocation as a priest within the Catholic Church, from his close study of Oratorian sources during his noviciate in Santa Croce in 1847, up to his last recorded Chapter Address in Birmingham in 1878 on 'Continuity and Change' as the basic law of community life.

Besides this historical interest of Newman's own life as a priest, these Papers offer an illuminating example of what is nowadays called *aggiornamento,* i.e. the renewal in religious life by a return to the original ideas of the Founder. The Italian Oratory of St Philip Neri, a sixteenth-century form of priestly life, might well have seemed an unpromising Institute to introduce into the backstreets of Birmingham in the 1850s. Only Newman's deep docility to the spirit, and bold freedom with the letter of the Oratorian Rule could have harmoniously effected a successful transplanting of the Italian shoot to English soil. Newman's historical tact, his unerring discrimination between the essential and the accessory, together with his stubborn realism—these were the indispensable factors of his work, and provide a fascinating study for anyone who is involved in the post-Conciliar renewal.

The third and final lesson which these Papers convey is that we need nowadays spiritual reading 'with a difference.' We tire of books which merely teach; we feel that if spiritual reading is to be valid, it cannot be worked out on paper alone —it should be written first of all on the living tissue of men's hearts and lives. But to attempt this difficult task is tò expose oneself to the risk of tensions, dissensions, opposition and even separation. Newman had more than his share of these, and even from the very first year of the existence of the English Oratory he had to set himself to exercising endless patience in his desire to preserve the 'weaponless state' of the Oratory. In his capacity as Superior, Newman set himself out to elicit the obedience of his subjects as a free voluntary act, constantly renewed in personal imitation of Christ, and not restricted by any legal restraint or bond of vow. The obedience which he prized above all was not so much the formal carrying out of orders, nor even the conscientious fulfilment of allotted duties, but a loving submission of each to all and at all times—'Santa Comunità.' Here he anticipates a great idea of our own day— that of community—but he does so, never losing sight of the fact that a community is composed of responsible persons, and that the smooth running of the whole is committed to the tact and discretion of each one's sensitivity to an unwritten law of love, which alone can bind hearts in unity over a long span of years spent living together.

Seen in this light, these Oratory Papers, which at first sight might seem to be just a miscellaneous collection of purely domestic interest, acquire a significance and a cogency which makes them immediately relevant to the life of the Church today, far beyond the walls of the Birmingham Oratory. In the present crisis of authority, Newman may well yet be a prophet pointing out afresh the way of filial—in preference to legal— obedience, ensuring at the same time full consideration for each member in his total dedication to community.

The editor's aim has been to reproduce as faithful a transcript as possible of the original autographs, all of which are preserved in the Birmingham Oratory Archives. A considerable portion of the documents has been transcribed for the first time here, the details being indicated in the appropriate place. Any significant alterations made by Newman have been included; any spelling or other slight mistakes on his part have been reproduced as they stand. A brief introductory note has been supplied to each paper; the numbering of the Papers (by the editor) follows, with a few exceptions, the chronological order.

While these Papers are the indispensable source for any study of Newman as an Oratorian, they become fully intelligible only in the light of a close theological examination of the spirituality of the priesthood in Newman's life, both in the Church of England and in the Oratory. Such a study was the starting point of the present work, and was suggested to me during my theology course in Rome (1939–42) by my then Professor of Dogmatic Sacramental Theology, Dom Augustine Mayer, O.S.B., later Rector of Sant' Anselmo, and now Abbot of Metten (Bavaria). The pressure of manifold other duties has protracted the completion of this work, which at one stage or another has been my companion for more than twenty years until its presentation for the degree of D.D. to the Theological Faculty of Sant' Anselmo, Rome.

The edition of the Oratory Papers, undertaken at the request of the Fathers of the Birmingham Oratory, grew out of the happy chain of coincidences which led me early on in my research to the Birmingham Oratory, where both the domestic traditions of the House and Newman's own MSS were put generously at my disposal. This prolonged contact with Newman's own House was vital in my attempt to come to grips with his spirituality as a priest—a subject on which he had published relatively little. I am deeply indebted to the successive Superiors and the other members of the Oratory for their fraternal hospitality extended over so many years, while in particular the two Archivists of the Newman MSS, the late Father Henry Tristram and his successor, Father C. S. Dessain have been indefatigable guides to the Archives and indeed to all matters relating to Newman.

My grateful thanks are due to all those in Glenstal, Birmingham and Rome who have made the completion of this work possible. In particular, however, I feel I must single out the late Abbot Joseph Dowdall and his successor Abbot Augustine O'Sullivan without whose encouragement, interest and support the book would not have reached its final stage.

Glenstal
21 February 1968.

ABBREVIATIONS USED BY NEWMAN IN THE ORATORY PAPERS

Annals *Memorie Historiche della Congregazione dell' Oratorio,* raccolte dal P. Giovanni Marciano, prete della stessa Congregazione, 5 vols. fol. Naples, 1693–1702.

Bacci *Vita di S. Filippo Neri Fiorentino, fondatore della Congregazione dell' Oratorio.* (Newman's copy is of the 1631 ed.) For an account of the English translations, see Trevor, *Apostle of Rome* (1966), p. 356.

Pregi *Pregi della Congregazione dell' Oratorio de San Filippo Neri,* 2 vols. Venice, 1825. (English translation: F. A. Antrobus, *The Excellences of the Congregation of the Oratory of St Philip Neri,* London, 1881.)

Marciano same as *Annals* (above)

vid see

ABBREVIATIONS USED IN THE FOOTNOTES

Apo.	*Apologia pro Vita Sua*, ed. 1889.
A.W.	John Henry Newman: *Autobiographical Writings*, ed. H. Tristram. 1956.
B.Or.Ar.	Birmingham Oratory Archives.
Brilioth	Y. Brilioth, *The Anglican Revival, Studies in the Oxford Movement*, 1925.
Dev.	*An Essay on the Development of Christian Doctrine*, ed. 1878.
D.T.C.	*Dictionnaire de Théologie Catholique.*
L.D.	*The Letters and Diaries of John Henry Newman*, ed. at the Birmingham Oratory by C. S. Dessain, Vols. XI–XVIII 1961–8.
Or.P.	Newman's Oratory Papers, in the present edition.
P.S.	*Parochial and Plain Sermons*, I–VIII, ed. 1868.
Trevor I	M. Trevor, *Newman The Pillar of the Cloud*, 1962.
Trevor II	M. Trevor, *Newman Light in Winter*, 1962.
Trevor, Apostle of Rome	M. Trevor, *Apostle of Rome, A Life of Philip Neri, 1515–1595*, 1966.

In transcribing the MSS, the following signs have been used:

    ( ) : for Newman's parentheses.

    [ ] : for editorial matter.

    ⟨ ⟩ : for Newman's references to his authorities, and also for his interlinear corrections and additions.

BIBLIOGRAPHY

1. MSS of Newman's other than the Oratory Papers

(References are to catalogue numbers in the Birmingham Oratory Archives)

Prayer for First Communion Day as an Anglican, 17 November 1817, *A.10.4.*

Weekly Prayer intentions, 1824, *C.5.12.*

Unpublished MS Sermon, 22 March 1829, *A.50.5.*

Unpublished MS Sermon, 20 March 1831, *B.3.6.*

Memorandum on the Exercises of St Ignatius, 1842–43, *A.11.6.*

Original MS Text of *Apologia*, 1864, *A.36.1.*

The three Mass Notebooks, *C.5.12.*

Memorandum on his attachment to the Church of England, November 1877, *Sundries A.46.3.*

2. Printed works of Newman's

John Henry Newman: Autobiographical Writings, edited with Introductions by Henry Tristram, 1956. Anglican Period covers pp. 1–245; Catholic Period is on pp. 245–333.

The Via Media of the Anglican Church, illustrated in Lectures, Letters and Tracts written between 1830 and 1841, two volumes, 3rd ed., 1877.

The Church of the Fathers (1833–36), 4th ed. 1868.

Lectures on the Doctrine of Justification (1838), 6th ed., 1892.

Correspondence of John Henry Newman with John Keble and Others, 1839–1845, edited at the Birmingham Oratory, 1917.

Parochial and Plain Sermons (1834–42), eight volumes ed. 1868.

'The Catholicity of the Anglican Church' (1840) Essay No. 10 in *Essays Critical and Historical,* Vol. II, 10th ed., 1890.

'The Greek Devotions of Bishop Andrews' (sic), 'Translated and Arranged' (1840), *Tracts for the Times,* No. 88.

'The Tamworth Reading Room' (1841) *Discussions and Arguments*, 1872, pp. 254–305.

Sermons preached before the University of Oxford (1843), 1872.

Sermons on Subjects of the Day (1843), 1872.

Select Treatises of St Athanasius in controversy with the Arians (1842–44), two volumes, 1881.

An Essay on the Development of Christian Doctrine (1845), 1878.

The Letters and Diaries of John Henry Newman, edited at the Birmingham Oratory with notes and an Introduction, Volumes XI–XVIII, 1961–68.

Loss and Gain: The Story of a Convert (1848), 9th ed., 1886.

Discourses addressed to Mixed Congregations (1849), 7th ed., 1886.

Difficulties felt by Anglicans in Catholic Teaching (1850, 1865 and 1874), two volumes, ed. 1910.

The present Position of Catholics in England 1st ed., 1851 under the title: 'Lectures on Catholicism in England'.

The Idea of a University defined and illustrated (1852, 1856 and 1858), 1898.

Callista, a Sketch of the third Century (1856), ed. 1876.

'Remarks on the Oratorian Vocation'. *Sanctus Philippus Birminghamiensis*, printed privately 1856.
   Italian Translations:— *Note sulla Vocazione dei Filippini*, Tipografia Cuggiani, Rome 1918, *Lettere sulla vocazione dei Filippini*, Quaderni dell' Oratorio, N 1. Rome 1962.

Sermons preached on Various Occasions (1857), 3rd ed., 1870.

On consulting the Faithful in Matters of Doctrine (1859), edited with an Introduction by John Coulson, 1961.

Historical Sketches, three volumes (1872).

Apologia pro Vita Sua (1864), 1889.

Verses on Various Occasions (1868), ed. 1903.

An Essay in Aid of a Grammar of Assent (1870), 4th ed., 1874.

A Letter addressed to His Grace the Duke of Norfolk on the occasion of Mr. Gladstone's recent Expostulation (1875).

Meditations and Devotions of the late Cardinal Newman (1893). A new edition is now available: M. Trevor, 1964.

Addresses to Cardinal Newman with his Replies, etc., 1879-82, ed. W. P. Neville, 1905.

Sermon Notes of John Henry Cardinal Newman, 1849–1879, ed. Fathers of the Birmingham Oratory, 1913.

Catholic Sermons of Cardinal Newman, edited at the Birmingham Oratory, 1957.

3. Anthologies of Newman Texts

LILLY, W. C., *Characteristics from the Writings of John Henry Newman*, 2nd ed. 1875.
KARRER, O., *Kardinal J. H. Newman, Die Kirche*, Einsiedeln and Köln, two volumes, 1945.
PRZYWARA, E., *A Newman Synthesis*, London, 1930.
RICKABY, J., *Index to the Works of John Henry Cardinal Newman*, London, 1914.
ROUCOU-BARTHELEMY, A., *John Henry Cardinal Newman, Pensées sur L'Eglise*, Paris, 1956.
TRISTRAM, H. *The Living Thoughts of Cardinal Newman*, London, 1948.

4. Bibliographies on Newman

BECKER, W. 'Newman, J. H.': *Lexikon für Theologie und Kirche*, 2nd ed., Freiburg, 1962, Vol. VII, 932–936.
BOEKRAAD, A. J., 'Continental Newman Literature': *Philosophical Studies* (Maynooth), 7 (1957), pp. 110–116.
DAUPHIN, H., 'Autour de Newman': *Revue d'Histoire ecclésiastique.* LIX (1964), pp. 112–118.
DUPUY, B-D., 'De l'ombre à la lumière: Introduction aux écrits spirituels de Newman': *La vie spirituelle*, No. 461, May 1960, pp. 540–562.
DUPUY, B-D., 'Bulletin d'histoire des doctrines: Newman': *Revue des Sciences Phil. et Théol.* 45 (1961), pp. 125–176.
Nédoncelle, M., *Dictionnaire de Théologie Catholique, Tables Générales* (1967). Cols. 3301–4.
Symposium, *Newman-Studien*, Volumes I-VI, Nurnberg, 1948–1964.
TRISTRAM, H. and BACCHUS, F., 'Newman': *Dictionnaire de Théologie Catholique* XI, 1 (1931), cols. 327–398.

5. Biographies

BELLASIS, E., *Coram Cardinali*, London, 1916.
BOUYER, LOUIS, *Newman, His Life and Spirituality*, London, 1958.
CROSS, F. L., *John Henry Newman*, London, 1933.
DESSAIN, C. S., *The Letters and Diaries of John Henry Newman*, XI (1961), pp. xv–xxiii.
DESSAIN, C. S., *John Henry Newman*, London, 1966.
HARROLD, C. F., *John Henry Newman: An Expository and critical study of his Mind, Thought and Art*, London–New York–Toronto, 1945.

HONORÉ, JEAN, *Itinéraire spirituel de Newman*, Paris, 1964.

HUTTON, R. H., *Cardinal Newman*, 2nd ed. London, 1892.

MIDDLETON, R. D., *Newman and Bloxam: An Oxford Friendship*, Oxford University Press, 1947.

MIDDLETON, R. D., *Newman at Oxford: His Religious Development*, Oxford, 1950.

ROSS, J. E., *John Henry Newman, Anglican Minister: Catholic Priest: Roman Cardinal*, London, 1933.

TRISTRAM, HENRY, *Newman and His Friends*, London, 1933.

TREVOR, MERIOL, *Newman the Pillar of the Cloud*, London, 1962.

TREVOR, MERIOL, *Newman Light in Winter*, London, 1962.

Symposium, *Newman and Littlemore: A centenary Anthology and Appeal*, Oxford, 1945.

WARD, MAISIE., *Young Mr. Newman*, London, 1948.

WARD, WILFRID., *The Life of John Henry Cardinal Newman*, two volumes, London, 1912.

6. Particular Points

BARMANN, L. F., "The Spiritual Reading of Newman's early Sermons": *The Downside Review* 80 (1962), pp. 226–242.

BARMANN, L. F., "Newman on the Psalms as Christian Prayer": *Worship* xxxviii (No. 4, March 1964), pp. 207–213.

BECKMAN, J. F.. "Another View of Newman": *The American Ecclesiastical Review*, cxxxviii (January 1958), pp. 37–48.

BLEHL, V., "The Holiness of John Henry Newman": *The Month*, 1958, pp. 325–334.

BREUCHA, H. "Newman als Prediger": *Newman-Studien*, I (1948), pp. 157–177.

CARROLL, M. G., *The Mind and Heart of St Paul. A Newman Anthology on St Paul*, London, 1959.

COLERIDGE, H. J., "A Father of Souls": *The Month*, October 1890, pp. 153–164.

CULLER, A. D., *The Imperial Intellect. A Study of Newman's educational Ideal*, New Haven and London, 1955.

COULSON, J., "Newman's Idea of an educated Laity—the two Versions": *Theology and the University*, (London, 1964), pp. 47–63.

DAVIS, H. F., "Newman and Thomism": *Newman-Studien* III (1957), pp. 157–169.

DAVIS, H. F., "Cardinal Newman": *English Spiritual Writers* (ed. C. Davis), London, 1961, pp. 123–135.

DAVIS, H. F., "Newman, Theology of the Word in Christian Life": *Blackfriars* 42 (1961), pp. 150–156.

DAVIS, H. F., "Newman and the Theology of the Living Word": *Newman-Studien* VI (1964), pp. 167–177.

DESSAIN, C. S., "The Newman Archives of Birmingham": *Newman-Studien,* III (1957), p. 269 ff.

DESSAIN, C. S., "Cardinal Newman on the Theory and Practice of Knowledge. The Purpose of the *Grammar of Assent*": *The Downside Review* 75 (1957), pp. 1–23.

DESSAIN, C. S., "The Holiness of Newman (Père Bouyer's Study)": *The Tablet,* 211 (1958), p. 208.

DESSAIN, C. S., "Newman's Spirituality. Its Value Today": *English Spiritual Writers* (ed. C. Davis), London, 1961, pp. 136–160.

DESSAIN, C. S., "Cardinal Newman and the Doctrine of uncreated Grace": *The Clergy Review* 47 (1962), pp. 207–225 and pp. 269–288.

FENTON, J. C., "Some Newman Autobiographical Sketches and the Newman Legend": *The American Ecclesiastical Review,* cxxxvi (June 1957), pp. 394–410.

FENTON, J. C., "Newman's Complaints examined in the light of Priestly Spirituality": *The American Ecclesiastical Review,* cxxxviii (January 1958) pp. 49–65.

FENTON, J. C., "The Newman Legend and Newman's Complaints": *The American Ecclesiastical Review,* cxxxix (1958), pp. 101–121.

JOHNSON, E. J., *The Psalm Piety of Cardinal Newman as revealed in his Christian interpretation of the Psalter,* (Dissertation), two volumes, Trier, 1960.

KARRER, O., "Newman Weg in die Kirche und sein Weg in der Kirche": *Sentire Ecclesiam (ed.* J. Daniélou and H. Vorgrimmler), Freiburg, 1961, pp. 676–742.

LAMM, W. R., *The Spiritual Legacy of Newman,* Milwaukee, 1934.

McGRATH, F., *Newman's University Idea and Reality,* London, 1951.

McGRATH, F., *The Consecration of Learning.* Lectures on Newman's *Idea of a University,* Dublin, 1962.

McMANUS, L., 'Newman and the Newman Legend': *The American Ecclesiastical Review* cxxxix (1958) pp. 93–100.

MOSELEY, D. H., 'Newman and the Roman Breviary': *Worship,* xxxiv (No. 2, January 1960), pp. 75–78.

PADOVANO, A. T., *The Cross of Christ the Measure of the World.* A Study of the Theology of the Cross in the Life and Writings of J. H. Newman, Rome, 1962.

RENZ, W., *Newman's Idee einer Universität,* Probleme höherer Bildung, Freiburg (Schweiz), 1958.

THEIS, N.. 'Newman als anglikanischer Seelsorger': *Beilage zum Kirchlichen Anzeiger,* Luxemburg, 1962, pp. 7–13.

TIERNEY, M., (ed.) *A Tribute to Newman, Essays on Aspects of his Life and Thought,* Dublin, 1945.

TRISTRAM, H., (ed.) *John Henry Newman: Centenary Essays,* London, 1945.

WALGRAVE, J. H., *Newman the Theologian,* London, 1960.

ZENO, Dr, 'The Reliability of Newman's Autobiographical Writings': *The Irish Ecclesiastical Record,* 86 (1956), pp. 297–305; 87 (1957), pp. 25–37.

7. Theological Studies

BRILIOTH, Y., *The Anglican Revival. Studies in the Oxford Movement,* London, 1925.

CLARK, F., *Anglican Orders and Defect of Intention,* London, 1956.

CLARK, F., *Eucharistic Sacrifice and the Reformation,* London, 1960.

COURTOIS, G., *The States of Perfection according to the Teaching of the Church.* Papal Documents from Leo XIII to Pius XII, Dublin 1961.

FONCK, A., *Perfection chrétienne, D.T.C.,* XII, I (1933), cols. 1219–1251.

FRISON, B., *Selection and Incorporation of Candidates for the Religious Life,* Milwaukee, 1962.

GY, P.-M., 'Bulletin de théologie dogmatique: Sacrement de l'Ordre': *Revue des Sciences Phil. et Théol.* XLVII (1963), 322–29.

HILDEBRANDT, F., *I Offered Christ: A Protestant Study of the Mass,* London, 1967.

MENNESSIER, A.-I, 'Conseils évangéliques': *Dictionnaire de Spiritualité* 11, 2e partie (1953), 1592–1609.

SEJOURNÉ, P., 'Voeux de Religion': *D.T.C.,* XV, 2 (1950), cols. 3234–3281.

SEMPÉ, L., 'Vocation': *D.T.C.,* XV, 2 (1950), cols. 3148–3181.

SPICQ, C., *Spiritualité sacerdotale d'après St Paul,* Paris, 1954.

Symposium, *The Sacrament of Holy Orders:* Some Papers and Discussions concerning Holy Orders at a session of the *Centre de Pastorale Liturgique,* 1955, London, 1962.

THILS, G., *Sainteté chrétienne. Précis de théologie ascétique,* Tielt (Belgium), 1958.

VEUILLOT, P., The Catholic Priesthood, Dublin, Vol. I (1957), Vol. II (1964).

Enchiridion de Statibus Perfectionis, Rome, 1949.

8. Historical Studies

BATTISCOMBE, G., *John Keble, A Study in Limitations,* London, 1963.

BODINGTON, C., *Books of Devotion* (The Oxford Library of Practical Theology), London, 1903.

BORRELLI, M., *Le Costituzioni dell' Oratorio Napoletano,* Naples, 1968.

BUTLER, C., 'The Record of the Century': *The Downside Review,* Centenary No., 1914, pp. 49–51.

CHAPMAN, R., *Father Faber,* London, 1961.

DAVIES, H., *Worship and Theology in England from Newman to Martineau,* 1850-1900, London, 1962.

DE LIBERO, G., *Vita di S. Filippo Neri, Apostolo di Roma,* Grotta-ferrata, 1960.

FABER, F. W., *Notes on Community Life in the Oratory,* Derby, 1867.

GÜLDEN, J., 'Vom Geist und Leben des Oratoriums vom heiligen Philipp Neri': N. Greinacher (ed.), *Priestergemeinschaften,* Mainz, 1960, pp. 213–239.

HÄRDELIN, A., *The Tractarian Understanding of the Eucharist,* Uppsala, 1965.

MARCIANO, G., *Memorie Historiche della Congregazione dell 'Oratorio,* 5 vols. fol. Naples, 1693–1702.

NEILL, S., *Anglicanism.* London, 1960.

O'RAHILLY, A., 'The Irish University Question': *Studies* 50 (1961), pp. 353–370.

PONELLE, L. and BORDET, L., *S. Philippe Néri et la société romaine de son temps.* Eng. trans, by F. Kerr, London 1932.

Anon., *Pregi della Congregazione dell' Oratorio di San Filippo Neri.* 2 vols. Venice, 1825. English Translation:— F. A. Antrobus, *The Excellences of the Congregation of the Oratory of St Philip Neri.* London, 1881.

Instituta Congregationis Anglicae Oratorii S. Philippi Nerii. Rome, 1847.

TREVOR, M., *Apostle of Rome, A Life of Philip Neri, 1515-1595,* London, 1966.

NEWMAN THE PRIEST

Introduction

THE aim of this study is to portray as accurately, as fully and as realistically as possible the spirituality of the priesthood in Newman's life. The question it sets out to answer is, What kind of priest was Newman, in fact, in his own existence?

The spirituality of the priesthood is a wide and flexible reality, which admits of many variations, resulting from a priest's own personality, his background, the circumstances of his life and the role he is called upon to play in the life of the Church at large. Some priestly characteristics will be brought into relief, others will be left unemphasized in the manifold interaction of a man's own talents and the demands of life, and although the grace of Orders is one and the same throughout the Catholic priesthood, in practice, however, notable differences occur, so that it is justifiable to speak of different types or schools of spirituality. Vocation, the sanctifying power of the priesthood for the priest himself, the pastoral and liturgical exercise of the ministry and the conscious elaboration of a spiritual way of life—all these traits taken cumulatively differentiate one type of priest from another, while of course within the same type, individual characteristics will mark off one man from another.

What of Newman? What was his priestly spirituality? It was of the Oratorian type but with an Anglican substratum resulting from his long ministry of over twenty years as an Anglican priest. The main concern of the pages which follow is to demonstrate in detail the identity and continuity between Newman's spirituality as an Anglican and as an Oratorian, between the Vicar of St Mary's and the Father of the Birmingham Oratory.

Within its modest limits the present study may claim to be the fruit of personal research pursued independently for almost a quarter of a century (1942–1964) at a time precisely when many of the great modern authorities on Newman were being written. It is based on first-hand acquaintance with the primary sources—Newman's Oratory Papers— acquired during prolonged visits to the Birmingham Oratory and has the benefit of an intimate knowledge of the domestic traditions of Newman's community.

The method followed throughout has been avowedly and explicitly deductive and not *a priori:* I have deliberately refrained all along from judging Newman by any standard readymade pattern of priestly spirituality. It is not the general but the particular which has been consistently pursued in this research; avoiding generalizations, I have everywhere striven to substantiate what I have to say by an appeal to the sources.

Of all existing works on Newman the present study is indebted above all to two in particular, both emanating from the Birmingham Oratory. Father Henry Tristram's edition of the *Autobiographical Writings*[1] has been ever at hand, but more than any other publication, it is the monumental edition of *The Letters and Diaries of John Henry Newman*[2] by Father C. S. Dessain which provides the indispensable documentary basis for most of my work.

With regard to the general line taken here of the central place of the priesthood in Newman's life, Father Henry Tristram had already led the way. For many years in charge of the Newman Archives at the Birmingham Oratory, he had an unrivalled knowledge of all things relating to Newman and always urged the research students who came to the Oratory to look on Newman as a 'Father of Souls'—the title of Father Coleridge's appreciation of the Cardinal published shortly after the latter's death. It was Father Tristram who first turned my attention specifically to Newman as an Oratorian and who

---

[1] See bibliography, p. XIX.

[2] See bibliography, p. XX. This critical and complete edition of all Newman's letters in chronological sequence is, perhaps, the most important primary source for Newman studies that has appeared since the Cardinal's death. Most opportunely for the present work, the edition begins with the letters of the Catholic period, from 7 October 1845 onwards, thus enabling us to follow as intimately as possible, the progress of Newman's own thoughts on his vocation almost day by day.

first put me in touch with the Oratory Papers. Louis Bouyer's *Newman: His Life and Spirituality*[3] benefited greatly from Father Tristram's guidance, as the author himself tells us.

In Germany, as far back as 1922, Dr Matthias Laros had singled out the priesthood as the great unifying force in Newman's life, and he held that Newman was a priest rather than a thinker, writer or orator—or rather, he wished to show that these different activities were only various manifestations of a single mission which was first and foremost that of a priest. To a certain degree, Przywara's *Newman Synthesis*[4] was a reaction against Laros, in re-affirming the image of Newman the thinker, though it does this in an over-systematic way[5].

In the present decade, the large-scale biography by Miss Trevor[6] deals exhaustively with all the vicissitudes of the English Oratory under Newman and so provides a full historical background to the present study. Reviewers have criticized Miss Trevor's championing of Newman throughout, but no refutation has been forthcoming, in particular of her minute treatment of the quarrel between the two Oratories[7],—a crucial point which had been glossed over in the hitherto standard biography of Newman by Wilfrid Ward. I find myself in substantial agreement with Miss Trevor's main picture; in presenting a less crowded canvas, I have tried to illuminate the portrait of Newman from inside his own soul without, if

---

[3]See bibliography, p. XXI. Reviews of this work in: 'A Portrait of Newman': *The Times Literary Supplement* (Religious Book Section) 23 May 1958; C. S. Dessain, 'The Holiness of Newman (Père Bouyer's study)': *The Tablet*, 211 (1958), p. 208.

[4]See the appreciation of the original German edition of Przywara's *Einführung in Newmans Wesen und Werk* by H. Tristram, 'On Reading Newman': *John Henry Newman: Centenary Essays* (1945), pp. 230, 240.

[5]This account of Laros and Przywara is indebted to R. Grosche, 'Der Wandel des Deutschen Newman Bildes', *Newman-Studien* IV (1960), pp. 331–44.

[6]*Newman The Pillar of the Cloud* (London, 1962); *Newman Light in Winter* (London, 1962), abbreviated in these Notes as *Trevor I, Trevor II*.

Does *Trevor* supersede Ward's *Life of John Henry Cardinal Newman* (1912)? For the purposes of the present study the answer must be yes, on account of the better chronological arrangement of the work, and particularly on account of the fullness of treatment accorded to the Oratory in Newman's life. This does not mean that I endorse all Miss Trevor's opinions; but her two volumes remain the best background for this study of Newman the Priest.

[7]'Conflict within the Oratory (1855-1857)': *Trevor* II, pp. 73–165.

possible, distorting any of the figures in the background. Jean Honoré's study, *Itinéraire spirituel de Newman*[8] was available to me during the revision of my text. Although a sensitive and sympathetic study—particularly of Newman's Oratorian life —it fails to use the newer material available both in the *Letters and Diaries* and also in Miss Trevor's volumes, and so does not affect the main positions of the present work.

That there should be room for this fresh study of Newman the priest, in addition to the authors already mentioned, and in spite of the vast output of modern publications about Newman, is to be ascribed chiefly to the new documentation on which it is mainly based, viz. the Oratory Papers alluded to above, and of which the present volume contains a full edition undertaken at the request of the Fathers of the Birmingham Oratory.

Although a number of these Papers had already been available both in the original MSS and in typescript in the Oratory Archives, it has, nevertheless, been my good fortune to have been able to add to the number by identifying several important MSS which up to now had passed unnoticed by Newman students. This new material is not merely of quantitative significance in making available further writings of Newman's; it is, moreover, of decisive importance in the precise problem with which this book is concerned.

For the kernel of the problem about Newman as a priest is the mature spirituality of which he gives evidence right from the beginning of his Oratorian career. He speaks with all the definiteness and assurance of a second founder of the Oratory after St Philip. This is perplexing when one reflects how relatively brief his preparation for the priesthood had been, how cursory his novitiate under Fr Rossi in Rome[9], how rapid the initial growth of the Oratory in England, and how many collateral duties, engagements and trials of all sorts crowded in on him during his first years as a Catholic. Whence then this wisdom, this confidence in his own idea of the Oratory?

No satisfactory answer was forthcoming to this central

[8]Editions du Seuil, Paris 1964.

[9]On this point, see below, *Or. P.*, No. 24, *Remarks on the Oratorian Vocation: Rough Draft.*

problem for many years until finally when, so to speak, scouring the Oratory Archives for ever more material (under the direction of Father C. S. Dessain) I began to re-examine some MSS which had been catalogued simply as 'Materials for the Life of St Philip.' I cannot claim to have discovered these MSS, but I may say that I unearthed them. If these Papers have hitherto passed unnoticed by students of Newman, it may be because they look uninviting. Unlike many other of Newman's MSS which are extant in a relatively legible and finished state, many of these Papers are more like the rough notes a man makes for private use. On attentive examination, however, they provide the fullest collection of *Oratoriana* from Newman's hand,—and supremely important for my quest, they at last yielded up the secret key to Newman's view of the Oratory, which he worked out for himself in Rome in 1847, and from which he never afterwards wavered.

I have named them the 'Santa Croce Papers' from a note on the first page, signed by Newman on 15 January, 1852, saying that they had been drawn up by him at Santa Croce in August or September 1847[10]. Furthermore, I was able to identify four lengthy and important Chapter Addresses, dating from early in 1848, which Newman delivered to his first Oratorians in the first weeks of the Oratory's existence before Faber and his Wilfridians were received by Newman into the Oratory. In view of the later differences between Faber and Newman about the ethos of the Oratory, it is highly significant to be able to demonstrate from these newly-discovered Chapter Addresses how fully Newman had worked out the idea of the Oratory before Faber had even donned the Oratorian cassock. A last lot in the bundle of MSS was an unfinished fragment of the Life of St Philip; this, too, is of considerable interest, as showing Newman's dissatisfaction with the existing *Lives*, and indicating the lines along which he felt it should be written.

With the aid of this new material, an admirable starting-point was provided for a study of Newman as a priest of St Philip Neri's Oratory, but no sooner had this problem been solved, than another—and in some ways more complex—

[10]It was only many years later that I discovered that Newman himself had used this very name 'Santa Croce Paper'. See Introductory Note to *Or. P.*, Appendix I.

subject of inquiry unfolded itself, viz. how far was Newman's
Anglican ministry the matrix of his Oratorian spirituality?

It became increasingly clear to me as the inquiry proceeded
that one cannot understand Newman the Catholic priest
unless one is fully aware of the positive spiritual values he had
acquired during his ministry in the Church of England, and
which had become part of himself, and were finally put to use
again during his long life as a Catholic priest. In the light of
modern ecumenical theology, this study of the interplay
within Newman's Oratorian life of his Anglican past and his
Catholic present became one of absorbing interest.

It is true to say that Newman learned to live as a priest
while still an Anglican. With the help of the *Autobiographical
Writings* and other still unpublished MSS, both of his Anglican
and his Catholic ministry, it was possible to trace in some detail
the identity and continuity of his priestly life as an Anglican
and as a Catholic, without thereby equiparating Anglican
Orders and the Catholic priesthood or implying that Newman
as an Anglican had all along been a concealed Catholic or
that, as a Catholic, he maintained a lurking Anglicanism.

In order to depict a spiritual portrait of Newman as an
Anglican priest, with a matured spirituality which led into his
Oratorian vocation, four major areas of his Anglican ministry
—the Care of Souls, Preaching, the Eucharistic Ministry and
finally, Prayer—have been closely examined both in themselves
and in their renewed appearance in Newman's Catholic life.
Each facet is examined separately, due respect being had at all
points for Newman's doctrinal development from Evangelicalism to Sacramentalism.

With such a faithful delineation to hand, one has no longer
the feeling of a *tabula rasa* when one comes to examine Newman's vocation to the Oratory.

Where was this rich priestly nature to fit into the Catholic
Church after his submission to Rome? Should he, so to speak,
'become a priest once again'? This was a crucial question for
Newman, since he believed that although the English Church
was in schism, his Anglican Orders were valid and that he was
already truly a Christian priest in virtue of them. His whole
attitude to the validity of Anglican Orders has been described

here at length, not as an isolated and general theological problem, but as a particular and highly personal anguish.

Once he had decided on going forward for ordination, the whole question remained as to what kind of priestly life he should follow. I have dealt with this whole process of his choice of the Oratory step by step, since the abundant source material available in *The Letters and Diaries*[11] gives an authentic and invaluable insight into his whole idea of priestly spirituality. The very hesitations he experienced are no mere negative rejection, but speak to us clearly of what his heart was seeking. He found it in St Philip Neri's Oratory, and although this was a meeting of heart with heart, it was based not on emotional impulse, but on a distinctly prudential choice.

With the help of the MSS material, it is now possible to get down to rock bottom on Newman's idea of the Oratory, based as it was on contemporary practice in the Roman and Naples Oratories, and on the precedents of early Oratorian history.

Newman's Anglican priestly heritage and his vocation to the Oratory already indicate the kind of priest he was likely to be, and our anticipation is confirmed when we examine from close-by his Oratorian spirituality as it existed in practice from his return to England at Christmas 1847 until his death in 1890.

What is attempted in the final chapters of this study is a theological appraisal of this Oratorian spirituality in the light of the historical circumstances through which he lived it. One must bear in mind that although Newman was the 'onlie begetter' of the English Oratory, nevertheless the accession of Faber and his group within the first few weeks of the Oratory's existence profoundly modified not only the course of development, but the very image of Oratorianism in England, the London House with Faber as its head, tending to a different type of spirituality from Newman's.

A basic point of difference between Faber and Newman was on the scope of the Oratory: was it to be an apostolate by gentlemen for gentlemen (only)? This view was urged on Newman by Faber in view of a phrase in the papal Foundation Brief which mentions an apostolate to the upper classes, the

[11]Excellently indexed, s.v. *Oratorians: L.D.* XI, p. 349; XII, p. 436; XIII, p. 516; XIV, pp. 549, 550; XV, pp. 562, 563.

ordo honestior. I have developed at length Newman's unqualified disallowance of Faber's view in this matter. That candidates for the Oratory should have had the education of a gentleman before entering the Oratory was indeed a constant principle with Newman: it is important, however, to realize that what he desiderated in his novices was not social rank but an educated mind. His reasons for this were partly historical (St Philip's first recruits had been drawn mainly from the educated classes), partly of necessity (if they are to be ordained on their patrimony, which presupposes private means), but chiefly supernatural. Only those, he felt, who had had the natural refinement of a superior education would have the requisite basis on which to build the delicate structure of Oratorian *carità,* the 'weaponless state'[12] of the Oratory as he calls it.

Newman wanted educated priests in the Oratory for an apostolate, not to the world of fashion, but to the world of thought, and particularly to the religious problems which face the intellect of modern man. This apostolate to the intellect is the key to Newman's lifelong responsibility for souls and of his view of secular education as a pastoral care. Several excellent studies of Newman's work in education have helped me considerably as background reading for this important aspect of his pastoral work; I should mention in particular A. Dwight Culler, *The Imperial Intellect, A Study of Newman's Educational Ideal* (1955), Wolfgang Renz, O.S.B., *Newmans Idee einer Universität, Probleme höherer Bildung* (1958), and the two studies by Fergal McGrath S.J., *Newman's University Idea and Reality* (1951), and *The Consecration of Learning: Lectures on Newman's Idea of a University* (1962). It was not necessary for my purpose to cover again the technical ground made good by these authors; my concern was to emphasize the pastoral motive in Newman's involvement in education.

And what of the Oratory itself as a means of Christian perfection for its own members? We must examine whether Newman's moulding of the English Oratory was a true development of the existing Oratorian tradition. The most germane standards by which to judge this are, of course, his own tests of

---

[12]*Or. P.,* No. 31. (end of text), below.

what constitutes a true development, mainly logical sequence, preservation of type and continuity of principles.

The first test, that of logical sequence, reveals a profound consistency from first to last in his understanding of the Oratorian idea; the second, that of preservation of type, shows us Newman as a humble and willing learner in St Philip's school, but also as the bold originator of a modern form of Oratorian apostolate; the third test—continuity of principles—shows us his grasp of the specific nature of Oratorian life, distinct on the one hand from the regulars and on the other from the seculars.

The foregoing outline of the nature, contents and scope of this work may be usefully supplemented by a final word about the method followed. This has been, by explicit choice, predominantly analytical, not to say phenomenological. The aim throughout has been to elicit from Newman's life and writings at first hand the various facets of the spirituality of the priesthood *in the order in which they appear in his experience*. This may at first sight seem to be less complete than would have been an alternative method, i.e. a systematic treatment following the plan of a standard treatise on the priesthood. Such a static and textbook approach would at every single step risk being an alien and ill-fitting garment for Newman's thought which is at once so rich, so consistent with itself, so highly personal and so deeply marked by the note of constant growth and development.

The method I have opted for, in eliciting each doctrine at the point of time where it really appears in his life, does slowly but surely cover the whole range of ideas involved in priestly spirituality. Thus, his responsibility for souls is already fully with him by his ordination as an Anglican deacon. Much was still lacking in Newman's own soul at this time, in particular a full doctrine of sacramental efficacy. A good deal, however, was already present, especially his lifelong habit of intercessory prayer. I have shown how both these ideas—the care of souls and prayer—grew throughout his Anglican days and came over into his Catholic life without a hiatus, continuing in the selfsame line as before.

The ministry of preaching was his earliest priestly work: here I have suggested a fresh approach to the famous *Parochial and Plain Sermons*. A new selection from these sermons shows us that Newman had a profound grasp of pastoral liturgy, expressing already as an Anglican some of the deepest liturgical insights which are being rejuvenated in the Catholic Church today.

The eucharistic ministry is, of course, the central thing in priestly spirituality. At this point I have analysed in detail his Anglican faith in Holy Communion, in order to illustrate the wealth of biblical insights on the Eucharist to which he had already attained as an Anglican. The passage to Catholicism impinged painfully on him with regard to Anglican Orders: he still believed in their validity, even after he had become a Catholic. This was a first major roadblock to be circumvented in his quest for his vocation within the Catholic Church: I have pinpointed here, particularly from the *Letters and Diaries,* his subsequent change of attitude to Anglican Orders.

In his quest for his vocation the note of supernatural prudence emerges above all others; Newman was a reasoner not only in thought but also in life. Once the decision was taken, another trait emerges—that of the sense of tradition. He really took Oratorian history seriously to heart as normative for his own life, while at the same time vigorously adapting existing Oratorian practice to English ways.

In the final part of this study—the examination of his spirituality in the light of his Oratory Papers—the investigator must resist, more than anywhere else, the facile solution of judging Newman by readymade categories. The more laborious, but more rewarding, method is to attempt several different soundings, in the spirit in which Newman himself would have worked. In one of these Papers—the unfinished fragment on St Philip—he has indicated his preferences:

. . . there is another mode of considering the Saints and their doings . . . and that is the view of them as living and breathing men, as persons with personal attributes and a character of their own, and peculiarities of habit and feeling and opinion such as belong to him and not to another . . .

Speaking of St Philip, he says in words that are equally applicable to himself:

. . . I wish to be in possession of that living view of him, which shall be a living key of all, of whatever kind, which has been committed to tradition or writing concerning him . . . To enter into the meaning and the beauty of St Philip's life, I must compare together what he did when he was young and when he was old, when he was obscure and when he was an Apostle . . . He lives long enough to live two lives, he has two sets of friends. . . All these things are to be taken into account, if we would estimate him aright . . .[13].

[13]*Or. P.*, No. 17, Lent 1853, fragment: *Life of St Philip.*

1 Newman and the Care of Souls

THE sense of his responsibility for souls was a pastoral principle indelibly borne in on Newman in consequence of his ordination to the Anglican ministry. In June 1824 he was ordained deacon; the entry in his journal for Sunday June 13 reads:

> It is over. I am thine, O Lord; I seem quite dizzy, and cannot altogether believe and understand it. At first, after the hands were laid on me, my heart shuddered within me; the words 'for ever' are so terrible . . . Lord I ask not for comfort in comparison of sanctification . . .

The entry for the following day finishes:

> . . . 'For ever', words never to be recalled. I have the responsibility of souls on me to the day of my death . . .[1].

Although in the event nothing came of it, Newman at this time felt drawn to the life of a foreign missionary. The Journal records his conversations with Pusey on the missionary ideal, and his own resolve: '. . . as I think the Missionary office the highest privilege from God I can possess, though I speak blindly, it will not be wrong to pray to God to make me a Missionary—therefore in future I propose to do so[2].' It would

---

[1] *A.W.*, pp. 200, 201. The correspondence in *L.D.* XIV and XV furnish several fine examples of his responsibility for individual souls (cf. Indexes to these vols., s.v. *Spiritual Counsel*, pp. 549 and 562 respectively).

[2] *A.W.*, p. 194. L. Bouyer, Newman, *His Life and Spirituality* (1958) p. 74 speaks of 'how strongly the idea of missionary work abroad had appealed to him on the morrow of his conversion, and how the feeling that he was intended to live a celibate life was more or less connected with that idea.' It would seem more accurate to say that the idea of celibacy *preceded* that of missionary work, the former dating from the morrow of his conversion, the latter from the time when he was first on the Oriel foundation. Cf. the MS text of the *Apo.*, quoted by Bouyer, p. 28.

On Henry Martyn, the missionary whose life inspired Newman, cf. The *Oxford Dictionary of the Christian Church* (1958), p. 866. On Protestant missions generally, cf. ibid pp. 907, 908.

seem that during the winter of 1824–1825 the missionary ideal gradually faded from his mind[3]; nor do we possess, it appears, any explicit memorandum of his as to why it did so. In later years as an Oratorian, Newman dwells rather often on the incident in St Philip's life when, wishing to become a foreign missionary, he was told by the Cistercian father whom he consulted that 'Rome was his India'. There is a curious, if fortuitous, parallel here between Newman and St Philip, both thinking of India, both in turn fired by the examples of the missionaries of their own day, and neither in fact, in the event, becoming a missionary. When Newman later lingers on the phrase 'Rome was his India', it is surely not fanciful to detect there some overtones of his own case, turning from a foreign to a home mission; it was still the responsibility of souls, though exercised in a less heroic way.

For two years after his ordination as deacon, Newman worked actively as a curate in the parish of St Clement's; his position as Fellow of Oriel giving him academic rank, but no definite academic work. His Journal for 16 May 1824 contains the memorandum of his decision to accept the curacy of St Clement's "...When I think on the arduousness, I quite shudder. O that I could draw back, but I am Christ's soldier. Every text on the ministerial duty and my ordination vows, within the last day or two, come [sic] home to me with tenfold force."

Among his weekly intentions for private prayer in 1824–1825, those for Tuesday run:

> ... Intercede for flock at St Clements—churchmen—dissenters—romanists—those without religion—pious, wordly—rector, churchwardens and other offices—sick, old, young, women labouring with child—rich and poor—schools—that the church may be rebuilt and well—for unity—for the extension of godliness[4].

[3] By May 16, 1824 he had come to 'a most important determination'—to accept the curacy at St Clement's, *A.W.*, p. 198. There does not seem to be any definite entry in his Journal about a decision not to become a missionary. Later on, in his Roman sojourn 1846–47, Newman expresses admiration for the missionary students at Propaganda, *L.D.* XI, 296.

[4] MS, Oratory Archives, C.5.12. cf. Father Neville's remarks on Newman's autograph books of private prayers, as giving 'impressions of him which are not to be got elsewhere,': Ward, *Life of John Henry Cardinal Newman* (1927) II, pp. 361–368.

This prayer is recopied verbatim into his later Mass note-book[5], with the understandable omission of "romanists."

After two years' hard work in St Clement's, Newman gave up parochial ministry in favour of the tutorship at Oriel. In effect, however, by his appointment as Vicar of St Mary's, the University Church, in 1828, he had a parochial charge concurrently with his work as tutor; in fact it outlasted the tutorship by another decade (1832–1843), and provided the setting for his Parochial Sermons in St Mary's and his pastoral care among the people at Littlemore, where he built the church and got to know his parishoners one by one. Though not exclusively a parish priest, he nevertheless considered his parochial duties an integral part of his life and bestowed his energy on them, combining this work with his academic obligations as tutor, and later with his engagement in the wider fields of the movement.

Both as an Anglican and as a Catholic Newman had a great capacity for work, often of a varied nature; he always had his hands full. We need only recall Dr Ullathorne's letter written on the occasion of the *Apologia:*

> . . . It is difficult to comprehend how, in the face of facts, the notion should ever have arisen that during your Catholic life, you have been more occupied with your own thoughts than with the service of religion and the work of the Church . . .[6].

The bishop then proceeds (rightly) to point out that Newman's literary labours as a Catholic represent but a portion of his work, and that in the second half of his period of public life. He then refers to four undertakings, "each of a distinct character, and any one of which would have made a reputation for untiring energy in the practical order[7]," viz. the founding of the Oratory, the establishment of the Catholic University, the pastoral work on the Birmingham mission, and finally the Oratory School.

[5] On these Mass notebooks, see below, pp. 61–63.

[6] *Apo.*, pp. 368–370.

[7] *Apo.*, p. 369. Newman's combination of practical gifts and intellectual power may be seen in the fact of his composing the *University Discourses* in the midst of the anxieties of the Achilli trial. The varied correspondence 1852-53 contained in *L.D.* XV is very revealing from this point of view.

To return now to his Anglican ministry. The unpublished sermon No 290 "On the object and effects of preaching," lets us see in what spirit he undertook the pastoral ministry at St Mary's:

> . . . God gives His blessing to those who diligently seek Him . . . Those gifts which He lodges by ordination in His servants for the good of His people, He lodges deep within them—They cannot, if they would, display them all at once . . . The Gospel is a Spirit dwelling within us—we can only communicate it, while we give out our own character the while[8].

Even though an integral part of his ministry, parish work was not to be the specifically characteristic note of Newman's care for souls. Secular education considered as a pastoral care was his true field, and this for his whole life. In 1879, among his replies to Addresses made to him on the occasion of his cardinalate, there is one brief but pregnant text of his (in reply to the members of the Catholic Poor School Committee) which bears out that an apostolate to the intellect was a life-long concern of his: ". . . . Long before I was a Catholic Priest . . . When I was Public Tutor of my College at Oxford, I maintained, even fiercely, that my employment was distinctly pastoral . . .[9]."

Three times in his long career Newman was engaged in an educational project: his tutorship at Oriel (1826–1832), the Catholic University at Dublin (1851–1858) and the Oratory School at Edgbaston (opened in May 1859). In each of these ventures he was concerned with the education of laity for the world, not of clergy for the Church; notwithstanding this, he considered—both as an Anglican and a Catholic—that this work of secular education was a directly ministerial office for a priest.

When in 1826 he was appointed one of the public tutors of Oriel and resigned his curacy at St Clement's, he expressed in a note in his Journal for his twenty-fifth birthday the feelings with which he entered on his tutorship:

[8]Newman's ministry at St Mary's has been frequently studied, among others by R. D. Middleton, 'The Vicar of St Mary's': *John Henry Newman: Centenary Essays* ed. H. Tristram (1945), pp. 127–138; L. Bouyer, *Newman* (1958), pp. 174–190; *Brilioth* pp. 211–259.

[9]*Addresses to Cardinal Newman with His Replies etc.*, ed. W. P. Neville (1905).

. . . And now, O Lord, I am entering with the new year into a fresh course of duties (viz. the Tutorship). May I engage in them in the strength of Christ, remembering I am a minister of God, and have a commission to preach the Gospel, remembering the worth of souls, and that I shall have to answer for the opportunities given me of benefitting those under my care[10].

After a month's experience of tuition he notes:

It is my wish to consider myself as the minister of Christ. May I most seriously reflect, that, *unless* I find that opportunities occur of doing good to those over whom I am placed, it will become a grave question, whether I *ought* to continue in the Tuition . . .[11].

Newman has described in detail the collision of views that occurred between Dr Hawkins, the Provost of the College, and himself over this view of the tutorship as a ministerial office. Broadly speaking, we may say that in this quarrel Hawkins wished to hold Newman down to an accepted system of lecturing, then in use at Oriel, while Newman wished the tutors to have discretionary rights over the nature of their office, particularly in giving personal tuition to their own pupils, in preference to giving open lectures to an indiscriminate collection of undergraduates.

However, beyond this question of educational method, there lay the deeper issue of the religious bias which Newman wished to give to the tutor's office. Consider his position. He was at this time a young clergyman, just ordained, not much older than his pupils, towards whom his attitude was not merely disciplinary, nor yet merely that collateral one of what we should now call a spiritual director. He was willing to train them for academic honours (and hastened to make up the leeway in his own competence in Classics for this purpose), but in addition he wished to discharge the obligation on his ordination "vow" by being a minister of Christ towards them. He did not see the point of all his time and energy being devoted to tutorial work, if this were to be a merely secular job of coaching undergraduates in the Classics and nothing more. This all the more so, since many of the young men were rich

[10]*A.W.*, p. 209
[11]*A.W.*, p. 209

and profligate. In a resident university, with all the students nominally at least Anglican (Oxford being closed at the time to Dissenters and Catholics), misbehaviour of this type would, of course, set a tone within the College walls which would nullify the merely teaching office of tutors, if these had no effective say in the moral formation of their charges.

It would have been unlike Newman to consider the Classics course merely as an (indifferent) means to a (spiritual) end, and not an end in itself; a pretext, so to say, for keeping in touch with his charges, so that he could "look after their souls". Such a dichotomy and a negation of natural values would not have been in Newman's line, nor do we need to anticipate any of his later statements from the Dublin Discourses to dispel it.

In Newman's view, the tutorial office at Oriel could be a pastoral cure of souls for a clergyman, because he would form the minds of his pupils by competent tuition and form their hearts by living with them. But even in the process of forming their minds, he was able to make the Classics teach a moral lesson, since they exhibit human nature as it existed without grace before the advent of Christianity[12]. We should note that in the balance between professional competence and priestly zeal, Newman's position differed as an Anglican from that as a Catholic later on. As a young Fellow of Oriel, at the time of his election, he was not as good a classical scholar as some of the other competitors, though their superior in powers of mind[13]; his mission as a tutor was novel in its moral rather than its intellectual tone. As a Catholic, the position was reversed: he desiderated not greater moral earnestness in English Catholics, but a wider and deeper intellectual basis for their traditional faith. This may be seen in one of his earliest observations as a Catholic:

> The more I understand it, the more the Oratory seems the proper
> thing for England at this moment—the object of St Philip was to

[12]H. Tristram, 'Newman and the Classics': *A Tribute to Newman, Essays on Aspects of his Life and Thought,* ed. M. Tierney (1945) p. 272. We should note that Newman's own formation prior to ordination had been that of a Classics Degree, without anything corresponding to a seminary training. See C. S. Dessain, *John Henry Newman,* (1966), p. 6.

[13]Cf. a letter from Bishop Copleston to Dr Hawkins under the date of May 2, 1843 quoted in *A.W.*, p. 64.

educate a higher class of priests for parish work—most of his followers were highly educated men, corresponding precisely to the fellows of our English Universities. There is abundance of piety and zeal in the English Priests at present, but they want education . . .[14].

In the event, Dr Hawkins gradually negatived Newman's policy as tutor, cut off his supply of pupils, so that the tutorship lapsed in 1832, leaving Newman, now aged thirty-one, still a Fellow of Oriel (an inalienable right) with an assured income on the foundation of the College, but without any office as College tutor or lecturer, or professorship in the university. It was this comparative leisure of Newman's at this turn of his life, which left him free to throw himself vigorously into the nascent Oxford movement.

As 'Santa Comunità' was one of the basic ideals of Newman's later Oratory, it is interesting to see how far he had anticipated this in his Anglican life, particularly because the first group of English Oratorians had been Newman's Anglican companions at Littlemore. Newman was never, strictly speaking, a solitary recluse in Oxford; the Littlemore period before his conversion was the nearest approach of his to a solitary life, but even there he was not alone.

In a letter to Newman of 31 August 1833, his intimate friend Hurrell Froude sketched a project "for reviving Religion in great towns." The letter was published by Newman after Froude's death, among the latter's *Remains*, and it is curious that Wiseman, reviewing this book at length in *The Dublin Review* of 1839 should have picked on this short passage for comment out of a large, essentially miscellaneous volume. Froude had written:

> It has lately come into my head that the present state of things in England makes an opening for reviving the monastic system . . . Certainly colleges of unmarried priests, (who might, of course, retire to a living, when they could and like) would be the cheapest

[14]*L.D.*, XII, p. 101. This is a familiar thought in the Santa Croce Papers. See below Appendix 3, paper n.
Already in 1849 he had noted the ineffective mental training given in Catholic education, judged by the inability of most English Catholics to write well:' . . . How few Catholics can compose! for instance, Dr Ullathorne's style! it is a reductio ad absurdum of the very argument to which it ministers . . .' *L.D.*, XIII, p. 6.

possible way of providing effectively for the spiritual wants of a large population . . .[15].

The future casts its shadow over the pages of Wiseman's lengthy comment since he takes up Froude's idea and explicitly suggests the Oratory of St Philip as the answer to it. Since this is the first traceable reference to the Oratory in Newman's life, the passage is worth preserving on record, though there is no evidence to show that even after Wiseman's article, Newman adopted in any way, while as yet an Anglican, either St Philip's Institute of the Oratory or its spirit. There was indeed at Littlemore a copy of an earlier English translation of the Oratorian Rule, but if Stanton's *Reminiscences* are trustworthy on this point[16], this was procured after the conversion, when Wiseman, now in a totally different capacity as Coadjutor of the Central District in which Littlemore lay, suggested the Oratory as a vocation for the converts. If Newman had already at Littlemore the in-folio copy of Brockie[17] now in the Oratory library, we cannot exclude the possibility that he had, as an Anglican, some acquaintance with the text of St Philip's Rule. This would explain Newman's words of 1849 in his dedication of the *Discourses addressed to Mixed Congregations* to Wiseman:

> . . . the service of St Philip, of whom I had so often heard you speak before I left England, and whose bright and beautiful character had won my devotion, even when I was a Protestant[18].

I have been unable to trace any more specific evidence of this devotion of Newman in his Anglican period to St Philip, but it should not be forgotten that the sixteenth century was already then one of his fields of study, both on the theological and the devotional side.

[15]Quoted by Wiseman in his review of Froude's 'Remains' in the *Dublin Review*, vol. VI (1839), p. 429. For the stormy reception accorded to Froude's 'Remains', cf. G. Battiscombe, *John Keble, A Study in Limitations* (1963), pp. 201–205; C. S. Dessain, *John Henry Newman*, (1966) p. 63.

[16]"Some Reminiscences of the Early Days of Cardinal Newman's Catholic Life":The *Dublin Review*, Third Series 24. No. XLVIII, October 1890, pp. 402–08. The edition of the Rule was *The Institutions of the Congregation of the Oratory, at St Maries in Vallicella, within the City of Rome, Founded by St Philip Nerius*. Printed at Oxford, 1687.

[17]*Codex Regularum* (1759).

[18]*Discourses addressed to Mixed Congregations*, 7th ed., 1886, p. vi.

When, however, he attempted community life at Littlemore in his last years as an Anglican, he included many practices more of a penitential than an Oratorian observance. These he discarded when an Oratorian, since, as he observes in his very first Chapter Address in 1848, St Philip "preferred Prayer, Preaching and the Sacraments to fastings, watchings, silence and psalmody."[19] Already in his Notes during the Retreat before ordination to the priesthood at S.Eusebio in April 1847, he had written:

> Amplius;—quando in recessu meo degebam cum aliis quibusdam, viam vitae quaerens, varia observare soliti sumus, quae Catholicorum propria sunt, jujunia, meditationes, exercitia sacra, Breviarii usum, et alia vitae ecclesiasticae, vel potius regularis. Et nunc re-actionem illam, quam vocant, subii, neque fortem animum habeo ad ea agenda quae libenter egi in Ecclesia Anglicana[20].

When he became a Catholic, his ideas of community life harked back rather to comfortable Oxford than to austere Littlemore. One of the earliest Chapter Addresses—all the more significant because delivered at Maryvale where the circumstances befitting an Oratory were as yet unrealized— gives us his preference in unmistakeable terms:

> Now I will say in a word what is the nearest approximation in fact to an Oratorian Congregation that I know, and that is, one of the Colleges in the Anglican Universities. Take such a College, destroy the Head's House, annihilate wife and children, and restore him to the body of fellows, change the religion from Protestant to Catholic, and give the Head and Fellow missionary and pastoral work, and you have a Congregation of St Philip before your eyes . . . An Oratorian has his own rooms, and his

[19] *Or. P.* No. 3 (17 January 1848), below.

[20] *A.W.*, p. 241, translated by the editor ib. p. 248: "Further;—when I lived in my retreat with certain others, seeking a way of life, we were accustomed to observe many things which are proper to Catholics,—fasts, meditations, retreats, the use of the Breviary, and other practices belonging to the ecclesiastical, or rather to the religious life. And now I undergo a reaction, as they say, and have not the courage to continue those things which I did willingly in the Anglican Church."

On Newman and Littlemore cf. *Newman and Littlemore: A centenary Anthology and Appeal* (Oxford, 1945).

On religious life in the Church of England cf. "Religious orders in Anglicanism": *Oxford Dictionary of the Christian Church*, ed. F. L. Cross (1958), pp. 1150, 1151.

4

own furniture . . . They do not form a cell, but a nest. He is to have his things about him, his books and little possessions. In a word he is to have what an Englishman expresses by the distinctive word *comfort*. And this characteristic of the Oratorian's private room is but a specimen of every part of an Oratorian establishment . . .[21].

As an Oratorian, Newman wished to live a community life modelled on that of an Oxford College, not only in its comfortable setting, but in the mutual relations between its members. As the Oratory has no vows, and very few rules, some common bond must imperatively be found. This can only be *"carità"*, but charity itself will find its best expression in terms of human refinement and tact such as would obtain between educated men.

Newman indeed at Oxford was a declared enemy of donnishness, the assuming of "state and pomp" as Hawkins did on becoming Provost of Oriel[22], the "courting the society and countenance of men of rank and name, whether in the world, or in the state, or in the Church[23]." Speaking in the *Apologia* of his own Oxford days, he claims that he had had "a lounging, free-and-easy way of carrying things on . . . I had lived with my private, nay, with some of my public, pupils, and with the junior fellows of my College, without form or distance, on a footing of equality[24]." And in the *Autobiographical Writings,* speaking of the relations between his undergraduate pupils and himself as tutor he says:

> With such youths he cultivated relations, not only of intimacy, but of friendship, and almost of equality, putting off, as much as might be, the martinet manner then in fashion with College Tutors, and seeking their society in outdoor exercises, on evenings, and in Vacation[25].

Later on, as Superior of the nascent Oratory he held up this ideal of English gentlemanlike manners and refined feelings as the norm of Oratorian community life. He considers the

[21]*Or. P.,* No 5. Early 1848 Chapter Addresses: Third Address.
[22]*A.W.,* p. 97.
[23]*A.W.,* p. 97.
[24]*Apo.,* p. 58.
[25]*A.W.,* p. 90.

objection "what have gentlemanlike manners and refined feelings to do with religion?" and proceeds to answer:

> . . . we are not here contemplating refinement of mind by itself, but as superadded to a high religious perfection . . . and it does not follow, because refinement is worthless without saintliness, that it is needless and useless with it. It may set off and recommend an interior holiness, just as the gift of eloquence sets off logical argument . . . the gift of words is necessary to be able to persuade; and so the gift of manners may be necessary to win . . . though Christian excellence is abstractedly most refined, most winning, yet from various circumstances . . . it may not possibly be so . . . And if this may be true even of saints, so much the more will it be true of a multitude of good men who are not saints, in whom from infirmities of various sorts, from natural temper, from the bad habits of childhood . . . the meek, loving and considerate Spirit of Christ does not flow from the heart to the eyes and the tongue and the other instruments of external communication . . .[26].

Although Littlemore, by the force of events, was more of a country seclusion than an apostolic centre, nonetheless the experience of community life there—and after the conversion, in Maryvale, which in Wiseman's idea was to be "Littlemore continued[27]"—was the seedground for the English Oratory. Now, it is a remarkable fact that, apart from the personal contacts made there and continued in the Oratory, the one pivotal principle for Oratorian life which Newman brings away with him out of Oxford and Littlemore is the necessity for an Oratorian to be a "gentleman". Since he staked the working of the Oratorian idea so much on this basis (confirming his own conclusions with illustrations from early Oratorian history), it may be well to examine closely why he should attach so much importance to this point, and how he conceives it as a help to Christian perfection, and an efficacious instrument of the apostolate. This is all the more important since Newman's own sensitiveness and disagreements with people have not only been variously interpreted by his biographers, but have in the recent past been criticized as running counter to true priestly spirituality.

[26]*Or. P.*, No. 5. Early 1848 Chapter Addresses: Third Address.

[27]Memorandum of a "satisfactory talk" with Wiseman, included in a letter of 28 November 1845, *L. D.*, XI p. 47.

The fundamental thing to be kept in mind about Newman's idea of a gentleman, is that "gentlemanlikeness", as he quaintly calls it, is the hallmark of a liberal education rather than a badge of social rank. Thus in the *Remarks on the Oratorian Vocation*, having treated of "rank" as one of the qualifications of a Father of the Oratory, he then poses the question that if this be so, may they not have to wait too long for recruits, since very few of such rank will be forthcoming. His reply is, that since St Philip's day, a whole new class of society has come into being, so that nowadays a priest who has the education, if not the ancestry, of a gentleman, fully answers in our day to the idea of a gentleman.

Of the cathartic effect of this quality of gentlemanlikeness, he expressed himself finely in one of the early 1848 Chapter Addresses:

> There is a far greater tendency to misunderstandings, jealousies, irritation, resentment and contention, when the mind has not been cultivated or what is called enlarged, than where books and the intercourse of society and the knowledge of the world have served to put things in their true light, to guard the mind from exaggeration, to make it patient of differences, and to give it selfcommand amid differences of opinion and conduct. I do not mean to say that these virtues I have mentioned are necessarily Christian—but they are Christian *in* a Christian—When a Christian mind takes them up into itself they cease to be secular, they are sanctified by their possessor, and become the instruments of spiritual good[28].

He then continues, reflecting on the regrettable results which the lack of such education brings about among religious:

> . . . we have but to reflect upon the petty quarrels which are apt to divide religious houses, the rivalries, the punctilios and the misconceptions, and then again which exist in such very various and aggravated forms in the world at large to[29] the influence of a liberal education and the experience of life in enabling the mind to be at once calm yet observant and versatile[30].

[28] *Or. P.*, No. 6. Early 1848 Chapter Addresses, Stae Apolloniae.

[29] MS: "feel" (but there is some illegible correction, in Newman's hand, written over it).

[30] See above, note 28.

The Fellowship at Oriel entailed for Newman the obligation of celibacy for the duration of the office, and the normal termination of a Fellowship was to resign in view of marriage, and accept an appointment to some benefice. Newman, however, never considered celibacy in this purely technical light— as one of the conditions of his remaining a Fellow; he had early felt the call to the single life, and speaks of it in a well-known passage of the *Apologia*[31]. The MS of the *Apologia* is more explicit here than any of the printed editions and enables us to see the inner development of his choice of virginity in preference to marriage. We must remember that he had a sensitive love of the virtue of purity in his youth:

> . . . I had a strong persuasion that offences against the rule of purity were each of them visited sharply and surely from above: I have still extant prayers and memoranda of the years 1816 and 1821, showing my distress at the thought of going to dances or to the theatre[32].

There is a passage in the *Autobiographical Writings*, in Latin, dating from the "End of 1816," where in a dialogue with himself he condemns, *condemno*, dances and all such gatherings, not setting himself up as a pious model, but avoiding them in self-defence . . . "Et quo vulto possum ego dormiturus exclamare Deo, 'Ne duc nos in tentationem?'[33]."

Coupled with this delicate love of purity for its own sake, there had come to him in the autumn of 1816 the "deep imagination" that he should lead a single life. This imagination:

> . . . was not founded on the Catholic belief of the moral superiority of the single life over the married . . . but arose from my feeling of separation from the visible world, and was connected with a notion that my mission in life would require such a sacrifice as it involved[34].

Here we have an attraction to celibacy arising from a setting apart from things visible and a devotion to a mission in life;

---

[31]*Apo.*, p. 7.
[32]MS of *Apo.* (Oratory Archives A. 36. 1); part of this text is available in L. Bouyer, *Newman, His Life and Spirituality* (1958), p. 28.
[33]*A.W.* p. 153.
[34]See above, note 32.

there is not yet "the high severe idea of the intrinsic excellence of Virginity . . the Blessed Virgin its great pattern," which was the next stage in his development and which he owed to his friend Hurrell Froude[35]. Although Newman had an unequivocal devotion to Our Lady while still an Anglican[36], his thought on Christian virginity is centred more on Christ than on Mary. The references available are only slight, since Newman did not flaunt his personal choice of celibacy in a Church and among a clergy where marriage was the normal state of life. It should be noted, however, that in the *Essay on Development*, when speaking of the Virgin Life in the early Church as an anticipation of its future growth throughout the history of the Church, he links virginity directly with Christ. Among the patristic texts he has collected there, we should note particularly the phrase of Tertullian's of being "married to Christ[37]".

As a correlative to this personal call to celibacy in his Anglican days, we should note among his weekly prayer intentions, dating from 1824, those of Wednesday:

Pray for *Purity*, sobriety—chastity—temperance—self-denial—simplicity—sincerity—truth—openness—candour—Pray against excess,—uncleanness—worldlymindedness—lying—insincerity[38].

This list reappears in his later Catholic Mass notebook with some slight modifications "excess in eating, uncleanness in though, word, or deed."

After February 1829 he had "the continuous will and resolution, with divine aid, to live and die single. I determined to be 'a pilgrim pale in Paul's stern girdle bound'[39]." And yet, he could in a Memorandum written eleven years later admit to himself that though he willingly gives up the sympathy which only a wife can give "Yet, not the less do I feel the need of it[40]."

[35]*Apo.*, p. 25.

[36]Cf. *Dev.*, "Devotion to the Blessed Virgin", pp. 423–434. Also, P. Schneider, O.S.B. "Das Marienbild des anglikanischen Newman": *Newman-Studien* II (1954), pp. 103–119.

[37]*Dev.*, p. 407, quoting Tertullian, *De Virg. Vel.* 16 and 11.

[38]MS, Oratory Archives, C. 5. 12.

[39]MS of *Apo.* (Oratory Archives A. 36. 1).

[40]*A.W.*, p. 138.

In this same Memorandum, while admitting the loneliness of the single heart, Newman expressed his own feelings about a married clergy:

> All my habits for years, my tendencies are towards celibacy. I could not take that interest in this world which marriage requires. I am too disgusted with this world—And, above all, call it what one will, I have a repugnance to a clergyman's marrying. I do not say it is not lawful—I cannot deny the right—but, whether a prejudice or not, it shocks me . . .[41].

From the Catholic period we have ample evidence of his regarding Our Lady as the pattern of purity, the closing pages of *Discourses addressed to Mixed Congregations* being a *locus classicus*. There is, moreover, a splendid, almost lyrical address of Newman's on Virginity, delivered in 1854 on the occasion of the religious profession of Maryanne Bowden, the daughter of one of his earliest friends. This address is all the more telling, because in it Newman speaks so feelingly of marriage, and is aware of the dreariness of that celibacy which is not based on the Gospel,

> . . . a state of life . . . melancholy from its unrequited desolateness . . . unamiable from the pride and self-esteem on which it is based.
>
> This is not the Virginity of the Gospel . . . The Virginity of the Christian soul is a marriage with Christ . . . ours to love, ours to consult, ours to minister to, ours to converse with, ours to gaze on. Ours so fully that it is as if He had none to think of but each of us personally . . . And this it is to be married to Jesus . . . it is to be His, while He is ours . . . that Day will reassemble us . . . the wise virgins will take their lamps . . . and He will take them up to the everlasting banquet—and there will be the mother of Jesus, with the flagons of celestial wine . . .[42].

---

[41]*A.W.*, p. 137.

[42]*Or. P.*, No. 18. Newman had no Anglican precedents for his ideal of virginity; his theological sources for it are patristic, not Anglican. There is a discreet reference to the monastic ideal in the sermon "The Apostolical Christian" (*Sermons on Subjects of the Day*, ed. 1871, pp. 290, 291). It is significant that this sermon dates from very late in his Anglican career—February 1843 (cf. ib. p. 417).

2 Newman's Legacy of Anglican Liturgical Preaching

MUCH has been written in praise of the *Parochial and Plain Sermons,* and all the well-known anthologies of Newman draw heavily on them to illustrate his thought on a wide range of topics[1]. Their value as an appropriate model for liturgical preaching, particularly in the light of Article 52 of the Constitution of Sacred Liturgy (1963) needs to be emphasized, since hitherto attention has been focussed mainly on their ethical content and their consummate English style.

We must not gloss over the fact that these sermons were composed by the Anglican minister, not by the Catholic priest—in the service of the Anglican, not the Catholic liturgy. Nevertheless with due precautions, we may look on this *corpus* of sermons (and more particularly of the new selection of them offered here) as one of the most precious legacies which Newman himself has saved for us from his Anglican days. Few readers today will ever have seen the original edition of the Sermons; the eight-volume sets with which we are familiar date from after the *Apologia* period, when Newman eventually, in 1868, put them back in circulation by having them re-issued —unaltered—by an Anglican editor and publisher. Newman himself, early on, had been aware of the difficulty of using his Protestant works for a Catholic purpose, as may be seen in a letter of October 1848[2]. Early in 1849 Volume IV of the *Parochial and Plain Sermons* was published by Burns with the

[1]Cf.v.g. E. Przywara, *A Newman Synthesis* (1930); *John Henry Cardinal Newman, Pensées sur l'Eglise.* Trad. française par A. Roucou-Barthélemy (Paris, 1956).

[2]Writing to Dr Newsham on 27 October 1848: "The question I have to ask you is this:—Supposing a Catholic *Priest* has a work which he wrote as a *Protestant,* and which he believes on the whole to *promote Catholicism,* and which has in fact promoted it . . . *Can he,* alteration thus being impracticable, *sell the copyright* of such a work? *L. D.,* XII, p. 313.

text "so far altered as they contained any thing contrary to
Faith and Morals[3]." This was the only corrected volume
issued, and it was never reprinted. A one-volume selection of
about fifty sermons published in 1878 is rather ethical than
theological, designed to contribute to the promotion of mutual
sympathy between estranged communions and alienated
hearts.

As regards doctrine, we shall have very few reservations to
make, and these only perhaps in those passages dealing directly
with the Anglican Holy Communion[4]; on all other doctrinal
points, the dates given in the volume of *Sermons on Subjects of the
Day*[5] will be a sufficient guide to guarantee orthodoxy; by 1830
Newman's course of patristic reading was well under way, and
his grasp of the sacramental principle in Christianity was more
and more clear. Where he speaks of such leading topics as
Regenerating Baptism, of the mystery of the Resurrection, of
the role of the Spirit, we may be practically always assured
that the teaching is a distillate of his patristic dogmatics and
his own contemplative musing over the Scriptures, and is
equally valid in a Catholic context now as it was in an Anglican
setting then.

The selection of Sermons offered below provides an admirable working model of the true liturgical homily, except
perhaps in length. Fourteen pages (an average length) would
run to about three quarters of an hour in delivery, which, of
course, would be far too long under modern conditions; the
abbreviation which is called for can be easily made. In all
other respects, however, these Sermons can hardly be surpassed
as liturgical preaching.

Basically dogmatic, and using the traditional patristic theology
of the Incarnation, Redemption and the Trinity, they are,
moreover, thoroughly liturgical, arising in every case out of the
liturgical celebration and keeping in mind the assembled
congregation. Five basic traits are in evidence throughout: the
awareness of the Easter cycle as the great sacramental season;

---

[3]*L. D.*, XII, p. 341, note 2.

[4]See below, chapter 3, *The Eucharistic Ministry*, pp. 46–52: "The Spiritual Role
of the Eucharist in Newman's Anglican Teaching."

[5]ed. 1871, pp. 411–424.

of the eschatalogical Day inaugurated by the Resurrection of
Christ; of the new range of Christian feelings aroused by the
mysteries of Christ's life as commemorated in the liturgy; of
the Presence of the Risen Christ to his Church, and of the
understanding of sacred history as doctrine.

It would be difficult to name any other collection of liturgical
homilies (in any language) composed in the last century and a
half, which could compare with this in quality and quantity.
The five basic traits mentioned above may be illustrated by
some characteristic passages. Thus, in the sermon "Keeping
Fast and Festival", preached on Easter Day, he begins by a
finely drawn picture of the nature of Easter joy:

> ... at Easter our joy is highly wrought and refined in its character
> ... it has a long history before it, and has run through a long
> course of feelings before it becomes what it is. It is a last feeling and
> not a first ... They (Christians) are disposed rather to muse and
> be at peace, than to use many words; for their joy has been so
> much the child of sorrow, is of so transmuted and complex a
> nature, so bound up with painful memories and sad associations,
> that though it is a joy only the greater from the contrast, it is not,
> cannot be, as if it had never been sorrow[6].

Contrasting the attitude of the world at large with that of the
Christian, he says of worldly people:

> To them, one season is the same as another, and they take no
> account of any ... To them the Gospels are but like another
> history; a course of events which took place eighteen hundred
> years since. They do not make our Saviour's life and death
> present to them: they do not transport themselves back to the
> time of his sojourn on earth. They do not act over again, and
> celebrate his history, in their own observance ...[7].

This, then, is the great purpose of the Church festivals and
particularly of Easter—to "act over again" Christ's mysteries
in our commemorations. Elsewhere he calls the Easter cycle the
"Sacramental Season" in which we are specially called to
faith[8].

[6]*P. S.*, IV, Sermon XXIII, pp. 334, 335.
[7]ib. (see preceding note), pp. 337-338.
[8]*P. S.*, VI, Sermon XI, 'The Eucharistic Presence', p. 136.

In the Sermon on "The Spiritual Presence of Christ in the Church," he speaks in scriptural terms of present history before the return of Christ as a "Day", the Day of the Gospel, the Day of grace:

> The Day then, that dawned upon the Church at the Resurrection, and beamed forth in its full splendour at the Ascension, that Day which has no setting, which will be, not ended, but absorbed in Christ's glorious appearance from heaven to destroy sin and death; that Day in which we now are, is described in these words of Christ as a state of special divine manifestation, of special introduction into the presence of God . . . He who was once on earth, has now departed from this visible scene of things in a mysterious, twofold way, both to His Father and into our hearts . . .[9].

This absence and presence of Christ arouses a completely new range of feelings in the Christian heart:

> Now how was it, that when nature would have wept, the Apostles rejoiced? . . . There was no sorrow in the Apostles, in spite of their loss, in spite of the prospect before them . . . For Christ surely had taught them what it was to have their treasure in heaven; and they rejoiced, not that their Lord was gone, but that their hearts had gone with Him[10].

The presence of the Risen Christ to his Church in the liturgical mysteries is finely developed in another sermon on the same theme of the Ascension:

> But when Christ has come, suffered, and ascended, He was henceforth ever near us, ever at hand, even though He was not actually returned, ever scarcely gone, ever all but come back . . . Christ's priests have no priesthood but His. They are merely His shadows and organs, they are His outward signs; and what they do He does; when they baptize, He is baptizing; when they bless, He is blessing. He is in all acts of His Church, and one of its acts is not more truly His than another, for all are His . . . since historically speaking, time has gone on, and the Holy One is away, certain outward forms are necessary, by way of bringing us again under His shadow; and we enjoy those blessings through a mystery, or sacramentally, in order to enjoy them really[11].

[9]*P. S.*, VI, Sermon X, p. 123.
[10]*P. S.*, VI, Sermon XVI, 'Warfare the Condition of Victory', pp. 225, 226.
[11]*P. S.*, VI, Sermon XVII, 'Waiting for Christ', p. 242.

Newman has a passage very similar to this in his *Lectures on the Doctrine of Justification*[12], to which in 1874 he added the rider: "It is true that there is but one Priest and one Sacrifice under the Gospel, but this is because the Priests of the Gospel are *one* with Christ, not because they are *improperly* called Priests[13]." Granted this corrective, I do not know where one could find in liturgical literature of the nineteenth century so close an anticipation of the doctrine of the Constitution on liturgy of Vatican II about the presence of Christ in the liturgy through his paschal mystery. Article 7 of the Constitution, though not having any direct literary dependence on Newman, reads almost like a paraphrase of his thought as expressed in the sermon quoted above and in the parallel text of the *Lectures on the Doctrine of Justification*[14]. The true significance of this would surely seem to be that Newman's insights into the deeper meaning of the liturgy can be an excellent guide to the spirit of the Constitution.

The idea of sacred history as doctrine—the "history of salvation" as it is called nowadays—and as such being con-

---

[12]6th ed., 1892, pp. 196–198: "Henceforth whatever is done is His doing, and it is called what it is. As He is the unseen source, so must He be acknowledged as the Agent, the present Object of worship and thanksgiving in all that is done; and His instruments are not even so much as instruments, but only the outward lineaments of Him. All is superseded by Him, and transmuted into Him . . . There were mediators many, and prophets many, and atonements many. But now all is superseded by One, in whom all offices merge, who has absorbed into Himself all principality, power, might and dominion . . . He is the sole self-existing principle in the Christian Church, and everything else is but a portion or declaration of Him . . . There is under the Gospel but One proper Priest, Prophet and King, Altar, Sacrifice, and House of God. Unity is its characteristic sacrament; all grace flows from One Head, and all life circulates in the members of One Body . . .."

Newman has a further patristic note on the Priesthood of Christ in his *Select Treatises of St Athanasius* (2nd ed., 1881), pp. 245, 246. Besides the collection of liturgical sermons grouped below, pp. 40–42 of the present work, we should also note Sermon V "The three Offices of Christ" in *Sermons on Subjects of the Day* (ed. 1871, pp. 52–62). This should in turn be compared with his Essay on the three Offices of the Church contained in the "Perface to the Third Edition" of the *Via Media* (1877).

In the present study I have concentrated more on the practical, pastoral aspects of Newman's spirituality as a priest in his own life, rather than on his dogmatic teaching about the priesthood of Christ of which the passages quoted above furnish the essentials.

[13]6th ed., 1892, p. 198.

[14]See above, note 12.

tinued in the Christian liturgy and in Christian life, is another cardinal point of the new Constitution, and it is a thought which was familiar to Newman, and recurs constantly in these Anglican sermons. In the sermon on "The Indwelling Spirit" he sums it up clearly:

> (The Spirit) inspired the Holy Evangelists to record the life of Christ, and directed them which of His words and works to select, which to omit; next, He commented (as it were) upon these, and unfolded their meaning in the Apostolic Epistles. The birth, the life, the death and resurrection of Christ, has been the text which He has illuminated. He has made history to be doctrine; telling us plainly, whether by St John or St Paul, that Christ's conception and birth was the real Incarnation of the Eternal Word,—His life, 'God made manifest in the Flesh,'—His death and resurrection the Atonement for sin, and the Justification of all believers[15].

This is the first stage—salvation as wrought out in the life of Christ, and as recorded in Scripture. Newman's thought, however, does not stop short at this, but presses on to the Spirit's "sacred comment in the formation of the Church" and finally to the "conveying of this system of truth, thus varied and expanded, to the heart of each individual Christian in whom He dwells[16]."

This sense of the history of salvation continued in the liturgy comes out incidentally, but perspicuously in the opening passage of a sermon on the Trinity[17], where Newman clearly draws the distinction between the mysteries in themselves and our liturgical celebration of them. We do not, he says, celebrate the mysteries simply because they are mysterious, but because they are saving mysteries. Trinity Sunday is an exception: on that day we celebrate the mystery for its own sake, not for our sake. Here, once again, with a sure touch, he has pointed out

---

[15]*P. S.*, II, Sermon XIX, p. 227.

[16]ib. (cf. preceding note), p. 228

[17]*P. S.*, VI, Sermon XXIII: "Faith without Demonstration," p. 327: " . . . the present Festival has this peculiarity in it,—that it is the commemoration of a mystery. Other Festivals celebrate mysteries also, but not because they are mysteries . . . we celebrate them not on this account, but for the blessings which we gain from them . . "

a truth which is axiomatic among liturgists today, that the true
purpose of a liturgical feast is not to celebrate an "idea" but
a "fact". This is a basic principle for the modern revision of the
liturgical calendar[18].

Newman's handling of Scripture throughout these sermons
in singularly fresh and "undated", although they were delivered
well over a century ago. He had been indebted to Scott the
"Commentator" for early evangelical impressions; there is,
however, little or no trace in Newman's own sermons of
dependence on any exegetical school or system. He simply
brings his own native intelligence to bear on the sacred text;
there is, of course, always in the background his grasp of the
patristic treatment of the great doctrines of the Incarnation and
Redemption.

His homiletic method will be best understood if we realize
that he treats his subject after the manner of scriptural themes,
comparable to that of v.g. the *Vocabulaire de théologie biblique*[19];
he is not making a descriptive meditation on Scripture scenes,
but elucidating the hidden harmonies of the sacred text. One
of the best examples is his sermon on "The Gift of the Spirit",
where his analysis of the idea of "glory" approximates very
closely to the best modern scholarship on the biblical idea of
doxa[20]. To quote:

> Such reflections as these are calculated, perhaps, to give us some-
> what of a deeper view than is ordinarily admitted, of the character
> of that Gift which attends on the presence of the Holy Ghost in
> the Church, and which is called the gift of glory . . . The gift is
> denoted in Scripture by the vague and mysterious term 'glory';
> and all the descriptions we can give of it can only, and should
> only, run out into a mystery . . . illumination, the heavenly gift, the
> Holy Ghost, the Divine Word, the powers of the world to come;
> which all mean the same thing, viewed in different lights, viz.,
> that unspeakable Gospel privilege . . . a present entrance into the
> next world, opened upon our souls through participation of the
> Word Incarnate, ministered to us by the Holy Ghost[21].

[18]J.A. Jungmann, S. J., *Pastoral Liturgy* (1962), pp. 395–99.
[19]ed. Xavier Léon-Dufour, (Paris, Les Editions du Cerf, 1962).
[20]C. Mohrmann, *Etudes sur le Latin des chrétiens* (Rome, 1958), pp. 277–86.
[21]*P. S.,* III, Sermon XVIII, pp. 260–3.

Two procedures characterize Newman's homiletic method, by which he rejoins modern Scripture study: the constant appeal to parallel passages and the habitual use of the Old Testament—particularly the Prophets—to explain the great themes of the New. In the sermon we have been considering, "The Gift of the Spirit", both these traits are conspicuous. We should note too, that like the best commentators among the moderns, Newman is not content with verbal parallels, but seeks everywhere for similar ideas. Nor does he fail to include the individual as well as the ecclesial dimension of the doctrine, as v.g. when he says:

> . . . it may be asked, how far the gift is also imparted to every individual . . .? It is imparted to every member on his Baptism . . . By this new birth the Divine Shechinah is set up within him, pervading soul and body . . . raising him in the scale of being, drawing and fostering into life whatever remains in him of a higher nature, and imparting to him, in due season and measure, its own surpassing and heavenly virtue[22].

An unpublished sermon (No. 290) "On the object and effects of Preaching (on the anniversary of my living), St Mary the Virgin, S.A. 20 March 1831, 15 March 1835" gives us Newman's reflections on the relation between his ministry of preaching and the Church's public prayer.

Taking as his text "Do the work of an evangelist" (2 *Tim.* 4:5), after an introduction, he proceeds to distinguish between the broad comprehensive sense which "preaching" connotes in the New Testament, and the narrow meaning it had acquired in his own day of meaning one type of public instruction:

> . . . In Scripture to preach is to do the work of an evangelist, is to teach, instruct, advise, encourage in all things pertaining to religion, in any way whatever. All education is a kind of preaching—all catechizing, all private conversation—all writing. In all things and at all times is a Christian minister preaching in the Scriptural sense of the word . . . and in all matters and pursuits of this world as truly, though not as directly as when engaged in religious subjects[23].

---

[22]ib. (cf. preceding note), p. 266.
[23]Oratory Archives, Early Sermons B.3.6.

The public instruction provided in sermons is only a means
to an end: an incentive to prayer. Baptized Christians are not
in the position of heathens, catechumens or backsliders, he
continues; when they come to church, it is not to hear a human
preacher merely, but to pray together:

> . . . Men . . . speak as if hearing so-called preaching was *the* great
> ordinance of the Christian religion, whereas the great ordinance
> . . . is joint prayer and praise together . . . it is the peculiar office
> of *public* prayer to bring down Christ among us, it is as being
> many collected into one that Christ recognizes us as His . . .
> preaching (i.e. public instruction,) being added but only as a
> means of our praying better and living better. But prayer is an
> end, for it is devotion, an acceptable sacrifice, the Christian's
> life itself . . .[24].

The last-quoted text above gives us the clue where to look
for the true counterpart in Newman's Catholic life to the place
occupied by the *Parochial and Plain Sermons* in his Anglican
period. It is in Part III of the posthumously published *Meditations and Devotions* that the characteristic tone of the *Parochial
and Plain Sermons* comes to light again, this time in a context of
prayer, not of preaching. The most recent edition of the
Meditations and Devotions has wisely put Part III at the beginning
of the book; an examination of the MSS shows that this section
(beginning at the §III. "God and the Soul") is an independent
MS in a separate copybook, most probably written for
Newman's own private use[25]. Like the *Parochial and Plain
Sermons* these prayers are written in scriptural terms within a
liturgical framework (some pencil markings in the MS bear
this point out: Lent I, Lent II, etc. These pencil markings are
in Newman's hand).

Newman's idea of virginity being a marriage with Christ
may be seen in his own case throughout these prayers. Here we
see Newman himself "consulting, conversing with, gazing on
Emmanuel[26]"—his favourite title of Christ in this MS. There
is a faintly decipherable note in Newman's handwriting

---

[24]ib. (cf. preceding note).
[25]It is significant that this copybook was never made public by Newman himself.
[26]Cf. Newman's Address on Virginity, *Or. P.*, 18.

opposite the first "Meditation": "O if in this day He shall say, I *asked* his love and he would not give it me. I courted him"— this gives the *leitmotiv* of the whole. It is not a description of a mystical union through infused contemplation; but the awareness in the light of faith of the shortcomings of the soul in its love. *Thou wooest me*[27], *O my only true Lover*[28], *the only Lover of my soul*[29], *O my all-sufficient Lord, Thou alone sufficest*[30]— these and many other haunting phrases are the soul's response in this "marriage with Christ." Here we have all the earnestness of the *Parochial and Plain Sermons,* their sobriety, their restraint, their realism, pitched now in a more intimate key of personal prayer.

Newman's Catholic sermons—apart from some of the *Occasional Sermons*—disappoint us today in this respect. We feel a hiatus between his Anglican and his Catholic sermons, perhaps because he felt obliged to fall into line with Catholic practice, even where no principle of faith or discipline was involved. Thus, for example, he tells us himself that one of the sermons in the volume *Discourses addressed to Mixed Congregations,* is based directly on St Alphonsus Liguori[31].

The following selection of the *Parochial and Plain Sermons,* on a rigorously liturgical (and not merely ethical) basis, has been compiled by the present writer, in view of what was said above. The Sermons have been arranged in groups according to the liturgical seasons. Within each group, the order follows

---

[27] *Meditations and Devotions of the late Cardinal Newman* (2nd ed., 1893), p. 512: "And now Thou biddest me love Thee in turn, for Thou hast loved me. Thou wooest me to love Thee specially, above others. Thou dost say, 'Lovest Thou Me more than these?' . . . Thou hast done that for me, O my love, which ought to make me love Thee with all my powers."

[28] ib., p. 483.

[29] ib., p. 483: " . . . Thee will I love now, that I may love Thee then."

[30] ib., p. 505.

[31] "As to the Sermon on Calls and Warnings, it is a saying of St Philip's that no one can hope for heaven, who has not feared hell and contemplated damnation— and in the said Sermon I have but made easy-going Catholics in danger of hell. But the best joke is that the Sermon (the only one in the Volume) is taken from St Alfonso's for the 1st Sunday in Lent on 'The number of sins beyond which God pardons no more—' with text 'Thou shalt not tempt the Lord thy God.'" Newman to Faber, 14 December 1849, *L. D.,* XIII, p. 341.

the date of delivery, following the dates given, as has been suggested above, in *Sermons on Subjects of the Day*[32].

I. EASTER

1. *Christ, A Quickening Spirit*, Vol. II, Sermon XIII, 3 April 1831.
2. *The Resurrection of the Body*, Vol. I, Sermon XXI, 22 April 1832.
3. *Witnesses of the Resurrection*, Vol. I, Sermon XXII, 24 April 1831.
4. *Christian Reverence*, Vol. I, Sermon XXIII, 8 May 1831.
5. *Keeping Fast and Festival*, Vol. IV, Sermon XXIII, 15 April 1838.
6. *The Spiritual Presence of Christ in the Church*, Vol. VI, Sermon X, 6 May 1838.
7. *The Eucharistic Presence*, Vol. VI, Sermon XI, 13 May 1838.
8. *Difficulty of Realizing Sacred Privileges*, Vol. VI, Sermon VIII, 31 March 1839.

II. HOLY WEEK

9. *The Humiliation of the Eternal Son*, Vol. III, Sermon XII, 8 March 1825.
10. *The Incarnate Son, A Sufferer and a Sacrifice*, Vol. VI, Sermon VI, 1 April 1836.
11. *The Cross of Christ, the Measure of the World*, Vol. VI, Sermon VII, 9 April 1841.
12. *The Crucifixion*, Vol. VII, Sermon X, 25 March 1842.

III. THE ASCENSION

13. *Mysteries in Religion*, Vol. II, Sermon XVIII, 1834, end of year.
14. *Rising with Christ*, Vol. VI, Sermon XV, 1836 or 1837.
15. *Warfare the Condition of Victory*, Vol. VI, Sermon XVI, 24 May 1838.
16. *Waiting for Christ*, Vol. VI, Sermon XVII, 29 November & 6 December 1840.

[32]See above, p. 31.

IV. PENTECOST

17. *The Visible Church an Encouragement to Faith,* Vol. III, Sermon XVII, 14 September 1834.
18. *The Indwelling Spirit,* Vol. II, Sermon XIX, 1834, end of year.
19. *The Kingdom of the Saints,* Vol. II, Sermons XXI–XXII. 1835, January or February; 1834, end of year.
20. *The Gift of the Spirit,* Vol. III, Sermon XVIII, 8 November 1835.
21. *The Visible Church for the sake of the Elect,* Vol. IV, Sermon X, 20 November 1836.
22. *The Communion of Saints,* Vol. IV, Sermon XI, 14 May 1837.
23. *The Church a Home for the Lonely,* Vol. IV, Sermon XII, 22 October 1837.
24. *Christ manifested in Remembrance,* Vol. IV, Sermon XVII, 7 May 1837.
25. *The Visible Temple,* Vol. VI, Sermon XX, 22 September 1840.
26. *Christian Manhood,* Vol. I, Sermon XXVI, 15 May 1831.

V. TRINITY

27. *The Christian Mysteries,* Vol. I, Sermon XVI, 14 June 1829.
28. *The Mysteriousness of our present Being,* Vol. IV, Sermon XIX, 29 May 1836.
29. *Faith without Demonstration,* Vol. VI, Sermon XXIII, 21 May 1837.
30. *The Mystery of the Holy Trinity,* Vol. VI, Sermon XXIV, date not known.

VI. ADVENT AND CHRISTMAS

31. *Worship, a Preparation for Christ's coming,* Vol. V, Sermon I, 2 December 1838.
32. *The Incarnation,* Vol. II, Sermon III, 25 December 1834.
33. *The Mystery of Godliness,* Vol. V, Sermon VII, 26 March 1837.
34. *Remembrance of past Mercies,* Vol. V, Sermon VI, 22 September 1838.

35. *Christian Sympathy*, Vol. V, Sermon IX, 17 February 1839.
36. *Christ hidden from the World*, Vol. IV, Sermon XVI, 25 December 1837.

VII. Epiphany

37. *The Glory of the Christian Church*, Vol. II, Sermon VIII, 1834, end of year.
38. *Righteousness, not of us, but in us*, Vol. V, Sermon X, 19 January 1840.
39. *The Season of Epiphany*, Vol. VII, Sermon VI, 17 January 1841.

VIII. The Saints

40. *Use of Saints' Days*, Vol. II, Sermon XXXII, 30 November 1831. See the many Sermons for Saints' Days in Vol. II, none of these being later than 1835[33].

---

[33]See *Sermons on Subjects of the Day* (ed. 1871), p. 412.

3   *The Eucharistic Ministry*

I T is only natural that we should, at this point, ask ourselves what doctrinal consistency lay behind this care of souls, these deep insights into the true nature of liturgical preaching. What of the heart of the liturgy itself, the Eucharist, and its ministry at the hands of an ordained priesthood? What did Newman, as an Anglican, believe about the Eucharist and about his Anglican Orders? How far may we consider his own reception and celebration of Anglican Holy Communion from youth to middle age as the matrix of his eucharistic faith and experience as a Catholic and a priest?

Many closely connected and delicate problems need to be unravelled if we wish to render faithfully all the different nuances in this picture. We are looking deep down into the soul of a living man, who had spent a lifetime in devotion centred on the Anglican Holy Communion before he came to the Catholic Church and the Mass. As a Catholic he did not simply write off what he had lived as an Anglican; after his conversion, speaking of his faith as an Anglican, he could write: ". . . And when I was at the early Eucharistic Service at St Mary's (I thus specify it, because I am appealing to my memory distinctly) I had an absolute and overpowering sense of the Real Presence . . .[1]."

The only satisfactory way of doing justice to all sides of this complex problem is to trace out the growth within Newman's own life of his thought and faith about the Eucharist: any other approach, particularly a schematic and ready-made summary of headings, would be a clumsy and ill-fitting suit of armour—Newman himself used complain like David, of the weight of the king's armour.

[1]Letter to Henry Wilberforce, 27 January 1846, *L. D.*, XI, p. 101.

A basic point in this whole matter is his doctrinal development in the decade 1823–1833, when he abandoned his early
evangelical positions and came to hold firmly a foundation of
dogma, as he has described it in the *Apologia:*

> . . . that there was a visible Church, with sacraments and rites
> which are the channels of invisible grace . . . after reading Anglican
> divines on the one hand, and after prosecuting the study of the
> Fathers on the other . . .[2].

According to Brilioth, Newman's "acceptance of the
doctrine of Baptismal Regeneration indicates his defection
from Evangelicalism[3]." As regards the Eucharist, we may take
it that Newman, as editor of Froude's *Remains,* fully endorsed
the remarkable essay on priesthood and sacrifice which this
book contains: his theological position may be fairly described
as a belief in the Real Presence, and in the Eucharist as a
sacrifice, though without accepting the doctrine of Transubstantiation. In a controversial letter supporting Froude's views
on the Eucharist, he defends the doctrine of the Real Presence
as being that of the Church of England Catechism and Homilies
as well as that of the Anglican divine, Hooker, stating the
problem as follows:

> . . . three questions offer themselves for consideration; first,
> whether there is a Real Presence of Christ in this Holy Sacrament,
> next what It is, and thirdly where . . .[4].

Having then quoted official Anglican formularies on the
Presence, he concludes:

> . . . these passages seem to determine that the Body and Blood of
> Christ are not absent, but present in the Lord's Supper; and if
> really, and in fact Christ's Body be there, His Soul is there, and
> His Divinity . . . Nor does any one doubt of His Presence on our
> altars as God, for He is everywhere; but the question is whether,
> His human nature also is present in the Sacrament . . .[5].

[2]*Apo.,* p. 49.
[3]*Brilioth,* p. 307.
[4]*The Via Media* (3rd ed., 1877), II, p. 220.
[5]ib. (cf. preceding note), p. 221.

He next examines the problem of what is meant by saying that Christ is really present, yet not locally:

> Presence . . . is a relative word, depending on the channels of communication existing between the object and the person to whom it is present. It is almost a correlative of the senses . . . As sight for certain purposes annihilates space, so other unknown conditions of our being, bodily or spiritual, may practically annihilate it for other purposes. Such may be the Sacramental Presence. We kneel before the Heavenly Throne, and distance vanishes; it is as if that Throne were the Altar close to us[6].

To this first suggestion he now adds another, which bears out the note he added later as a Catholic ("His Presence is substantial, spirit-wise, sacramental; an absolute mystery, not against reason, however, but against imagination, and must be received by faith[7]"):

> Our Lord . . . now that He is in Heaven . . . is not subject to the laws of matter, and has no necessary relations to place, no dependence on its conditions . . . His mode of making himself present on earth, of coming and going, is as different from the mode natural to bodies by locomotion,—nearness being determined by intervals and absence being synonymous with distance,—as spirit is different from matter. He may be literally present in the Holy Eucharist, yet, not having become present by a movement and a transit, He may still be continuously on God's right hand[8].

Thirdly, he considers the relation of the consecrated elements to those realities of which they are the outward sign. Here he shrinks from the doctrine of Transubstantiation (which, as he admits in a later note, he misconstrues) but continues to maintain the reality of the Presence. Speaking of this pamphlet in the *Apologia*, he says: '(It was) an attempt at placing the doctrine of the Real Presence on an intellectual basis. The fundamental idea is consonant to that to which I had been so long attached: it is the denial of the existence of space except as a subjective idea of our minds[9].'

---

[6]ib. (see note 4, above), pp. 227, 228.
[7]ib. (see note 4, above), p. 220, note 6.
[8]ib. (see note 4, above), p. 228.
[9]*Apo.*, p. 73.

With this theological basis of the Real Presence in mind, let us now examine Newman's teaching on the spiritual role of the Eucharist. We have fortunately two exquisite eucharistic sermons of his, one dating from 1832, the other from 1838— these dates, it should be noted, being significant, since within that period Newman had not yet thought of leaving the Anglican Church. We have here then, his Anglican faith in the Eucharist expressed with greatest feeling. The two sermons are respectively "The Resurrection of the Body"[10] and "The Eucharistic Presence"[11], and they may be taken not only as representative samples of his thought, but as the most explicit statement of it.

The Resurrection of the Body (*P.S.* I, Sermon XXI)

In this sermon he is concerned with the *effect* of our eating Christ's flesh. In what real sense is the consecrated Bread his body? We do not know, we may not enquire, all we are concerned with is the effect on us of eating it. This doctrine is addressed to faith, not to our reason: just as in the doctrine of the resurrection from the dead—we know so little of the extent of God's power that we have nothing to reason upon, we have no means or ground of argument. This, however, is not a blind uncertainty: we *know* we eat his Body and drink his Blood; 'but it is our wisdom not curiously to ask how or whence, not to give our thoughts range, but to take and eat and profit thereby'.

[10]Preached on 22 April 1832, cf. *Sermons on Subjects of the Day* (ed. 1871) p. 411. For a different appreciation of Newman's eucharistic doctrine as an Anglican, see *Brilioth* pp. 318 ff: " . . . When, in 1838, Newman treats the subject in two sermons, one feels that the theme did not specially inspire him. One, 'The Gospel Feast,' puts together Biblical passages, which can be explained as types of the Eucharist, and adds to them a very tame conclusion. In another, 'The Eucharistic Presence,' there is a very dry presentation of the correct doctrine of a Presence of Christ, which is real, without being corporal, thus rejecting Transubstantiation: while a typically Tractarian warning is added, not to neglect this means of grace; it may contain more than we now see in it."

This meagre appreciation of Newman's eucharistic doctrine surprises one in Brilioth, who usually displays a keen insight into Newman's mind. Perhaps his interest in Pusey's doctrine made him unwittingly belittle Newman's. See *loc. cit.*, pp. 318ff.

[11]Preached on 13 May 1838. Cf. *Sermons on Subjects of the Day* (ed. 1871), p. 415.

In examining Christ's promise of life through the Eucharist, Newman rejoins modern biblical insights about the unity of man's nature. We are apt to speak of "soul and body" as if we could distinguish between them, but for the most part we use words without meaning. Soul and body make up one man, which is born once and never dies. Christ's Blessed Supper is food to us altogether, *whatever* we are, soul, body and all; it is not given to us to distinguish what he does for our different natures, spiritual and material.

The eschatalogical promise of life in the Eucharist should come home to us with greater force in a church round which the dead are buried. This dust will one day become animate, life to the living God. In the Communion Service we magnify God together with the Angels: if our eyes were opened like Elisha's servant, we would perceive the Angels in their ministrations to the Christian dead.

The conclusion drawn in this sermon is that the body is not the source of sin; sin is a disease of the mind, of our whole nature; Christ has redeemed our whole nature, both sinful soul and body. We should lay up year by year the seed of life proferred to us in the Eucharist, believing that it will one day bear fruit.

There is nothing in this sermon incompatible with Catholic theology, except perhaps an over-insistence on our inability to penetrate the mystery, emphasized to the point almost as if we had to renounce all theological investigation of it. The thought processes of this very sermon itself, however, show us Newman himself exercising his own mind on the implications of the text of *Luke* 20:37–38 ("God is the God of the living") and its eucharistic overtones. The treatment of the Eucharist in this sermon as the seed of life and of immortality, in default of explicit references, may nevertheless be confidently referred to the Epistles of St Ignatius for its inspiration.

It may not be out of place here to wonder how many Catholic sermons on the Eucharist preached at the time in England or elsewhere gave such a faithful echo of the biblical and patristic understanding of the meaning of "life", the "unity" of the human person, the eschatalogical dimension of the eucharistic celebration.

The Eucharistic Presence (*P.S.* VI, Sermon XI)

One preliminary mental corrective is needed when reading this sermon: Newman as an Anglican had no idea of the Presence in the Reserved Sacrament[12]; he is referring therefore to the Presence of Christ during the celebration of the mystery, not to the "Blessed Sacrament" in the tabernacle. Incidentally, we should note that after his conversion to Catholicism he found great consolation in his faith in the Reserved Sacrament[13].

The sermon—which contains a wealth of insights which sound surprisingly modern—opens by referring to the time from Ash Wednesday to Trinity Sunday as the sacramental

---

[12]i.e. outside the time of celebration, the custom of Reservation not existing at that time among Anglicans. Cf. v.g. *Apo.* 35: " . . . I was aching to get home; yet for want of a vessel I was kept at Palermo for three weeks. I began to visit the Churches, and they calmed my impatience, though I did not attend any services. I knew nothing of the presence of the Blessed Sacrament there . . ." *The Oxford Dictionary of the Christian Church* (1958) has the following remarks s.v. *Reservation:* " . . . As a matter of history, the practice had died out in the Church of England, except in very rare instances, before the beginning of the nineteenth century, but it has now been widely restored . . . The rubrics which would have permitted the practice in the proposed English Prayer Books of 1927 and 1928 largely contributed to the defeat of the Prayer Book Measure in Parliament" (p. 1156).

[13]The following gleanings illustrate Newman's personal devotion to the Blessed Sacrament. In a letter of 4 October 1846 to Mrs Bowden, written from Milan in the course of his journey to Rome, he writes: " . . . here are a score of Churches which are open to the passer by, . . . in each of which . . . the Blessed Sacrament ready for the worshipper even before he enters. There is nothing which has brought home to me the Unity of the Church, as the Presence of its Divine Founder and Life wherever I go—All places are, as it were, one . . . " *L. D.,* XI, p. 254.

Again to the same correspondent in July 1851 about her daughter's vocation: " . . . The vow of obedience is the difficult vow. It is very complex—it is not merely obedience to one Superior, but to a state of things, resignation to companions she may not like etc etc. An intense devotion to the Blessed Sacrament will overcome every trial." *L. D.,* XIV, p. 307.

In the stress of the Achilli trial (1852), Newman spent most of his time praying before the Blessed Sacrament "in the tribune at the King William Street chapel." (*Trevor,* I, p. 595).

Later on in 1860, writing in his Private Journal about the difficulty of not being appreciated by his ecclesiastical superiors, he says: " . . . This has naturally made me shrink into myself, or rather it has made me think of turning more to God, if it has not actually turned me. It has me feel that in the Blessed Sacrament is my great consolation, and that while I have him who lives in the Church, the separate members of the Church, my Superiors, though they may claim my obedience, have no claim on my admiration, and offer nothing for my inward trust . . ." *A. W.,* pp. 251, 252.

season of the year. We are called to faith in an exceptional way at this time. The greatest and highest of all sacramental mysteries which faith has been vouchsafed is Holy Communion. Christ who died and rose again for us, is in it spiritually present in the fullness of his death and resurrection. We call his presence in this Holy Sacrament a "spiritual" presence, not as if "spiritual" were but a name or mode of speech, and he were really absent, but by way of expressing that he who is present there can neither be seen nor heard; that he cannot be approached or ascertained by any of the senses; that he is not present in place, that he is not present carnally, though he is really present. And how this is, is of course a mystery. All that we know or need know is that he *is* given to us, and that in the Sacrament of Holy Communion. The sermon is based on *John* 6:50, and Newman takes this sixth chapter of St John as treating of the Last Supper, and as being in fact a comment upon the account of it given by the other three Evangelists: St John explains as a doctrine what the other Evangelists deliver as an ordinance. When Christ used the words given in St John's text, he was prospectively describing that gift, which, in due season, the consecrated Bread and Wine were to convey to his Church for ever. This announcement in St John looks on towards and is accomplished in the consecrated Bread and Wine of Holy Communion.

It is not conceivable that he who is the Truth and Love itself should have used difficult words when plain words would do. Which is more likely, that his meaning is beyond us, or his words beyond his meaning? The opposite feelings of St Peter and the disciples to Christ's "hard saying" give us a token of our Saviour's real meaning.

We next consider our Lord's allusion to the manna. Some persons explain our eating Christ's flesh and blood as merely meaning our receiving a *pledge* of the *effects* of the *Passion* of his Body and Blood, i.e.; in other words, of the favour of Almighty God: but how can Christ's giving us his Body and Blood mean merely giving us a pledge of his favour? These awful words are far too clear and precise to be thus carelessly treated. Christ would not use such definite terms did he intend to convey an idea so far removed from their meaning and so easy of expression in simple language. Now it increases the force of this consideration to observe that the manna, to which he compares his gift, was not a figure of speech, but a something definite and particular, really given, really received. The manna was not simply health, or life or God's favour, but a certain something which caused health, continued life and betokened God's favour. Manna was a gift external to the Israelites, and external also to God's own judgment of them and resolve concerning them, a gift created by him and partaken by his people. What therefore the manna was in the wilderness, that surely is the spiritual manna in the Christian Church; the manna in the wilderness was a real gift, taken and eaten; so is the manna in the Church. It is not God's mercy or favour; it is not a state of grace, or the promise of eternal life, or the privileges of the Gospel, or the new covenant; much less is it the doctrine of the Gospel or faith in that doctrine; but it is what our Lord says it is, the gift of his own precious Body and Blood, really given, taken and eaten as the manna might be (though in a way unknown), at a particular time, and a certain particular spot; namely, at the time and spot when and where the Holy Communion is celebrated.

The preacher now examines the significance of our Lord's rebuking the multitude for not dwelling on the miracle of the loaves *as* a miracle. Christ generally represses the Jews' desire for signs, but here he stimulates it. He finds fault here, because they did not dwell upon the miracle. Now supposing the Eucharistic Gift is a special sign, this will account for the difference between his conduct on this occasion and on others, it being as unbelieving to overlook signs when given, as to ask for them when withheld.

Next, the incomprehensible nature of the miracle of the loaves is a kind of protection of the mystery of the Eucharist against objections with which men are wont to assail it. As to Christ's other miracles, they are, it may be said, intelligible, though supernatural, but to speak of five thousand persons being fed with five loaves may be speciously represented to be almost a contradiction in terms. How could it be? Did the substance of the bread grow? Or was it the same bread here, there and everywhere, for this man and that, at one and the same time? Or was it created in the shape of bread, in that ultimate condition into which the grain is produced by the labour of man, and this again and again created out of nothing till the whole five thousand were satisfied? If the marvellousness of the miracle of loaves is no real objection to its truth, neither is the marvellousness of the Eucharistic Gift any real difficulty in believing that gift.

Further, the identity of the gestures which Christ used in multiplying the loaves and at the Last Supper, shows us that the feeding of the multitude with loaves interprets the Lord's Supper.

Christ, at the end of the discourse, in appearance withdraws his words. Allowing for argument's sake that he seems to qualify the wonderful words he used at first; what follows from such an admission? Only this, that God's rule of dealing with unbelief is illustrated again here as if he said "It is by a Divine Gift that you believe; beware, lest by objections you provoke God to take away from you his aid, his preventing and enlightening grace."

A sermon such as this certainly gave the fullest possible eucharistic content to the Anglican Communion Service, and as such, in relation to its historical setting and background, the reader of today can only applaud and assent. What, however, is its value judged by absolute standards of Catholic belief? It is a sermon, not a treatise; no preacher—and least of all Newman—ever covers all the aspects of his subject. (In fact, Newman used to reproach both the Evangelicals and the Catholics with the particular weakness of wanting to hear everything said in every sermon[14]). He is here confining himself to treating of the reality of Christ's presence during the celebration of the Eucharist. He calls this presence "spiritual" —but he immediately qualifies this by saying that it is not to be misunderstood in the sense of being equivalent to unreal. His argument from the parallel between the manna and the Eucharist hits upon the exact term of comparison: the concrete particular nature of both—not merely a doctrine, but a gift.

---

[14]*L.D.* XII, p. 372: " . . . indeed I have thought Catholics almost puritanical in their horror of onesided views in Sermons—like the Evangelicals, who want all doctrine to come into every sentence."

He has grasped the significance of the "signs" addressed to faith, and has seen in the incomprehensibility of the miracle of the loaves a protective veil of the eucharistic mystery. He has rightly seen that *John* 6 interprets the Synoptic accounts of the Last Supper for us. His last point about God's dealing with unbelief is in line with the doctrine of the Epistle to the Hebrews about not hardening one's heart.

All the above constitute a valuable accumulation of perfectly valid insights into a theology of the Eucharist, at once biblical and sacramental. Does Newman, however, fall short of complete Catholic doctrine in failing to affirm that the Eucharist is not only a gift *from* God to the Church, but also a sacrifice, an offering of Christ *to* the Father? He does not explicitly propound this, but such omission of itself would not in his case betoken denial of this truth, since he did not consider it necessary to say everything in every sermon. We should, too, note carefully the phrase: "Christ, who died and rose for us again, is in it spiritually present, in the fullness of his death and of his resurrection[15]." This phrase (so reminiscent of Casel's "Mystery Presence"), combined with Newman's theology of the Real Presence, goes a long way towards a sacrificial concept of the Eucharist[16].

[15] *P.S.* VI, Sermon XI, p. 136.

[16] In *Tract* 90 Newman made one last supreme effort to reconcile a Catholic sacrificial doctrine of the Mass with the official formularies of Anglicanism, particularly with Article xxxi of the Thirty Nine Articles. He held that "the sacrifice of the *Mass* is not spoken of, in which the special question of doctrine would be introduced; but 'the sacrifice of *Masses*,' certain observances, for the most part private and solitary, which the writers of the Articles knew to have been in force in time past, and saw before their eyes, and which involved certain opinions and a certain teaching." (*Via Media*, 3rd ed., 1877, vol. II, p. 315).

In re-editing the Tract (in the edition referred to above), Newman, now a Catholic, repudiated this distinction: 'I do not see then how it can be denied that this Article calls the sacrifice of the Mass itself, in all its private and solitary celebrations (to speak of no other), that is, in all its daily celebrations from year's end to year's end, toto orbe terrarum, a "blasphemous fable."' (*loc. cit.* p. 316, note 1).

One might refer at this point to Francis Clark, S.J., whose study *Eucharistic Sacrifice and the Reformation* (London, 1960) has as its main thesis that the English Reformers (and hence the Anglican Church) had really rejected the Catholic doctrine of the sacrifice of the Mass (and not merely the alleged medieval abuses of the Mass), see especially p. 514, and also F. Hildebrandt, *I Offered Christ*, London 1967, p. 56.

After 14 October 1843 Newman "regarded himself as no longer a priest in the service of the Church of England . . ." Brilioth tells us[17]; it is important, however, to realize that he still regarded himself as a priest, and this in virtue of his Anglican ordination. What then were his precise views on his Anglican Orders at the time of his conversion and in the years immediately subsequent to it? There would seem to have been a definite development and change in his thought on this point between October 1845 and July 1848: a change from a belief in their validity in his own case to a belief in their non-validity in general. Writing on 9 October 1845—the day he was received as a Catholic—he says:

> The Church of Rome has never acknowledged English Orders, though she has never formally denied them. Practically, I am a layman in her eyes[18].

Again, in the *Apologia* he writes: "For a while after my reception, I proposed to betake myself to some secular calling[19]." There is, however, no trace as far as one can see in his day-to-day correspondence of any practical steps taken by him to take up a secular calling, nor does he, in the *Apologia*, give any reason of his proposal to himself to do so.

The real reason for this resolution was not that he did not feel himself called to be a priest in the Catholic Church, but that believing himself to be a priest already in virtue of his Anglican ordination, he felt a scruple in exposing the Sacrament to sacrilege by re-ordination. He refers to this in a letter of 11 April 1846 to Dalgairns:

> . . . Nor would a director overule and ride over the sort of scruple, which and which alone I had to receiving orders[20].

Writing a week later to Mrs Bowden he says:

> . . . I forget whether I told you, that when I was in London at Christmas, Dr Griffiths quite removed my difficulty about re-

---

[17]*Brilioth,* p. 172. We might note incidentally that in his protest in 1841 against the establishment of an Anglican bishopric in Jerusalem, Newman styles himself "a priest of the English Church and Vicar of St Mary the Virgin's." *Apo.,* p. 146.

[18]Letter to Miss Parker, *L.D.,* XI, p. 15.

[19]*Apo.* p. 235.

[20]*L.D.,* XI, p. 148.

ceiving ordination. My difficulty of course had been that I could not say that Anglican orders were invalid. It seems that the *conditional* administration of the Sacraments is of late introduction in the Church, the condition being implied, in such cases as it was necessary, in the *Church's* intention . . . The Catholic authorities then treat Anglican orders, which they consider only doubtful, in no other way than they treat their own when doubtful[21].

His views had not changed even by January 1847, as the following passage from a letter written from Rome to Mrs Bowden shows:

> . . . As to ordination, among their other privileges here, they can confer the different degrees of ordination without interval—so that probably we should be ordained sub-deacon, deacon, priest in the course of 10 days, and just before our return. I am glad of my liberty, for the responsibilities of orders grow greater and greater upon me, as I approach them—and this without seeing any great ground in reason to think differer, ly of my Anglican orders than before . . .[22].

Newman was ordained priest on Sunday 30 May 1847; there is no evidence to show any change of mind, by that date, of his view on Anglican orders from that quoted above from the letter of 13 January 1847. We know from a letter written a year and a half later that the question of the validity of Anglican orders was never put to him "*by* or *from* any one in authority in Rome[23]." In this same letter he repudiates as a calumny the assertion "that I could not get ordained, because I would not deny the validity of Anglican orders[24]." It would not, however, be correct to say that he was ordained "conditionally", if we were to imply thereby that some special or preferential treatment were shown to him in deference to his own conviction of the validity of his Anglican orders.

After his ordination as a Catholic priest, he seems to have taken a stand rather soon against the validity of Anglican orders. Thus already on 21 July 1848 he writes to a correspondent:

[21]*L.D.*, XI, p. 151.
[22]*L.D.*, XII, p. 15.
[23]*L.D.*, XIII, p. 73: Letter to Henry Wilberforce, 28 February 1849.
[24]*loc. cit.* (preceding note), p. 72.

... I cannot help saying that I do not think the established Church is better off, as regards the Sacraments, than other non-Catholic bodies which have not renounced baptism . . . No wonder I say this, considering I have the greatest misgivings of the validity of Anglican orders; nor do I see how a Catholic, fairly read in Catholic doctrine and Anglican History can be without them. If the Anglican Church has not orders it has no Eucharist . . .[25].

In a letter of 11 October of the same year he writes:

... If the English Church has the Sacrament of the Eucharist, I cannot imagine anything more frightful than Priests consecrating and people receiving who *do not believe*, the careless disposal of Christ's own flesh, the crumbs under which it lies left on the plate, the pieces suffered to fall about and kicked aside, the blood drunk as a refreshment or a treat after the Service, or poured back into the bottle . . . and certainly it is an argument, which has for some time weighed with me, in corroboration of other more direct ones, in proof that the Anglican Church has not the Apostolical succession[26].

Theologically, then, one may say that his attitude to Anglican Orders in the period immediately preceding and subsequent to his ordination to the Catholic priesthood was as follows. The only scruple he had about receiving Catholic Orders was, that by so doing, he might expose the Sacrament (which he had already received) to sacrilege, since re-iteration of Orders would be sacrilege. His fears on this score were allayed by Dr Griffith's explanation of the Church's attitude in the conditional administration of the Sacraments. The condition was implicit in the Church's intention, when conferring orders in a case where existing Orders (whether Roman or Anglican) were doubtful. Within five months before his ordination, he yet could not see any great grounds, in reason, to think differently of his Anglican Orders than before. However, within a year after his ordination, he speaks definitely against their validity, and anticipates already the argument from broad historical facts in preference to minute antiquarian research,

[25]Letter to Robert Monteith, *L.D.*, XII, p. 249.
[26]Letter to Catherine Ward, *L.D.*, XII, p. 293.

6

such as he develops in his letter of 5 August 1868 to Father Coleridge[27].

As to the workings of grace in the hearts of many Anglicans, on the occasion of their 'ordinances', he does not deny the fact in their case (nor in his own memory of his own case), but will not admit that it is given through the ordinance itself, but only through the inward energetic act of the recipient. Thus in a letter of 25 September 1848 he already uses the distinction between *ex opere operato* and *ex opere operantis* (though not in these terms):

> . . . Nor does it avail to say that grace seems among Anglicans to be given *through the Sacraments,* and that Dissenters do not even pretend to this. It is impossible to ascertain whether it is given *through* ordinances, or in answer to the *good feelings and thoughts* existing during their administration . . . Surely to say that God's grace works outside the pale of the Church, is not to speak against that grace. We adore His mercy the more, *because* He is merciful beyond His promise. When He gives grace to those outside the Church, it is not to keep them outside, but to bring them into it. As He gave grace to Abraham or to Cornelius, not to keep them where they were, but to bring them on where they were not[28].

This thought is developed in the *Difficulties felt by Anglicans in Catholic Teaching*:

> . . . if you merely mean to say that the supernatural grace of God, as shown either at the time or by consequent fruits, has

---

[27]*Essays Critical and Historical,* II (10th ed., 1890), p. 110. Essay X in this volume "The Catholicity of the Anglican Church" written by Newman as an Anglican is followed by a "Note on Essay X" written when a Catholic, in which he arrives at an unfavourable judgment on the validity of Anglican Orders. On this "Note" cf. *D.T.C.,* XI (1931), col. 368, 369.

The whole question of the validity of Anglican Orders has been discussed since Newman's day, particularly in the light of the Papal Bull *Apostolicae Curae* (13 September 1896) of Pope Leo XIII. There is a concise defence of the Anglican point of view in *The Oxford Dictionary of the Christian Church* (1958), s.v. *Anglican Ordinations* p. 54. There is an exhaustive treatment of the invalidity arising from defect of intention in F. Clark, S.J., *Anglican Orders and Defect of Intention* (London, 1956). One of the men on the Catholic side at the time of *Apostolicae Curae* was Edmund Bishop. It is interesting to see that Bishop takes Newman's line of an appeal to the 'argument of visible facts.' See N. Abercrombie, *The Life and Work of Edmund Bishop* (London, 1959), p. 229. See further, J. J. Hughes, 'Recent Studies of the Validity of Anglican Orders': *Concilium,* Vol. 1, No. 4, January 1968, pp. 68-73.

[28]Letter to Catherine Ward, *L.D.,* XII, pp. 271, 272.

overshadowed you at certain times, has been with you when you were taking part in the Anglican ordinances, I have no wish, and a Catholic has no anxiety, to deny it.

Why should I deny to your memory what is so pleasant in mine? . . . Can I forget,—I never can forget,—the day when, in my youth, I first bound myself to the ministry of God in that old Church of St Frideswide, the patroness of Oxford? nor how I wept most abundant and most sweet tears, when I thought what I then had become; though I looked on ordination as no sacramental rite, nor even to baptism ascribed any supernatural virtue? Can I wipe out from my memory, or wish to wipe out, those happy Sunday mornings, light or dark, year after year, when I celebrated your communion-rite in my own church of St Mary's, . . . Yet what has this to do with the matter in hand? I admit your fact; do you admit, in turn, my explanation of it . . .[29].

He then proceeds to compare evidences of sanctity among Methodists (through preaching, not through sacraments) in order to bring out the force of the argument that grace may be conferred *ex opere operantis*. He does not, as far as I can ascertain, go on to the further difficult point to explain how the graces received in the Anglican Holy Communion are recognizably "eucharistic" graces, an almost perfect parallel to the graces received at Catholic Mass. To any one who ponders Newman's own Anglican Eucharistic writings, this problem cannot fail to present itself and to tease the reader's mind for a satisfactory solution. The paradox remains, that we can now apply in a Catholic sense (and particularly in the light of modern liturgical theology) what he wrote originally for Anglicans and with the Anglican Communion service in mind. Reference may be made here to Schillebeeckx's treatment of the religious value of the sacraments in the separated Christian Churches, though he is dealing with continental Protestantism rather than with Anglicanism. Schillebeeckx considers that an Evangelical Christian in celebrating the Communion Service undoubtedly possesses a "Eucharist of desire", and thereby participates—though not to the full—in the *res sacramenti*. He goes on to add that there is more than a subjective religious value in the Protestant ceremony of the Lord's Supper, though

[29]*Difficulties felt by Anglicans in Catholic Teaching,* (1910) I, pp. 81, 82.

he is careful to say that he does so, subject to any eventual decision of the teaching authority of the Church on the matter. "The rite of Communion service" he says, "(though it is not even partly a valid sacrament) is therefore a quasi-sacramental manifestation of an explicit eucharistic desire, which, moreover, implicitly looks forward to the true fruits of the Catholic Eucharist[30]."

[30]E. Schillebeeckx, O.P., *Christ the Sacrament of Encounter with God*, (London, 1963), pp. 239–243.

It will be apposite to quote art. 23 of the decree of Vatican II on Ecumenism:—

'The ecclesial Communities separated from us lack that fullness of unity with us which should flow from baptism, and we believe that especially because of the lack of the sacrament of orders they have not preserved the genuine and total reality of the Eucharistic mystery. Nevertheless, when they commemorate the Lord's death and resurrection in the Holy Supper, they profess that it signifies life in communion with Christ and they await His coming in glory'. (*The Documents of Vatican II*, ed. Abbot, p. 364.) See the Latin text in *Sacrosanctum Concilium.Vaticanum II, Constitutiones, Decreta, Declarationes*, Rome, 1966, p. 272. Cf. also *Instruction on the Worship of the Eucharistic Mystery* (25 May 1967), C.T.S.I. rans. 1967, §8 *The Eucharistic Mystery and Christian Unity*.

4 Prayer and the Ministry

Τ H E innermost core of continuity in Newman's priestly life, as an Anglican and a Catholic, was undoubtedly an intimate habit of prayer, cultivated from early boyhood and maintained throughout all the vicissitudes of a long life. This habit of prayer has particular importance for an understanding of his Anglican ministry, since it was in large measure the norm of his early evangelical faith, such as he was up to and for some time after his ordination. His practice of prayer pre-dated his full sacramental belief, and coalesced with it once he had come round to this "foundation of dogma[1]."

When he went up to Oxford as yet two months short of sixteen, he was destined not for the Church but for the Bar. Nevertheless we can see from his Private Journals and other private notes that as a lay undergraduate he was living a very real life of prayer; this continued after his decision to take Anglican Orders; and still more important for our purpose, we are able to show that as a Catholic priest, he kept on using a type of intercessory prayer which he had composed for his own use as an Anglican. As an Oratorian, he maintained, even within the very *Memento* of the Mass this pattern of prayer which he had practised as an Anglican minister; we should note, however, that it was not a Church of England formulary as such, but a form of private prayer congenial to himself.

This deep-seated continuity in prayer becomes absolutely clear when we compare some private memoranda of 1817–1845 with three small notebooks which he kept later in life; the model of some of these prayers may be traced to the manual of *Private Devotions and Meditations* of the Anglican Bishop of Winchester, Lancelot Andrewes (1555–1626), composed orig-

[1] *Apo.*, p. 49.

inally in Greek[2], and which Newman himself as an Anglican had translated and published as Tract No. 88.

One prayer, dated from the day of his first communion in the Anglican Church—November 17, 1817—he recopied many years later into one of these three small Mass notebooks. It runs as follows:

> Lord I praise Thee for calling me to the light of Thy Gospel—for my birth in a country where Thy true religion is found, and for Thy goodness in enlightening my soul with the knowledge of Thy truth, that, whereas I was proud, selfrighteous, impure, abominable, Thou wast pleased to turn me from such a state of darkness and irreligion, by a mercy which is too wonderful for me, and make me fall down humbled and abased before Thy footstool. O let me so run the race that is set before me that I may lay hold of everlasting life, and especially let me make Thee, O Holy Jesus, my pattern in my pilgrimage here, that Thou mayest be the portion of my soul to all eternity[3].

Sixty years later, the memory of that first Anglican Communion was still vivid to the old Oratorian, who had now been a Catholic priest for thirty years. In November 1877 he jotted down in a stray Memorandum:

> Do you love, my dear Self, or don't you, your active abidence time past (*sic*) in the Church of England? E.g. you have a photograph of Trinity Chapel before your eyes daily, and you love to look at it. Yes—and it is in great measure an abstract—yet it is not the Church of England that I love—but it is that very assemblage, in its individuals concrete, which I remember so well, the times and places—the scenes, occurrences—my own thoughts, feelings and acts. I look at that communion table, and recollect with what feelings I went up to it in November 1817 for my first communion . . . but the Church of England as such, does not come into my tender memories[4].

[2] *Tracts for the Times.* No. 88, *The Greek Devotions of Bishop Andrews* (sic), publ. March 25, 1840. For an account of these *Devotions* cf. *Oxford Dictionary of the Christian Church* (1958) s.v. Andrewes; C. Bodington, *Books of Devotion* (The Oxford Library of Practical Theology), Longmans 1903, pp. 164–174; H. Tristram. "With Newman at Prayer": *John Henry Newman: Centenary Essays* (ed. H. Tristram) 1945, p. 113; L. Andrewes—J. H. Newman, *Geheiligte Woche. Biblisch-liturgische. Gebetbuch, eingeleitet und übersetzt* von O. Karrer (Ars Sacra, München), n.d. (reviewed in *Archiv für Liturgiewissenschaft* V/2, 1958, p. 437).

[3] Oratory Archives, C.5.12 (copied from A.10.4).

[4] Oratory Archives, "Sundries" A.46.3., pp. 111, 112.

On his own admission then to his "dear Self" his memory had lingered—even daily—on his Anglican past, but not on the Church of England as such; there was psychological continuity, but no misplaced loyalty—he had a tenaciously retentive memory, stretching back unbroken over his own "thoughts, feelings and acts" of the years that had expired.

There exist in the Oratory archives, as has been mentioned above, three small notebooks which he used, when a priest, for "Preces ante et post Missam." One of these contains prayers compiled from standard Catholic sources as preparation for and thanksgiving after Mass, with the surprising inclusion of the *Dies Irae*. He has copied them out in his own hand, and must have used the book for many years since the pages bear the thumb marks such as Breviaries do after constant use.

Along with the prayer from his first communion day as an Anglican, mentioned above, he recopied a list of intentions arranged for each day of the week, which he had composed between June and September 1824, i.e. from the months just following his ordination as an Anglican deacon. He recopied this list with some abridgements into his Mass intention notebook at some later date (perhaps about 1875, as an entry in the same firm script follows under this date); we must conclude that he copied them for use, not merely as a reminiscence, seeing that this little black notebook bears all the signs of familiar daily use. The intentions are set out in an identical pattern for each day of the week:

> Pray for . . .
> Pray against . . .
> Intercede for . . .

We should note the prayer for Friday:

Friday—Pray for *Zeal*—Pray for In church—singleness of heart —1 Cor. x, 31 2 Cor. iii. 5 Gal. vi. 14. Phil. iv. 13 a view to God's glory—simple dependence on the grace of Christ—regarding myself as an *instrument*. For liveliness and fervency of prayer—for a deep sense of the awful nature of my sacred office—regarding myself as the voice of the people to God, and of God to the people, for the spirit of devotion, affection towards my people—love, faith, fear, confidence towards God . . . for strength of body, nerves, voice, breath &c—earnestness of manner, distinctness of delivery[5].

This is remarkably akin to the later passage in *Meditations and Devotions* where the recurring phrase "in asking for fervour" hammers home his prayer until the final demand:

> Lord, in asking for fervour, I am asking for Thyself . . . Thou art the living Flame . . . enter into me and set me on fire after Thy pattern and likeness[6].

The latest entry in the notebook is an almost illegible scrawl dated "Jan 7 1889" with some names of people to be prayed for. Thus here within the covers of the same private notebook we find prayers composed by the young English boy of sixteen, the youthful Anglican deacon of twenty-three and the aged Oratorian Cardinal of almost eighty-eight. Here, if anywhere, we can find that intimate continuity and identity which make the Vicar of St Mary's, the Father of the Oratory and the Cardinal of the Roman Church into one and the same man.

The second notebook is even more revealing, containing as it does lists of names of persons to be prayed for, the dates ranging from 1850 to 1864 and up to 1882. The names are entered under short headings:

> Auld lang Syne
> Protestants (1864)
> Dear to me; Kind to me; Cold to me; No how to me
> Godchildren
> Cousins
> St Mary's and Littlemore
> Faithful Women
> Old and Catholic
> Old and Protestant (*cancelled*)
> With claim on me
> Loyal to me
> Catholics 1; Catholics 2; Catholics 3
> Benefactors to Congr.
> Irish friends

[5]Oratory Archives, C.5.12.

[6]*Meditations and Devotions* (2nd ed., 1893), Part III: "Meditations on Christian Doctrine", p. 599.

About Oratory
Ecclesiastical
Converts
The Dead.

The interesting thing about these Mementos is that we have similar lists of prayers for individuals, dating from 1839 and 1840, also classified under headings (pencilled, in Greek) together with lists dated "March 15, 1840" and "March 21, 1845 Good Friday." On page 6 of the latter bundle there is the revealing note: "up to this point gone through and written again in Private Journal 1846—on Aug. 27, on going abroad[7]." Here is another filament, light as gossamer indeed, but all the more valuable for being "most private and personal" as the label on the copybook proclaims; he carried over in prayer into his Catholic life in 1846, at the very moment of setting out for the continent en route to Rome, all his Anglican friends and associates who had been the objects of his prayer in 1840 and 1845. He was still praying in the same way, and often for the very same persons.

Newman then had nothing to unlearn as regards inter-. cessory prayer, when he passed from the Church of England to the Catholic Church, all the more so as this intimate life of prayer, after his first conversion in the autumn of 1816, was based on the genuine doctrine of the Blessed Trinity and its Indwelling through the role of the Holy Spirit in the soul[8]. All these were authentic graces in his baptized soul; they were equally valid after his passage to Catholicism, although they had come to him without much direct contact with Catholics: "Catholics did not make us Catholics; Oxford made us Catholics[9]."

[7]Oratory Archives, C.5.12.

[8]cf. C. S. Dessain, "Cardinal Newman and the Doctrine of Uncreated Grace," *The Clergy Review*, vol. XLVII, 1962, pp. 207–225 and pp. 269–288.

[9]Letter of Newman's to Canon Estcourt, 2 June 1860, quoted in Wilfred Ward, *The Life of John Henry Cardinal Newman* (ed. 1927), II, p. 57. This remark raises the whole question of Newman's attitude to ecumenism, particularly as a Catholic, and its relevance for ecumenical work today. An excellent and comprehensive study of this is available in C. S. Dessain, "Cardinal Newman and Ecumenism", *The Clergy Review*, vol. L. 1965, pp. 119–37 and pp. 189–206. Also in John Coulson, A. M. Allchin, Meriol Trevor, *Newman: A Portrait Restored*. An Ecumenical Revaluation. London, 1965.

The practice of intercessory prayer, begun before his ordination to Anglican Orders, was reinforced as a consequence of it. He treats of this type of prayer in several of the *Parochial and Plain Sermons,* of which those on "The Christian Ministry" and on "Intercession" furnish us with his most characteristic thought on the role of intercessory prayer in the Christian Ministry. He notes that "the office of intercession . . . though not a peculiarity, is ever characteristic of the Priestly Order, is spoken of in Scripture as a sort of prerogative of the Gospel ministry[10]", and he proceeds to instance this by the "ministering" mentioned in *Acts* 13:1-2 (the preparation on Saul and Barnabas for the work); as well as the passage in *James* 5:14-15, "which seems to invest the Elders of the Church with the same privilege of the priesthood[11]."

It is, however, the sermon on "Intercession" which is Newman's most explicit teaching on this type of prayer as "characteristic of Christian worship, the privilege of the heavenly adoption, the perfect and spiritual mind"[12]. In structure this sermon resembles all the *Parochial and Plain* series. First of all, a *catena* of New Testament texts, in this case taken from St Paul; then follows a reference to the "instances of prayer, recorded in the book of Acts" being "of the same kind, almost entirely of an intercessory nature, as offered at ordinations, confirmations, cures, missions and the like[13]." Then follows his own reflections on this New Testament teaching:

> Such is the lesson taught us by the words and deeds of the Apostles . . . Nor could it be otherwise, if Christianity be a social religion, as it is pre-eminently. If Christians are to live together, they will pray together; and united prayer is necessarily of an intercessory character, as being offered for each other and for the whole, and for self as one of the whole . . . Intercession becomes a token of the existence of a Church Catholic[14].

[10]*P.S.,* II, Sermon XXV, pp. 312, 313. This sermon dates from 14 December 1834.

[11]ib. (see preceding note), p. 313.

[12]*P.S.,* III, Sermon XXIV (22 February 1835), pp. 350, 351.

[13]ib. (see preceding note), p. 352.

[14]*P.S.,* ib. (see above, note 12), p. 352.

His thought then proceeds to show that where Scripture records the prayers of good men, not yet Christians (as Cornelius), that these were not intercessory, but were prayers for themselves only. He concludes that "Intercession is the kind of prayer distinguishing a Christian from such as are not Christians[15]."

At this point he reaches out further to show that sinners must first pray to be rid of their sin, before they could presume to busy themselves about the salvation of other men. Nature tells us that "God heareth not sinners"; but none but God himself could tell us that he will hear and answer those who are not sinners. The preacher then turns to our Lord's own words in the discourse at the Last Supper and finds that "consistent obedience . . . is therein made the condition of power in Intercession[16]."

It is typical of Newman's feel for Scripture, and his sense of the unity of Revelation, that he should branch off here to a consideration of Old Testament instances, and particularly that of Abraham, to illustrate the Scripture truth that separate rewards attend on separate graces, and that in accordance with this law of God's dealings with men, Intercession is the prerogative of the obedient and holy.

Like a mounting eagle, having circled over the familiar terrain of Scripture, he now looks steadily into the full light of the mystery, and reads in Christ's death the supreme meaning of the Christian's mandate of Intercession:

> He died to bestow upon him that privilege which implies or involves all others, and brings him into nearest resemblance to Himself, the privilege of Intercession . . . He is made after the pattern and in the fulness of Christ—he is what Christ is. Christ intercedes above, and he intercedes below[17].

Then follows the pressing lesson on the need to use this gift. And we see incidentally, that his thought right to the end is thinking of common prayer, the Church's ministry of prayer

[15]*P.S.*, ib. (see above, note 12), p. 353.

[16]*P.S.*, ib. (see above, note 12), p. 356.

[17]*P.S.*, ib. (see above, note 12), p. 362.

"How can we complain of difficulties . . . if we have but lightly used the intercessions offered up in the Litany, the Psalms, and in Holy Communion?[18]"

A sermon such as the foregoing is a statement of the ministerial role of Intercession, such as is valid under the Christian dispensation of any century. Newman makes no reference in it to his own practice; in fact, the printed *Parochial and Plain Sermons* contain, on the whole, few personal references, in contrast to the still unpublished Anglican sermons preserved in MSS in the Oratory archives. This makes the allusion in the sermon on "The Daily Service" all the more valuable. He is referring to the introduction of daily Morning Service at St Mary's in 1834; this was a non-eucharistic service, as is clear from his letter of 21 June 1834, in which he mentions this intended daily morning service, he also speaks of a weekly celebration of the Lord's Supper, as not being yet feasible.

He wishes to let his congregation into the reasons why he lately had begun the Daily Service:

> *This*, then, is what I felt and feel:—it is commonly said, when week-day prayers are spoken of. 'You will not get a congregation, or you will get but a few;' but they whom Christ has brought near to Himself to be Stewards of His Mysteries depend on no man . . . He is the one effectual Intercessor for sinners at the right hand of God. And what He is really, such are we in figure; what He is meritoriously, such are we instrumentally . . . allowed to depend on Him, and not on our people; allowed to draw our commission from Him, not from them . . .[19].

Here he is envisaging the possibility that he would have no congregation, while he performed alone the Common Prayer of the Church, and he justifies his action by the fact that the Christian minister, in virtue of his priesthood "is the spokesman of the saints far and near[20]." If the sermon on 'Intercession' spoke of the gift of Intercession as a privilege of all obedient Christians within the Church, here we see it presented as a commission given by Christ to his priests:— "they are allowed

[18]*P.S.*, ib. (see above, note 12), p. 365.
[19]*P.S.*, III, Sermon XXI (2 November 1834), p. 314.
[20]*P.S.*, ib. (see preceding note), p. 313.

to be centres, about which the Church may grow, and about which it really exists, be it great or little[21]."

In the unpublished sermon No. 191, where he makes it clear that public preaching is no adequate substitute for what we should now call private contacts, he goes on to express his regret at the tendency to make the Church's prayer private, not public:

> . . . As usage has made teaching merely public, not private, so there is a tendency in these times to make the prayers of the Church private when they ought to be public. Hence it is that persons so often wish that their children should be baptized at home, when no good reason can be pleaded for such departure from received practice, or they are unwilling . . . that their children should be baptized in the sight of the congregation (as the Church directs) when they have the opportunity and no reason preventing it . . .[22].

Both these deviations from the true norms of the Church: public teaching instead of private, and a private instead of a public use of Common Prayer—he ascribes to the same root, viz:

> . . . an unwillingness which exists in towns to conform to the parochial system, i.e. to that system which associates persons together as one body or small Church of Christ under the superintendence and instruction of one or more of His ministers[23].

It is astonishing to reflect that Newman should have had such a clear grasp of the leading principles of pastoral liturgy— the primacy of liturgical prayer, the subordination of preaching to prayer, the importance of the parish as a grouping of the faithful around their priests into an *ecclesiola* and the peculiar difficulty of realizing all this in a town parish—and that he should have seen all this so clearly before 1840, when we must admit that it is only since 1940 or thereabouts that the same basic principles have been clearly seen in Catholic liturgical circles. Newman took no misleading by-roads into the cul-de-sac of Ritualism, as many of the Anglican liturgists were later to do.

[21]*P.S.*, ib. (see note 19), p. 314.
[22]Oratory Archives, A.50.5.
[23]Oratory Archives, ib. (cf. preceding note).

Since it is the considered judgment of this study that Newman's Anglican ministry was the spiritual matrix of his later
Oratorian vocation, it may be well to recapitulate here the
leading traits of this spiritual portrait of Newman as an Anglican
priest, such as they emerge from the four areas chosen for
investigation, viz. The Care of Souls, The Legacy of Liturgical
Preaching, The Eucharistic Ministry and Prayer and the
Ministry.

His Anglican ordination impressed on him his responsibility
for souls—though at the time of his ordination his doctrinal
position was more evangelical that sacramental. Although he
engaged in parochial work assiduously, his real ministry lay in
an apostolate to the intellect, which found its first characteristic
exercise during his tutorship at Oriel. In the last years of his
Anglican life he practised at Littlemore a form of living in
community, with considerable ascetic rigour. This, however,
did not serve as a direct model for his Oratorian ideal; rather
he deliberately went back in mind to an Oxford College,
when proposing an analogy in modern times to St Philip's
idea of the Oratory. The mutual charity which he strove to
pursue as an Oratorian ideal, he aimed to have embodied in
the English ideal of gentlemanlike behaviour towards one
another.

Although he exercised the ministry of the Word with great
regularity and singular success, both in oral delivery and in
written composition, he looked on public preaching as subordinate to public prayer, and considered private contacts
between priest and people more salutary than sermons. We
have seen too that a fresh selection of the *Parochial and Plain
Sermons* on a strictly liturgical basis reveals a surprising affinity
between Newman's doctrinal standpoint and that of the new
Constitution on Sacred Liturgy.

His sacramental theology underwent a complete transforma-
tion during the decade 1823–1833 from an evangelical (non-
sacramental) bias to a fully sacramental belief, first in Baptismal
Regeneration, then in the Eucharistic Presence (and most
probably, in the sacrifice.) As a Catholic he gradually came to
doubt the validity of Anglican Orders, and since he held that
there can be no true Eucharist where there are no true Orders,

he contested the sacramental reality of the Anglican Holy Communion. But as an Anglican himself, he had had an over-powering sense of the Real Presence in the Anglican Eucharist. He explains the presence of such graces as coming *ex opere operantis*.

In his personal priestly life as an Anglican, Newman never married, though clerical celibacy was not common practice among the Anglicans of his day; early in life he embraced celibacy as a positive choice, though not unaware of the sacrifices it would involve.

A habit of prayer, practised from boyhood, remained constantly with him, and, judging from his private MSS and prayer notebooks, seems to have continued along the same lines, without any break, from his Anglican to his Catholic life. This prayer was predominantly intercessory. He sees in intercessory prayer, not only the Christian's greatest likeness to the mediatorial role of Christ, but the priest's closest imitation of Christ: "What He is meritoriously, such are we instrumentally . . .[24]"; this does not exclude—rather it includes—the ministry of the Eucharist[25].

We might round out this spiritual portrait by a short poem of his, dated "Oxford 1834," and written therefore before his adherence to the Anglican ministry showed any signs of wavering;

'The Priestly Office"

—from St Gregory Nazianzen[26].

In service o'er the Mystic Feast I stand;
I cleanse Thy victim-flock, and bring them near,
In holiest wise, and by a bloodless rite.
O fire of Love! O gushing Fount of Light!
(As best I know, who need Thy pitying Hand)
Dread office this, bemired souls to clear
Of their defilement, and again make bright.

---

[24]*P.S.*, III, Sermon XXI, 'The Daily Service', p. 314.

[25]cf. *The Via Media* II (3rd ed., 1877), p. 204, quoting Bramhall on the Eucharist.

[26]Verses on Various Occasions (ed. 1874), p. 193.

5 Newman in Quest of a Priestly Vocation (1845-47)

THAT Newman as a Catholic should have become an Oratorian can be explained in the last resort only as a meeting of heart with heart, of Newman and St Philip Neri; but it would be a mistake to conceive of this choice as a vocation based largely on an emotional attraction to a congenial Patron Saint or his Institute. In fact, nothing is more marked in the whole process of his vocation (and he was, later, at great pains to insist that life in the Oratory was a real vocation), nothing—we may notice—is more discernible than the deliberate and eminently rational nature of his procedure. In the process of choosing a suitable way of priestly life for himself and his companions, he reasons very closely on the implications and possible consequences of every solution proposed. Ward looks on the relevant letters as 'almost tiresomely fussy from their realization of objections to any plan and their balancing of alternative considerations[1]'; a truer insight into Newman's character would realize that he was a reasoner not only in intellectual matters, but also—and particularly so—in the conduct of his own life situations. In fact, this is probably the root of the later deep-seated difficulties between Newman and Faber as Oratorians: unlike Faber, Newman never allows impulse to obliterate reason, he carries forward with him into each new situation the hard-won convictions of each preceding stage of his quest, and keeps a tenacious grip all the while on things as a whole. His conduct may be illustrated from a remark in *Loss and Gain*:

> . . . he (Reding) should certainly think that Christ had called him in the way and method of careful examination—that prudence was the divinely appointed means of arriving at the truth[2].

[1]Wilfrid Ward, *The Life of John Henry Cardinal Newman* (ed. 1927), I, p. 17.
[2]*Loss and Gain* (ed. 1886), p. 122.

This careful examination of practically all the forms of priestly life then available in the Church will issue for Newman only in a negative conclusion: they were not, he felt, suitable for himself and his companions, and for the other prospective converts from among English university men. This negative conclusion, however, in itself, implies a positive side: it delimits the range within which Newman's priestly life will be exercised: not as a Jesuit, nor as founder of a theological Faculty for England, nor as a Dominican, nor a Lazarist, nor a Redemptorist, nor as a missionary priest (as the secular clergy were then called in England). Sharing the same priesthood, and to a certain extent the same tasks as all these others, he nevertheless will have to find his own way, bringing a new Institute slowly into shape, and guiding his own Birmingham Oratory to the end of his life.

One might be tempted to ask, would it not have been more generous, more supernatural for Newman simply to seek ordination for the ecclesiastical district in which he found himself, and let himself be absorbed in a self-effacing way into the rank and file of the "missionary" clergy of England (we must remember that the dioceses were not yet re-established in England at the moment of Newman's conversion)? Was there not something of self-importance, of self-seeking in thus setting about to introduce a new Institute into England in order to provide himself and his associates with a congenial sphere of priestly activity? Aware as they explicitly were of their superior advantages of education as compared with the run of secular priests, was the Oratory to be just a natural scheme, on the natural plane, of keeping the converts together, and not to be a supernatural vocation to a specific form of priestly life?

Several clear distinctions need to be made before we can give the true answer to this fundamental and challenging question. First of all, Newman had no intention of making the Oratory an enclave of converts within the Catholic Pale: he was eager for recruits from among the old Catholics and the Irish. Thus when, in 1862, Father Stanislas Flanagan (an Irishman) left the Oratory, Newman looked on it as "the most tragical event which has befallen the Oratory since it was set up."[3]

Besides, he deprecated any assumption of a superiority complex by the Oratorians towards their fellow-Catholics and fellow-clergy; he has stated his thought on the matter forcefully and unambiguously in one of the early Chapter Addresses, that of 17 June 1848, delivered that is, within the first six months of the Oratory's existence in England:

> . . . There is a very great danger I am persuaded of our body getting (and partly justly) a character of uppishness, flippancy, criticalness and the like, from neglect of mortifying those tendencies which lead to these odious results . . . You will then infallibly look down on other people (not as moral beings but intellectually) . . . you will have almost your party tenets, your favourite doctrines, you will go against other people and bodies, and you will be a school, instead of a modest courteous Congregation of St Philip . . .[4].

So much for "behaviour towards those without" as this Address is headed in the MS. Newman was not aiming at forming an exclusive club of ex-university men turned priest, provoking irritation and jealousy among their fellow-clergy by their superior airs.

To turn now to the problem of the "supernatural" character of Newman's choice of the Oratory as a vocation. A recent author has described admirably in what sense one should look for the supernatural in a priestly or religious vocation, describing vocation itself as:

> . . . a reality, which in all its truly significant and operative elements is supernatural. It embraces, however, all that is naturally adaptable within the human personality . . . It is the sum total of the human person's character, temperament, and bodily and spiritual qualities as these . . . have been . . . transformed and elevated by the continued operation of God's grace. In this conception divine vocation is the whole human person viewed as the end result of the formative influences, natural and super-

[3] see *Trevor* II, p. 272.
[4] *Or.P.*, No. 7. Chapter Address, 17 June 1848, below.

natural, which have contributed to his making, and of his own myriad responses to these influences[5].

This passage of Dr Frison's is an excellent and flexible view of the complex reality which any individual vocation must necessarily be, and it throws a valuable theological light on Newman's case.

At this stage (1845–1847), Newman was a man in the middle forties, facing into the second half of life, not knowing what expectancy of remaining years he could count on; in the letters of these years he often speaks as if he were beginning a new life in the end of his days[6]. The idea of his age and past attainments was a considerable factor with him when he was examining the various possibilities of vocation; in particular, he sought for some solution that would allow him to be "a continuation of his former self[7]", to speak his own words, as coming from himself, and not as becoming a "sort of instrument of others, and so clean beginning life again[8]." It took him about a year and a half to decide on the Oratory. While it would be difficult to say whether he now felt again an imperative call to a definite work, such as had sustained him in his illness in Sicily twelve years earlier[9], still he was well aware that his acquired experience, his talents, his reputation could all combine to enable him to do some work which he alone might be able to do.

Wiseman, who was now Newman's immediate ecclesiastical superior, concurred in this view[10]. One cannot but admire the

[5]B.Frison, C.M.F., *Selection and Incorporation of Candidates for the Religious Life* (Milwaukee, 1962), p. 10.

[6]*L.D.*, XIII, p. 16, letter of 24 January 1849 to Henry Wilberforce.

[7]*L.D.*, XI, p. 306, letter of 31 December 1846 to J.D. Dalgairns.

[8]ib. (see preceding note), p. 306.

[9]*A.W.*, p. 127: "God has still work for me to do."

[10]*L.D.*, XI, p. 47: " . . . I had then a very satisfactory talk with Dr Wiseman, as far as talks can be satisfactory. He distinctly stated that 'he wished Old Oscott to be Littlemore continued—' this was 'precisely his view.' He wished laymen there—he wished anyone to be there who otherwise would have come to me. He wished it to be 'a place of refuge.' . . . What he wanted, he said was this—a body of men educated above the common run—not for ordinary purposes, but for extraordinary;—principally for two objects—first to meet the growing Germanism and infidelity of the times by literature—next to be preachers . . ."

generous welcome to the Catholic ranks which Wiseman offered to Newman and the Maryvale group. Here was no jealous authority, suspicious of these newcomers, anxious to make them toe the line and be like everybody else. Realizing that they were not like everybody else, he wished to put their particular gifts to full and congenial use. In Newman's search for his own vocation, this express wish of his superior was, one may feel, a sufficiently supernatural motive to justify his ultimate choice of the Oratory.

It is important, for justice' sake, to give Wiseman due credit for this initial welcome and suggestion, since the later cool relations between the two men might make us overlook it. Newman had had already some acquaintance with Wiseman through the Roman visit of 1833, and since then through the articles and reviews in the *Dublin Review*. However, personal contacts with Wiseman during Newman's early years as a Catholic were unsatisfactory. His impressions of Wiseman noted here and there in the correspondence of 1845–1847 tally with the deliberate judgment committed to the Private Journal in 1863:

> . . . so slow to throw himself into other minds, so sanguine, so controversial and unphilosophic in his attitude of mind, so desirous to make himself agreeable to the authorities in Rome[11].

and after Wiseman's death in 1865:

> . . . the two chief persons, whom I felt to be unjust to me, are gone—the Cardinal and Faber[12].

We may say then, that in deferring to Wiseman's suggestions for his future, Newman deferred to his position, not to his person. When we remember how, in later life, when crises arose, Newman sought for and was really guided by the opinions of reliable friends, we readily see that he never put himself in this relationship with Wiseman. Later on, in the light of mutually strained relations, he saw Wiseman's role in his own choice of vocation in an unfavourable angle:

> . . . 'I broke my staff'; and the Cardinal did not hinder it. Rather he co-operated, and I was fixed in Birmingham[13].

[11]*A.W.*, p. 258.
[12]*A.W.*, p. 260.
[13]*A.W.*, p. 258.

The whole process of his choice of vocation was by examination and elimination. He was not choosing for himself alone; he was thinking, in a sense, of a group vocation, for his companions at Maryvale as well as for himself; and even after the final choice, he still could sigh:

How much happier for me to have no liabilities (so to speak) but to be a single unfettered convert[14].

The unrealized projects of vocation were, broadly speaking, three (once he had decided to enter the ecclesiastical state afresh and not go off to some lay profession); it was a choice between starting a theological college for England, or joining one of the modern congregations or the Jesuits. He never considered the purely secular (missionary) clergy as a suitable solution for his own case and that of his fellow-converts[15].

Wiseman's character and position had prompted Newman in July 1846 to adumbrate a scheme of making Maryvale a Divinity School for the whole of England. This scheme never got beyond a paper existence in Newman's correspondence with Dalgairns, though the idea was still with him during his stay in Rome that autumn, as he notes in the Memorandum over thirty years later[16]. The idea had originated with Newman from his observing the unsatisfactory bustle and fuss reigning at Oscott on account of its dual purpose as a boys' school and a theological seminary under a man of Wiseman's character:

... he is fond of boys; he is everything to the boys, but the divines suffer. They complain they don't see him once in three months ... Oscott is a place of dissipation. Tribes of women, and hosts of visitors ...[17].

Newman's idea was to separate the two functions of Oscott: leaving the boys' school above in Pugin's new building and

---

[14]*L.D.*, XII, p. 243, letter of 12 July 1848 to Ambrose St John.

[15]See *Or.P.* No. 2. In his letter to Cardinal Fransoni of 14 February 1848 he writes: " ... at nostra indoles contra, et vitae praeteritae consuetudo, et mens interior, et maturissimae cogitationes, nos avocant clarissimis indiciis, à vitâ omni ex parte saeculari" (i.e. "our character, and the habits of our former life, and our way of thinking and ripest reflection seem quite clearly to turn us away from a fully secular life"). *L.D.*, XII, p. 37.

[16]*Or.P.*, No, 36. 10 May 1878, *Paper on the choice of vocation in Rome after conversion.*

[17]*L.D.*, XI, p. 195, letter of 6 July 1846 to J.D. Dalgairns.

bringing the divines down to the seclusion of Maryvale, where he and his companions would have formed the teaching staff. Having considered various objections to the scheme, he concludes by saying "I see nothing except that the notion of a theological school is a great idea . . .[18]."

It is, perhaps, useless to speculate on what might have been, but it is difficult not to regret that Newman's Catholic career did not include this scheme of a theological college. He had all the requisites: he himself was in his prime, many of his companions were theologically able men, while he had at his disposal a fine library of patristic and positive theology (still at the Oratory today). It was not unthinkable that converts should be entrusted with such a college: Ward, as a convert and a married man, was professor at St Edmund's. Newman as an energetic head of an English theological faculty would have been able to give several generations of English priests the benefit of his wide learning and his acute grasp of the great problems facing Christian faith in modern times. However, all this was not to be; to this day England has not yet got her own faculty of theology at a level comparable to those of the continent; while Newman himself as a Catholic devoted his intellectual efforts more to apologetics and education rather than to theology proper, with the result that we today often find more rewarding theological insights in his Anglican than in his Catholic writings.

In the same letter of 6 July 1846 to Dalgairns in which he throws out the suggestion of the Divinity School, Newman adds that he had been thinking lately of founding an Institution with the express object of propagating the faith and opposing heresy: "I sketched out the faint outlines of a community under the patronage of St Mary . . . with the object of first, adoring, second, defending the *Mysteries* of Faith[19]."

This "faint outline" consists of a page and a half, dated June 15/46, on a projected "Congregatio de SS Trinitate," and is interesting as being Newman's only personal sketch of a possible congregation, while they were still in the first stage at

[18]ib. (see preceding note), p. 196.
[19]*L.D.*, XI, p. 196, letter of 6 July 1846 to J. D. Dalgairns.

Maryvale, before the journey to Rome. Although only a faint outline, this is an intelligible sketch, and one which adumbrated in several particulars the future shape of the English Oratory, though Newman is probably harking back in spirit to Littlemore when he speaks of a "country seclusion, with a library." This scheme, however, did not get beyond a paper existence, just like that of the Divinity School. Compared with Faber's Rule for his *Brothers of the Will of God,* of which a copy (together with Newman's comments) exists in the Oratory archives, one may see in miniature the incompatibility of temperament between the two men. Newman's outline is a basic 'brief', Faber's a fussy composition, elaborating on details of organization and devotion, written with all the meddlesome insistence of an enthusiast.

In his letters of this period, Newman's thoughts on the religious Orders and Congregations of his day are expressed with all the uninhibited frankness of intimate correspondence by a man who is looking for a realistic and practical solution for himself, his companions and their future ministry in England. These remarks should not give offence to the members of these same Orders today, or worse still, alienate them from sympathy with Newman's person or thought; in each case they should be looked on in their context—he was not writing a panegyric on the various Orders, but examining them from a very practical standpoint 'How would it suit us?'

This is particularly necessary when assessing his running comments on the Dominicans in an exchange of letters with Dalgairns in the course of 1846–47[20]. It is ironical to think that Dalgairns, of all people, should have been the person to press the claims of the Dominicans on Newman, and this on intellectual grounds. Dalgairns was the very man who, having been one of Newman's companions in Littlemore, was ordained priest in France, came out to join the first Oratorian group in Rome, and later criticized Newman bitterly for his inclusion of intellectual work as an integral and traditional Oratorian activity. One of Newman's later Oratory Papers—that of 31

[20]Letters of 6 July, 21 July, 18 October, 22 November, 8 December and 31 December 1846, all of which are to be found in *L.D.*, XI. In addition, 10 January 1847 and 22 March 1847 in *L.D.*, XII.

August 1856—gives us the measure of the anxiety and distress which Dalgairns as an Oratorian caused to Newman.

Newman never warmed to the idea of becoming a Dominican. The references to the Dominicans as a possible vocation are mainly confined to the correspondence with Dalgairns, and in it Newman is all the time parrying Dalgairns' suggestions. Newman's elimination of the Dominicans, as seen in this correspondence, might seem somewhat summary, off-hand, impatient and prejudiced. His setting aside of the Dominicans as a personal vocation was not equivalent to a rejection of Thomism; the excellent study by Monsignor Davis 'Newman and Thomism' makes it clear that although Newman differed from St Thomas in method, he was at one with him in his fundamental 'world view[21].' It is clear that his criticisms of the Dominicans are directed against the French and Italian Dominicans of his own day: they were uncongenial to his own temperament. He is not finding fault with St Dominic's ideal or with St Thomas' theology; he fully allows the part played in St Philip's life by the Dominicans; and later in life he himself was to become very friendly with Mother Margaret Hallanan and her Dominican community. His well-known essays on the Benedictine centuries were to have been followed by similar ones on the Dominicans—circumstances, however, prevented the writing of these.

Newman's letter of 31 December 1846[22] to Dalgairns, while giving us the most explicit statement on his part of what rendered him averse to the Dominican spirit, incidentally gives us a valuable insight into his own cast of mind, and the type of priestly institute he was seeking. Admittedly the Dominicans were an intellectual body, but he found them too technical, too doctrinaire, too much of a closed school, too averse to the milder moral theology of St Alphonsus Liguori. One phrase of his in this connection, all the more valuable in that it is *obiter dictum*, reveals Newman's devotion to Our Lady as the 'Seat of Wisdom': ' . . . Our whole line . . . has been a sort of domestic one—easy, familiar and not rigid—with a

[21]*Newman-Studien*, III (1957), pp. 157–169.
[22]*L.D.*, XI, pp. 303–307.

special devotion to St Mary, the special patronness of such habits of mind, so far as they are virtuous—and the Dominican school is utterly contrary to it[23].'

As regards Newman and the Jesuits, we must remember that already as an Anglican he was acquainted with and practised the Exercises: he made a real attempt at apprenticeship, if not of discipleship, only to abandon it later. He wrote a lengthy Memorandum at Littlemore, March 15, 1843 'Memorandum drawn up from St Ignatius's Spiritual Exercises, the Directorium upon them of the Society, and Rosmini's Manual;' another MS consists of 'Annotations for the better understanding of the following Exercises, 1842–1843[24].' There is nothing original in these notes; they are merely careful summaries of the books used. The *Autobiographical Writings* contain Newman's notes made during retreats at Littlemore and Maryvale (1843, 1846) along these lines[25]. As an Oratorian, however, he does not seem to have considered the Exercises suitable for Oratorian spirituality, as may be seen clearly in a passage from one of the early 1848 Chapter Addresses[26]. This is curious, as showing that one of the few Catholic practices which Newman had anticipated as an Anglican, was laid aside by him as a Catholic.

Although he genuinely admired the Jesuits at Propaganda, and remained on friendly terms with them later in England, he never took any steps to apply for admission to the Society. In fact, he had to contradict an article in *The Quarterly Review*

---

[23]ib. (see preceding note), p. 305. On Newman's devotion to Our Lady while he was still an Anglican cf. P. Schneider, O.S.B.: "Das Marienbild des anglikanischen Newman", *Newman-Studien* II (1954), pp. 103–119.

Newman's characteristic devotion to Mary is to her as 'Sedes Sapientiae' (this was the title chosen by him for Mary as the patroness of the Catholic University in Dublin later). He looks on her as our model for the reception of faith and its development in the soul.

Many years earlier, in a sermon preached on 25 March 1832 on "The Feast of the Annunciation of the Blessed Virgin Mary, The Reverence due to her", he emphasized the close connection between devotion to Our Lady and faith in the Incarnation. In spite of some hesitations and reservations, this text already shows Newman's reverence for Mary.

[24]Oratory Archives, A.11.6.

[25]*A.W.*, pp. 222–236; pp. 236–239. See H. Tristram, "With Newman at Prayer": *John Henry Newman: Centenary Essays*, (1945), pp. 115, 116.

[26]*Or.P.* No. 6.

many years later which said that he had once offered himself for admission to the Jesuits and had been refused[27]. It may be of interest to remark here that, in the Mass notebooks already referred to, Newman placed the Jesuits second on the list of his intentions for prayer on Mondays—'The Household of the faith.' (The Passionists, it should be noted, come first, out of a sense of *pietas* to Fr Dominic Barberi, one supposes—the Benedictines are not mentioned.)

Bearing all this in mind, we may more impartially assess one of the hitherto unknown Newman texts, i.e. the last of the early 1848 Chapter Addresses, dated "Stae Apolloniae", (Oratory Papers, No. 6)[28]. In this he draws out a detailed contrast between the Jesuit and the Oratorian spirit. In his whole concept of the Oratorian vocation, Newman greatly stresses the absence of vows, and constantly differentiates the Oratorians from the 'Regulars' on this point, and he considered the Jesuits 'nearly the only regulars now, for the Benedictines etc. are scarcely more than local institutions now[29].' We should understand this sharp contrast, not as personal animosity against the Society, but as Newman's effort to describe an *idea* (the English Oratory was not yet six months old) as against an existing institution, though perhaps he does less than justice to Jesuit practice in the course of his comparison. His correspondence of 1846–1847 contains many shrewd comments on the Jesuits as a body, such as he was able to observe them in Rome, where he considered them to be in the same unpopular position as the Conservatives of 1830 'continually making false moves, by not seeing whom they have to deal with[30].'

It was not, however, any lack of political *savoir faire* in the Jesuits which deterred Newman from joining them: it was a more personal feeling still, that of safeguarding his own personality: 'As—Jesuit, e.g. no one would know that I was speaking my own words[31]'. He dreaded the corporate spirit of

---

[27] *Or.P.* No. 36. *Paper on the choice of vocation in Rome after conversion.* 10 May 1878.

[28] The most striking passage is on pp. 207-12 below.

[29] *L.D.*, XII, p. 117, letter of 15 September 1847, to his sister, Mrs John Mozley.

[30] *L.D.*, XII, p. 103, letter of 25 July 1847, to his sister, Mrs John Mozley.

[31] *L.D.*, XI, p. 306, letter of 31 December 1846 to J. D. Dalgairns.

regulars which crushed the liberty and spontaneous action of the individual. He had expressed himself at length in the Chapter Address already mentioned, on this very point, comparing the Jesuits to the Greek phalanx and the Oratorian to the Roman legionary: ' . . . in the phalanx the soldiers were closely knit into each other, in the legion each stood and fought with free space for his weapons and his movements[32].'

Of the three possibilities considered so far—a Divinity School, the Dominicans and the Jesuits—we may say that for the first, circumstances were against it, and that as regards the other two, Newman shrank from what he considered Dominican rigorism and Jesuit corporate conformism. Two further possibilities envisaged were the Lazarists (i.e. the Vincentians) and the Redemptorists. In a letter of 20 August 1846 he speaks appreciatively of the former: '. . . At this moment I am more drawn to them than to any other[33].' A few months later, on 18 October 1846, he writes: 'What we saw at Paris rather blunted our zeal in favour of the Vincentians[34]', and this change of attitude is explained in a later Memorandum: '. . . we seemed to feel that though a most important body of religious, they did not give to theology and literature that place in their system which we wished[35].'

The other possibility was that of becoming Redemptorists. Newman makes no mention of being attracted by Redemptorist spirituality: the argument in their favour was theological, but

---

[32] *Or.P.*, No. 6. See above Note 28. The same thought is expressed by Newman in a letter to T. F. Knox, on 10 September 1847:

" . . . Do you recollect Pericles's contrast between the Athenians and Spartans in the Funeral Oration? We are Athenians, the Jesuits Spartans. Ours is in one respect more anxious and difficult—we have no vows, we have fewer rules—yet we must keep together—we require a knowledge of each other, which the Jesuits do not require. A Jesuit is like a soldier in the phalanx—an Oratorian like a legionary—he fights by himself—he guides himself by 'carità'—which means by tact, self-knowledge, knowledge of others. This requires a specific training—more, it requires training *with* those with whom he is to live . . ." (L.D. XII, p. 113).

Newman seems to have borrowed this idea of the Oratorians as "free troops" from the opening pages of Marciano, *Memorie Historiche della Congregazione dell' Oratorio* (Naples, 1693–1702).

[33] *L.D.*, XI, p. 227, letter to T. F. Knox.

[34] *L.D.*, XI, p. 263, letter to J. D. Dalgairns.

[35] *Or. P.* Appendix 4. Memorandum 9 June 1848: Early Days of the Oratory.

this, on examination seemed to be negative praise[36]. Again, he felt that Dr Wiseman would not approve of their becoming Redemptorists. Newman then, did not get very far in his examination of the Redemptorists as a possible vocation; and it faded away in proportion as the idea of the Oratory grew stronger with him. At a later date, in the *Apologia,* he dissociates himself deliberately from St Alphonsus on the casuistry of 'Equivocation', preferring the English rule of conduct better[37].

The late Father Henry Tristram once wrote: 'I have often wondered why Newman did not become a Benedictine. It would have seemed the obvious thing, and yet it did not come up for consideration[38].' Abbot Butler had asked himself, in the centenary issue of *The Downside Review,* the same question with regard to the Tractarian converts in general, and came to the conclusion that the English Benedictines at the time were not ready to assimilate the converts, because they did not correspond 'to the ideas the Tractarians would naturally hold of a Benedictine monastery and Benedictine work[39].' There is no evidence whatever in Newman's case that he either looked to the English Benedictines of his day for such a way of life, or that he was disappointed in his quest. His sympathetic studies on 'The Mission of the Benedictine Order' and 'The Benedictine centuries' (one of the immortal phrases coined by Newman), do not mean that Newman was in any sense a Benedictine *manqué;* he was studying the records of the past history of the Benedictines, not their function in the contemporary world. This interest in Benedictine learning was almost certainly motivated by the parallel with the writings of the Italian Oratory[40].

[36]*L.D.,* XII, p. 6, letter of 10 January 1847 to J. D. Dalgairns: " ... About St. Alfonso I hear this, that the praise given him is not really praise, perhaps the contrary, viz that there is *nothing wrong* in his writings."

[37]*Apo.,* (ed. 1889), p. 273; cf. ib. pp. 348–363, Note G "Lying and Equivocation."

[38]Private letter, 18 June 1944.

[39]"The Record of the Century": *The Downside Review,* Centenary No. (1914), p. 49.

[40]In the marginal summaries of the articles on the Benedictines, as they originally appeared in *The Atlantis* we read: "On the whole, what literature not Benedictine, not polemical, nor metaphysical nor systematic. Contrasted with that of the French Oratorians, of Jesuits, as being Biblical, patristical, antiquarian, and documentary. Like the Italian Oratory." (*The Atlantis,* No. 1, January 1858, pp. 44–45).

We should note further the passage on the Benedictines in the unfinished fragment of the *Life of St Philip,* p. 261 below.

Concurrently with this examination of the various forms of priestly life in view of his vocation, Newman himself became a student at Propaganda, which he entered on 9 November 1846. While in retrospect he looked on his sojourn at Propaganda as a happier time than that under Father Rossi the 'dreary' Oratorian Novice Master[41], it was really no more than an interlude in his life, with little organic connection either with his Anglican past or his Oratorian future. Although Newman worked conscientiously on theological problems during this stay in Rome[42], the year in Propaganda added little or nothing to his stock of theological learning; he did only one out of the four years of the course of lectures, and became so impatient at the system of drawling through a few tedious pages at a time that he gave up attending the lectures and read on his own[43].

One must, however, take into serious consideration two negative conclusions which were deeply borne in on him during his theological course in Rome, and which had a close bearing on all his future work as a priest. He became aware of the 'iron form' as he called it prevalent in Roman theology at the time,

[41]*A.W.*, p. 256: " . . . And then how dreary (after the happy months, thank God, at Propaganda) how dreary Fr Rossi and Sta Croce, 1847."

[42]Newman's theological papers of this period will form part of a projected edition of his theological and philosophical papers.

[43]In a letter of 13 January 1847 he writes: "First we went to Lectures here, but we found it a loss of time, and have abandoned them. We read by ourselves (*L.D.*, XII, p. 15)." Writing to Stanton the next month he says: "Again, (let me say it to *yourself*, for I don't like to say it aloud) you will not, cannot, get education here—not simply from the many objects there are to take you off your studies, but because you are not a boy. The lecturers are men quite up with their subject, but the course takes *four* years—if you don't stay that time, you only go through a part of it—and anyhow you go, lecture after lecture, to drawl through a few tedious pages—All this is quite necessary for boys, not for grown men. I seriously think (still in confidence) you will do as much sitting at home at Maryvale (*L.D.*, XII, p. 48)." He had much the same opinion about S Sulpice: ". . . and from what I hear of the stiffness and dryness of the text-books in use I suspect by the end of one, two, three years, you will be very uncomfortable there. Besides, it is not a place for those who like you or ourselves have been forced to exercise the intellect so carefully in the English Universities—so long a course of slow reading is utterly unfit for us and a mere waste of time, keeping you from important duties when you are intellectually fit for them . . ." (*L.D.*, XII, p. 97, letter of 17 July 1847, to T. F. Knox).

which militated against any real deepening of views[44]. The other conclusion he came to was the inadequate acquaintance of even the leading Roman theologians with the facts of the case in England. Speaking of Perrone, whom he admired as a dogmatic theologian, he says: 'It was rash (for him) to undertake England, knowing neither English language nor English character[45].'

Not only did he find the Roman system of lectures unfit for grown men, but he also judged the general formation of the students unequal to the stresses of future life as it awaited them outside the seminary. At the end of his stay in Propaganda, he made bold to write a letter to the Rector about the discontent he found rife among the English-speaking students in the college. He says he has studied the rules of the house to see if he could find a justifiable reason in them for this dissatisfaction. The only criticism of the rules which occurred to him was the too rigid shielding of the students, even of the older ones, from all outside contacts. He did not understand, he confessed, how these same students were later expected, in one go—*uno saltu*—to learn how to deal with the outside world from which they have been so carefully withdrawn.

This, however, he felt, was not the root of the matter. Not even the tenderest charity—let alone rules—can nourish a starved and restless intellect. Young men are not looking for an encyclopaedic formation, but for the capacity to judge of things as they come before them— to expound and solve

---

[44] In a sad strain in a letter of 8 February 1847 to J. D. Dalgairns, he concludes a list of emendations for the French translation of his *University Sermons:*

"And now after reading these Sermons I must say I think they are, as a whole, the best things I have written, and I cannot believe that they are not Catholic, and will not be useful. Indeed there are times (I mean after reading them and the like) that feelings come upon me, which do not often else, but then vividly —I mean the feeling that I have not yet been done justice to—but I must leave all this to Him who knows what to do with me. People do not know me—and sometimes they half pass me by. It has been the portion of Saints even; and may well be my portion. He who gives gifts, is the best Judge how to use His own—He has the sole right to do as He will, and He knows what He is doing. Yet sometimes it is marvellous to me how my life is going, and I have never been brought out prominently—and now I am less likely than ever—for there seems something of an iron form here, tho' I may be wrong—but I mean, people are at no trouble to deepen their views. It is natural". (*L.D.*, XII, p. 32).

[45] *L.D.*, XII, p. 21, letter of 17 January 1847 to Bishop Wiseman.

difficulties, to compare things one with another, to form a judgement of men and events, nations and cities, to acquire a critical faculty in judging books, examining authors' opinions, investigating religions and religious bodies, developing the principles of philosophy, poetry, politics—they need some fellow-countryman to open their minds, to inform them, to direct them—and someone who is not in any disciplinary position in the College[46].

In this letter to the Rector of Propaganda, we have in germ Newman's own view on the need for integrating scientific and religious training into a coherent whole, much as he expressed it in the sermon preached before the Catholic University a decade later on 'Intellect, the Instrument of Religious Training[47]'. Man is not only a moral but an intellectual being, and young men

> feel a consciousness of certain faculties within them, which demand exercise, aspirations which must have an object, for which they do not commonly find exercise or object in religious circles . . . I want the intellectual laymen to be devout, and the devout ecclesiastic to be intellectual[48].

The Propaganda system did not really recognize its future priests not only as moral, but also as intellectual beings, so it was no wonder that Newman found the intelligence of the English-speaking students under such a system to be 'starved and restless' for lack of appropriate nourishment, *intellectui famelico et irrequieto cibum dare*. We have here a measure of how he himself would have conducted the proposed Divinity School for England, which in fact did not come about.

Ordination, in the normal way of things for a Catholic priest, comes as the climax to his years of philosophy and theology, during which his systematic training in the spiritual life will have gone hand in hand with his human development in the opening years of manhood. Newman's case was different: he was not only a late vocation, but a convert with twenty years' ministry in the Church of England behind him. Ordina-

---

[46]*L.D.*, XII, pp. 88–90, letter of 30 June 1847 to Antonio Bresciani, S.J.

[47]*Sermons preached on Various Occasions* (3rd ed., 1870), pp. 1–14.

[48]ib (see preceding note), pp. 12, 13.

tion came to him after a brief six months in Rome when he
was already a mature man of forty-six; and although, as we
have noted above, he worked conscientiously at his theological
course in Propaganda, it can hardly have been woven into the
texture of his mind as it would have been into the minds of the
young students among whom he lived. Although in these
early years of his Catholic life, he was fond of referring to
himself and his companions as 'neophytes[49]', he was conscious
to himself of the loss of resiliency, buoyancy and simple faith
caused by the wear and tear of the passing years.

This impression pervades the lengthy self-analysis written in
Latin during the Retreat for ordination, at St Eusebio in
Rome, 8–17 April 1847. He is there occupied in a psychological survey of his spiritual resources, a description of a
many-sided wound or cancer which might prevent him from
being a good Oratorian,

> . . . when I began to apply my intellect to sacred subjects . . .
> although what I wrote was for the most part true, nevertheless . . .
> I lost my natural and inborn faith, *fidem meam naturalem et ingenuam
> perdidi,* so that now I am much afraid of the priesthood, lest I
> should behave without due reverence to something so sacred . . .[50].

It is interesting in this light to compare his two ordinations,
Anglican and Catholic: twenty-two years almost to the day
lie between them, Sunday 29 May, 1825 in Anglican Orders,
and Trinity Sunday 30 May, 1847 as a Catholic priest. The
early Journal contains the following passage about his Anglican
ordination:

> I have this day been ordained priest. What a divine service is
> that of Ordination! The whole has a fragrance in it: and to think
> of it is soothing and delightful[51].

There is no detailed entry in his diary for his Catholic
ordination; just the bald note: 'Trinity Sunday 30 May

---

[49]cf. v.g. his reply to F. W. Faber of 30 October 1845: I had no wish at all to
avoid any responsibility nor do you think it—but of course one feels it is impossible,
as a neophyte, to do otherwise, if one speaks, than to speak as others would speak;
not from one's own judgment, if judgment I could have. (*L.D.,* XI, pp. 22, 23).

[50]*A.W.,* pp. 247, 240.

[51]*A.W.,* p. 205.

ordained (St John and I) priests by Cardinal Fransoni[52].' We get some glimpse of his inner feelings of joy in the early days of his priesthood from an incidental remark in the Chapter Address of 22 December 1852:

> It is the very rule then, my dear children, under which we live, if we are God's own, to sow in tears that we may reap in joy. When I was first a priest, and kissed the Cross on my maniple, and said *Merear, Domine, portare manipulam fletus et doloris*, I used to say to myself, 'Where is the sorrow? where the tears[53]?'

[52]*L.D.*, XII, p. 84.
[53]*Or.P.*, No. 11.

6 Newman, Founder of the English Oratory (1847-48)

THE decision on the Oratory was Newman's own, though he was deciding not for himself only, but for his friends too, as he notes in a retrospective Memorandum:

> . . . and then, after other enquiries and speculations, I said (in words I have elsewhere used, perhaps in my address to the Wilfridians on admitting them into the Oratory on Febr. 14, 1848) 'Dear me! I have forgotten St Philip,' and then at once I began acquaintance with him, finding out his Church as the first step. I should add I was choosing *for my friends* as well as for myself, and had to consult them with this purpose[1].

One may line up the various elements that influenced his final decision somewhat as follows. In the background was Dr Wiseman, whose original idea it had been that Newman and his friends should join some such body as the Oratorians[2]. In the final stages, however, Wiseman was a remote and unsatis-

---

[1] *Or.P.* No. 36, Cf. the letter to F. W. Faber of 31 March 1847:
"Do not for an instant fancy our plans will clash . . . At the same time I am surprised to find that our general plans are more the same than I thought at first. I know how great a devotion you have to St Philip and that he is one of your patrons; but I had fancied that both in devotional exercises upon which you fell back and in the great prominence given to your lay brothers, you differed from him essentially. Besides, the very fact that you had not become an Oratorian when you might, was quite enough to put me off the idea that in becoming Oratorians we should interfere with you. This was our feeling when, after a good deal of beating about, we finally determined to offer ourselves to St Philip". (*L.D.*, XII, p. 66).

[2] *L.D.*, XII, pp. 19, 20, letter of 17 January 1847 from Newman to Bishop Wiseman:
"It is curious and very pleasant that, after all the thought we can give the matter, we come round to your Lordship's original idea, and feel we cannot do better than become Oratorians".
See ib., p. 20, note 1, the references collected by the editor, to Wiseman's early interest in the Oratory as a project for England.

factory correspondent in England[3], and cannot be said to have clinched the matter. Although Wiseman had been instrumental in offering Maryvale to Newman almost immediately after the latter's conversion, he never in fact was Newman's Ordinary after Newman's return to England, having been by that time moved to London. It would not then be quite correct to say that Wiseman 'brought' the Oratory to England, in any other sense than that he suggested the idea originally, and welcomed Newman's final step. Wiseman reappears later in the story of the English Oratory in connection with the London House, whose side he espoused in their ulterior differences with Newman.

Three of the Roman Oratorians were involved in different ways in Newman's enquiries about the Oratory: Theiner, whose zeal appeared to Newman as 'tactless'[4], next Rossi, the Novice Master, who in retrospect seemed 'dreary[5],' and finally Cesarini, the Superior of the Roman Oratory, whom Newman later discovered to be 'a great man for the Rule,' and therefore did not want the English group at the Chiesa Nuova[6]. All this goes to show that there was no outstanding figure among the Italian Oratorians at the time, to whom Newman could have opened his soul, as he had been accustomed to do with Keble in the years preceding his conversion. This isolation only emphasizes all the more Newman's own role: he was, in fact, the 'onlie begetter' of the English Oratory.

[3]*L.D.*, XII, p. 41, Newman's letter of 14 February, 1847 to Bishop Wiseman:
. . . It is sad work corresponding at a distance of 1,400 miles—and that when one is in a place for but a few months and that place Rome; and events and daily occurrences, and new introductions crowding upon one and changing the whole view of things. I thought you felt this yourself and for that reason did not write to me.

[4]Augustine Theiner (1804-74). See the biographical note on him in *L.D.*, XI, pp. 357, 358. For Newman's impressions of him, see *L.D.*, XII, pp. 71-4, especially p. 73: '. . . extremely zealous and useful as Theiner has been to us, he seems to be pushing on too fast . . .'

[5]Carlo Rossi (1802-83). See the biographical note in *L.D.*, XII, pp. 437, 438. The reference to his 'dreariness' is *A.W.*, p. 256: 'And then how dreary . . . how dreary Fr Rossi and Sta Croce, 1847 . . .'

[6]Pacifico Cesarini (+ 1851). See the account of him in *L.D.*, XII, p. 109, note 4. It was at a later stage that Newman discovered that Cesarini had been opposed to taking the English group at Chiesa Nuova. Cf. *L.D.*, XVII, p. 125.

There were likewise three men in Curial circles connected with his choice of the Oratory: Monsignor Palma 'a true friend, the only friend I had in Rome[7],' and who ultimately obtained the Papal Brief for him. Then there was Brunelli, Secretary of Propaganda, and finally Barnabò who succeeded Brunelli as Secretary of Propaganda, and with whom Newman found fault at two later stages—in 1856 and 1867, at the time respectively of the breach between the London and Birmingham Oratories, and the quashing of the Oxford Oratory scheme[8].

There was, finally, Pius IX, to whom all credit is due for the practical steps of arranging for the noviciate of the English group at S Croce, the provision of Fr Rossi as Novice Master, the issuing of the English Oratory Brief, and even for some financial assistance when they were returning to England.

We are able to pinpoint the end of January and the first week of February 1847 in Rome as the definite time of conception of the English Oratory. From that moment on, it passed through an accelerated gestation and came to birth almost exactly twelve months later on 1 February, 1848[9]. In a later Memorandum Newman says, speaking of their time in Rome and referring to the end of January 1847:

> At this time we began to think definitely of introducing the Oratory into England. My reasons were such as these: that, whereas the tastes of all of us were very different, the Oratory allowed greater scope for them than any other Institution; again it seemed more adapted than any other for Oxford and Cambridge men[10].

It would seem then that what Newman got hold of around Christmas 1846 and the following weeks in Rome, was the *idea* of the Oratory, rather than any practical existing model of an Oratory which could have been transplanted from Italy to a mid-nineteenth-century English town. At this point we are not reduced to conjecture, since we still have in the Oratory

[7]Giovanni Battista Palma (1791–1848). See the detailed note on him in *L.D.*, XII, pp. 436, 437.

[8]Alessandro Barnabò (1801–74). See the biographical note in *L.D.*, XIII, p. 510.

[9]Cf. the entry in Newman's diary under this date: "... Began with solemn Vespers, then admitted 9 members (5 Fathers, 1 novice, 3 laybrothers) thus setting up the Congregation . . ." *L.D.*, XII, p. 165.

[10]*Or.P.*, Appendix 4.

archives the 'Santa Croce Papers' written by Newman in the autumn of 1847, and which constitute a practically complete working plan of the Oratory, based on his close study of authentic Oratorian documents and his attentive observation of the Roman and Naples Oratories at the time.

Since Newman published relatively little about the Oratory[11], these Papers are vital for our understanding of his idea of it, being more systematic and documented than anything he wrote or said about the Oratory in later years. It is indisputable that these Papers are Newman's own body of Oratorian precedents and principles culled in the main from the sound historical work of Marciano[12], and the then still fairly recent *Pregi*[13]. That they are not something taught him by Father Rossi the Novice Master is borne out by the existence of another MS in Newman's handwriting, which gives us Father Rossi's 'Suggestions for reforming the Constitutions of the Oratory[14].' The ideas contained in this paper are absolutely different to those of Newman's, and in fact they are quite 'unOratorian', since they recommend centralization. There is

[11]The most considerable publication of Newman's on the Oratory is Sermon XII in *Sermons preached on Various Occasion* : "The Mission of Saint Philip Neri" (3rd ed., 1870, pp. 199-242). One could also add from *Discourses addressed to Mixed Congregations* (7th ed., 1886), Discourse XII "Prospects of the Catholic Missioner", and Discourse III: "Men, not angels the Priests of the Gospel." There are also some verses in honour of St Philip in *Verses on Various Occasions*.

Two sermons on St Paul are also relevant because of the angle from which Newman presents the character of St Paul—his gift of sympathy. This is thoroughly in keeping with St Philip's spirit. The sermons are Nos. VII and VIII in *Sermons preached on Various Occasions*, pp. 91-120. M. G. Carroll has published a useful "Newman Anthology on Saint Paul": *The Mind and Heart of Saint Paul* (London, 1959).

Newman draws a close parallel between St Paul and St Philip both in their work and their manner of acting. Spicq's study *Spiritualité sacerdotale d'après St Paul* (1954), particularly chapters X and XI (La mansuétude du prêtre, la benignité du prêtre), rejoins Newman's analysis of St Paul's gift of sympathy.

[12]G. Marciano, *Memorie Historiche della Congregazione dell' Oratorio*. 5 vols. fol. Naples, 1693-1702. Newman made copious use of Marciano in the 'Santa Croce Papers', usually referring to the work as the "Annals."

[13]Anon., *Pregi della Congregazione dell' Oratorio di San Filippo Neri*. 2 vols. Venice, 1825. English translation: *The Excellences of the Congregation of the Oratory of St Philip Neri*. London, 1881.

A solid, if somewhat naïve, systematic treatment of Oratorian spirituality.

[14]Oratory Archives (The Cardinal's room), B.9.3. Catalogue note: "Written by Fr Rossi. In JHN's handwriting."

a final decisive point in favour of Newman's authorship of the 'Santa Croce Papers', in the note on the top right-hand corner of page 1 'This has no authority, beyond what comes of its having been drawn up by the Father and assented to by the rest at Santa Croce in August or September 1847. JHN. Jan 15/52.' (In Oratorian usage, 'the Father' means the Superior, and here refers to Newman himself.)

It is interesting to follow in these MSS Newman's mind at work on an 'idea'—in this case the idea of the Oratory. By an 'idea' Newman meant not the verbal expression of a concept, but a transcript from life as lived—expressed, of course, in words, but not resting in them—going straight to persons, to facts, to things and events as they actually happen and have happened (and will be likely to happen) in real life. Hence his minute scrutiny of what might seem trivial in itself—sayings and examples traditional in the Oratory. In his quest of the 'idea' of the Oratory, he maintains a delicate balance between historical facts, the current practice of the Roman and Naples Oratories, and the circumstances of his own group of friends and the religious state of England generally. He is almost fussily exact in establishing facts, down to the details of spelling a proper name. He never extracts an idea as an abstract principle to be applied without reference to the original fact in which it was embodied. When once he has got hold of a principle, he is immediately concerned to back it up with reliable evidence from his sources. He does not attempt to dovetail one principle into another at the risk of spoiling both; he is more concerned with bringing out to the full all the shades of each particular principle, even at the cost of some very close reasoning and nice distinctions, e.g. how the Oratory is *not* a religious body, and yet is like one.

Having thus penetrated to the centre of things and seized on the heart of the Oratorian idea, he could all the more easily shed its outward Italian complexion; he never promoted an Italianate jargon in community or devotional life; as the event showed, he was able to introduce the Oratorian idea into English Catholic life, without any direct supervision, direction, support or backing from Italy. Since there was no direct Italian tutelage, the English Oratory—in as far as it remained under Newman's guidance—never experienced what other foundations from the continent so often undergo, viz., a revulsion of feeling from continental ways in favour of a national expression. Newman's Oratory was thoroughly English from the first, and the Birmingham Oratory, at least, continued to be so. That the London Oratory took a different tone, came about when it separated from Newman.

The need for adaptation of the Oratory to English conditions appeared imperative to Newman from the first, and he carried out this adaptation in the spirit of what we now call *aggiornamento,* i.e. not the mere transmission—even the faithful transmission—of an existing religious tradition, but the return in spirit to the founder's life and ideals, and applying them in a fresh and bold way to modern conditions. In the later controversy between the London and Birmingham houses[15], it seems fair to say that Newman was bent on safeguarding the idea of the Oratory such as he had distilled it from past precedent and contemporary practice, and which he, as founder, had had embodied in the adaptation of the Rule to England.

Though in a sense, Newman shared the Oratorian venture *in solidum* with his companions, yet he reveals himself in the Santa Croce Papers as the thinker, the leader, gifted with a far-seeing sense of strategy. Many of the points into which he entered with so much historical detail might seem otiose, but future events justified him for having taken history so seriously; in the light of the past, he had anticipated almost uncannily the problems which lay ahead. None of his companions could really be called a co-founder with him of the English Oratory; Ambrose St John was his closest friend and confidant, but this intimacy between him and Newman was only one segment of the circle of Newman's preoccupations as founder. As for Faber, he was a complete outsider at this moment, the moment which was decisive above all others in the genesis of the English Congregation. He had not the remotest share in the enterprise at this stage, being busy at home in England with his 'Little Brothers of the Will of God'.

Once the decision on the Oratory was reached, all traces of

[15]See below, pp. 100–2.

hesitation, of marking time, of weighing up possibilities fade away from Newman's correspondence and Memoranda. It would, perhaps, be too much to say that from now on he became a man of one idea, and that that idea was the Oratory, just as he himself has said of St Philip:

> We must not indeed call the Congregation of the Oratory specially his work, for he was Apostle of Rome independent of it[16].

But having decided on the Oratory as his vocation, he henceforth bends all his energies towards carrying it into effect. The remainder of his sojourn in Italy is taken up with his Oratorian training, the procuring of the Foundation Brief, a visit to the Naples Oratory, the examination and declining of a scheme to give the English party an Oratorian House in Malta. The same activity on behalf of the Oratory occupies him on his return to England; his first work—with priority in time and intention—is to establish the Oratory in England, and, of course, to live the life of an Oratorian himself.

In so far as the design of his life lay in his own choosing, it was henceforth to be set in an Oratorian pattern. Within that pattern itself, many unexpected twists were to appear, particularly in relation to the London Oratory; but the Oratory as such was never just a collateral activity among others for Newman; it was his home, his *nido*. He had hit on this idea very early on, as we see from one of the early 1848 Chapter Addresses (delivered within the first weeks after his return to England):

> The Congregation is to be the *home* of the Oratorian. The Italians, I believe, have no word for home—nor is it an idea which readily enters into the mind of a foreigner, at least not so readily as into the mind of an Englishman. It is remarkable then that the Oratorian Fathers should have gone out of their way to express the idea by the metaphorical word *nido* or nest, which is used by them almost technically[17].

Indeed, many of the well-known incidents of his public life as a Catholic, in particular the Achilli trial, were mere accidents, extraneous elements which occupied a great deal of time,

[16]*Or.P.*, No. 3.
[17]*Or.P.*, No. 5.

and caused serious anxiety, but once over had no continuing place in his life[18]. Even the Catholic University was no exception, as the Memorandum of 1870, written in the calmness of solitude and retrospect clearly shows[19]. It was different with the Oratory. Writing in his Private Journal in a sad moment (1860), he prays:

> Let not the contempt which comes on *me*, injure the future of my *Oratory*—about this I am anxious, though I ought to put it, and do put it simply, into Thy hands, O Lord[20].

No study of Newman as an Oratorian may evade a consideration of Faber's role in the English Oratory. Can Faber be called in any true sense a co-founder with Newman? As events turned out, Faber did ultimately share with Newman the task of shaping the fortunes of the Oratory in England by his lifelong superiorship of the London House. But it must be emphasized once more, as has been established above[21], that he had had not the slightest share in the initial stage in Rome, or in the choice of the Oratory as a group vocation for the Maryvale men (of which he was not a member), or in the drafting of the

[18]See *A.W.*, p. 256: "As to what followed in 1851-2, I mean the Achilli matter, it is abnormal (except as regards Wiseman's conduct) in any life, and I do not count it in."

Vol. XV of *L.D.* shows Newman concentrating on all his current engagements, particularly the composition and delivery of the *University Discourses* in spite of the acute anxiety caused by the Achilli affair.

[19]University work in itself never rivalled the Oratory in Newman's view of his own vocation, as the following extracts from this Memorandum show:

"... It is true that I had hoped to found an Oratory in Dublin; it is true also that Dr Cullen and his friends were so little opposed to it, or rather so favoured it, that they wished and expected the whole Birmingham Oratory to pass over to Dublin and to take possession of the new University house. Of course that never entered into my thoughts, though I think it was one of the supposed baits with which Dr Cullen thought he was tempting me to undertake the Rectorship ... And what was an additional difficulty on my own side was my double allegiance. I was bound not to leave England, yet bound to reside in Ireland, and, if my being Rector of the University necessarily involved my presence in Dublin, my absence from my Oratory was the breach of a duty as primary and sacred, as that breach was in the event of evil consequences to our Congregation. The Pope expressed a wish that I should be both in Dublin and Birmingham, but to be in both was to be in neither..." (*A.W.*, pp. 308, 286).

[20]*A.W.*, p. 253.

[21]See pp. 92, 93. Cf. the rather ironical chapter in *Trevor* I, pp. 425-40: "1848 Faber arrives."

letter to Cardinal Fransoni[22], the novitiate in S Croce, and
the study of the history of the Oratory from the Annals; in a
word, as has been already said, he had had nothing to do with
the genesis of the English Oratory.

One very important point from the early years of the Oratory
in England merits close examination, not only as a sample of
the incompatibility of temperament between Newman and
Faber, but because it explains a great deal about the background of Newman's life for the rest of his days—namely, why
Newman should have settled in Birmingham, of all places.
The point at issue was the scope and location of the first
English Oratory—should it be in Birmingham as the Brief
directed, or should it be in London where there was more
likelihood of finding the *ordo honestior,* the educated class, also
mentioned in the Brief as a special mission for the Oratory?

When Newman landed back in England at Christmas 1847,
Wiseman presented him with 'a most choice Christmas gift[23]'
of Faber and his group who wished to join the nascent English
Oratory. Many years later, in the light of bitter experience,
Newman confided to his Journal: 'And then when I came
home, at once Faber was upon me, to bully me, humbug me,
and make use of me . . .[24].'

The normal habitat of an Oratory is a large town. Newman
started the Oratory, on his return from Rome, in Maryvale
(at that time somewhat outside the main town area of Birmingham)—which, because of its position, would perhaps have not
been fully suitable as a definitive home for the Oratory, but
provided at least a first *nido* for the fledgling Congregation, and
entailing no expense beyond that of the maintenance of its
members. Within the first fortnight Faber and his 'Wilfridians'
also climb into the nest, with protestations of complete surrender:

> Our wishes are that you should consider us as giving ourselves
> over to you in the spirit of surrender— that you should take us as

[22]See the comment on this, below, pp. 135, 151.

[23]Newman's letter to Faber, 2 January 1848, *L.D.,* XII, p. 145.

[24]*A.W.,* p. 256. A controversy has arisen in recent years about the tone of this
and other remarks in Newman's private journals. See V. Blehl, "The Holiness of
John Henry Newman": *The Month* vol. 19, No. 6 (June 1958) pp. 325–34.

so much raw materials for Oratorianism, and make what you can of us in the way you think best, and fuse us down as you think will be most convenient, into your existing body[25].

Not a word here of any liabilities attaching to the new group, as a group. The House and Church of the Wilfridians, Newman writes: 'were offered us, I think, to do what we would with—without conditions[26].' It soon transpired, however, that there was a triple liability attaching to the House and Church, viz., (i) The patronage of the Earl of Shrewsbury, who (ii) held himself responsible for the maintenance of a community to look after the Catholic mission in the neighbourhood hitherto catered for by Faber and his companions, (iii) in addition the Wilfridians had sunk £7,000 into the property, and this obviously would not be recoverable, if, on joining Newman, they abandoned St Wilfrid's. Since St Wilfrid's (Cheadle) lies in a completely different district, it could not possibly have served as a first nucleus of a Birmingham Oratory.

Here was an unexpected entanglement in the very first months of the Oratory's existence. In order to understand Newman's attitude, as revealed in the correspondence about St Wilfrid's, one should realize clearly the role played by the "House" in the idea of the Oratory[27]. Though not a monastery in the technical sense of the word, it is more like a monastery than like the house of a modern religious congregation, in this sense that it is not only the residence of the Fathers, but also the place of their apostolic work. Oratorians were not to be like secular priests serving missions, nor yet like Regulars who could be sent away on long-distance assignments: the Oratory, as a body, should find its work on its own doorstep. Its normal

[25]*L.D.*, XII, p. 143.

[26]*L.D.*, XII, p. 179. See the concise summary of the case by the editor, ib. p. 177, note 2. To quote:

A misunderstanding latent in the admission to the Oratory of the Wilfridians had already begun to cause embarassment. Newman understood that they brought their house and church with them without conditions. See next letter and that of 28 March to Faber. It was too expensive to keep up both Maryvale and St Wilfrid's, but it became known that there was an obligation to Lord Shrewsbury to serve the latter mission, and that if it was abandoned the £7.000 which the Wilfridians had sunk in it would be lost. Faber suggested as an alternative that Maryvale, to which the English Oratorians had been sent by their Papal Brief, should be given up.

[27]See *Or.P.*, No. 20 pp. 285–8.

habitat is in the *urbes ampliores,* the large towns and cities, as mentioned in the Brief.

Now, if Newman were to take on St Wilfrid's and its rural mission, he might indeed do spiritual good to a handful of souls (for whom he originally had had no direct responsibility), but he would be jeopardizing the true development of the Oratory, which of its nature is an urban thing. On the other hand, by drawing Faber and his companions off to Maryvale, he would be denuding the Cheadle district of its Catholic clergy, and would appear to be doing a disservice to the cause of religion, all for the sake of preserving the theory of the Oratory. In addition, he would have to cope with the displeasure of the patron, Lord Shrewsbury, and the bishop, Dr Ullathorne. Were he to take on Faber and his followers, with their white elephant of a property, he would be saddling himself with an almost insoluble financial burden.

The three-cornered correspondence between Newman, Faber and Lord Shrewsbury reveals in anticipation all the difficulties with which Newman was to be beset in his future dealings with Faber. As regards Lord Shrewsbury, Newman is able to say:

.. the correspondence between Lord S. and me is simply one of money matters[28].

With Faber, however, the matter is different. The impartial reader has a rather uncomfortable feeling that, objectively speaking, Faber is not telling the truth[29]; while, subjectively, Faber seems unable to see the facts of the case, except as reflected in the prism of a wounded sensibility. It is difficult not to sympathize with Newman, particularly in the light of the whole development of his Oratorian vocation step by step, and of his concern to set the true course of the new Oratorian venture in England. He was not just looking for a solution of expedience to a bothersome problem about alternative disposal of the properties of Maryvale or St Wilfrid's.

Newman made the sacrifice, relinquished Maryvale, went through the whole laborious process once more of shifting

---

[28]*L.D.,* XII, p. 190, Newman's letter of 27 March 1848 to Faber.
[29]See v.g. Faber's letter of 19 January 1848, and Newman's comments on it: *L.D.,* XII, p. 191, note 1.

house, and went out to St Wilfrid's to live. This, of course, on account of its rural situation, could not become the site of a city Oratory, and so we find Newman on 26 January 1849, founding the first Oratory in Birmingham at Alcester Street, leaving part of the community at St Wilfrid's.

The same 'restless spirit' among the *giovani* and Faber soon led to a creeping campaign pushing for a London foundation. Here again, Faber fixes on a disingenuous interpretation of the Brief, while Newman, with his full knowledge of the origins of the Brief, sticks doggedly to the facts of the case, and tries to shape his course accordingly.

When Newman in Rome on 27 November 1847 had eventually received the Foundation Brief from Pius IX, he discovered one phrase in it, which he had not suggested in the letter to Cardinal Fransoni, and which now in England in 1849 was to prove a further point of tension in the development of the Oratory—the mention of an apostolate to the upper classes[30]. Faber now held that the fixing of Newman and the first English Oratory at Birmingham was accidental, and that the clause which Pius IX had inserted in the Brief, praising Newman and his companions for their resolution to promote religion among the 'splendidior, doctior et honestior ordo', was incompatible with it, and could only be fulfilled if Newman and the Oratorians moved to London. 'You sacrifice,' urges Faber 'what the Pope suggested to you for what you suggested to the Pope[31].'

Newman replies, going back patiently over the facts (and not indulging in subjective impressions); but he is obliged to do more than state the facts, he must interpret them anew, to counteract Faber's facile assumption:

When the Pope *added* 'ordo honestior etc,' of course one wishes to obey him *literally,* i.e. to see that his purpose is fulfilled; but I am persuaded that he meant merely to *fulfil* what *I* had set down. What can the Pope know of the constitution of English political society? to him ordo doctior, honestior, was in *great measure* synonymous with the classes I had specified—so that *if there* be a class in Birmingham of sharp intellects, who are the recipients of political power, and who can be made Catholics, I think we are

---

[30] See the relevant passage of the Papal Brief, Appendix 2.

[31] *L.D.,* XIII, p. 50, note 1.

fulfilling the Brief, not only in letter as to Birmingham, but in spirit as to the ordo honestior[32].

To anyone who ponders dispassionately these two contrary interpretations of the Brief, he cannot but award the judgment to Newman's side of the case; all the antecedent facts being in his favour, and his interpretation of the additional phrase being based on the whole context of the Brief which, after all, does specifically mention Birmingham, and is silent about London. Moreover, when one reflects that Birmingham as such had no claims on Newman's personal interest or admiration, if he sticks doggedly to it as the place intended for the first Oratory, one must admit that he does so out of loyalty to his commission as Founder. He had always realized the limitations of Birmingham (such as it was in the mid-nineteenth century) as a field for an apostolate among the educated classes by comparison with London. As early as 9 November 1845 he had written to Dalgairns from Littlemore:

London is a centre—Oxford is a centre—Brummagem is no centre . . .[33].

When an opening presented itself for a London House, Newman could still have availed himself of the opportunity of Wiseman's invitation, and gone to London as the head of the new foundation. On the balance, however, he settled himself in Birmingham in preference to London because it afforded him leisure for intellectual in addition to missionary work, his most explicit statement on the reasons motivating his choice being that of 29 March 1849[34]. Of course, by remaining behind in Birmingham, he cut himself off, practically speaking, from any sustained and permanent contacts with the London 'ordo honestior'[35].

The thorniest point in Newman's whole Oratorian life is the estrangement between him and his London foundation, arising out of steps taken by the London House to get a ruling in Rome on a point of the Oratorian Rule. The affair had been glossed over in Ward's *Life* of Newman, but the full facts of the

[32]*L.D.*, XIII. p. 50: Newman's letter of 16 February 1849 to Faber.
[33]*L.D.*, XI, p. 30.
[34]*L.D.*, XIII, pp. 94, 95.
[35]See Newman's letter of July 1857 quoted in *Trevor* II, p. 162.

case are now available in Volume XVII of Newman's *Letters and Diaries,* while a telling presentation in Newman's favour has been given by Miss Trevor in her volume *Newman: Light in Winter*[36].

It is the considered judgment of the present writer, in the light of the Oratory Papers—a factor which has not hitherto been sufficiently taken into account in the debate—that Newman never had the slightest desire to make himself a *Preposto Generale* over the English Oratories. This was the burden of the Londoners' complaints against him. Further, one must concur in Miss Trevor's admirable statement of the intrinsic importance of the case—far transcending the actual occasion of the quarrel over nuns' confessions[37].

While granting Newman full exoneration on these two scores, what is one to think of his attitude to Faber and the London community, judged from the standpoint of Oratorian spirituality, or indeed of Christian charity? Here I think, Fr Walgrave's study of 'Newman's Personality' as a critique of O'Faolain's *Newman's Way,* might be quoted with profit:

> His (Newman's) truthfulness tolerated no inner falsehood, not even a pious one. He distinguished clearly between the social community with its many duties and that intimate community of confidence and union which is the real domain of the person. His opinions of Cardinals Wiseman, Manning, Barnabò, and even of the Pope as a person were not caused by personal resentment, or a spirit of insubordination or irreverence, but by his uncompromising realism, his truthfulness, and his lively sense that the inner personality and its domain, where 'heart speaks to heart', was of its nature, and so in the Church too, something sacred and inviolable. I am not obliged to have any personal confidence in the Pope and to open my heart to him, because he is Pope. Those are the things the human person does freely only to other persons he deems worthy of confidence[38].

In any estimate of Newman's attitude to the London House, particular importance should be given to his Chapter Address

---

[36] *Trevor II,* pp. 73-165.

[37] *Trevor* II, pp. 73, 74. See Newman's letter to St John, 9 November 1855, *L.D.,* XVII, p. 44. "Alter the Rule essentially, and you alter the vocation for the Oratory".

[38] J. H. Walgrave, O. P., *Newman the Theologian* (London, 1960), p. 326.

of 31 August 1856 after the departure of Dalgairns from the Birmingham community[39]. This is a lengthy survey of Dalgairns' character, with its salient trait of disquiet, and his unsettled and unsettling second period in the Birmingham Oratory. Critics of the Birmingham Oratory, Newman felt, thought that Dalgairns had been providentially sent to the Birmingham House in order to infuse in it the spirit of the London Oratory, and that the London Oratory was going to be towards the General Congregation of St Philip (*mutatis mutandis*) what St Bernard and Citeaux were to the Benedictine Order. The general tone of this patient Address makes it clear that by this time Newman felt that the London House had a different spirit to his, but that he was not going to abdicate his own view of the Oratorian vocation in favour of theirs. It is in this light that we should judge his later relations with them.

In the Oratory Papers Newman dwells more than once on the propagation of the Oratory: that although St Philip himself never thought of extending his work outside Rome, nevertheless the early history of the Oratory bears witness to a fecund proliferation of Houses. The question immediately arises, Why are there only two Congregations of the Oratory in England? Did Newman want not only *small*, but *few* communities? Early on he had spoken sanguinely of 'covering England with Oratories'[40], and even at the time of the setting up of the London community, he had wanted to leave himself free for other possible foundations within a short-term future[41].

Was it in the event, commensurate with all the effort Newman had made to get the Oratory going, for him to end up as

---

[39]The following extract is relevant here: ". . . When he implied that *we* had not St Philip's spirit, he meant that we had not the spirit of the London Oratory—and he has been used by the London Oratory to new-make us after the pattern of the London Oratory . . ." *Or.P.*, No. 27.

[40]See "Notes on future plans for the Oratory, made during Retreat", *L.D.*, XII, pp. 392–394 (July-August 1848). The phrase 'cover England with Oratories' occurs *L.D.*, XIII, p. 330.

[41]cf. v.g. *L.D.*, XIII, p. 92; "Moreover, if I am thus to be loose, which on this plan I certainly must be . . . then it may happen at the end of my time that there is an opening at Manchester or Edinburgh, and I shall be the only one of the Congregation free, loose to set off then, and begin a house. We cannot anticipate the future . . ."

Superior of just one House, and as a discarded founder of a second? Why was the development of the Oratory limited in this way? The answer is not that there were not enough priests with private means in England at the time to man several Oratories. The early correspondence shows clearly that Newman's Birmingham Oratory was not originally composed of wealthy priests, particularly, after the separation into two communities[42]. The real reasons which stopped the growth of the English Oratory at the second bud on the tree are largely connected with the genesis and personnel of the London House, with Faber's presence as head of the latter, and Newman's absence in Dublin. Newman's energies since 1847 had as their main objective the Oratory and its establishment; after 1851 the university with its frustrating and time-consuming delays became a second major objective. The Achilli trial too, absorbed his time. All this put a brake on any direct expansion of the Birmingham Oratory into other Midland towns. London could have been considered large enough to contain a second Oratory, but Faber's decided antipathy to any possible Irish version of the Oratory in London—which is already revealed in the 1849–50 correspondence[43]—pruned away what might have been a vigorous shoot. Two other possibilities of Oratories connected with universities—at Dublin and later at Oxford— never came to realization. During Newman's difficult years, numbers at the Birmingham Oratory were low: the famous dedication at the end of the *Apologia* mentions each member of the community by name—only six in all. At this period Newman confessed to a feeling of 'recklessness' about not having

[42]cf. *L.D.*, XIII, pp. 119, 121 (22—23 April 1849):
We have hardly any good payers in our House—William, Frederic, Austin and Stanislas are below the mark—Robert and McQuoin have nothing . . .
. . . Indeed, it is very hard indeed to help being extravagant, for economy consists in scraping cheese instead of paring it, and similar littlenesses. This is what makes it so unpleasant—and so hopeless too, for we find it difficult to believe that what in each particular is so small will in the heap come up to any thing of consequence. I think it is the nature of all of us University men to spend, and it is only by a continual effort and a forced jealousy and stinginess that any of us can be got to act conformably to our place and profession.

[43]See *L.D.*, XIII, p. 104, note 1, letter of Faber to Newman 3 April, 1849: ". . . Never take another Irishman, Padre mio . . ."cf. also *Trevor* II, p. 127 for Newman's later impressions of Faber (in 1856, during the dispute with London).

9

novices⁴⁴; things finally improved with the entry of the first
generation of vocations from the Oratory School, already in
Newman's lifetime. But by then the time was past when he
could have been at the head of a dynamic Institute multiplying itself in numerous offshoots. It was then the extrinsic
difficulties outlined above, rather than any lack in the Oratorian
idea itself which limited the English Congregation to the
Birmingham and London communities.

Newman's vocation to the Oratory was worked out altogether
on the plane of supernatural prudence, after several unrealized
projects of vocation had been examined and abandoned. His
idea of the Oratory was largely self-taught, from a minute
study of the Annals of the Oratory and from a close observation
of the two major Italian Oratories—those of Rome and Naples.
His life as a priest was cast in an Oratorian pattern, but the
accession of another religious leader (Faber) with an already
existing group of followers, gave the English Oratory a
development it would scarcely have had, if Newman alone
had been the central figure of the new Institute. The painful
estrangement between Newman and the London House must
not be blamed on Newman, since he had a just and canonical
claim on his side of the quarrel. His attitude to the London
House subsequent to the quarrel was motivated by prudence
and not by resentment.

Newman's formation for the priesthood was not carried out
under Oratorian auspices, but under the Jesuits who were in
charge of Propaganda College in Rome. He was keenly aware
of the shortcomings of the Propaganda system of preparation
for the priesthood, particularly of its lack of genuine mental
training for the students. His own intellectual and spiritual
acquirements from his Anglican ministry continued with him
throughout this brief period of Roman training, and re-appear
after it. At the time of ordination he was no longer a young man,
and he was acutely aware of the loss of spiritual resiliency in his
own soul due to the wear and tear of the years.

⁴⁴See *A.W.*, p. 260 (22 February 1865):
    ... I have got hardened against the opposition made to me, and have not the
soreness at my ill treatment on the part of certain influential Catholics which I had
then—and this simply from the natural effect of time—just as I do not feel that
anxiety which I once had that we have no novices—I don't know that this recklessness is a better state of mind than that anxiety ...

7 Newman's Oratorian Spirituality: Preservation of Type

NEWMAN himself has explained what he meant by 'Preservation of Type' as the basic test of the true development of an idea[1], and Father Walgrave has drawn attention to the fact that this invariability of type is not to be taken too strictly, and that 'this note . . . no longer relies on the definition of the idea in its essence, but on the visible form and the attitude which express it[2].'

We have then to examine whether, due allowance being made for the immense differences between sixteenth-century Italy and nineteenth-century England, Newman's English Oratory is recognizably of the same *type* as that of St Philip.

An initial difficulty confronts us here: did Newman himself outshine St Philip in the eyes of the first group of young English Oratorians to the point that one might say their idea was to join Newman, rather than the Oratory? In a letter of 16 February 1849 to Faber, when the project of a London House —with the consequent division of the members into two

[1] See v. g. *Dev.* p. 178:

An idea then does not always bear about it the same external image; this circumstance, however, has no force to weaken the argument for its substantial identity, as drawn from its external sameness, when such sameness remains. On the contrary, for that very reason, *unity of type* becomes so much the surer guarantee of the healthiness and soundness of developments, when it is persistently preserved in spite of their number or importance.

See *ib.* p. 207:

. . . whereas all great ideas are found, as time goes on, to involve much which was not seen at first to belong to them, and have developments, that is enlargements, applications, uses and fortunes, very various, one security against error and perversion in the process is the maintenance of the original type, which the idea presented to the world at its origin, amid and through all its apparent changes and vicissitudes from first to last.

[2] *Newman the Theologian* (1960), p. 264.

separate communities—was coming to the boil, Newman writes:

> Recollect, my dear F. Wilfrid, what I have already urged on you —your own words, that *I* am the bond of union among those who otherwise would not have come together. F. William, says the same this morning 'You know it is not to be Oratorians, but to be with Newman that we are met together—we came not seeking the Oratory but you[3] . . .'

One need not attach too much importance to F. William Penny's phrase, particularly as in the event he did not persevere in the Oratory[4]; nevertheless, it does reveal the fact that some of the younger recruits followed Newman personally, even to the point of joining the Oratory with him, once he, after careful consideration, had decided on the Oratory as their common vocation. Such a preponderance of personal influence was in itself quite in the Oratorian tradition, especially as Newman did not set up shop for himself. He had written from Rome on 21 February 1847 to Mrs Bowden:

> . . . Certain it is, we shall do our best to import a tradition, not to set up something for ourselves, which to me is very unpleasant . . .[5].

There need not be any difficulty then in admitting that Newman's personality attracted recruits, if we establish firmly that he did not attract them to himself, but to St Philip, and so to Christ.

Of this there can be no reasonable doubt: far from 'newmanizing' St Philip Neri, Newman's one aim in the Santa Croce Papers had been to put himself to school at St Philip's feet, and adapt the 'Philippine' Oratory to his own and his companions' vocation in England.

We must recollect that as an Anglican Newman had had an intellectual difficulty about the place of the saints in Catholic worship, even until the last years at Littlemore[6], although he

[3] *L.D.*, XIII, p. 51.

[4] See *L.D.*, XIV, p. 500: "Appendix 2. Decree of 30 January 1851 accepting W. G. Penny's Departure from the Oratory." See below p. 458.

[5] *L.D.*, XII, p. 45.

[6] See *Correspondence of John Henry Newman with John Keble and Others*, 1839–1845 (edited at the Birmingham Oratory, 1917), p. 356.

had already written *The Church of the Fathers* in 1833. There had been a certain deliberateness and gradualness in his coming to St Philip; we really do not know anything about his knowledge of St Philip, while he was still an Anglican. At the outset of his Oratorian career he had grasped clearly the outlines of St Philip's idea, as we see it in the Santa Croce Papers and the early Chapter Addresses of 1848. The Oratory had originally been a set of exercises, a means of reformation of Rome: it was a local Roman thing, not at first intended for any place else. The early history of the propagation of the Oratory after St Philip's death, was, as has been pointed out above[7] the catching influence of an example rather than a planned development of subordinate houses. As each new Oratory came into being, it realized in itself, whole and entire, the idea of the Oratory, without dependence on any central house or General: nothing except the 'few rules' and the spirit of St Philip. This Italian type of Oratory is diametrically opposed to the Jesuit type of organization and ethos, and is, moreover, far removed from the French type of Oratory which was a centralized body, adapted to each different diocese as regards its rules, and devoted chiefly to the conversion of Protestants, while the Italian type on the whole avoided controversy, was chiefly pastoral, and was distinguished by its daily ministry of the Word[8].

It is only natural that the Italian Oratories founded after St Philip's death, would give a place in their spiritual scheme of things to St Philip, which the Founder naturally enough would not have thought of allotting to himself. This is the normal filling out of the Founder's role in the memory of his successors, and is a legitimate development in any religious Institute. That Newman was second to none in this cultivation of the Founder's role may be deduced from a consideration of his Oratory Papers—one can see that Newman's study of the Oratorian idea included at its core an assimilation to the spirit of St Philip, and this not merely in personal devotion but in his specific function as Founder and Superior of the Oratory.

[7]See p. 102.
[8]See *Or.P.*, No. 24, and also Appendix 1. Paper O 'Oratorii Italici typus.'

This fidelity to St Philip, not merely in devotion but in function, is seen at its best in those Papers which immediately follow the stress of the Dalgairns' dispute, viz., the Chapter Addresses of 1856 and 1858[9]. Here Newman is battling for the very existence of the idea of the Oratory, such as he has understood it:

> . . . when once we have apprehended that distinction . . . I mean, the difference of living . . . to ourselves and living to St Philip, we shall see our duties in a new light. As Christians we have given ourselves to Christ; to make this more sure and definite, we have, as Oratorians, given ourselves to St Philip—we are not our own property, but his, and we must please, not ourselves, but him . . .[10].

Besides this conformity to St Philip as Father and Founder of the Oratory, there is, one feels, discernible in Newman's devotion to him, a more personal note as the weight of years and of crosses begins to tell. He leans more heavily on St Philip's arm, wistfully begging some share in Philip's marvellous gift of graceful and winning old age. 'Forma Senectutis' (Picture of old age) is one of the invocations in the litany of St Philip composed by Newman. The Journal for 15 December 1859 expresses this:

> . . . as years go on, I have less sensible devotion and inward life . . . I more and more wonder at *old* saints. St Aloysius or St Francis Xavier or St Carlo, are nothing to St Philip. O Philip gain me some little portion of thy fervour. I live more and more in the past, and in hopes that the past may revive in the future[11].

Another significant invocation in the litany is 'Vir prisci temporis' (Man of primitive times). Newman is intimating here that affinity between St Philip and the Church of Antiquity, which he has treated of in many passages, though perhaps nowhere more explicitly or fully than in the fourth of the early 1848 Chapter Addresses[12]. Newman's own personal preference for the ethos of primitive Christianity, such as he has given

[9]*Or.P.*, Nos. 26, 27, 28, 31, 32.

[10]*Or.P.*, No. 26.

[11]*A.W.*, p. 249.

[12]See the second paragraph of this Address, *Or.P.*, No. 6.

expression to in the much-quoted passage of his *Eirenicon*[13], far from being a distortion of St Philip's spirituality by a former Anglican patristic scholar, was thoroughly 'Philippine' in character.

Granted then that Newman preserved the type of Italian Oratory in the devotional role allotted to St Philip, may one say as much about the intellectual tone—did he give an undue emphasis to intellectual, as distinct from pastoral work? This was one of the first controversies that arose in the nascent English Oratory, during the summer of 1849. Shortly after the foundation of the London Oratory, when Newman was trying to find some lucrative use for the 'white elephant' of the St Wilfrid's property, his suggestion that it be used as a place for educating boys was hotly contested by Dalgairns on heated views which went beyond the facts of the case[14]; that Newman was proceding on the lines of the French not the Italian Oratory, and following Cardinal de Bérulle instead of St Philip. In the correspondence which ensued, Newman restates his position on the legitimate place for intellectual work in the Italian Oratorian tradition, on the lines on which he had already studied it for himself in the Santa Croce Papers, and had

---

[13] *Difficulties felt by Anglicans in Catholic Teaching* (1910), II, pp. 24-5.

[14] cf. v. g. Newman's letter of 20 June 1849 to Dalgairns, *L.D.*, XIII p. 177. We should note in this connection Newman's distinction between different "views" about the Oratory and different "lines" within it. He is referring to the Dalgairns case:

"NB. I don't mean to let off F. Bernard answering me—don't *tell him* this, for I suppose he will—but, if he don't, make him. We must not go out on different *views* as regards the Oratory, though as *individuals* we may, and must, if my view of the O. is right, go out on different *lines*." (*L.D.*, XIII, p. 184; letter of 22 June 1849 to Faber).

Newman develops this thought of the necessity of having the same views in community in a letter of 18 February 1850 to Antony Hutchinson:

"I am truly rejoiced to hear on all hands so good an account of the London House— I mean internally. That it has the spirit of carità, I know quite well. What I am very anxious it should cultivate, if possible, is another spirit besides —not obedience, for it has that too—but a third. There are three bonds of a community, carità, obedience, and intellectual agreement. St Paul speaks of this third, when he prays for his converts that their *charitas* abundet in scientiâ et omni *sensu*, and that they may be perfecti in eodem sensu et in eâdem sententiâ. It is astonishing how much men get over who have the same *views*. It is *the* way in which good kind of people get on together, and is no mean support of the religious principles of love and obedience . . ." (*L.D.*, XIII, p. 426).

expressed it in the early Chapter Addresses of 1848 and later repeated in the *Remarks on the Oratorian Vocation.* Furthermore, the English Oratory, though a daughter of the Italian, was expressly empowered by its constitutions to take care of schools, seminaries and universities 'in cases of grave necessity[15].'

Dalgairns' (and Faber's) view that purely intellectual work, not directly pastoral, was un-Oratorian was based on a misunderstanding of St Philip's maxim of *mortificazione del razionale.* This, in Newman's view, did not mean a deadening of one's thinking powers, but a submission of one's judgment in practical obedience to the commands and wishes of the Superior. Newman's considered judgment on early Italian Oratorian history as normative in this matter is (in the light of facts which he had diligently compiled), fair and straight-forward. The crucial question, however, remains, whether Newman's own particular intellectual field was in a true sense Oratorian. Was there a dichotomy here between his priestly life and his intellectual work? Did he accept St Philip's Rule and Institute as the norm for his devotion, but just go his own way in the things of the mind? Would he have been the same great thinker and writer, with precisely the same tonality, even if he had not been an Oratorian?

This is a very serious question which searches very deeply into the reality of his Oratorian vocation. Intellectually, he had not been formed in an Oratorian tradition; Oxford, not the Oratory, had trained his intellect. In the 'Advertisement' to the *Sermons preached on Various Occasions,* he tells us what his anticipations about his intellectual work as a Catholic had been—philosophy or ecclesiastical history, but that dogmatics would have been incongruous in one who had 'freely taught and published error in a Protestant communion[16].' This cultiva-

---

[15]"Cum sint multi in Ecclesia Dei, qui audiendis Monialium confessionibus aut dant operam, aut dare optime possunt; propterea nequis ab instituto Congregationis nostrae proprio possit abduci, statutum est, ne nostrorum aliquis sese obliget aut dedat confessionibus audiendis, moribus reformandis, rebusque earum gerendis. Idem dicimus de Seminariis, Collegiis, Congregationibus, Societatibus, aut aliis Universitatibus, rebusve earum, sine gravi necessitate, tractandis." (*Instituta Congregationis Anglicae Oratorii S. Philippi Nerii.* Rome, 1847, p. 30, "Decretum LXX.")

[16]3rd ed., 1870, p. ix.

tion of historical in preference to dogmatic theology was indeed in the Oratorian tradition, but Newman's own interests were not precisely those of the erudite labours of the learned Maurists or early Oratorians. He was interested in the great religious questions of the day; now it is a question how far the Oratorian ethos allowed scope for the uninhibited use of the intellect in these agitating problems—it would seem rather to point to the quiet backwater of a placid, soothing intellectual life, such as Newman himself suggests that of the primitive Benedictines to have been, and in which he sees a parallel to the work of the Italian Oratory[17].

Our crucial question still remains: was Newman's own intellectual work Oratorian, in the sense of being in line with Oratorian tradition? Broadly speaking, we may say that his interests and work lay in two great fields: in education (in its broadest sense) and in the philosophy of religious belief. Now both these interests necessarily bring a man out into direct contact with the problems of his own day, rather than seclude him in an erudite study of the past. To deal adequately with contemporary problems, one cannot live at one remove from life.

At this point we should, perhaps, appeal to a further note of a true development (in Newman's sense), that of assimilative power. From the Oratorian point of view, one should recognize that there never had been a writer quite of Newman's type in the history of the Italian Oratory; his work was a development, a new beginning, not a copying of what went before. The only question is, was it a genuine and legitimate development, or a corruption of the Oratorian idea? In all fairness, we must hold that it was a true development, since it was an apostolate compatible with the general tenor of Oratorian life (community living in a town) and was adapted to the particular needs of the time. It was an apostolate to the intellect, for which Newman explicitly invokes the pattern and patronage of St Philip, who:

> . . . preferred to yield to the stream, and direct the current, which he could not stop, of science, literature, art and fashion, and to sweeten and to sanctify what God had made very good and man

---

[17]See Chapter 5, note 40, above, p. 82.

had spoilt . . . he perceived that the mischief was to be met, not with argument, not with science, not with protests and warnings, not by the recluse or the preacher, but by means of the great counter-fascination of purity and truth . . . For me . . . so far I can say for certain that, whether or not I can do any thing at all in St Philip's way, at least I can do nothing in any other . . .[18].

[18] *The Idea of a University* (ed. 1898), pp. 235–8.

8 Newman's Oratorian Spirituality: Continuity of Principles

HAVING settled the fact that Newman preserved, while developing, the Italian type of 'Philippine' Oratory, both in functional and devotional attachment to St Philip, and in exercising an active apostolate to the contemporary intellect, let us now examine how far he maintained the continuity of Oratorian principles.

The Santa Croce Papers contain the following Latin note: 'Essentialia Congr. Orat. principia duo sunt—unum ut voto ne obstringatur patres (et fratres); alterum ut ne plures fiant in domo quàm admittit illa inter se familiaritas et summa conjunctio quam supra explicuimus[1]'. That is to say, the two basic principles of the Oratory are (i) Absence of vows; (ii) A small community bound together by mutual attachment.

Newman seems to have been much exercised to work out a doctrine of perfection to be achieved in community life without religious vows—it is a frequent theme in the Oratory Papers—and in the process, he (at times, at least) seems to undervalue the vows, as if there existed a contrast between 'voluntary' obedience (without vows) and 'vowed' obedience (where the action of the moment would seem to be less voluntary, because done under the constraint of a past vow).

Our interest here is focussed on Newman's mind working out a point of practical spirituality, as a constituent principle of the Oratory, distinct from religious life on the one hand, and from the secular priesthood on the other. The whole question really hinges on obedience as the backbone of community life: where there are no vows, there must still be obedience, if the back of the body is not to be broken. Does this mean that such

[1] *Or.P.*, Appendix i. Paper "O".

obedience is limited, because not binding under vow? In a letter to Faber of 8 January 1850, Newman writes of a 'nasty unphilippine jansenistic' of yielding a so-called 'Oratorian' obedience, as if this were to be less comprehensive than vowed obedience. He then quotes St Philip's maxim 'Aut pareat aut abeat[2].'

Newman then shows himself quite exigent about the full scope of obedience for Oratorians, nor would it be fair to him to impute this to a desire to reinforce his own authority over his community. Though the Brief nominated him Superior for life, he had not fully realized this in the very early days[3]: when he speaks of obedience then, he includes himself as a possible subject. This idea of total obedience had been a clear trait in St Philip, and Newman was continuing a genuine principle in enforcing it. The question remains, however, whether he ranked this ideal of Oratorian obedience as higher than that of the vowed obedience of religious. Is the Oratorian's obedience 'voluntary' while that of the religious is 'vowed'— and therefore not quite so voluntary?

The most explicit of Newman's texts on this point is the hitherto unpublished Chapter Address, dated 'Stae Apolloniae' of 1848, in which he develops his line of thought that St Philip returned to the fervour of apostolic Christianity, forming a community without vows, and almost without rules, by forming in his disciples a certain character instead.

> . . . It was St Philip's object therefore, instead of imposing laws on his disciples, to mould them, as far as might be into living laws, or, in the words of Scripture, to write the law on their hearts . . . The Oratory has never degenerated, but is at this day faithful both its tradition and spirit. It is still conducted on the free spirit of St Paul, and walks forward to its work, with the law written on the heart, not so much by external precepts, as by the light and truth within it . . .[4].

[2]*L.D.*, XIII, p. 374: "How can you *trust* a man's *perseverance*, who is confessed not to have the *principle* of obedience in him? Till he gives up his will, till he relinquishes that nasty unphilippine jansenistic notion of 'yielding an Oratorian obedience.' I cannot trust him."

[3]An early entry in the Birmingham Oratory Decree Book mentions elections at which Father Newman was re-elected Provost. Cf. *L.D.* XVII, p. 124.

[4]*Or.P.* No. 6.,

The precise point of contrast between Oratorians and all others, whether seculars or regulars, lies in a willing submission to the ascesis of community life as the great means of perfection. This contrast is stated even more forcefully in a passage of the *Remarks on the Oratorian Vocation,* where Newman even goes so far as to say:

> . . . Again, even suppose regulars to be *bona fide* in a community, as is often the case with women; well, but it is because they cannot help it. They conform, they obey, because they are under a *vow.* There is nothing to show that they have the gift of living together as such, and for its own sake. They obey, not for the sake of obedience, but from a past act which binds them. There is, then, as distinct a difference of vocation and of perfection, between us and regulars in this respect, as there is between us and secular priests . . .[5].

Newman has not really examined the relative merits of a vowed and an unvowed obedience as a point of abstract doctrine; he is concerned with concrete situations, with the type of ethos which, *in fact,* religious obedience tends to produce compared to the more inward, loving and refined ethos which St Philip (and the Oratory after him) succeeded in effecting through unvowed obedience. Are Newman's observations valid, even at this existential level? If what he says were true, by and large, it would almost amount to saying that, in practice, religious life can produce obedience rather than love, which would be a very serious indictment of the practice of religious life.

We should, perhaps, distinguish here between the facts which Newman cites, and his interpretation of them. Undoubetdly, most communities of men in England in his day (apart from the Cistercians at Mount St Bernard) were not living in fixed unchanging communities, and he was then correct in placing the distinguishing mark of Oratorian life as stable residence in community. To say, however, as he does that women observe community life 'because they cannot help it', that they 'obey (only) from a past act which binds them' may be questioned first of all on the ground of fact: is it true?

[5]*Or.P.,* No. 25, pp. 334, 335.

Whatever about the ground of fact, which will necessarily
present limitless variations, we may question Newman's as-
sumptions on the level of doctrine. St Thomas has shown that
the obligation of vowed obedience comes not from compulsion,
but from the constancy of the will:

> . . . auctoritas illa est intelligenda de necessitate coactionis, quae
> involuntarium causat, et devotionem excludit . . . necessitas autem
> voti per immobilitatem fit voluntatis; unde et voluntatem
> confirmat, et devotionem auget . . .[6].

In the same article, ad 3, St Thomas has convincingly
maintained the advantage of vowed over unvowed obedience
in this radical commitment of the will which the vow imparts
to the whole future of a man's life.

Newman, for his part, has rightly seen that charity is the
great aim of community life, and that vows are only a means—
and not the only means—of arriving at community charity.
One must recognize that the religious state as we know it with
its three essential vows of religion, although recommended by
the weight of a tradition of many centuries, is only one successful
solution among many other possible ones. Newman was
intensely concerned with one of the other possible ways: the
Oratorian way. Far from despising religious life, he was attempting to achieve its characteristic note of Christian perfection,
but without using the vows of poverty and obedience. Admitting
the distinction between vow and virtue, we must allow that he
exacted the full measure of the virtue of obedience, without
basing it on an obligation arising out of a past vow: he wanted
an obedience which was the immediate result of a free, spontaneous charity. If, in passing, in the passage quoted above
from the *Remarks on the Oratorian Vocation*, he has overstepped
the limits of justice somewhat with regard to regulars we must
admit that his grasp of the full value of the religious vows seems
to be inadequate.

Would this be a case of lingering Anglicanism in his make-up?
As an Anglican he had no prejudices against religious or monastic life, as the frequent references in his correspondence

[6] *S. theol.*, IIa, IIae, q.88, a.6. ad 1.

show; he does, however, already in one passage of his Anglican days, rate a voluntary higher than a vowed religious act[7].

Unlike St Thomas who solved the problem at the level of theological principles, Newman does not seem to go beyond the psychological level, as the following extract from a letter would indicate:

> . . . In a religious house no regard (except accidentally) is paid to the feelings of each other, whereas in the world society gets on, and a family gets on, by a refined system of mutual concession. Society is like a carriage going on springs, where every collision and jar is anticipated. Such is necessarily the case in any voluntary community—it is necessarily the principle of the Oratory even if St Philip had not prescribed it, directly vows are excluded . . .[8].

To conclude this point on the vows, we may state the case somewhat as follows. Newman's whole concern was to build up an Oratorian community on Oratorian lines, and therefore in his preference for the Oratorian way, and his contrasting it as a way of voluntary love in comparison with the vowed obedience of regulars, he is but echoing the early Oratorian tradition of which he had made extracts in the Santa Croce Papers. In a community where there is not the bond of vows, charity must be the bond. This charity needs the 'virtue of humanity' distinct from charity, though subordinate to it, its object being human nature in itself, its mind, its sentiment, its history. This virtue in turn is normally produced by a refined education, and here he found priests and religious wanting:

> . . . add to this the utter want of taste, arising from the absence of education, and you have your dish smoking hot. (Theology, as mathematics or metaphysics does not give taste) . . . The same is seen in a parallel way in the after dinner conversation of priests,

---

[7] Cf. *Letters and Correspondence of John Henry Newman*, ed. A. Mozley (1891), II, pp. 310, 311. And from his Catholic period cf. *Sermons on Various Occasions* (3rd ed 1870), p. 225, and *Historical Sketches*, III, p. 88.

[8] *L.D.*, XV, pp. 402, 403, letter of 27 July 1853 to Lady Georgina Fullerton.

and the recreations of nuns. They are to be cheerful and they have *nothing* to be cheerful upon. So they are boisterous or silly[9].

The human refinement which he hoped for in Oratorians would largely derive from their previous education: Newman aimed to foster and supernaturalize this human refinement in order to make it a lasting bond of 'Santa comunità.'

Newman never wavered in his preference for a small Oratory, feeling that one cannot really love (intimately) a large number of persons with the supernaturalized but still human affection traditional in the Oratory. One of the few Italian phrases which he cherished was that of 'Santa comunità', a maxim traditional in the Oratory, and one that sums up the heart of Oratorian life. He never wished for numbers for mere numbers' sake—they would only render impossible the type of community life wished for by St. Philip. Small numbers alone make it possible for the Oratory to be a home. This thought was uppermost in his mind when, after an anxious journey, he was at length able to return to Birmingham in July 1879 after he had been made a cardinal in Rome. In the brief Address which he made at the Oratory on his return, he dwells on this idea of 'home', as having been consecrated for them by their patron and founder St Philip, for he made the idea of home the very essence of his religion and institute[10].

Two practical consequences flow from the principle of 'Santa comunità': one being the necessity for each Oratory of

[9]*L.D.*, XIV, p. 183, letter of 28 December 1850 to Henry Wilberforce.
See the excellent remarks on Newman's "virtue of humanity" in Walgrave, *Newman the Theologian* (1960), p. 327.
[10]*Addresses to Cardinal Newman with his Replies etc.* ed. W. P. Neville (1905), pp. 103–05:
'...To come home again! in that word 'home' how much is included. The home life—the idea of home—is consecrated to us by our patron and founder, St Philip, for he made the idea of home the very essence of his religion and institute. We have even a great example in our Lord Himself; though in His public ministry he had not where to lay His head, yet we know that for the first thirty years of His life He had a home, and He therefore consecrated, in a special way, the life of home. And as, indeed, Almighty God has been pleased to continue the world, not, as angels, by a separate creation of each, but by means of the family, so it was fitting that the Congregation of St Philip should be the ideal, the realization of the family in its perfection, and a pattern to every family in the parish, in the town, and throughout the whole of Christendom. Therefore, I do indeed feel pleasure to come home again ... I feel I may rejoice in coming home again—as if it were to my long home—to that home which extends to heaven, 'the home of our eternity'....

maintaining—though in no narrow sense—its own house spirit. The other is the assimilation by new members of this same house spirit, as they find it, and to which by natural predisposition they were attracted even before entering. Both points receive full treatment in the Chapter Addresses of 20 February and 8 March 1858. A Memorandum of April 1857 dealing with the (then unsettled) vocation of Ignatius Ryder deals with this natural predisposition of a novice as a possible sign of vocation:

> . . . It is probable then, that either he has been told, or will be told, that his human feelings indeed lead him to *us*, but his supernatural motives *elsewhere*. He will have to consider, whether he has any better proof urged on him that grace leads him *elsewhere*, than the fact that nature leads him *here*. But this is no proof, for it may easily happen that grace and nature lead the same way . . . If then he feels an habitual affection for us, a love of our ways, and a fear of annoying or displeasing us, or of losing our good opinion, all which in themselves are natural feelings, such a circumstance does not prove that they are not St Philip's instruments for protecting supernatural charity. Any how they are not inconsistent with it, unless human nature and divine grace are essentially opposed to each other[11].

As we ponder Newman's treatment of the theme of perfection in his Oratory Papers, a certain feeling of disappointment creeps over us: his handling of this great idea seems meagre, not to say jejune. The most characteristic text is the Chapter Address of 27 September 1856, which had already appeared (substantially at least) in print in the original editions of *Meditations and Devotions* as 'A Short Road to Perfection[12].'

To do justice to his almost bald outline ('He then is perfect who does the work of the day perfectly'), we should remember that he is not, in these papers, elaborating a theological analysis of Christian perfection. For such an analysis we should have to go to the *Parochial and Plain Sermons*, the *Lectures on the Doctrine of Justification* and, above all, to the precious collection of tiny essays on patristic theology collected together in the second volume of his *Select Treatises of St Anthanasius*. All these

[11]*Or.P.*, No. 30.
[12]*Meditations and Devotions* (2nd ed., 1893) pp. 379–383.

had been works of his Anglican period, but by re-editing them as a Catholic he endorses their teaching once more. A recent study by C. S. Dessain on Newman's doctrine of grace shows what deep insights Newman has to offer us on the nature of grace and consequently of Christian perfection[13].

In the Oratory Papers, on the other hand, his aim is severely practical. In the brief length of time at his disposal in a community meeting, he has to recall in a telling way one or other basic point of Oratorian life. He does so, writing out his text in a few pages of clear script, with no apparatus of learning, the only alterations being stylistic, with a view to greater perspicuity or accuracy. It is in this light that we should read them, filling out what he leaves unsaid by a perfectly legitimate appeal to his other, more formal writings. These intimate informal papers on the other hand, have their own peculiar and irreplaceable value. They are first-hand evidence from life of his own earnest effort at perfection. They have a biographical more than a theological interest, i.e. they tell us a great deal about Newman, even if they do not tell us a great deal about the spiritual or priestly life in the abstract. The following passage is characteristic of this earnest personal tone:

> It is easy to have vague ideas what perfection is, which serve well enough to talk about it, when we do not intend to aim at it —but as soon as a person really desires and sets about seeking it himself, he is dissatisfied with any thing but what is tangible and clear, and constitutes some sort of direction towards the practice of it[14].

The answer to our problem then would seem to be that, when replaced in its setting of his own Oratorian life, Newman's idea of perfection is theologically adequate, even though the actual texts of the Oratory Papers limit his treatment to an ascetical exhortation towards daily perfection. This perfection would lie essentially in the two basic principles outlined above: community life without vows as the setting for total mutual charity in the spirit of 'Santa comunità'.

---

[13]See C. S. Dessain: "Cardinal Newman and the Doctrine of uncreated Grace": *The Clergy Review* 47 (1962), pp. 207–225 and pp. 269–288. We should note too, in particular, Newman's *Or.P.* No .10, where he develops this idea of daily duties well done, as being the safest road to Perfection.

[14]*Or.P.*, No. 28.

9 Conclusion

IT may be helpful to outline here the main positions adopted in this study, the chief problems encountered and the leading solutions arrived at. As has been pointed out in the Introduction, the book consists of two distinct but closely related parts: it is a study of Newman's spirituality as a priest, in the light of his ministry in the Church of England and of his hitherto unpublished Oratory Papers. The Anglican ministry has a value in itself, but its chief value for this study has been to furnish a demonstration of how these same pastoral principles were carried over into Newman's Oratorian life and ministry.

By a mere process of deduction one might already conclude *a priori* that large areas of Newman's feeling and thinking would have been—unconsciously perhaps—carried over from his Anglican to his Catholic life, particularly on account of the short interval which separates his Anglican from his Catholic ministry, and this at an age when a man is usually settled in his ways. In Newman's case, we are not reduced to conjecture, as the minute study of four such areas—the care of souls, liturgical preaching, the eucharistic ministry and prayer—carried out in Part I of this study has shown, and which may be summarized as follows.

Right from the beginnings of his Anglican ministry, Newman considered the Christian priesthood above all from a pastoral —one might almost say, a practical—standpoint as a lifelong 'responsibility of souls.' This pastoral note is the great underlying bond of continuity and identity between his ministry before and after his conversion. In Newman's work, this care of souls became largely a care of minds, an apostolate to the intellect, recognizably the same before as after conversion. Thus his apostolic attitude to his tutorship at Oriel is in the same line as his letter about the intellectual formation of future priests at Propaganda, while his treatment of the problem of faith in his Catholic period arises directly out of his basic positions in the Oxford *University Sermons*.

As a Catholic priest, he directed the apostolate of the Oratory in two major directions,

> . . . first of the educated world, scientific, literary, political, professional, artistic—and next of the mass of town population, the two great classes on which the fortunes of England are turning: the thinking, speaking and acting England[1].

In choosing an apostolate to the rising industrial towns as the nerve centre of England's political power, he was by-passing any direct rivalry with the Anglican Church, since its influence in these new towns had hitherto been negligible. In labouring for the conversion of England he was not primarily envisaging corporate re-union of the Anglican with the Roman Church[2]; in his Oratory's work for the people of Birmingham he was labouring for souls as in a mission-field, and the newly-published *Letters and Diaries* reveal what a generous share he took in this missionary activity[3].

It was, however, in his work for Catholic education both in the University and in the Oratory School, that the principles he had acquired as an Anglican came again most clearly into play. He wished to 'raise the status of Catholics, first by education, secondly by a philosophical basis of argument[4].' As

---

[1]*Catholic Sermons of Cardinal Newman* (1957), p. 125. In this sermon—preached at the opening of St Bernard's Seminary, Olton, 2 October 1873—Newman is not speaking directly of the work of the Oratory. Nevertheless, the passage quoted in the text sums up what he has said elsewhere, particularly in the early years after his conversion. Cf. p. 151, the letter of 14 February 1847 to Cardinal Fransoni.

[2]See the note on Newman and Ecumenism, note 9 to Chapter 4, p. 63.

[3]This may be followed in detail throughout the correspondence dating from Newman's establishing himself at 40 Alcester Street, Birmingham at the end of January 1849. See *L.D.* XIII *passim*. See also *Trevor* I, pp. 494–510.

[4]*A.W.*, p. 259. Two samples of his description of the education he desiderated for Catholics may be cited: the closing lectures of both the *Lectures on the Present Position of Catholics in England* (1851) and of *Nine Discourses addressed to the Catholics of Dublin* (1851). In the former case—that of Catholics in England labouring under Protestant prejudice—the remedy was for Catholics to force a true knowledge of the Church on their opponents, and to do so in their own locality. In the latter he pleads that if a university is to be a direct preparation for this world, let it be what it professes. "It is not a Convent, not a Seminary . . ."

regards education, he wished to give a large and active role to the laity in the university, not, of course, in order to give a secularist or liberal bias to education, but because he considered the role of the Oratory (and his own role) to be like that of St Philip, one of influence rather than of rule.

A further facet of this responsibility for Christian minds in a world where infidelity was rapidly increasing, is contained in his correspondence with individual inquirers. Two types of soul had special claims on his sympathy: those Anglo-Catholics, former followers of his, who were thinking of becoming Catholics, and those other educated Englishmen (often non-Catholics) who doubted not merely about the true Church but even about the truth of Christianity itself. Some of Newman's replies amount to treatises in miniature, elicited by the difficulties of his correspondents[5]. Nor should one overlook his two novels, *Loss and Gain* and *Callista* where one may find his thought on the true Church and on Christian faith expressed in non-technical language.

The Oratorian tradition of preaching the Word of God was undoubtedly one of the elements which attracted Newman, who had already behind him more than twenty years' experience as one of the greatest of English preachers. Circumstances, however, in the Catholic Church at the time could not provide him either with a liturgical climate or an audience of culture comparable to that in which his Anglican sermons had been preached. His expository gifts re-appear not in the pulpit, but on the platform of the public lecture. It is remarkable how many outstanding books of Newman's Catholic period consist of a series of lectures: *Difficulties felt by Anglicans in Catholic Teaching, The present Position of Catholics in England* and *The Idea of a University defined and illustrated* (in its original form). The Anglican counterpart to these was the volume *Lectures on the Doctrine of Justification.*

[5]Three of these inquirers were women—Mrs William Froude, Mrs J. W. Bowden and Catherine Ward—and all three became Catholics. Newman's letters to them contain many lucid statements of the nature of the act of faith, expressed in terms that do not call for a technical knowledge of theology. He felt a particularly anguished sense of responsibility towards those who had become Anglo-Catholics through his influence, and who were unsettled by his passage to Rome. See his letter to Mrs Froude, *L.D.,* XII, p. 228.

It has been pointed out above[6] that it is only in his *Sermons preached on Various Occasions* that he again, as a Catholic, reaches the high-water mark of the *Parochial and Plain Sermons*. He did moreover, as a Catholic, salvage the latter for further use by arranging for their re-issue from 1868 onwards. A fresh approach, rigorously liturgical, has been suggested above to these Sermons, since of all Newman's Anglican heritage perhaps no part is more apposite for the Church today than his liturgical theology as contained in this *corpus* of Anglican preaching. He here reaches and gives expression to a deep insight into the real nature of the liturgy, which is astonishingly close to that of the Constitution of the Second Vatican Council on the Sacred Liturgy. By this very fact these Sermons provide abundant material for the true liturgical homily—a part of the liturgy most in need of renewal.

Newman's theology and spirituality of the Eucharist when an Anglican has been illustrated above[7] from *The Via Media* and from a close analysis of two of the *Parochial and Plain Sermons*. His view of the Eucharistic mystery abounds in biblical and patristic insights, assents to the doctrine of a Real Presence, and goes a long way towards a sacrificial concept of the Eucharist. When he passes over to Catholicism and looks back on the Anglican Eucharist, he explains the workings of grace on the occasion of the Anglican ordinance as coming *ex opere operantis*, not *ex opere operato*. As a Catholic he did not make any notable original contribution to the theology of the Mass[8]; the practical place which Mass took in his day-to-day life may be gleaned from the *Letters and Diaries*, while devotion to the Blessed Sacrament reserved in the tabernacle was a marked characteristic of his piety.

[6]See p. 38.

[7]See pp. 43-58.

[8]A passage of *Loss and Gain* (pp. 327-29 9th ed., 1886) has often been quoted, and indeed over-quoted, where Newman describes the celebration of Mass as taking place without external active participation on the part of the faithful present, but with real individual participation nevertheless. People often take this passage as the most characteristic thing of Newman's on the Mass. Surely this is to give a false perspective to his eucharistic doctrine. Would it not be more to the point to quote the passage in *Meditations and Devotions*, (2nd ed., 1893, pp. 560-70) on "The Holy Sacrifice"?

Closely connected with the Eucharist was, of course, his view on Orders. His attitude towards the validity of Anglican Orders has been discussed in detail above[9], since it had a significant bearing on his choice of vocation as a Catholic.

Particular importance attaches to Newman's early practice of prayer as an Anglican, both because it remained the pattern of his prayer as a Catholic, and also because his habit of prayer was antecedent to his faith in the efficacy of the sacraments as grace-conferring rites.

Several unpublished MSS, both Anglican and Catholic, have been drawn on at this point to illustrate the predominantly intercessory nature of Newman's own prayer, the role of prayer in the ministry and the precedence of prayer over public preaching[10]. The prominence of prayer in St Philip's idea of the Oratory is realized in Newman's case by this lifelong habit of prayer, which continued along the same lines after his conversion as before.

The emphasis given above[11] to intercessory prayer in Newman's thought may be borne out by that passage of the *Eirenicon* on the belief of Catholics in the intercessory power of Our Lady. The same leading ideas occur here as in the Anglican sermon on Intercession[12], and are here developed with reference to Our Lady's mediation.

One might ask, in what true sense these gifts of Newman's were specifically Anglican—were they not rather *vestigia Catholica* lingering on in Anglicanism from pre-Reformation days, and as such can hardly be called 'Anglican' elements in Newman's priestly spirituality?

To answer this question in all fairness, one must reply in the concrete, not in the abstract. Taking the concrete situation of Anglicanism as it was in Newman's early life and young manhood, one must candidly admit that this concrete assemblage of persons, institutions and traditions had by now, after three centuries of independent existence, a life of its own parallel to

[9]See pp. 53-8.
[10]See pp. 61-7.
[11]See pp. 64-6.
[12]See *Difficulties felt by Anglicans in Catholic Teaching*, (1910), II, pp. 68-76: "Belief of Catholics in her Intercessory Power."

and no longer dependent on the Roman Church. It was within this closed, self-contained community that Newman's rich, many-sided religious personality developed, a flower of spirituality on Anglican soil, within the 'garden enclosed' of Oxford.

It would be merely theoretical to claim the spiritual fruits of Anglicanism, as exemplified in Newman's ministry, to be due to an antecedent Catholic tradition—they were the cumulative result of generations of Anglicans who had lived and died out of communion with Rome. All the distinctive and imponderable touches, which in real life differentiate one type of spirituality from another, are to be found in these Anglican traits of Newman: to assert the contrary would be chimerical, and unjust both to the Anglican communion from which he came, and to the workings of divine grace which brought him out of such a communion (in spite of all its prestige) into the modest Catholic community of the England of the 1840s.

The great broad central fact in Newman's life after his reception as a Catholic was his quest for his vocation, firstly as to whether he should be a priest and then what kind of a priest. The only scruple which held him back from seeking ordination was his settled conviction that his Anglican Orders were truly valid, and that hence he was a priest already. To seek re-ordination would, he felt, expose the sacrament of Orders already received, to sacrilege; on the other hand, he considered that the Catholic Church would treat him practically as a layman in spite of his Anglican Orders. When he was reassured that the practice of re-ordaining ex-Anglican clergymen involved (at that period) no definitive judgment of the Church against the validity of their Orders, his scruple was allayed, though his reason continued to cling to their validity until a year or two after his ordination in the Catholic Church.

He never felt drawn to becoming a secular priest since he felt the need of a rule of life over and above the exercise of the ministry. This did not imply an insensitivity in evaluating the work of the secular clergy, as is maintained by a reviewer of one of the volumes of the *Letters and Diaries*[13]. It was not his vocation, so far as he could judge by the habits of his past life: in his

[13]*L.D.*, XIV, reviewed in *The Irish Theological Quarterly*, XXXI, No. 4, October 1964. p. 341.

Anglican ministry, his background had always been the College, not the parsonage.

No form of priestly life to be found in England at the time of his conversion appealed to him, and the prime object of his Roman sojourn (1846–47) was to come to a decision about his vocation. He passed carefully in review the spirit of several Congregations (though not the more severe among them, as v.g. the Passionists), but did not at any stage envisage a monastic life for himself. Newman never had a monastic vocation, though he staked the whole working of the Oratory on one of the central ideas of cenobitic monasticism, viz. common life in a stable community.

It was at the end of this lengthy enquiry, and not as a result of a first impression that he finally chose the Oratory as his vocation. At the time of his decision (1847) the Oratory appealed to him mainly because of its suitability for the group of English university converts: it was adapted to the habits of educated men, and seemed most likely to allow of a free development of their combined talents in their priestly work for Catholicism in England. Later on, under the stress of disagreements with the London House, he dwelt more on the Oratory as a vocation, not only as a setting for apostolic work, but in itself a genuine way of perfection, through the exercise of supernatural charity in obedience in community life without the obligation of vows.

The vocation to the Oratory which Newman had chosen in Rome in 1847 remained the central core of his life in the Catholic Church until his death in 1890. He makes indeed only few references to his Oratorian life throughout his written works—a fact which has to some degree veiled the true significance of his Oratorian vocation even from those who study his writings with sympathy. The publication, since 1961, of the monumental edition of his *Letters and Diaries*[14] has restored the true perspective, and lets us see how largely the Oratory and its concerns loomed in his life and thought.

Against this closely-filled day-to-day correspondence we may now place his Oratory Papers in order to follow the

[14]Details of the edition, given in Bibliography, p. xx.

development of his vocation. We discern an initial period of almost feverish activity in the foundaticn years, with a gay and almost youthful readiness to tilt a lance even with the Old Catholics and Dr Ullathorne. Faber's peculiar personality without in any way modifying Newman's own richer and more balanced mind, did nevertheless in some measure polarize the active side of Newman's nature in these early years. This polarization faded away after the separation into two communities, one in Birmingham, the other in London. The sharp disagreement between the two communities arising out of the London House's *démarche* in Rome, elicited from Newman his most formal statement on the nature of the Oratorian vocation. The painful experience of Fr Bernard Dalgairns' return to and eventual departure from the Birmingham Oratory about the same time, was a further occasion for Newman to make explicit what (on his own witness) he would have preferred to have left unsaid.

There follow two long and difficult decades (1858–78) when he passes beyond his prime into old age, living out his vocation, often under painful and trying circumstances. He adds little in these years to his writings about the Oratory: his business is to live it. When finally, the cardinalate comes his way and he changes over from being 'Father Newman' to become 'Cardinal Newman' he is already in advanced age and continues quietly in his own beloved *nido* of the Oratory to the end.

The circumstances of Newman's Oratorian life limited him to one small community in an undistinguished, if prosperous, Midland town. His Oratorian vocation itself was a limitation, and the acute disagreement between the two English Oratories was a further circumscription of his sphere of influence. All these factors reduced the scale on which he worked, but they in no way affect his legacy to the Catholic priesthood.

Viewed historically, that legacy may be said to consist primarily in the foundation of the Oratory in England. This was of importance not only for English Catholicism, but also for the Oratory, since the two English Houses are among the most flourishing today. Moreover, the dynamic modern German Oratory, in its first beginnings after World War I, was directly modelled on Newman's Birmingham Oratory.

Viewed in terms of the problems and needs of our own time, Newman's spirituality has much to offer to priests generally. The basic traits of his Anglican priesthood show us what spiritual values can exist to a highly developed degree among our separated brethern. The continuance of these traits in his Catholic ministry indicate how spiritual values acquired outside the Catholic fold may find a legitimate place within the Church. His intelligent and yet thoroughly traditional adaptation of the Italian Oratory to English ways is an excellent example of the energetic renewal that is called for in so many spheres of Church life today. His generous apostolate to an industrial population is consonant with the pastoral work of many priests in the modern Church. His legacy of liturgical preaching, saved over from his Anglican days, is quite unique of its kind and particularly opportune in the present restoration of the homily as an integral part of the Mass.

It is, however, in his lifelong service of truth, both in education and in personal religious inquiry, that his most characteristic legacy lies. This responsibility for Christian souls and minds, assumed by him in virtue of his Anglican ordination and exercised so faithfully in Oxford, resumed anew in Birmingham and in Dublin, under the patronage of St Philip Neri, Apostle of Rome, continues still wherever his writings are read. Heart speaks to heart while Newman still lives in the Church, a mighty Father of Souls.

NEWMAN'S ORATORY PAPERS

RULES OBSERVED IN EDITING NEWMAN'S ORATORY PAPERS

1   Newman's original autograph, when it still exists, has always been used as the editor's source. This is the case for all the Papers provided here, the only exception being Oratory Paper, Nº 18, and for this Paper the best available copy has been supplied. Where more than one autograph exists, as in the case of Oratory Paper, Nº 20, the text chosen is that which the editor judges to be most definitive. As regards Oratory Paper, Nº 25, the text prepared by Newman himself for printing has been given (together with its punctuation) in preference to the autograph copy marked 'Original, sent from Dublin,' since the printed text represents his own final choice.

2   Newman's paragraphs, punctuation and spelling have been reproduced exactly as they stand, even when they are inconsistent or obsolete. No alterations have been made except in Oratory Papers, Nºs 3, 4 and 5, where the numerals he has used so frequently have been spelt out in full. Further, following C. S. Dessain in his edition of Newman's *Letters and Diaries*, a parenthesis or quotation that Newman began with the proper mark but failed to complete, or completed but did not begin, is supplied. All other punctuation marks supplied by the editor are enclosed in square brackets.

3   A list of the abbreviations used by Newman in the Oratory Papers, and of the editorial marks used in the present edition is given above, pp. xvii, xviii.

Introduction to the Oratory Papers

HAVING considered the Anglican basis of Newman's priestly spirituality, and the choice of the Oratory as a way of life, it now remains to examine his Oratorian spirituality, particularly in the light of the whole *corpus* of his Oratory Papers—a task which has not yet been attempted among the multifarious publications on Newman.

This has proved to be by far the most difficult portion of the present work ısince, in a sense, it was a matter of wresting Newman's secret from him. He himself was quite aware of keeping his secret to himself, St Philip's phrase, *secretum meum mihi*[1]. It was only under the stress of disagreement that he wrote the *Remarks on the Oratorian Vocation* as an outline of a reasoned statement on the nature of their vocation.[2] What is attempted here then is something which even Newman himself did not formally do—a presentation of his thought on the spirituality of the Oratory in an ordered whole.

What Newman himself has written on the Oratory has been fragmentary—the Oratory Papers are essentially a miscellaneous collection, elicited as they were by the vicissitudes of life. In order to respect this fragmentary character, and nevertheless attempt a synthesis of their contents, we cannot do better than adopt some of Newman's own 'Notes' of the genuine development of an idea, as employed in his *Development of*

[1] *Apo*. p. 1:
"It may be easily conceived how great a trial it is to me to write the following history of myself; but I must not shrink from the task. The words 'Secretum meum mihi' keep ringing in my ears . . ."

[2] See *Trevor* II, p. 94 quoting Newman's letter of 8 November 1855:
"It is not necessary that any member of the Oratory should be able to talk fluently about its peculiar vocation."

Christian Doctrine, particularly those of 'Logical Sequence', 'Preservation of Type', and 'Continuity of Principles'. No more congenial patterns of thought could be found for Newman himself than these which are of his own making.

The application of these 'Notes' will enable us to see whether, in the event, Newman made a faithful transcript of St Philip's idea or not. At the same time it will let us take Newman's true measure as a priest in the practice of his own life, since the central fact in his priestly life was the founding and fathering of the English Oratory. He will have realized the special role of the priesthood in his own life, in the degree in which he will have lived up to his destiny as Founder of the Oratory in England.

'Logical Sequence' as understood by Newman as a Note of true Development

By 'logical sequence' Newman means that body of thought which grows round and coalesces to an idea which has become embedded in the mind. External circumstances elicit the manifestation of different facets of the idea in turn, but they do not form them; logic is only brought in to arrange and inculcate what no science was employed in gaining. As is well known, Newman gives an illustration of this by the developments which follow on a consideration of sin after baptism[3].

The application of this note of logical sequence to Newman's Oratory Papers, in their chronological order, reveals to us the growth in Newman's life of the idea of the Oratory, from its beginnings as a possible project on to its experience in the trials of community life. Beginning in books, it ends in men, bringing in its train all the anguish attendant on the misunderstandings that arise even between the best-intentioned of men.

---

[3] See Newman's remarks on this Note of "Logical Sequence" in *Dev.* pp. 189–195, particularly the passage:
"... minds develop step by step, without looking behind them or anticipating their goal, and without either intention or promise of forming a system. Afterwards, however, this logical character which the whole wears becomes a test that the process has been a true development, not a perversion or corruption . . ."

The Letter to Cardinal Fransoni, 14 February 1847[4]

This remarkably well-drafted letter is Newman's first formal statement of the scope and purpose of the proposed English Oratory. Written before he himself was ordained priest or even accepted as an Oratorian novice, it nevertheless is a clear statement of his view of the Oratory, and one to which he adhered even under opposition from some of his own future fellow-Oratorians in England. Some salient points should be carefully noted, viz. his attitude of carrying out no frontal attack on the Anglican Church, his selection of the new industrial towns as the focus of political power in English life and the most promising field for the development of Catholicism, his readiness to adopt an apostolate to working class youth, and finally, his care to include literary and theological work within the scope of the Oratory. Each of these points recurred in one way or another in the years following, and Newman's attitude to them as outlined in this letter remained consistently the same. Incidentally, we may note his grasp of social conditions in England (the 'two Englands' of Disraeli's novel), and his readiness to throw in his lot with the—to him new and uncongenial—industrial areas. A comparison is often made between Newman and Manning on this point, to Newman's disadvantage, as if he did nothing for social problems; such a judgment overlooks the broad fact of Newman's voluntary apostolate to the *populosiores urbes*.

This letter to Cardinal Fransoni, in its clear statement of the actual situation in England, and its proposal of a method of conversion, is a considerable advance over the paper on *Congregatio de SS Trinitate*[5] of the previous year, and shows how far he had progressed in the meantime in giving a definite shape to his vocation.

The 'Santa Croce Papers', August or September 1847

In presenting these MSS of Newman's to the public for the first time, the present study may modestly claim to have made available to students the rock-bottom foundation of Newman's

---

[4] The text (in Latin) is published in *L.D.*, XII, pp. 36–40.

[5] See p. 149.

thought on the Oratory. A general sketch of their importance has been provided above[6]; it only remains here to indicate the major lines of Newman's analysis of his Oratorian sources, as they appear here, and re-appear in the later Oratory Papers. Almost every possible aspect of St Philip's institute is covered in these Memoranda, and they may be grouped for convenience' sake under the three great heads of history, canonical status and spirituality. Considering the nature of the Santa Croce Papers to be more documentary than discursive, the present editor has placed them as an Appendix to the collected Oratory Papers, pp. 395–420, where they are available for consultation without hindering the readable flow of the other Newman Papers.

(a) *The Notes on Oratorian History:* These are contained in the passages: 'Propagation of the Oratory'; 'The Four Associated Oratories' and 'Anomalies, Mistakes &c.[7].' The main trend of Newman's interpretation of the Oratory in the light of its history is that it was the spread of an idea rather than the extension of a system. St Philip himself was concerned solely with Rome, his Oratory was a set of spiritual practices, not a religious Institute. If the Oratory developed—and rapidly— this was due to the catching influence of example: no two Oratories had similar origins. These thoughts are worked out more consecutively in the second of the Early Chapter Addresses of 1848[8].

The note on 'The Four Associated Oratories' (viz. Rome, Naples, Lanciano, S.Severino) is of the utmost significance in view of the later controversy between the Birmingham and London Houses. This lay behind his suggestions in the correspondence of 1849[9] that for a time, until things were stabilized,

---

[6] See pp. 90–2.

[7] *Or.P.*, Appendix 1. Paper n and Second Paper.

[8] *Or.P.*, No. 4.

[9] See *L.D.*, XIII, p. 52 (letter of 16 February 1849 to F. W. Faber):
". . . Moreover I have proposed alleviations, one seems unpopular, the other you have not taken notice of. The first was that here and at London we should for a time be one Oratory, with the members moving to and fro—the other a certain number of our members should be *fixed* in London, with the prospect of being formed into an Oratory at the end of a given time—in both cases my being their Superior till the separate Oratory is established."

he should act as Superior of the two groups, divided between the two houses, but remaining one community. By analogy with the Four Associated Oratories of early Oratorian history, this would have been a temporary measure, not a permanent arrangement. In point of fact, it did not come off, and already on 9 October, 1850 Newman released the London Oratorians from their connection with the Birmingham Oratory. To accuse him, five years later, of wishing to become a General over the English Congregation, can only be put down to the disingenuousness of ingratitude.

(b) *Notes on the Canonical Status of the Oratory:* The basic point here is that the Oratory is not a 'religion' (Newman constantly uses the word in this context with this technical canonical meaning). Simply speaking, of course, the Oratory was not a religion, since St Philip would not hear of having vows in the Oratory. On the other hand, its community life resembled the community life of regulars, not the domestic life of secular clergy, and perfection for the Oratorians was to be sought in living community life for a motive of love.

Newman enlarges on the point that St Philip did not write any lengthy Constitutions: the Oratory was to live largely by unwritten rules. The interplay of power within the Oratory is not based on a rigid system of sub-delegation of authority, but on the New Testament ideal of mutual service in the respective functions of the members.

(c) *Notes on the spirit of the Oratory:* His notes on the Oratorian spirit arise out of the historical circumstances of its origin and its peculiar canonical status: secular priests living in a sense like religious. Vows are replaced by love, not in name only, but as the only possible working hypothesis for such a way of community life. There was to be an absence of the *appearance* of government; the whole action of the community was to be, as it were, spontaneous and natural, as if things went on of themselves. As mortification of selfwill is the vital principle of the Oratory, so *obedience* is the essential and necessary means by which it is exercised, and this obedience is to proceed from love. This voluntary, yet perfect, obedience is to be based on the example of our Lord. Newman remarks here, in an aside, that this is probably what is meant by St Philip's special love for St Paul's Epistles—for, if there be one aspect of Christianity which the Apostle delineates beyond others, it is that of *voluntary obedience* after the pattern of Christ[10]. This necessity of the mortification of private judgment and of one's own will arises out of the nature of the community, which if it be really such (and not just a mere lodging house) has a will of its own, to which the wills of individuals must be subordinate. A voluntary submission of the will to the Congregation is, as it were, the definition of good membership[11]. To be an Oratorian is directly to consult for the life of the community, to postpone one's wishes and will to its welfare.

Many of these ideas re-occur in the later *Remarks on the Oratorian Vocation,* almost verbatim, and would seem to suggest that Newman had the Santa Croce Papers by him in Dublin when he was composing the *Remarks.* The recurrence of the same ideas based on the same arguments, adapted to new circumstances, illustrates the point made above[12] that Newman was a 'reasoner' in the affairs of life, and carried over into each new stage the hard-won convictions of the preceding period of life's journey.

The Early Chapter Addresses of 1848

Here we see the raw material of the Santa Croce Papers worked into coherent form. These addresses are chiefly historical —they give us Newman's view of the rise and propagation of St Philip's Oratory. Delivered as they were in the course of three weeks (20 January to 9 February 1848) they present in a synthetic way the view of the Oratory as analysed in the Santa Croce Papers. These Addresses were delivered before the reception of Faber and his followers into the Oratory, which took place on 14 February 1848[13]. It should be noted that the

---

[10]See pp. 114–8, for a full discussion of Newman's idea of Oratorian obedience as "voluntary" in contrast to the "vowed" obedience of regulars.

[11]See *Or.P.*, No. 25, p. 335.

[12]See p. 70 on the role of prudence in Newman's own choice of vocation.

[13]See *L.D.*, XII, p. 169: "Monday 14 February admitted Faber etc Oratorians . . ."

present study is the first occasion on which these MSS of Newman's have been presented to the public, and hence they provide new light on his idea of the Oratory.

There are four Addresses in all, three of them dated by the feast on which they were delivered (these datings bear no relation to the contents of the papers). As the English Oratory was formally erected in the course of the weeks in which these Addresses were given, they throw a valuable light on Newman as captain of the enterprise taking his bearings as he sets out from port on his spiritual voyage though, of course, it would be too soon to expect to find any log of the difficulties of the journey.

The first Address: 'In fest. S.Antonii/48.'

This first address considers St Philip's Oratory in its historical connection with other forms of community life, both in the primitive Church and in the sixteenth century. St Philip went a step further than the contemporary congregations, by not having vows; his characteristic apostolate was that of Sacraments, Preaching and Prayer, and of these he singled out preaching and hearing sermons especially, perhaps as being less common in his time.

One of the most remarkable points in St Philip's life is the deliberation with which he was carried on to the fulfilment of the work which was committed to him. We must not indeed call the Congregation of the Oratory especially his work, for he was Apostle of Rome independent of it. He heard confessions, he preached, he conversed, he formed institutions in the town, he trained saints, while his Congregation was but slowly coming into existence. He never put before him that Congregation as the end of his labours. Still, in fact, it is what his life has resulted in, and it is curious to contrast the slow growth of the formation of an Institution, which was to do so much, with the rapidity with which some other saints have been urged, and proposed through their labours. Newman then sketches the life of St Philip, laying great stress on the saint's reluctance to foster new foundations from his Oratory. He concludes:

. . . may the Santo Padre himself, who with such caution, deliberation, prudence, judgment and success guided the course of his nascent Congregation, be with us now in England, and bind us together in that his own spirit of love and gentleness, which is better than all vows, and adorn us with his own beauty of holiness and amiableness of word and deed, which is an influence stronger, wider, surer, than the most cunningly organised association[14].

The second Address: 'SS. Fabian et Sebastian'

This address is devoted almost completely to a historical sketch of the early propagation of the Oratory in Italy, particularly in the States of the Church and in the Kingdom of Naples. Newman is at pains to show how very various were the circumstances under which the Oratory began in different localities, and found consolation in this chequered history for himself and his friends, who even though they had the best promise of success, yet nevertheless were beset with the perplexities inseparable from any new undertaking.

The third Address

(not dated, but follows immediately on the second Address in the MS).

This Address is extremely important, since it permits us to see how distinct Newman's idea of the Oratory was even in the details of its ethos, already when the English Oratory was only in its infancy. Having given in the two preceding Addresses an account of the rise and propagation of the Oratory, he now proceeds to describe its ecclesiastical object and position. He enlarges on the idea of gentlemanliness as inherent in St Philip's ideal, on the Oratory as the only *nido* or home of each member of the community, on mutual love as the community bond, on the uncontroversial temper of Oratorian studies and writing, and on the Oratory as being a bond of union between seculars and regulars.

The fourth Address: 'Stae Apolloniae'

The fourth Address, Stae Apolloniae, continues in the same strain as the third: it is a study of the inward characteristics of

---

[14]*Or.P.*, No. 3., conclusion of Address, p. 171.

the Oratory. This MS is full of re-drafting and cross-references, betraying Newman's concentrated effort of fixing in words the spirituality of the Oratory—a more difficult task than that of tracing its outward history. Two important themes are treated here: the contrast between Jesuit and Oratorian spirituality, and his view of Oratorian 'unvowed' obedience as a return to the primitive spirit of Christianity. We should see the sharp contrast by Newman between Jesuits and Oratorians, not as any personal animosity against the Society, but as his effort to describe an *idea* (the English Oratory was not yet six months old) in contrast to an existing body of facts, though perhaps he does less than justice to the Jesuit practice of obedience in the process. The momentous significance of this discourse lies above all in its date—Newman had a completely clear view of the specific ethos of the Oratory in its absence of vows, its mainspring being personal influence as distinguished from the type of obedience current among regulars—and all this in February 1848.

The Chapter Addresses of Summer 1848

These three Addresses date from the first summer, when the newly-formed community was still at Maryvale[15]. The first Address is a warning against superciliousness on the part of the Oratorians towards their less-educated fellow-Catholics. The second, given on the feast of St Paul, is an exhortation to fraternal charity; the third an appeal to make their faith in their vocation explicit. This last Address is of particular importance, stressing as it does the need for faith in one another in community life. It would be a mistake to try to begin with charity; for although charity is the building, faith is the foundation. So many good religious projects wither away because of this lack of faith.

The Addresses to the Birmingham Oratory

All the remaining Addresses and Memoranda concern the Birmingham House alone, after the foundation of the London

---

[15]See *L.D.*, XII, p. xiv: "31 Oct. (1848) Maryvale is given up and Newman moves to St Wilfrid's, Cotton, until the opening of the Oratory in Birmingham after the new year."

Oratory. As we have been discerning all along a gradual descent on Newman's part from the general to the particular in the logical sequence of his teaching on the Oratory, so from now on this characteristic becomes accentuated, and we may safely say that all the remaining Addresses are motivated by some definite circumstances connected with the Birmingham Oratory. They fall into four groups: (i) Addresses during the Achilli trial in the winter 1852–53, (ii) Memoranda dealing with the dismissal of Brother Bernard, (iii) The two Addresses on the House and the Refectory, (iv) Addresses, Memoranda and the *Remarks on the Oratorian Vocation* arising out of the troubles occasioned by Fr Dalgairns' criticism of the lack of 'spirituality' in the Birmingham community. Although circumscribed by the narrow confines of one small community, these Addresses are a valuable indication of Newman's view of Oratorian life in practice.

(*a*) *Addresses during the Achilli trial, winter 1852–53:* These four Addresses, all in close consecutive order, show Newman troubled at the enigma of the Achilli affair—troubled from the supernatural point of view. He had deliberately, and only after prayer, embarked in God's cause on his attack of Achilli, and now God seemed to be abandoning him, and to let him be the victim of evil men. His real discouragement and trouble was that he felt no religious good was accruing to him from the external trial.

(*b*) *Memoranda dealing with the dismissal of Brother Bernard, winter 1852–53:* At the same time as the Chapter Addresses of winter 1852–53, there took place, in Newman's temporary absence, the dismissal of a certain Brother Bernard from the community. The incident has been described in full by Miss Trevor[16]; all we need to do here is to draw attention to Newman's indignation at the injustice done to the Brother. We should also note his compassion and lack of pharisaical self-righteousness in judging the moral fault of the Brother in question.

---

[16] *Trevor*, I, pp. 620–624.

(*c*) *Fragment on the Life of St Philip, 1853:* During this period of great mental stress, when he was awaiting the outcome of the Achilli trial, Newman prepared with his own hands extracts from Bacci's Life of St Philip for refectory reading, pasting the passages in a volume for the purpose. He has inscribed this book with a touching dedication, written in his own hand dated Epiphany 1853. It is significant that some months later, dissatisfied with the piecemeal treatment of saints' lives then current, and of which Bacci (an earlier writer) is a flagrant example, Newman should have set about writing of St Philip as a living and a breathing man. The Introduction on method is full and satisfying, quite as excellent as the well-known Introduction to the Essay on St Chrysostom[17]; but through force of circumstances the *Life* itself is only the barest sketch and peters out after a few chapters. It is revealing though, that he should have attempted such a work at such a time.

(*d*) *Addresses on the House and the Refectory:* After the community had taken possession, on Low Sunday, 1852, of the new house at Hagley Road (still the home of the Birmingham Oratory today), Newman addressed them in a discourse to which he gave great thought, since there are three different drafts of it, all in his own hand. The house and the community are correlative: the community must grow into the house as into its outward covering or shell. *Nulla dies sine linea*, 'No day without its touch' as St Philip was wont to say: every day must see a gradual progress in bringing into shape the Congregation and the house which it inhabits.

The Address on the Refectory[18] carries still further this idea of community and house fitting into one another. The nature of Oratorian work throughout the day is necessarily personal or isolated, or nearly so; the community meal taken in common[19] is one of the few occasions of solemn meeting day by

[17]*Historical Sketches* II (1873), pp. 217-31.

[18]See *Trevor* II, p. 155.

[19]In Newman's day there used to be two formal community meals daily in the Birmingham Oratory; at present there is only one, viz. the evening dinner. The characteristic feature of this meal is the propounding of theological cases (referred to technically as "doubts") on which each member of the community gives his opinion in turn.

day. A keen sense of gratitude to God for giving them such a noble home, and providing for all their wants, in spite of the great change that had taken place in their material prospects after conversion—this was the deepest feeling aroused in Newman's heart at the completion of the community Refectory.

(*e*) *The 'Remarks on the Oratorian Vocation'*: The difference with the London House, and the disturbing presence of Father Dalgairns within the Birmingham community constituted the greatest single challenge to the spiritual standards of Newman's Oratory, in fact to his own Oratorian spirituality. These two related incidents have been dealt with exhaustively by Miss Trevor[20]; one need not re-open the whole process here; it will be enough to see what was Newman's answer to the challenge. He points out that Dalgairns' restless spirit had nothing in common with St Philip. Further, Dalgairns' very opposition has revealed their own latent spirit to the Birmingham community:

> . . . Others have looked on us, perhaps, he himself has looked on us, as a number of priests, brought together by human motives, who had no view of the Oratorian vocation. Certainly, it has *not* been our way, it has been part of our idea of that vocation not to make it our way, to bring out importunately and officiously any scientific definition of what an Oratorian should be . . .[21]

Arising out of the whole dispute Newman had, however, given a 'scientific' definition of the Oratorian vocation in seven letters written from Dublin to Birmingham in March 1856. Dalgairns withdrew from the Birmingham community when agreement was to be voted on these papers[22], which were duly voted and subsequently printed in the booklet *Sanctus Philippus Birminghamiensis* as 'Remarks on the Oratorian Vocation'.

In these Remarks Newman draws out as a closely reasoned thesis the view of the Oratory which he had already analysed in the Santa Croce Papers and which he had expressed in the

[20] *Trevor* II, pp. 73–165: "Conflict within the Oratory (1855–1857)." See pp. 100–2 above on Newman's estrangement with Faber and the London Oratory.
[21] *Or.P.*, No. 27.
[22] *Trevor* II, pp. 142–149: "1856, Dalgairns leaves Newman."

Early Chapter Addresses of 1848. In substance he does not go beyond the positions acquired there; he makes no reference whatever to the embittering circumstances which occasioned the letters.

There are seven letters in all, ranging in date from 5 to 9 March, 1856. Whether Newman had with him in Dublin the MS of the 'Santa Croce Papers' or the *Early Chapter Addresses of 1848* is not quite clear; however, the rough draft of these letters in the Birmingham Oratory Archives (*Or. P.* No. 24) is much fuller than the final draft, and shows us once more Newman working over even a familiar subject thoroughly. Each letter clinches the matter on one precise point, from where the argument resumes in the next letter. The sequence of the complete argument is as follows: (Letter I) The Oratory is not a religious body, and yet is like one; its members aim at perfection, yet at a perfection different in its circumstances and peculiarities from that of regulars. (Letter II) Certain qualifications attaching historically to Fathers of the Oratory, by which they are distinguished from ordinary secular priests, viz. the breeding of a gentleman, the mental elevation and culture which learning gives, the accomplishments of literature, the fine arts and similar studies. (Letter III) The literary qualifications and liberal knowledge traditional in the Italian Oratory. (Letter IV) Various characteristics of a Father of the Oratory, both in how he differs from the ordinary run of secular priests, and how he differs from the type of a regular. Various counsels (of perfection) he does *not* pursue. (Letter V) The precise instrument of Oratorian perfection, is that he is 'a secular priest'; but not only so, but a secular priest 'living in Community'. (Letter VI) The duty of obedience to the Rule. (Letter VII) Obedience to the Superiors.

The kernel of the whole matter is Letter V on community living as the precise instrument of Oratorian perfection, on which we have commented more at length in chapter 7 above.

(*f*) *The Three Addresses of Summer 1856* (*2 August, 16 August, 27 September*): These Addresses, delivered after the departure of Dalgairns from the Birmingham community, seem to betray still in Newman the practical desire to answer the question:

how can an Oratorian of this Birmingham community reach
perfection? He no longer appeals to history (as in the *Remarks*)
nor to contemporary disputes (as in the Address on the departure of Dalgairns); his aim is positive and practical, not polemical. He fixes on the idea of doing the duties of the day
perfectly, particularly in the Address of 27 September.

(g) *Two Addresses to Novices, 20 February and 8 March 1858:*
These two chapters are of some importance, as being practically
the last extant Addresses to the community of any length for
the next twenty years—the reason for this silence being explained in the letter of 27 June 1854 to Henry Bittleston (*Or.
P.* No. 23), and also by the small numbers in the community
at this period. Although two years later than the Dalgairns
affair, these two chapters seem to contain explicit echoes of it,
at least in Newman's reflections on it. He insists on the existence
of smaller unities within the one vast unity of the Catholic
Church: the members of each of these unities must assimilate
themselves into their spirit. Oratories differ from one another
in spirit, and so

> . . . it is plain that the object or standard of assimilation is not
> simply the Rule, or any abstract idea of an Oratory, but the
> definite local present body . . . the only security and principle
> of permanence in an Oratory, is the submission of all of us one to
> another . . . the unarmed, weaponless state of an Oratorian body,
> involves the necessity of our being one in spirit . . .[23]

(h) *The Address of 1878:* The last step in logical sequence is
the preservation of continuity within the community in spite
of the changes occasioned by time. In 1878, when he himself
was seventy-seven years of age, Newman made a brief Address
to the community on 'change and succession' as the normal
state of community continuity. For thirty years the Birmingham
community had had few deaths—much fewer than the London
House; this note of identity with itself could never again be
recaptured in its history; the passage of time inevitable intro-
duces change as a second essential element in the normal state
of things:

[23]*Or.P.*, No. 31.

. . . That is no real succession which is not a continuation of what was before it; that is no identity, of which the elements are heterogenous and discordant. It is for this reason that I have never wished, I have never liked, a large Oratory. Twelve working priests has been the limit of my ambition. One cannot love many at one time; one cannot really have many friends . . . A large body can hardly help breaking from its own weight. The continuity of succession is snapped, not strengthened by its numerousness . . .[24]

And so within a lengthy span of thirty years (1848–78) in the apparently inconsequential succession of events of real life, Newman pursues his Oratory ideal, holding fast to the idea of the Oratory such as he had mastered it at Santa Croce, and living it out in all the successive circumstances, with a logical sequence which is truly remarkable from its clear-sighted fidelity and flexible adaptability.

[24]*Or.P.*, No. 35.

Newman's Oratory Papers

NEWMAN'S ORATORY PAPERS No. 1
15 JUNE 1846

INTRODUCTORY NOTE

This is the earliest extant plan of Newman's for his future work within the Catholic Church: a 'Congregation of the Most Holy Trinity', which in point of fact never came into being. The general background to Newman's quest for his vocation has been examined at length above pp. 70–87 and this pre-Oratorian project is dealt with on p. 76.

This Congregation would have been a fresh start, not linking up with an existing Catholic tradition like that of the Oratory. Although only embryonic, and not as yet explicitly Oratorian, it is on the whole in the general line of Oratorian life—with one important difference, that of living in a country seclusion instead of in a town.

We can detect here a mixture of Newman's heritage of Anglican devotion to the Blessed Trinity and to Our Lady as the 'Seat of Wisdom', combined with overtones of the current Catholic devotion to the Holy Family.

June 15/46

Congregatio de SS Trinitate[1].

The one object to practise and promote the loving adoration of the mysteries of Religion—especially that of the most Sacred Trinity.

[1] *B. Or. Ar.*, A.11.6.

Considering the rationalistic tone of the times, which is all based or exhibited in denial of mysteries, it seems of special importance to teach the contrary.

Hence the work of the Congregation will consist in reading, writing, teaching, catechising, preaching, controverting, all with a view to enforcing the mysteries of faith, and subjecting reason to faith.

The secondary object will be that of cherishing and enforcing a profound sense of our nothingness—1. as mortal men—2. as rational beings (e.g. the vanity of all things, the feebleness of reason etc.)

Its subjects all classes—its instruments all means of persuasion, whether intellectual or ethical—all kinds of learning, exegetic, philosophical, doctrinal etc.

Its place a country seclusion—with a library—where its members will write, and from which they will be sent out to give courses of sermons, (or if necessary ⟨?⟩ to dispute).

It will not have to do with retreats or direct religious works except for special reasons.

Its ejaculatory prayers 'O beata Trinitas' &c. &c. 'Pater &c charitas Spiritus Sanctus &c' from the Breviary—'Tu lux perennis Unitas &c'—and all that is sublime, majestic and mysterious.

The three great mysteries are the Holy Trinity, the Incarnation; the Eucharist; they will be lovingly adored *as* mysteries. All the prescribed worship of the B.S. will be directed to it as a mystery. St Mary will be honoured as the destroyer of heresies, Tu sola interemisti &c. The devotion of the infant Jesus, Mary and Joseph is an image of the Eternal Trinity.

As to music, no choir service ordinarily—but on festivals vespers, besides high mass.

Very few lay brothers—the superior elected first for 3 years, then perpetual—Every brother bound in conscience to choose another at the end of the 3 years, if it seems desirable.

As to penal work, one must be found in mixing with artisans, mechanics, &c and arguing with them—e.g. the Socialists.—another perhaps must be some humiliations at home—corporal discipline?

NEWMAN'S ORATORY PAPERS No. 2
14 FEBRUARY 1847

INTRODUCTORY NOTE

No English draft of this Latin letter of Newman's exists. The English translation given here was made by the editor for the convenience of readers. The aim was to produce a straightforward version; no conscious effort being made to reproduce Newman's style. Here and there some phrases of the Latin original have been reproduced in [   ], to enable the reader to check on some difficult passages. The Latin original appears in *L.D.* XII, pp. 36–40.

The central point which calls for comment is dealt with by Newman himself in Appendix F to the Memorandum of 9 June 1848 (see Appendix 4, p. 442). Whereas Newman had envisaged a pastoral mission aimed first of all at the working class youth of Birmingham, the Brief singled out pastoral work for the upper classes as a distinctive role of the future English Oratory. On all this, see above pp. 99-100.

Newman's attitude to the Anglican Church and to what he calls the 'sects' may seem somewhat harsh; this may be due to the necessity of making his point clear to Roman authorities who were unfamiliar with the details of the English situation.

His closing remarks about the Holy See are in the strain of similar remarks at the time of the Irish University; later, in the *A.W.* he distinguished between the Holy See's doctrinal place and its practical policies in the Church of the day.

For an analysis of this Paper, see above pp. 95-135.

[14 February 1847]

To His Eminence Cardinal Fransoni from some recent English converts.[1]

Since Your Eminence has furnished and continues to furnish so many proofs of your kindness towards us, we hope it will not

---

[1]Translated from the Latin text printed in *L.D.*, XII, pp. 36-40.

12

be out of place to lay before Your Eminence some reflections concerning ourselves, and the state of this England of ours, and of the way in which we conceive we may best promote the Catholic religion there.

In this regard, it should be noted first of all that our object in coming to Rome was, among other reasons, to discover under the tutelage of the sacred city and the protection of the holy places, God's will for us and our vocation. Further, it should be kept in mind that we have at home some associates and friends, who are also seeking their vocation; they are ten or twelve in number, but this number will increase, when they are able to see more clearly what becomes of us. Finally, we should add that able men whose opinion we value highly, have advised us that nothing would suit the Catholic cause in England better than if we were to take on some way of life resembling the Philippine Rule.

When therefore we had at length come to Propaganda College as into port, our constant aim was to look around sharply on all sides to see what would be best for ourselves and our dear country. We observed the Jesuit Fathers following out a lofty and excellent course, but there were many reasons, which we omit here, why we should praise that course, not follow it. But our character on the contrary and the habits of our former life, and our way of thinking and ripest reflection seem quite clearly to turn us away from a fully secular life, nor could we at first sight see any middle course suitable for ourselves, between adopting the Jesuit religious life or none at all. In this difficulty, the Rule of the Oratory, almost secular, but nonetheless a Rule, seemed to us—as it had already appeared to [some] Englishmen of sound judgment—to suit our needs exactly; moreover, it would be of such a nature (we hoped) that if it became ours, it would not forfeit us the patronage of Your Eminence nor that of the Sacred Congregation[2].

So much for ourselves; let us now consider this England of ours. Your Eminence is not unaware, that the densely populated cities there, devoted to manufacture, and where all the present or future dynamism of our Empire resides, are the

[2]Fransoni (1775-1856) was Cardinal Prefect of Propaganda. See further, *L.D.*, XII, p. 431.

dwelling place of infidelity and the hope of Catholics. This will be readily understood if we take account of the fact that the Anglican Church—the enemy of Catholics, the extirpator and devourer of sects—has only a feeble hold over those cities. That Church hates, suppresses, absorbs the dissent to which she gives birth; enjoying great wealth, possessed of no small measure of truth, to some she ministers a certain solace of religion, to others the bread of this world; some she excites by her illusions of high office [*alios suis dignitatum praestigiis percellit*], others she flatters by intimacy with men of rank. Words can scarcely express the influence exerted by the Anglican Church—of the royal household, established by law, moderator of extremists, heir of antiquity, a witness to and almost a pattern of Catholicity —in that steady, sober, stable Anglo-Saxon race. Not that they love her, but they love decency and order, and what is serious and decorous; the Establishment of religion promotes these things. This respectability in religious matters is missing, because the Anglican Church is missing, in that vast multitude of men, occupied in various trades, which here and there in the course of the last century, in the solitude almost of the country-side or of the seashore, or in an out-of-the-way corner of some parish, from a cluster of cottages [*ex magalium quasi concursu*] developed into a flourishing city and an important centre. Many sects, some of them professing Christianity, others at enmity with her—Methodists, Independents, Socinians, Chartists, Communists—thrive and pullulate there; all of them rivals of Anglicanism, some of them a match for her in their own locality [*nonullae in suis locis pares*], each of them feeble in itself, and extremely hostile towards the rest. See then this stormy land where many souls, alas, are seeking rest but as yet have not found it. See this centre, which the Catholic Church and none other, obviously not without the angry opposition of those sects, can safely, confidently and within her own right claim as her own.

To return now to ourselves and our concerns. We are living in Old Oscott College, formerly [the] school and seminary for the Central District, four miles out of the City of Birmingham, a most thickly populated place, remarkable for its recent flock of converts, but full of every sort of heresy, with its youth skilled in the trades but holding a false religion or none at all. This city was for many years the centre of those organizations which were actively hostile to the laws of nature and of society; and also of those Associations, the Mechanics' Institutes, devoted to the perverse cultivation of literature (good in itself), and of an unhealthy science [*bonis literis prave cultis et physicae malesanae deditarum*], which that English lawyer, Lord Brougham, for these twenty years has spread all over England, in order to teach the people Science, and make them unlearn their religion. Wishing to do what we can against these evils (if our companions at home are agreed, and if the Fathers of the Oratory permit it), we should like to take on the Rule of St Philip (abrogated or adapted in details, perhaps, to conditions in England) and exercise it particularly in the following way.

Let us have in the City some house or large hall which would be the Oratory. There the Exercises according to the Rule of St Philip would be carried out, not straight away every day, but first of all on Sundays and on some Feastdays, or more suitable weekdays. The audience will be male only, as is fitting; women are excluded[3]. We would start off with singing; then a lecture would follow, and discussion, treating always of theological and sacred subjects; but in a more intellectual or learned or more argumentative way than was the Holy Father's[4] practice in his own house; dealing at times with the same matter, scientific or literary, as those lectures in the Mechanics' Institutes. Or, what would please St Philip better, let something be read from Church History or the Lives of the Saints, or from some other book of the sort; on condition however that after the reading a discussion should follow, in which the sophistries of the Protestants should be propounded by some and refuted by others [of those present]. After the discussion would follow a sermon, leaving the field of argument and giving free scope to the affections; then singing, perhaps litanies, with which the Exercise will close. As time goes on, a kind of confraternity would be formed out of suitable members of the audience,

³This point was noted by Newman in *Or.P.*, Appendix 1, paper "n" "how far women were admitted." (The original Exercises of the Oratory were held in St Philip's private room, where no women were admitted.)

⁴i.e. St Philip Neri (1515–1595), founder of the Roman Oratory.

bound together by the ties of an upright life, the use of the Sacraments, and by customs both of piety and of recreation, which are suitable for such confraternities. Whether we should hold, not only an Oratory, but a Church, will be for others to judge. Moreover, if we get on well in the city of Birmingham, we should proceed to other towns, of which there are six or seven densely populated ones around our College. Or we might go up to London itself, most dear to ourselves as our birthplace, and the centre moreover of everything that is said or done in our Empire [the Latin reads: *emporio*, most probably a mistake for *imperio*].

The advantage of this suggestion is that since the tastes and talents of our companions are very various, here is opened the widest possible field of scope for each. For those of a logical turn of mind, there is discussion; for the eloquent, preaching; for those skilled in music, singing; for anyone interested in youth work, the confraternity; for those to whom the care of souls appeals, the hearing of confessions. From this it will probably follow that others also, who, one may hope, will from time to time join the Catholic Church from both English Universities[5], will find their place and their vocation in this Institute.

In addition, the more learned who devote themselves to study or to publishing books can also easily live in a Society of this kind. Since the Exercises of the Oratory belong only to the greater solemnities, and do not occupy simultaneously all those who are under the Philippine Rule, it is clear that a good deal of time remains which may be spent in reading and writing[6]. The brothers of the Congregation, relying on the divine assistance, may confidently hope to contribute something in the literary and theological line among Catholics.

Having said so much, we should like to mention only one thing further to Your Eminence; it is something which is in part disagreeable to mention, and in part unpleasant to listen to—in that unhappy disease under which the inner life of Catholicism is labouring in England[7], in the factions, alas,

[5] i.e. Oxford and Cambridge.
[6] See below, *Or.P.*, No. 26 (The Use of Time); also p. 100.
[7] See *Or.P.*, No. 7, and *L.D.*, XII, p. 159.

[which exist between] so many excellent men, in such contending party spirits [*in tot adversis studiis*], in the inveterate and envious apathy of some, in the great fear and suspicion with which the name of converts is held by many, how would it be possible for us insignificant men to undertake or carry through such great work, unless we were sustained by the protection of that sacred Citadel, where the weak and weaponless, fighting for the name of Christ and for the Church, have ever brought back their shield and buckler. The combat must be waged both hand to hand and far off, among the sects of heretics, amidst the quarrels of brothers; we are looking for help in a suitable time from the "Successor of the Fisherman and the Disciple of the Cross", whom we look up to most of all, whom alone we revere and love; nor can we believe that the See of Peter will look with contempt on those who wish to be its servants [and who have] the same ardour of soul, the same fidelity— even if not with the same hopes for the future or the same fame for virtue—through which the great men of old, members of our Anglo-Saxon race, St Wilfrid and St Boniface, regained England for, and added Germany to, the Apostolic See.

NEWMAN'S ORATORY PAPERS No. 3
17 JANUARY 1848

INTRODUCTORY NOTE

Summary

1. Community life in the sixteenth century.
2. Variations of this:—Theatines, Barnabites, Jesuits: all these had modified the traditional forms of community life, but still maintained vows. With St Philip vows are superseded.
3. History of St Philip, between his 36th and his 68th year:—
   Aged 36: daily conference at S Gerolamo,
   Aged 43: daily conference in the adjoining Church: the rudiments of Oratory life,

Aged 49: *Convitto* (Community life) at S Giovanni,
Aged 59: Oratory at S Giovanni,
Aged 68: Philip goes to the Vallicella.
4. Difference between 'Oratory' and 'Congregation'.
5. Propagation of the Oratory in St Philip's lifetime:—
   Philip's reluctance to extend the Oratory outside Rome—
   refuses Genoa, Fermo and Florence—yields reluctantly
   to S Carlo. Motives for the Naples foundation.
6. Similarity to conditions in England in Newman's effort
   to found the Oratory.

On this Address, see above pp. 139–40. The outline of St.
Philip's life culled by Newman mainly from Marciano *Memorie
Historiche della Congregazione dell'Oratorio* (1693–1702) may be
completed by reference to the appropriate chapters in the recent
biography of St Philip by Meriol Trevor: *Apostle of Rome*
(Macmillan, 1966).

[History of the Rise of the Oratory]

In fest. S. Antonii/48 [1]

The sixteenth century gave birth to several important
variations of the Cœnobitic or Community Life, which had
existed in the Church since the days of St Antony and St
Pachomius. The peculiarity of that life had been its ascetic
character, and the cœnobitic form had been taken from the
feeling that its severities could be better borne, when supported
by the sympathy of others, than in loneliness. There was indeed
a still more essential characteristic of the community life,
though more recondite, which from the nature of the case it
could never lose, the rule of obedience, for where many live
together there must be Superior and subjects; still fast, vigil,
silence, bodily chastisement devotional exercises, ceremonial
forms all that makes up the notion of asceticism, these, in the
eyes of an external spectator, are the life of a regular, and these
it was which were so seriously modified, so extensively re-
trenched in the coenobitic institutions which rose in the era in
question.

[1] *B. Or. Ar.*, B. 9.3.

The first great variation in the sixteenth century is the institution of Regular Clerks, which was commenced by the Theatines in Rome in the year 1524 ⟨Ranke t.l. p. 176⟩; who were followed by the Barnabites in Milan in 1533. ⟨Memor. de' Barnab. t.l p. 32 90.3⟩ the Jesuits in Rome in 1540; the Somaschini in Lombardy in 1568; the Camillites in 1591; the Fathers of the Scuole Pie in 1621. ⟨Mem de' Barnab. t i p 32⟩

All these institutions were under vows, and so far were in the condition of the Regulars before them, and they differed from the monastic orders in the greater freedom and pliability of their Rule. "They were priests with monks' vows," says Ranke. "Their aim was to establish a kind of seminary for priests; the charter of their foundation expressly permitting them to admit the secular clergy. They did not originally prescribe to themselves any precise form and colour of vestments, but left them to be determined by the usages of the clergy of each country. They likewise permitted the services of the Church to be performed everywhere according to the customs of the country. They thus emancipated themselves from many things which fettered the monks, expressly declaring that, neither in habits of life, nor in the performance of divine service, ought any usage what ever to be binding on the conscience. On the other hand, they devoted themselves to the clerical duties of preaching, the administration of the Sacraments, and the care of the sick." ⟨vol 1 p. 177⟩

"Then was seen again," continues the same author, "what had long fallen into disuse in Italy: priests appearing with the cap, the cross and the clerical gown in the pulpit, shortly after in the oratory, and frequently in the form of missions, in the streets. Caraffa and his associates, most of them men of noble birth, who might have revelled in the enjoyments of life, began to seek out the sick in their habitations and in hospitals; and to administer the last consolations to the dying." He adds, "The order of Theatines became in time the order of priests peculiar to the nobility, and, as it had been carefully remarked from the beginning that the new members were of noble extraction, at a later period proofs of nobility were in some places requisite to admission."

As to the Barnabites, he presently observes that "A Milanese Chronicle relates with what wonder these new priests were regarded in their homely dress and round cap, all with downcast eyes, all in the bloom of youth. They lived together in a house near St Ambrose" ⟨p 180⟩

The Jesuits, it need scarcely be said, carried the idea on which the Theatines and Barnabites were instituted into a wider development. They not only rejected the monastic habit, but they had no obligation to sing in choir, and instead of selecting one object for their exertions, as the Barnabites or Camillites, they equally addressed themselves to preaching, confession, direction, and education.

The second form of community life which owes its rise to the sixteenth century, is that which St Philip began or rather originated. It is very much the same as that of Regular Clerks which has been above described, with one important distinction, that vows are superseded. This then was a further departure from the religious discipline of St Benedict and St Francis.

St Philip was followed by the Oblates of St Charles, the Lazarists *or* Vincentians,[2] the Sulpicians, and others.

Widely as the Oratorians differ from the primitive Monks in their occupations, objects, and members, yet there are points in which they may considered a return to the rule of St Pachomius or St Basil. For they have no vows, they are under implicit obedience to their superior and others; and their houses are each complete in itself and independent.

St Philip's was not the first Oratory which had existed in Rome. In this, as in some other things, he was preceded by the Theatines, or at least by a collection of pious men, among whom the Theatines were conspicuous, Even as early as the date of Leo x, that is, in the first twenty years of the century there existed at Rome an institution which was called the Company of Divine Love, ⟨Mem. de' Barnab. t i. p 7.⟩ consisting of as many as fifty or sixty members, ⟨Ranke vol 1 p. 136⟩ for the most part of noble family or in ecclesiastical station ⟨Barnab. p 8⟩ who met in an Oratory in the Church of St Silvester and St Dorothy in the Trastevere. In their number

---

[2]Marginal note by Newman: they have vows?

was St Caietan, Caraffa, afterwards Pope Paul iv, Contarini, Lippoman, and Sadoleto.

What was the end of this Society does not appear, but probably it died a natural death by the distinct formation of the Theatines, and by the dispersion of its members into different parts of the Church. Ranke observes that there was a reunion of a portion of its members at Venice a few years later.

And here I will go out of the way to observe, that in other ways the Congregation of St Philip, and not only it, but other religious bodies also of that era were indebted to the Theatines. (Perhaps) there will be an opportunity hereafter of alluding to the share they had in the introduction of the Oratory into Naples. In like manner they assisted the Capucins in obtaining their foundation in the time of Clement vii: ⟨Barnab. p 10⟩ They lodged the Barnabites at Naples and assisted them in gaining a house there; and one of them was the director of the founder of the Clerk Regular Minors[3].

Now we proceed to the history of St Philip.

In the year 1551, when he was thirty six years of age, we find him in S. Gerolamo, with seven or eight penitents, who held a daily conference with him in his room, on moral and practical subjects, he sitting in his easy chair, and the conversation passing from one to another.

This room is still seen at Rome, having been converted into a chapel. It is perhaps ten feet by eight, and eight feet high— and considering the distress which heat occasioned to St Philip, and how insupportable a close cassock[4] was to him even in winter, it is inconceivable how he should have managed to live for thirty years in what is rather a prison than a cell.

In 1558, seven years after, when St Philip was forty three, he found the number of his hearers so increased, that he transferred them to a room, which also is still shown, above the vaulting of the aisle of the adjoining Church. It was at that time an empty place, and it was converted into the first Oratory. Here he permitted some of his disciples to discourse, (ragionare)

---

[3]Note by Newman in right-hand margin: On the other hand, it may be observed, that St Philip was the director of St Camillus, the founder of the Ministri degli Infermi, and of another founder of a family of Clerks Regular.

[4]Original draft: habit.

—for instance Tarugi, who was as yet a secular; Modio, a medical man:—then Fucci, and Baronio.

This exercise lasted three hours, and consisted mainly of reading, preaching, and discoursing; but soon afterwards, as it appears, St Philip opened the Oratory for evening prayer; at twenty–three o'clock (i.e. an hour before sunset) in the summer, at twenty-four (i.e. at sunset) in the winter.⟨Ann. t i. pp 20, 21⟩

And now St Philip's day contained in its rudiments the daily life of the Congregation after him—Mass and the Confessional, i.e. *Sacraments*, in the morning—*Preaching* in midday, (dopo pranzo), and *Prayer* in the evening. These three, Prayer, Preaching and Sacraments he said, he preferred to fastings, watchings, silence and psalmody. And of these three, he singled out preaching and hearing sermons especially, perhaps as being less common in his time: "Voluit consulere viris Congregationis suae," says Manni "ut per quotidianum auditum verborum Dei, haberent quod jejuniis, vigiliis, silentiis, psalmodiis contraponerent." ⟨Annal. t i. p. 27⟩

Six additional years passed away, and in the year 1564, when St Philip was forty nine, the Convitto, or Community Life, commenced; for hitherto, it must be observed, his disciples lived at their own homes, and merely came to him for devotional exercises. It commenced, however, on a very small scale; the rectory at St John of the Florentines, with its Church and house, was conferred on him; he remained himself at St Gerolamo, and placed five priests in the house to serve the Church; Baronio, Bordini, Fedeli, Tarugi, and Velli[5]. Besides these, were two, not Oratorians, one of whom he made Curato (or Vicar) of the Parish. And there was a youth of sixteen, who was under St Philip's care; and another, who was a pupil of Baronius's. S. Gerolamo, however, the residence of St Philip, was still the place where the Exercises were held, and members of the Community at S. Giovanni, for the long space of ten years, went three times a day from S. Giovanni to S. Gerolamo, in all weather, for Sacrament[6], Preaching and Prayer. Besides the Confessions, High Mass, Solemn Vespers,

---

[5]Note in right hand margin by Newman: Most of these had come to Rome to study the law, but on this occasion three of them received the priesthood.

[6]Original draft: Sacraments.

and Preaching at S. Giovanni, they had the cleaning of the Church, and all the work of the house, as having no servants. It was during this period that Baronius, in ridicule of his own employment, wrote on the chimney in the kitchen, Cæsar Baronius, Coquus perpetuus. They had no Superior in the house, St Philip apparently ruling them from S. Girolamo, they had a common purse, and seem to have been united in a most intense affection for each other.

We now come to the year 1574, when St Philip was fifty-nine. And here let me observe on what is one of the most remarkable points in St Philip's life, viz. the deliberation with which he was carried on to the fulfilment of the work which was committed to him. We must not indeed call the Congregation of the Oratory especially his work, for he was Apostle of Rome independent of it. He heard confessions, he preached, he conversed, he formed institutions in the town, he trained saints, while his Congregation was but slowly coming into existence. He never put before him that Congregation as the end of his labours. Still in fact it is what his life has resulted in, and it is curious to contrast the slow growth of the formation of an Institution, which was to do so much, with the rapidity with which some other saints have been urged, and prospered through their labours. He was thirty six years of age before he was tonsured, though then he proceeded on without the intervals to the priesthood and began his ragionamenti[7] in his room. Seven years more passed before he transferred them into his first Oratory over the Church of S. Girolamo—and six years more before he was put in possession of S. Giovanni and began his convitto or community. Ten years more passed, and we come to the year 1574, the sixtieth of St Philip's life. Then it was the Florentines, desirous to obviate the inconvenience to which he was exposed, of having his Community in one place and his Oratory in another, built him an Oratory at S. Giovanni.

To S. Giovanni then the Exercises were transferred, but they did not continue there long; calumnies were just at this time circulated about St Philip, and an opposition against him got up. An attempt was made to persuade the Florentines to dismiss him from S. Giovanni.

[7] i.e. discourses.

This was the fourth and last persecution, to which S. Philip was exposed, and it may be worthwhile briefly to enumerate them.

The *first* was directed against him, when he first had his exercises in his room at S. Girolamo.

The *second* took place in [S.] Girolamo, the year after he had opened the Oratorio there. He was brought before the Vicar General for going with his people to the Seven Churches.

The *third* lasted for three years, when he was accused to Pope Pius of unguarded doctrine in the Oratory.

And the fourth, at the date with which we are at present occupied, was the work of a member of the Community, whom St Philip dismissed, and who in consequence did what he could to bring his late associates into disrepute.

This was soon after the Oratory had been built at S. Giovanni by the Florentines, and St Philip, at this time sixty years of age, began to see that if his followers were to be in a state of security, they must not be dependent on others. Perhaps the revenues of S. Giovanni were not sufficient⟨?⟩; and at all events the Oratory was not theirs. They on the other hand, with natural feelings which he as naturally did not share, wished that, as St Philip was now in years, something should be done to perpetuate an institution which now for twenty four years had been profitable to so many souls. Accordingly Pope Gregory xiii gave him the Church of S. Maria in Vallicella, with the condition annexed, (of which perhaps the late internal disturbance showed the necessity,) that he should himself leave S. Girolamo and join his community.

The particular reason why this Church was chosen was, that it was "ubi frequentior habitantium multitudo, et accedentium occursus."

At the same time (1575) the Community was erected into a Congregation of Secular Priests.

They at once began rebuilding their Church, henceforth called the Chiesa Nuova, on which in St Philip's lifetime as much as 100.000 scudi (more than £20.000) were spent.

Two years after, in 1577, most of the Fathers took up their abode there—and on May 8 elected St Philip Provost. He still remained, however, at St Girolamo.

The new Institution began to prosper. Soon they ran up to as many as 130 in Congregation and Oratory, a distinction of terms which shall be explained hereafter.

Their homestead ⟨terreno⟩ spread—A priest, who lived next door to them, gave them his house, which was freehold—the stable became the new Oratory—Four years after, a small monastery of Clares, close to them, was given them; and the next year another house. A Chapel of St Cecilia had already fallen into them. At length on St Cecilia's Day 1583, thirty two years after he had come to St Girolamo, and twelve years before his death, when he was at the age of sixty eight, he removed to the Vallicella. Four years after [,] he was elected perpetual Superior, an office which he held for six years, and resigned two years before his death. He died in 1595 aged eighty.

Before going on to trace the course of his Institution after his death, I will briefly explain the difference between the Oratory and Congregation, which has already been implied. By the Oratory is meant the room, or the exercises, or the persons who assembled in it for them, first at S. Girolamo, then at S. Giovanni, then at Sta Maria in Vallicella. They might be of all classes and ages, to the exclusion of women. But when the Community or Convitto was formed at S. Giovanni, a smaller society was formed in addition to this and by a closer tie. Its members actually lived together, they were priests, or those who were training for the priesthood, and they served the Church. It was this Community which was erected into a Congregation, under the title of the Congregation of the Oratory.

The Oratory itself, however, remained as before, with its own rulers and members, taking the place of a sort of confraternity dependent on the Congregation, and governed by it, and for distinction sake being called the Oratorium parvum or the Oratorium externum. It still had possession of the building called the Oratorium, while the place of the Congregation rather was the Church, though of course it presided in the Oratorium also. But to proceed to the history of the *propagation* of the Congregation.

There were more than 150 Oratories founded after the pattern of the Roman in the course of the seventeenth century;

there are or have been Oratories throughout Italy, in Sicily, in Spain, in Portugal, in Poland; not to mention the French Oratory, which was not on St Philip's pattern and extended into Belgium and Germany; in Peru too, in Mexico, in Brazil, and in Goa and Ceylon;—yet the idea of propagation did not enter into the mind of St Philip. In his original idea, propagation was impossible, there was nothing to propagate, because he was introducing a set of Exercises, rather than a Community of men. When he went to the Cistercian Monk at the Tre Fontane, full of zeal to be sent out to preach the gospel in the East, he had been told to make Rome "his India", and he dedicated himself exclusively to Rome. His Exercises were a means of improving specially and only the Romans; they were suited, he conceived, to their case; and some of them, as the visits to the Seven Churches, could not exactly be practised elsewhere. He would consider that they could not take a formal shape, or be embodied in a permanent institution, any more than mere preaching or praying. They had nothing distinctive in them except what was local.

Moreover he had no wish to form an Order or Congregation, of which he considered there were enough in the Church already.

And he might think his own Community and its rules too recent, too little tried, to be made the subject of imitation in other places.

There was another very cogent reason, when the question of propagation came practically before him. It could not be carried into effect without his bestowing some of his own people to the place where a new Oratory was to be erected; and this he was unwilling to do. Rome was his India; he dedicated himself to Rome; to ask him to take interest in other places, was nothing short of asking him to intermit his exertions in behalf of Rome.

When then propositions came to him from other cities for the establishment of the Oratory in them, he answered that he could not spare his members for the purpose, and he bade either set up an Oratory for themselves, or apply to some other body, monastic and clerical.

Thus he turned a deaf ear to the pressing intreaties of his

friend the Bishop of Perugia; he always made answer che non poteva privarsi de' suoi soggetti per mandare altrovi.[8]

He refused the application of the Archbishop of Bologna, Paleotto, in 1580 and 1586.

He refused Genoa, though a rich man, who had lived at S.Giovanni, offered to be at the cost. He sent him and his money to the Theatines instead.

He also refused Fermo in 1580, yet he offered to receive two of the Priests of the place, who wished to set the Oratory on foot, into the Roman House for some months, and even to send back with them a Roman Father to set the new institution going.

He refused Naples in 1575.

Even Florence he refused, when it was proposed to aggregate a Company of St Thomas Aquinas to the Roman House; however, as in the case of Fermo, he offered to receive into the Roman Oratory two members of the Company in question to teach them the Exercises and mode of government.

However, it happened that he had yielded to one of the first instances made to him, but it came from a Saint. In 1572, while he was yet at S.Girolamo, and his Community at S. Giovanni, S.Carlo applied to him for some of his disciples to set up an Oratorian House in Milan. He yielded reluctantly; his chief difficulties being the moment and the distance— 'sebbene', as he writes in 1578, 'secondo la prudenza, non essendo le nostre cose cosi formate e stabilite qui in Roma, non pareva che dovessimo fare un passo tanto lungo la prima volta.[9] The plague followed, and he took occasion upon, or rather before it, to withdraw the father he had sent there. He did not send him back to Milan when the plague was over, and even writing afterwards to the Bishop of Fermo, he states that he had refused S Carlo. Perhaps S. Carlo may be considered to have founded his Oblates in place of the Oratory.

It would seem as if in 1581 the Duke of Bavaria was desirous of introducing the Oratory into his territory, and that St Philip

[8]i.e. he could not deprive himself of his subjects to send them elsewhere.

[9]'Even though, according to prudence, since our affairs here in Rome are not so formed and stabilized, it did not seem as if we should take such a long stride the first time.' Cf. full text in Bacci (Eng. tr. Antrobus), ii., p. 385.

had got the Pope to excuse him; ⟨this seems involved in an idea entertained by St Carlo⟩ for S. Carlo had an idea that the Oratorians were disobeying the Pope in having sent and then withdrawn Fathers from Bavaria, whereas the parties really were not Oratorians but chaplains of S.Girolamo della carità.

Nothing can place St Philip's reluctance to extend his operations in a clearer light than the circumstances under which he at length yielded to the prayers of his friends and followers. This was in favour of Naples. He had rejected a proposal from that city in 1575, as we have seen—but he gradually gave way in the course of the years 1583–1586. The circumstances of this change were as follows: Baronius, being carried there on ecclesiastical business in 1583, was hospitably entertained by the Theatines; and they, supported by the Jesuits, were earnest in their applications to him to gain from St Philip a Neapolitan Oratory. Baronius pleaded, as St Philip to St Charles, 'essere allora bambina la Congregazione di Roma';[10] Not long after his return to Rome, two of his hosts followed him on some business, and they expressed to St Philip the wishes which they had already urged upon Baronius; but St Philip 'non si può indurre a privarsi di soggetti per imprendere la novella fondazione,'[11] However Tarugi was troubled with sciatica, the hot springs of Pozzuoli are celebrated in that complaint, and the Theatines persuaded St Philip to allow him to try them. Tarugi went to Naples and began to preach and discourse in the peculiar style of the Oratory. He had great success, and, his visit being ended, he returned to Rome. The sulphur baths had been of great service to him, *but* had not perfectly cured him. Thus there was just a reason for going a second time; and a second time did the Theatines urge upon St Philip the establishment of an Oratory at Naples. Again St Philip refused their request; however, he not only consented to Tarugi's paying a second visit to the baths, but he allowed him to take with him two novices (giovani) and two fratelli or lay brothers as a conditional foundation. This was in 1584; St Philip even made Tarugi conditional Rector of the House,

[10]'The Congregation of Rome being then only an infant'.

[11]'Cannot be persuaded to deprive himself of subjects in order to undertake the new foundation.'

13

(Rector being a lower title than Provost) 'Il Padre Francesco Maria,' says the Decree of the Roman House, 'si costituisca Rettore della casa di Napoli, se al Signor piacera, che s'istituisca.' ⟨Annal t 2. p. 8.⟩ Tarugi set to work, and was in the midst of preaching and confessing, when suddenly in the following May St Philip recalled him.

Tarugi's success was so great as almost to frighten St Philip; 'a me mette qualche sospetto il troppo favore, e si gran principio.'[12] The Neapolitans actually bought a house and presented it to St Philip before they knew whether he would receive it. Yet St Philip's difficulties were not overcome. It was a new and difficult enterprise; it was the introduction of a new principle; it was making the Oratory a sort of religion, and a religion must have vows. There is an interesting letter written to the zealous Theatine Father in the name of St Philip by the secretary of the Congregation under the date of Nov. 9, 1585. ⟨Annal t 2 p 13⟩ 'Our apprehension,' he says, 'is great in proportion to the greatness of this undertaking, which imposes on us engagements, to which our weakness is unequal, both on account of the fewness and inadequacy of our members, who, compared to the numerous, holy, and learned religious (which are in the Church) are but as dwarfs compared to giants' . . . 'We consent⟨?⟩' he continues, 'to deprive ourselves, for a time, of Father Francis Mary, in order⟨?⟩ that every one may see how detrimental his absence is to our work at Rome; and your reverence is aware what difficulties and troubles are involved in the multiplication of a family.[13] If in formal religions, bound with vows so many embarrassments so often occur, so that one restless brain is sufficient to disquiet a whole religion, what will not happen where vows are not, and men are only united of free will?' This Letter is remarkable, as showing the connexion between the two decrees, which alone among those contained in the Oratorian Rule, are said to be immutable; that the Congregation should not be bound by vows, and that it should be confined to one locality. It is plain indeed, that nothing can possibly be a principle of harmony in conduct, in word and work, between man and man, but either a vow or

[12]'I am rather suspicious of too much popularity, and such a great beginning'.
[13]The question marks are in the MS in Newman's hand.

personal attachment, which cannot exist through the length and breadth of an order extended. St Philip, in one of the Decrees to which I refer, dwells much on this principle of attachment, stating that a community never must be so large that the faces of all are not known to each.

But to return:– St Philip gave up Tarugi only for a time, sending with him, apparently, to return also, one priest, four clerks, and two laybrothers. They began working; numbers crowded for admission, but St Philip advised caution in admitting them. 'He counselled', says Marciani ⟨Annal t 2.p 19⟩ 'that they should not be in a hurry to accept every one who asked admission into the Congregation; but that with much caution they should make long trial of their qualities and perseverance according to the provision in the Rules.'

What seems to have contributed to the removal of St Philip's reluctance was the circumstance that his disciples at Rome were so immediately in the eye of the Court that they could not escape promotion. By sending them out of the way, he kept them instèad of losing them. At least we find him using Naples as a place of concealment for his Fathers, within six or eight months of Tarugi's going there.

It will be observed, that even now we have not arrived, strictly speaking, at a *propagation* of the Oratory. The Naples Oratory was not a second House, but a continuation of the first, it was the Roman House continued into Naples. It was strictly under the authorities at Rome, but not as one House under another, but as a number of individuals, who belonged to the Roman Oratory, and happened to find themselves in Naples. This is shown from a variety of circumstances; the inmates of the two houses passed to and fro from one to the other; their property was common; the Naples House was bought for the Fathers of the Congregation of the Oratory of St Mary and St Gregory in Vallicella in Rome; the Naples members took orders, according as St Philip determined; the Superior of the Naples Oratory could be recalled by the Roman; novices of the Naples house were admitted by licence of the Roman; when the Naples House began the Quarant' Ore at the Carnival, they first consulted the Fathers at Rome; and for a while Baronius was apparently Superior of both Houses at once.

Nor did this continuation or expansion of the Roman Oratory cease with the instance of Naples. Two more Oratories sprang from the Neapolitan almost simultaneously with its own foundation. A new Church had been built at San Severino; the authorities of the place asked for Oratorians to take charge of it; the Roman Oratory consented, on condition that the Neapolitan should find members, which it did. Again, almost before its formal foundation, the Neapolitan Oratory was endowed with the Church of the Conception and the abbey of S. Giovanni in the Abruzzi. This gave St Philip and his two houses episcopal jurisdiction; he established in his diocese, for so it may be called, an episcopal seminary; and an Oratory followed three years after St Philip's death, and it was governed from Naples, not from Rome.

An expansion, such as this, tended to become a real affiliation or propagation of separate Oratories; and accordingly we find that at length the Houses of Rome and Naples were governed separately by two Rectors, under one Superior over both, who was called Provost General, and who also governed S. Severino, where there was also a Rector, and the Oratory of Lanciano. Such a state could not continue conformably to the idea and rules of the Oratory. Accordingly at the date of the publication (and confirmation)⟨?⟩ of the Rules (in 1612) the house of Naples was divided from Rome; at the same time that of Lanciano was suppressed. S. Severino had been suppressed some years before viz in 1601, and the Church made over to the Barnabites.

Here our historical sketch shall stop for the present;—all I will add is, that out present state in England is likely to be, mutatis mutandis, very similar to that in which the Oratory found itself in the time of St Philip. I mean, that probably we shall be for a time a floating mass or collection of Oratorians without definite and final location, passing here or there as circumstances may determine. Ultimately we trust we ⟨or our successors⟩ shall find our home in this or that town; meanwhile it is our protection and sanction and consolation, while we thus remain suspended and in suspence, to perceive from the example of our first fathers, that such an unsettled [in]determinate state arises from the nature of things, as it occurred as regards the

Catholic Church itself in the days of the Apostles. 'Instabiles sumus,' 'we have no settled home,' say St Paul.

Only may we have a portion of that grace and that blessing which rested on the first disciples of St Philip! Only may the Santo Padre himself, who with such caution, deliberation, prudence, judgment, and success guided the course of his nascent Congregation, be with us now in England, and bind us together in that his own spirit of love and gentleness, which is better than all vows, and adorn us with his own beauty of holiness and amiableness of word and deed, which is an influence stronger, wider, surer, than the most cunningly organized association.

———

NEWMAN'S ORATORY PAPERS No. 4
20 JANUARY 1848

INTRODUCTORY NOTE

Summary

1. History of the propagation of the Oratory in Italy after St Philip's death offers instructive precedents—Mode of its foundation very various.
2. In the States of the Church:—Fermo and its foundations— Fano, Camerino, Ripa Transoni, Macerata. Perugia and Bologna.
3. In the Kingdom of Naples:—Naples, Palermo, Aquila.
4. Brescia and other Houses in the north of Italy.
5. Several Oratories which set up of themselves.
6. The lessons of this history.

On this address, see above p. 140.

In the main, this is a developed treatment of the raw material collected in Paper 'n' of the Santa Croce Papers, and of which a summary is provided in the Introductory Note (below, pp 418–9).

One might compare this sporadic, unorganized, spontaneous development of the Oratory, with what Newman says of the growth of the Benedictine Order[1].

Particular attention should be given to the history of the Camerino Oratory, since Newman frequently returns to this case as a precedent for the absolute necessity of unity of spirit within each Oratorian community. Cf. v.g. the Chapter Address of 8 March 1858: 'The instance that rests most clearly on my mind is that of the Oratory of Camerino . . .'

SS. Fabian, et Sebastian[2]

The history of the rise and propagation of such an institution as the Oratory is of course interesting in itself, expecially to those who belong to it; but it is also valuable and instructive from the precedents it contains for the guidance of those who find themselves at this day in the circumstances of its first founders. And this is the reason why I now ⟨intend to⟩ make a point of directing your attention to it.

The mode of its foundation was very various in different localities, as might have been anticipated, when each house was independent of the other, and the first Founder refused to co-operate in its propagation—some houses were set on foot without any tradition from Rome, others by persons who had attended the exercises there, others with the advice and encouragement of the Roman Fathers, others by means of persons who were sent to Rome to learn the exercises, others by Fathers sent from the Roman House, others with, others without the countenance, or the furtherance of the diocesan, while others were old institutions which became Oratorian, and others were founded and failed, and then were begun a second or a third time.

Now to give a few specimens of this history,—and I will begin with Fermo, Perugia and Bologna, three of the most important in the States of the Church.

It may be recollected that Fermo petitioned for an Oratory

[1] 'The Mission of St Benedict', *Historical Sketches*, II, pp. 388–9.
[2] *B. Or. Ar.*, B. 9.3

as early as 1580. St Philip refused to give it members, though he offered to lend them a Roman Father, and to make two of their postulants novices at the Chiesa Nuova. It so happened that Ricci, one of the Roman Fathers was a native of the place, and it would seem, though I have not found it distinctly stated, that St Philip sent him there. Anyhow in the course of his life he visited the Oratory of Fermo as many as six different times. At first, however, they seem to have begun of themselves, having sent for the Rules from Rome. This was soon after their application, and after twelve years before St Philip's death. In the course of two years they had formed their Convitto or Community. It consisted of five priests and began October 13, 1585, all natives of Fermo, besides a clerk and a laybrother. They chose one of the five for their head. Of these five one had been much at the Chiesa Nuova, in the train of Cardinal d'Este, and St Philip had said, 'We shall have him one day;' the second had been known to St Philip, and perhaps his penitent; a third who already was familiar with the Chiesa Nuova, had been sent there for the sake of learning the practices of the Oratory. It is interesting to know that the House of Fermo, which was of as early or earlier date than the Neapolitan, is at this day the most exemplary in the Roman States. It is said always to have had Saintly men in it.

And it was as distinguished for its zeal in the foundation of Oratories in other cities. Among these it sent out directors to form the Congregations, more or less of Fano, Camerino, Ripa Transoni, Macerata, not to say Perugia in the Roman States and Rheggio [sic] in the Modenese.

The history of each of these is different from the others, and shall be briefly traced.

Fano was founded by Gabrielli; he was wealthy and noble and his family still dwells in the place and on a spot adjoining to the Oratory. He had already taken part in exercises of an Oratorian character, in a Chapel of St Girolamo, in the last days of St Philip. Encouraged by the Oratorian of Fermo, who has been above mentioned as known to St Philip, he began, in May 1597, to build an Oratorian House close by the Church of S. Pietro in Valle. At this time he was a layman, but he soon received the tonsure. On the first Sunday of the new year he was joined by the Rector of San Petro, and another, and the Rector became Superior. The Bishop patronized the attempt, and on the death of the Rector, his successor joined them, and Gabrielli, now priest, was made superior. A fourth had joined them in 98. There now was an accession of many more. Gabrielli laid out about £500 (2300 sc.) in buying and repairing some adjacent houses and a large sum in embellishing the Church. A painting by Guido, and another by Guercino, were among his gifts. Also he obtained of the Pope a new distribution of the parish—the cure of souls was divided among other parishes, and the Church and revenues annexed to the Oratory.It is on this account perhaps, that the Church is at present accounted almost the chapel of the Palazzo Gabrielli, which stands hard by. The Oratory was established by Bull in 1607. This Oratory was afterwards presented with a magnificent Library of as many as 10.000 bound volumes, on miscellaneous subjects, valued at about £5.000 (22.000 sc.), also with a museum of medals, and a collection of mathematical instruments.

(Fano was instrumental in founding the Oratory of Fossombrone. The citizens of Fossombrone having vowed a Church to their five saints, determined to put it into the hands of the Oratorians; but, when the Roman Fathers would not give, but only lend, members, they gave up the thought. Meanwhile a few priests, one from the Court of Rome, another from a Nunciatura, began an Oratory of the Blessed Sacrament every Saturday, and this at length becoming similar to the Oratory of St Philip, was put in possession of the new Church, which was called the Chiesa Nuova, as at Rome Some rooms were built close to it, and a convitto or community was formed. This seems to have been the work of the Duke D'Urbino, without the co-operation of the Bishop. Perhaps too they had done some things in an irregular way. A serious persecution followed, on the part of the secular priests⟨?⟩, and the Bishop took part against them; their Superior fell ill, and some of their members left them. At the end of six years a new Superior was chosen, in the formal Oratory with Deputies, the founder of the Oratory at Fano taking part in the proceeding. The Bishop too gave them a brief, which was soon followed by a brief from Rome, and they get legitimate possession of the Church which rightly or wrongly they had always used.)

A Father of Fermo took part in the establishment of the Oratory of Camerino; but it was founded by a remarkable man of the name of Matteucci. He was blind, and yet he was admitted to minor orders. For two years he had been at San Severino; and we find him with others stationed at a Church some little way outside the walls of Camerino. This was shortly after St Philip's death, and he communicated with the Fathers at Rome about setting up an Oratory. They encouraged him, especially Ancina and at the end of two years he began. After a while came a priest, who had known St Philip and joined the party, which soon mounted up to fourteen. They had no means, and, contrary to the Oratorian Rule, lived by the oblations of the people, laying under contribution not only Camerino but the neighbouring cities. Also contrary to the Oratorian Rule, they fasted rigorously three days in the week. F. Velli, at that time Superior of Rome, interfered; he told them that they must observe no fasts but such as were by precept, that experience showed that in an Oratory additional fasting was destructive of what was more important, though they might abstain if they wished.

Matteucci, though blind and only in minor orders, had been Rector till the coming of Grandi, to whom he first gave up the care of priests and novices, keeping himself the general government of the house, but in the course of a few years the post of Superior also. Distant as their present house was from the centre of population, they were led to accept another which was as much as four miles from the city, and there they posted some of their community. After this, a confraternity puts them in possession of a Church within the city, to which a small house was attached, and a brief was granted them by the Pope.

Eleven years past [sic], and at the end of twenty years from the commencement of the Community events occur, which make it probable that the unoratorian practices which had shown themselves in it were the work of the foreign priest Grandi who had succeeded the blind Matteucci as Superior. For at that date Matteucci is again chosen for the Provostship, in preference to Grandi. A change of policy followed; they gave up the two Churches which were outside the city, as contrary to the custom of the Oratory. Grandi in consequence left, and set up in Camerino a Congregation of his own, called the Congregazione del Ospizio. He was a man of great sanctity and his body was found entire fourteen years after his death, but he was apparently no Oratorian.

Following the Congregation into its new abode, we find them in straitened accommodation for as many as forty years. They lived in two rooms, over the Church, and in winter the snow came down upon their bolsters. They had no means, and, being unable in consequence to increase their laybrothers, they were obliged to put up with one old man, who could not even serve at Mass, from his ignorance of Latin. He therefore and the blind Superior served between them. They appear to have been without St Philip's Rule till the date of its publication (1612) which was a year after Matteucci was restored to the Headship; at this date too the Roman Fathers took them up. Two Houses were propagated from Camerino. The blind Matteucci's process was made out on his death for the Congregation of Rites.

The Oratory of Ripa Transoni was established by the Bishop of the place. He had originally contemplated introducing the Oblates of Milan, or the Barnabites, or Jesuits, not knowing the Oratory; and he had in his eye a religious person, rich and childless, who he hoped would give him means of his design. This person was unwilling to commit himself; meanwhile the Bishop was as much in want of men as of money. At length, hearing of the Oratory, he persuaded one of the Rectors of the city, with three other Priests, to begin a Community, and he obtained two Fathers from Fermo to set it on foot. Their only incomings were the incomings of the Rectory, which amounted to about £20 (90 sc.). They were obliged to borrow furniture. This went on for three years. The old man determined to found a monastery, but suddenly on a vision of St Philip, he endowed the Oratory.

Macerata was the first city which dedicated a Church to St Philip. Its Oratory was founded in 1615, but came to nothing. It was refounded in 1645 by a noble of the city of Fermo.

The Oratory of Reggio also had to struggle with serious

misfortunes in its commencement—was begun in 1629; it lasted but three years; the plague carried off all its members. In 1662 it recommenced—the Oratory of Fermo sent a Father to set it off—but, from want of funds, all its members dropped off but one, who, in spite of obstacles continued in his profession, till at the age of thirty, he was cut off by a fever in consequence of his excessive labours. A third time the Oratory begins with three members; it is patronized by a man of property, who builds them a Church and endows them.

I will refer to another Oratory which was visited in its first years by the same trial. All the Fathers at Casale but three were cut off by the plague in 1600. Before this they were visited by another misfortune, though of a different kind, the loss of their Church. At Casale, the good offices of a Capuchin, who was the originator of the undertaking, procured them large contributions from several neighbouring sovereigns. Scarcely had they built their Church with the sums thus collected, when it was objected to as affording a position for an enemy in event of war. Orders in consequence were given for its demolition. This is parallel to a new line of railroad going through a Church at this day. However it recovered these adversities—A new Church was built, the Congregation grew again—and in the time of of Marciani, who gives the account, it consisted of twelve Priests, two Clerks and six lay brothers.

While I am on the subject of misfortunes, I will mention a similiar trial which came on the Oratory of Trapani. The Fathers had just built their Church at the expense of 30.000 scudi, when it fell down with the loss of 300 lives. They soon built another at the same cost.

So much for Fermo, and four of the Oratories which may be considered to have sprung from it.

While Fermo is on the Neapolitan frontier Perugia lies towards the Tuscan, and was an offshoot at once of Rome and of Fermo. The Bishop of the place was a friend of St Philip, was desirous of establishing an Oratory there. ⟨He had already?⟩ supplied three members to the Roman House; and seems to have been desirous to have them returned to them [sic]. St Philip refused, though he offered to lend some Fathers for a time. In consequence the Bishop half addressed himself to the Barnabites, and proposed to bestow all his patrimony upon them. Two Perugians, however, at Rome, in the service of Spain, persuaded by one of the Fathers in the Oratory there, after a retreat at S. Andrea, came to a resolution of becoming Oratorians. This turned the Bishop's thoughts back to the Oratory; he obtained from Fermo the loan of two Fathers, and his infant community was joined by two other Perugians, a priest and a layman; also by a foreign priest—This brought it up to the number of five. The Bishop then erected the Oratory in 1615. At the same time a second of the three Roman (Perugian) Fathers above mentioned, paid them a visit. Three years after they gained a brief and indulgences from Paul v. In another three years they gained possession of the Church and Parish of St Gregory. Not long before this the third of the original Roman Fathers returned to Perugia for good; he was a pupil of Consolini's and had lost his health in Rome. He joined the Perugian Oratory and lived in it for forty four years. At length they were able to build a magnificent Church with pictures by Guido, Sacchi, Pietro di Cortona and others, and an ample sacristy.

Bologna, in the north of the Roman States, towards Lombardy, had attempted, but unsuccessfully, to gain an Oratory from St Philip, as well as Fermo and Perugia, but succeeded in at length erecting one in the same year as Perugia, which was the year of his beatification. Licinio Pio, a young Bolognese of the age of twenty eight, devoted to the pleasures of the world, and giving little promise of piety or devotion, went to Rome for the sake of living more at his ease then he could among those who knew him, and with the idea of attaching himself to the service of some Cardinal. He happened to lodge in the Monte Giordano, in the same house with a citizen of Bologna, who was a Tertiary of St Francis, and did his best to convert him. His prayers and his efforts were not without effect. One morning hurrying home, his shortest way lay through the Chiesa Nuova. The Masses were over; as he passed the Blessed Sacrament he dropped his knee in a careless way, as usual when he would hurry on. But he was arrested; he could not rise; he began to weep. His tears were sweet not bitter, and he heard a clear voice within him say, 'Become a priest, become a priest'. The voice was both sweet and strong, and, overcome by it, he promised to become one. He left the high altar, at which to this day the Blessed Sacrament is found, and passed to the Chapel of St Philip, and there he invoked the aid of that great Saint for the obtaining those graces which he well knew he needed for the fulfilment of his engagement. He then had recourse to a Confessor at San Girolamo, and at his direction began a daily attendance at the Quarant' Ore, at the Hospitals, and at the Exercises at S. Girolamo. At first he wished, like Baronius, to become a Capucin, but he left the disposal of himself to his Confessor, who, taking him by the hand, said with decision, 'not a Religious, but a Priest'. In consequence he received minor orders, the subdiaconate, and in due time ascended to the Priesthood.

He had just been ordained subdeacon, and was passing through the Chiesa Nuova, when Santolini, who did not know him, happened to be in the Confessional, rose up, put aside the crowd of penitents who surrounded him, walked all the way to him, and invited him to take part in the function on the following Sunday, there being time enough to learn the ceremonies in the interval of the Prefect of the Oratory. This led to his becom[ing] a regular attendant at the Chiesa Nuova, and to his taking Santolini for his director, who at length bade him introduce the Oratory into Bologna.

He returned there with the Rule, which had then been just approved by Paul V. At first he had no associates in his design. He succeeded in obtaining a meeting of prominent persons, ecclesiastical and lay, married and single, out of which he forms an Oratory for the Exercises—among these were three Canons, a Provost, four priests, two curates of parishes, a LL D, and a Senator. He became Superior with a layman, viz the Senator, for his associate. He appoints a secretary. They first met on Thursdays: there, being transferred into a church, on Monday, Wednesday, and Friday, introducing the ragionamenti.[3] Then they were taken up by the Archbishop, who soon became Pope Gregory XV. Now they begin in form; Licinio, being apparently the sole Priest does all the work. At present there is no community or Convitto, only the Oratorium parvum

[3] i.e. spiritual discourses after St. Philip's manner.

—At the end of a year he is joined by a Bolognese friend, now a Priest who had already attended the Exercises, and by others. At this time he was still under the direction of Santolini, who at one time paid him a visit. At length he was able to rebuild and embellish their Church. Such were the interesting beginnings of the Oratory at Bologna—which, after so long a continuance, is just at this time in a very languishing condition, if not on the point of expiring.

Let us now descend to the Kingdom of Naples the capital of which had succeeded in obtaining an Oratory from St Philip himself. Houses multiplied apparently so readily in this territory, that there is a Brief of the date[4] of forbidding the introduction of the Oratory into the smaller ⟨?⟩ cities or where ten Fathers could not be furnished with means of their own. Two Houses, however, deserve especially to be named as early foundations, Palermo in Sicily, and Aquila in the Abruzzi ⟨?⟩.

The house at Palermo was set up two years before St Philip's death. It began with five Fathers, two of whom were sent to Naples for six months to learn the Exercises and Rules. They were soon increased by four others. They attempted in vain to be aggregated to Naples the year of St Philip's death, and then they asked for one of the Neapolitan Fathers to come to them, which they gained.

In the beginning of the seventeenth century, when the Oratory of Aquila was founded, the clergy of the place were in a relaxed state, as seems to have been the case all through Italy at the time, and the Bishop seems to have made no great efforts to improve it. The Oratory originated, not with him, but with a lay-man of noble family of the city, who, at the advice of a Canon who had practised the Exercises at S Girolamo, went to Rome in 1606 for two months to learn the Exercises and Rules. On his return he passed a retreat in a hermitage which his ancestors had built and endowed. Having made over his property to his sisters, he had no means whatever, and met with many difficulties besides. He was dissuaded from his plan by prudent persons, while others accused him of pride, and others tried to keep back people who were desirous of joining him. Between January and March 1607 he had got

---

[4] A space was left for the insertion of the date.

together six persons besides himself; some of them at the time had parochial cures, and other engagements. By the end of April they got the use of the Church of St Jerome for their Exercises. The founder, though at this time only a clerk, is chosen for Superior, the rest being priests. For some months they practise by themselves, in the beginning of June they open their room to the town; that is they form the Oratorium parvum. Ten brothers join it, who proceed to choose their head, who is a LL D. and, contrary to the Rules, they first call him not Rector but Prefect—whereas the Prefect is one of the Fathers of the Congregation. They correct their mistake, and this leads them to give their Superior his proper title of Provost, whereas he had hitherto been called Rector. In a short time the brothers of the Oratory amount to seventy. As yet they seem to have lived by themselves, not in community—and two years elapse before they are put in possession of a house, entering it on Maundy Thursday April 16. Four days before their brief had come from Rome. Before this time F. Ricci of Rome had gained them the sanction of the Bishop of Aquila, and they had begun to preach in the Church on days of obligation. When they had been in their house a year, they were visited [by] two fathers from Rome, who perfect them in the Exercises and Rules.

It is observable that the Oratories, which were most distinguished for energy and success in the first years of the Institution, generally retain to this day the same character. Fermo, which sent out more houses from itself than any city in the Roman States, is still remarkable, as I have already said, for the excellent state of its Congregation. Naples is another instance. And Brescia, which I shall now speak of, is a third. It was the mother house of Verona, Udina [sic], Trent, Cremona⟨?⟩, Vicenja, and Como; and at this day, though Verona has the most striking establishment, Brescia is the most business-like and contains the best workers. The history of its origin is curious. We have already heard of an Oratory of S. Dorothea at Rome, called the Oratory of Divine Love, previous to the time of St Philip; a similar institution, of the same date, existed at Brescia, called the Congregation della Pace. They differed, however, from the Oratory in this important respect, that they lived in the country and with greater rigor than befits the Rule of St Philip. They amounted to more than fifty priests, and more than this number, fifty three, were cut off by the plague and other illnesses of the time. The new members, who came in their place, conceived the wish to become Oratorians, and at length the whole community resolved by a unanimous vote to adopt the Oratorian Rule. Some of them were very unwilling to give up their fasts, but the Roman Fathers obliged them 'abbracciare con allegrezza le Costituzioni senza diminuire nè alterare cosa alcuna'[5]. They were still popularly called the Congregazione della Pace.

Now I will mention several Oratories which set up of themselves, without the help of any existing Oratory, furnished however with the Statutes, and incorporated by Pope's brief.

The first was not an auspicious instance of this mode of proceeding. The Oratory of Lucca was founded in St Philip's time by a person who had once been the guest of St Philip for seventeen days, and is acknowledged as an Oratory, by the Neapolitan Register; in the year 1600 it changed into a religion⟨?⟩, and had a Church at Rome. In 1621 it introduced vows.

Forli was begun in 1637 by a nobleman, with a few others, under the direction of a Jesuit, and with the sanction of the Bishop. He got a Church lent him, and bought an adjoining house. He did not at first formally adopt the Roman Statutes, and his Exercises much resembled those which St Philip used in San Girolamo. Persecutions were raised against them, self interest imputed, threats held out. The Father General of the Jesuits is for a time persuaded to send away their director. However, they proceed, and by the end of twenty years had built a new Church, which they dedicated to St Philip.

At Jesi, a person who had no intention of becoming Oratorian, built a small Church to the Annunciata and St Philip. He serves it as priest for fourteen years. At the end of this time two priests inspire him with the design of founding an Oratory, and a Nun of Foligno injoins it. He gains two novices⟨?⟩, and all three clothe themselves in St Philip's livery on St Antony's day, 1644. They were very poor, but are described as clean and

[5]'To embrace with cheerfulness the Constitutions of the Oratory, without diminishing or altering anything.' *See* below, p. 332.

neat. Nor were they in force sufficient for carrying on the Exercises, and did not attempt more than evening prayer in public every day, and three times a week the discipline. When a fourth was added, they began to preach in the morning in the Oratorium parvum. The Bishop erected them into a Congregation.

At Cesena there was a celebrated writer and philosopher chiefly, I believe, on mathematical subjects towards the middle of the seventeenth century, the Cavalier Scipio Chiaramonti. When. he was eighty years old, he was ordained priest, and became the founder and a member of an Oratory in that city. He began to take his place in the Confessional like a younger man, and lived for eight years in his new life. The Congregation gained a Pope's brief towards the end of the century.

I may end, as I began, by directing attention to the very various circumstance under which the Oratory has begun in different localities. Sometimes the Bishop is the mover in its establishment, sometimes he is unfavourable to it. Now, it is a neighbouring⟨?⟩ prince, now a rich patron, or a man of literature and science, now the inhabitants of the place, now a Capucin, or a Jesuit, or a Theatine. At one time it is propagated from Rome or Fermo or Naples, at another it begins merely by initiative or by observance of the rules, or without the rules and is but gradually brought into the true Oratorian shape, or it is a pre-existing body which changes into an Oratory. Sometimes the first founder is a layman, sometimes rich, sometimes poor, sometimes the first Superior is a clerk, not a priest. Sometimes it begins with five priests, sometimes with four, sometimes six. Sometimes it is well endowed, sometimes it struggles with difficulties for years. Now it has a Church given it, now two or three, now it is inconveniently far from the town, now it has a parish, now a Church without cure of souls. One while the Convitto or Community is formed first, at another time the Oratory. Now it comes to an end and begins again; now it is thinned by pestilence; now it is endowed with lands and has ecclesiastical jurisdiction, now it is enriched with a library.

We can hardly name the difficulty or peculiarity, which has not its precedent; and this makes its history especially valuable

14

to persons like ourselves, who, though with the highest ecclesiastical sanction and the best promise of success, yet under the anomalies which must occur in a particular case, and the perplexities which can lie at the origin of undertaking [sic], are, (with humble reliance on the divine blessing,) attempting to introduce it into a new country.

NEWMAN'S ORATORY PAPERS No. 5
JANUARY/FEBRUARY 1848

INTRODUCTORY NOTE

Summary

1. What was the object of St Philip's Institution?

2. Providence and the projects of the Saints.

3. The Oratory, though originally in no sense a clerical exercise, becomes a pattern for the secular clergy.

4. The object then of the Congregation of the Oratory is to form good secular priests.

5. How the Fathers of the Oratory fulfilled this object:—
    i. By holiness and zeal.
    ii. By the fact that they are gentlemen.
    iii. A necessary word of explanation: What have gentlemanlike manners to do with religion?
    iv. No external austerity in an Oratorian House—an Oratory resembles a college in an English university.
    v. The Congregation as the home of the Oratorian—his *nido* (nest)—instances of this attachment.
    vi. The Oratory a local institution in the town in which it finds itself.
    vii. On the whole a learned institution, but undogmatic and uncontroversial.
    viii. The Oratory a bond of union between Seculars and Regulars.

On this ·Address, see above pp. 23–5; pp. 110–2; p.140. We have here a remarkable instance of Newman's gift of anticipating, by an analysis of his Oratorian sources, some of the crucial problems which lay ahead in the development of the Oratory in England, in particular the precise role of intellectual work for Oratorians. See the Chapter Address for 31 August 1856 on Father Bernard Dalgairns.

The Early Chapter Addresses of 1848[1] [: The Third Address]

3

When we see any new organization invented, or plan of action set on foot, our first and natural question is, What is the object of it? Men do not form into bodies, or begin a course of labour for nothing; what then was the *object* of that Institution which St Philip founded, and which was welcomed so warmly, and taken up so zealously and promptly, and spread so rapidly through the extent of Italy, to say nothing of its success in Spain? Some account then of the ecclesiastical object and position of the Oratory, naturally follows a sketch of its rise and propagation.

It continually happens in the history of the Church, that the immediate and direct notion which has stimulated holy men to begin their labour, is but a part of that work, or is not that work, which the event proves to have been their mission. They have had their own object before their mind, and Providence had led them on by means of it to accomplish His own. Their own humility would by itself be sufficient to keep them from beginning that to which He calls them; and thus they go out in faith and obedience not knowing whither they go. They begin a limited work, and they are led on to a great one. They have thoughts of their own neighbourhood or country, and God's grace and blessing has made them a light to the world. At other times they have sought scope for the zeal which devoured them in one set of objects, and Divine Providence has turned and satisfied it upon others. They have sought to convert

[1] *B. Or. Ar.*, B. 9.3.

pagans and have been employed in reclaiming the lapsed; they have at first have [sic] kindled an almost military ardour and have ended in creating some system of profound wisdom.

Both these remarks are illustrated in the history of St Philip. His first wish, as that of St Francis of Assisi and St Ignatius, was to preach in heathen countries; but he was told by the Cistercian at the Tre Fontane, that Rome was his India. Then he set himself to preaching, confessing, and directing in Rome; but to improve the laity seems to have been the extent of his design, or at least he did not contemplate the clergy specially. The Oratorio is in no sense a clerical exercise; it is not addressed to any particular class of men. All that St Philip worked for was an Oratory in that age in Rome. He did not like to give his mind to the thought of his institution being spread into other places. It was a Roman institution; it was the Roman Oratory. But it spread and rapidly through the cities of Italy, nay as high as Trent and down to Palermo and Trapani—nay and not only spread as an Oratory, but his Congregation served a distinct purpose; it became a pattern of the secular clergy in an age when it wanted a serious reform. And hence in the event St Philip has been considered the Reformer of the seculars, as St Ignatius was the reviver of the regular spirit.

There have been various eras in the Church, as is obvious, in which the state of the clergy, whether seculars or regulars, being relaxed or corrupt, it has pleased Providence, in fulfilment of the prophecies made to His Church, in one way or other to interfere and effect a reformation. Sometimes it has been done by the instrumentality of members of the body, as in many of the monastic reforms; thus St Odo or St Stephen reformed the Benedictines, and St Theresa the Carmelites. Sometimes a Pope has been raised up to do the work; and hence we celebrate St Gregory the viith as the great reformer of ecclesiastical discipline. Sometimes the old state of things has been simply superseded to make way for a new hierarchy or a new order, as St Benedict took the place of the monastic rules before him, and as the Saxon clergy were supplanted by the foreign seculars and regulars which followed the conquest of England by the Normans.

Such an era, first of relaxation of morals, then of reformation was the 16th century. We cannot well exaggerate the licence which prevailed in the clerical order in its earlier years. The life of St Carlo or any of the saints of Italy at the time will abundantly show it. Nay the title of St Philip, as the Apostle of Rome, itself is a proof of it; there cannot be a greater condemnation of at least the state of the population at that era, than that a title should be applied to St Philip, which those only bear who have laboured in heathen countries. And probably the holy Cistercian meant the same thing, when he called Rome St Philip's India.

It was this relaxed state of the Church in Italy, which accounts for the eagerness with which the Oratorians were demanded and welcomed in so many places. One is tempted to ask what was it that made the Neapolitans so importunate with St Philip, which made them subscribe so large a sum, buy a house before they knew he would accept it, and flock in crowds to the preaching of Tarugi? What was so attractive in the exercises of the Oratory, that for the sake of them they were willing to bring in to Naples the clergy of a foreign state? It was the need doubtless of good, zealous, hardworking, heavenly minded priests. Nearly all the present religious devotional and pious characteristics of Rome are traceable to St Philip. The teaching, the pilgrims, the devotion of the Quarant'Ore, the visits to the Seven Churches, the attendance at Hospitals, the Sunday Schools for children, and the confraternities of young men, are owing to him. Though he can scarcely be said to have had a Parish in Rome, he was the father of parish Priests. He was the most unwearied of Confessors, the most gentle and wise of directors. And what he was, such were his followers in their measure. When then the Neapolitans desired the Congregation of the Oratory among them, they were expressing a desire for exemplary pastors, who would fulfil the needful and solemn office which a parish priest has undertaken. And what was felt at Naples was felt elsewhere. A renovation of the clergy was required; and as the Benedictine monasteries of the Norman period in England were planted on the ruins of the Saxon clergy, so in Italy in the 16th century, the Priests of the Oratory formed centres round which a more zealous ministry collected itself after a time of relaxation.

This then, I conceive, to be the *object* of the Congregation of the Oratory; the formation of good secular priests, who shall at once be a blessing to the population among which they are placed, and a standard of the parochial clergy or missioners. And now having stated the *object* of the Institution, let us consider in what ways the Oratorian Father fulfilled it, or what there was in his character and circumstances adapted to fulfil it.

Now first it need hardly be said, that the first Oratorians, of whom I am speaking, were eminently saintly men. As many as eighteen of the first Fathers at the Chiesa Nuova have received the title of Venerable. The Oratory of Fermo again, down to this date has never been without exemplary members. The founders of the Oratories of Macerata, Jesi, Florence, Padua Forli, Camerino, and various others either wrought miracles or graces, or died in the odour of sanctity, or appeared in vision, or their bodies remained incorrupt, or their processes have been made out for canonization. The missionary labours of Santi of Padua, Magnanti of Aquila, and others were unbounded. And these are but a specimen of the multitude of holy men, who were members of the first Oratories. Holiness then and zeal formed the first and greatest and most necessary qualification by which they became a pattern to the secular clergy of their time.

A second characteristic of the first Oratories was this that their members were generally of a higher rank in life, and a higher education than was usually found among the parochial clergy. By the rule an Oratorian must be possessed of sufficient property to sustain himself, and the priests of the Oratorian Church are not supported by the parish or congregation. Thus they take a higher position in secular matters than the ordinary parish priest or a monk or friar. They are gentlemen. And this was perhaps the meaning of St Philip's humiliations of his disciples. He had gentlemen about him, and wished to keep them gentlemen, but at the same time wished to purge them of the fastidiousness, selfimportance, and loftiness which is commonly the characteristic of a gentleman. But anyhow the first Oratorians were by birth and education gentlemen; and such in a good measure they remain down to this day. We have found this the case at Rome, Naples, and Palermo, not to speak of Verona and others.

The instances are very frequent in the annals of the Congregation. At Rome St Philip's first disciples had for the most part come to Rome to study the law. Tarugi, Savioli, and Ricci were men of noble, rich and distinguished families. In like manner Gabrielli the founder of the Oratory of Fano, Santi of that of Padua, Nardi of Aquila, D'Aste of Forli, were men of family. Paccaroni, one of the original fathers at Fermo, had been in the train of the Cardinal d' Este; two of the first fathers at Perugia, had been in the service of the Spanish government; two at Fossombrone were the one from the Court of Rome, the other from a Nunciatura. Three out of the first four fathers at Naples were lawyers; the remaining father was a man of property. The founder of the Oratory at Bologna was a young man of property and (what we should now call) fashion, who was converted at the Chiesa Nuova. Fesolo, the founder of Lodi, was a man of property. The founder of the Oratory at Cesena, Chiaramonti was a man of rank and a celebrated writer.

Many more instances may be given; indeed considering St Philip's principle, already referred to, that every Oratorian was to live on his own means, it could hardly have been otherwise. At the very least, a certain number of the members of an Oratorian Congregation will ever be men of education and connexions. And this being so, we see another of the means of influence by which the institution of St Philip acted on the secular clergy.

Here a word of explanation is perhaps necessary. It will be asked what have gentlemanlike manners and refined feelings to do with religion? and how does it really raise the secular priest to bring him in contact with what sometimes is merely superficial, and at best is not more than a moral excellence. In answer to this objection I shall answer, first of all, that we are not here contemplating refinement of mind by itself, but as superadded to a high religious perfection. I have already spoken of the saintliness of the first fathers of the Oratory, and now I say in addition that they are gentlemen besides: and it does not follow, because refinement is worthless without saintliness, that it is needless and useless with it. It may set off and recommend an interior holiness, just as the gift of eloquence sets off logical argument. A bad speaker may be as firm a believer as the most accomplished of orators; yet the gift of words is necessary to be able to persuade; and so the gift of manners may be necessary to win. But further than this:—I suppose it may be said that true refinement of thought, word, and manners is the natural *result* of Christian holiness, and the necessary result when it is carried out into its full and ultimate effect. But so it is that few are able, so to carry it out; nay, though Christian excellence is abstractedly most refined, most amiable, most winning, yet from various circumstances it need not be so, or it may not possibly be so, in the case of individuals, nay of individual Saints. There are saints whose very mission has been to perform work of the severest character, and who could not, sometimes at least, without sin show the more gentle and courteous side of the Christian character. And if this may be true even of saints, so much the more will it be true of a multitude of good men who are not saints, in whom from infirmities of various sorts, from natural temper, from the bad habits of childhood, and the like causes, the meek, loving, and considerate Spirit of Christ does not flow from the heart to the eyes and the tongue and the other instruments of external communication. Hence it is that mere secular training, gentle nurture, good society, classical education, are of special benefit to the Christian, first as at least excluding their contraries, habits of rusticity or oddness or affectation and thus protecting and giving room for the unimpeded development of the saintly character in all its parts, as concurring in that development, encouraging and completing it, and lastly, when there is after all from some fault or other a deficient development, at least simulating it, and supplying from inferior principles and by secular instruments that refinement which ought to follow, and often does follow even in the humblest and least educated, from Christian faith and love.

It need not then surprise us to find that, accidentally, good birth, a liberal education, experience of good society, knowledge of the world, all those things which issue in what we familiarly mean by a gentleman, or in a word gentlemanlikeness, however attained, whether by these means or by any other, and still better if really flowing from the Christian spirit within, but what we mean by gentlemanlikeness, I say it is not wonderful, if this external polish and refinement, which is so valueless in itself morally, yet so useful as a sort of rhetoric in conduct, nay and valuable too, so far as it is a symptom and the product[?] of Christian excellence within, should have been one of the means by which the Oratory acted in the reformation of both clergy and laity at the time of its establishment.

3. And having got so far as this, we may be prepared to be told of some other peculiarities of the Oratorian character, which at first sight are somewhat removed from the popular and true notions of saintliness. To be a gentleman externally implies a number of habits and ways, which, it cannot be denied, savour of worldliness, and especially, to use an English word, of worldly comfort. Not that true gentility may not exist in the most abject poverty, as I have already said, not as if the meanest friar or the most emaciated hermit may not be a true gentleman (and for the proof of this we need by turn our eyes upon St Antony, whose sweetness of mind and manner shines forth the more conspicuous from the remarkable fact that his biographer, St Athanasius, had himself so much more call for the sterner and severer aspect of the Christian character—) but that, as the philosopher tells us that a state of temporal prosperity is the natural sphere for his good and happy man, though such prosperity is not an essential part of moral perfection, so certain external circumstances and a certain life are no part of real gentlemanlikeness, yet may be necessary for it perfect exhibition.

Now I will say in a word what is the nearest approximation in fact to an Oratorian Congregation that I know, and that is, one of the Colleges in the Anglican Universities. Take such a College, destroy the Head's house, annihilate wife and children and restore him to the body of fellows, change the religion from Protestant to Catholic, and give the Head and Fellows missionary and pastoral work, and you have a Congregation of St Philip before your eyes. And in matter of fact the Congregation is in the Annals sometimes called a College. And now I will put down some particulars which are implied in this account of it.

The Congregation is to be the *home* of the Oratorian. The Italians, I believe, have no word for home—nor is it an idea which readily enters into the mind of a foreigner, at least not so readily as into the mind of an Englishman. It is remarkable then that the Oratorian Fathers should have gone out of their way to express the idea by the metaphorical word *nido* or nest, which is used by them almost technically. The sanction for this idea is contained in the Rule, in one of the Decrees, which is one of the two which are said to be unchangeable. The Congregation, according to St Philip's institution, is never to be so large that the members do not know each other. They are to be "bound together by that bond of love, which daily intercourse creates, and thereby all are to know the ways of each, and feel a reverence for 'countenances of familiar friends.' " Familiar faces, exciting reverence, daily intercourse, knowledge of each other's ways, mutual love, what is this but a description of home? As the Poet says

"Sweet is the smile of home; the mutual look
Where hearts are of each other sure;
Sweet all the joys that crowd the household nook
The haunt of all affections pure."[2]

This is the principal idea conveyed in the word "nest"; but other things are to be added. An Oratorian has his own rooms, and his own furniture; and according to the traditions of the Chiesa Nuova, without being luxurious, they should be such as to attach him to them. They do not form a cell, but a nest. He is to have his things about him, his books and little possessions. In a word, he is to have what an Englishman expresses by the distinctive word *comfort*. And this characteristic of the Oratorian's private room is but a specimen of every part of an Oratorian establishment. The Church is to be handsome, the functions are to be performed with accuracy, and (if possible) with splendour, the music is to be attractive, the Sacristy is to be large and well furnished with vestments, the Refectory is in its way not to be inferior to the sacred buildings, and the table is to be abundant and respectable. Meanness, poverty, austerity, forlornness, sternness, are words unknown in an Oratorian House.

[2] John Keble, *The Christian Year*, The First Sunday of Lent, last verse.

Now this will seem at first sight a strange description of what, in some sense, professes to be a religious institution; and yet it may be seen at once, (though it would be a digression to have to do more than touch upon the subject,) that there are many things associated with the above description which involve mortification. For instance, though the Congregation is the home of the Oratorian, he gives up, (at least, according to the rule of the primitive Oratory,) all other home but this. The first Oratorian renounced his paternal roof, and was discouraged, almost prevented, paying it even an occasional visit. The Oratory was a compensation for his loss, not a mere club house, which he might frequent or not, as he pleased. And again, the community meal, though so well furnished and handsome, was eaten in silence, with, first, reading, then with the exposition of some moral question or text of Scripture. The fathers waited by turns, and the Superior gave penances to those who had incurred them. There is enough then at first sight in the Oratory to rescue its members from the merely secular life of a College. But to return:—

St Philip himself affords us an instance of that attachment to his home or nest, which was a characteristic of his Congregation after him. For thirty years and more he lived in one small room at St Girolamo, and he did not quit Rome for more than sixty years. Perhaps it is by a tradition from him that the Superior at the Chiesa Nuova is said never to quit Rome at this day. As to St Philip, we know how unwilling he was to leave his old familiar abode, when the Congregation was placed in the Chiesa Nuova; the command of the Pope was necessary to move him, and when he moved, he seemed by his way of moving to take a good humoured vengeance on his spiritual children who had brought the Pope upon him.

In like manner when F. Sensi of the Roman Oratory was obliged to betake himself to his native air for the recovery of his health, far from feeling comfort in returning to his country, we are told "So dear were to Father Sensi the walls of his beloved *nest,* where he had become the son of the Santo Padre, that, nothing moved by the pressing requests of the Bishop, he desired by all means to return to Rome, to try if that air and that climate would turn out more favourable to him than

before." ⟨Annal. t. 3. p 558⟩ And so of Amadei, a laybrother
of the Oratory of Perugia, we read that, when he was to transact
some business in his own country, which required leave of
absence, "immediately he had finished it, even without seeing
his own relations and friends, he returned to his own beloved
nest of the Oratorio." ⟨t. 3. p 596.⟩ When Licinio Pio, the
founder of the Oratory of Bologna, was in his last illness, and
had been taken into the country for change of air, "he made
instance to be taken into the city that he might die in his own
nest." ⟨t. 4. p 44.⟩ Morico, being drawn from the Oratory of
Fermo by a family feud or lawsuit, when he gained his cause at
Rome, "hoped to return to the beloved *nest* of his Congregation." ⟨t. 4. p 401 vid also pp 12, 129.⟩

But the most striking illustration of this affection of the home
of the Oratory occurs in the life of Cardinal Baronius. That
holy man, after having been taken from the Congregation,
sorely against his will, and made a Cardinal, at length obtained
from the Pope leave to return to it. He came back to the Chiesa
Nuova and took possession of rooms close to the church. "From
the time" says Marciano, "that Baronius was as though by
force torn from the bosom of his beloved Congregation, he had
never any other view than that of returning to its old walls;
and, whereas he was not permitted to put off the purple, being
now advanced in years and worn out with labours, he thought
of returning at least to the Vallicella, where he had it in mind,
with leave of the Pope, not only to preach to the people on
festivals, which he already did, but even on ferias, as he was
wont before he was Cardinal, with a design of discoursing upon
the Dialogues of St Gregory. Nay he wished to assist daily at
the Sermons of the rest in the Oratory, in order to take up again,
as far as he could, the ancient exercises, with which he had been
nourished by the Santo Padre, and there to render at the last
his soul to God, where he had received the first fruits of the
Spirit. Meanwhile he besought and gained of the fathers some
rooms contiguous to the Church, adapting them, as far as
could be, to his use. This took some time, and while the work
was proceeding, the old man urged it on, thinking every delay
long, which stood in the way of his seeing himself close to those
most dear walls, and saying often that he wished to die in the

hands of his fathers and brothers. Now, while his rooms were a preparing, he was minded one morning to go to dinner with the Fathers, as he oft was wont to do, and there chanced to be read at table the ninth chapter of Job, in which, that holy man, after having recounted the innumerable blessings, which from his youth upwards he had received from God, subjoins these words, "I said I will die in my nest, and as the palm tree I will multiply days," "Dicebam in nidulo meo moriar, et sicut palma multiplicabo dies"[3]. These words filled the Cardinal with gladness, for he thought he saw them verified in himself; accordingly, when the reading was ended, opening his eloquent mouth, he said, "Certainly, my dearest Fathers, with reason can I apply to myself the things which have been read, while I reflect on the years which are passed, and on those most happy days, when I was guarded by God, that is, when I dwelt in these domestic walls, when the lantern shined over my head, held and carried before by Blessed Father Philip, by light of which I walked amid the darkness of the world;—as it happened in the days of my youth, when God dwelt in secret in my tabernacle, and the Almighty was with me, and ye my brethren around me, when I washed my feet in butter (by means of the abundance of heavenly consolations wherein from spiritual exercises I abounded with you,) and the rock flowed for me with rivers of oil, (the rock, I mean, from which we (all) have been taken, our Blessed Father, from whose most sweet mouth and from whose holy breast, full of divine love, we drew, the most luminous maxims of salvation)[4]. At that time I too could securely say: 'In nidulo meo moriar, et sicut palma multiplicabo dies.' But, drawn thence by force, and sent forth from the ark, like the dove, and exposed to the stormy flood of this world, and not finding where to put my foot, I have ever been desirous of returning into the ark to your company; which I especially covet in these last days of my life, that I may die, as though in my own nest, in my Congregation. Wherefore I beseech you, O my dearest Fathers, that, after I have been tossed so long a time by so many storms and tempests, yet saved from shipwreck by God who piloted me,

[3] Vulgate text of *Job* 29:18. [Newman refers by mistake to ch. 9.]
[4] Baronius is embroidering here on the rather strange text of *Job* 29:6.

and brought at length to port, though with my bark broken and leaking, ye would be willing to receive me with that love, which, up to this day, though I be unworthy of it, ye have borne to me.' ⟨Annal t.l. p 319⟩.

Passages, like these, carry us on to another subject, exemplifying the mutual love which existed between the first fathers of the Oratory; but here I introduce them to illustrate the *extrrnal* character of the Congregation.

Another remark may be made. As the Oratory is the home of the individual Father, so the town in which it is placed is the home of the Oratory. A Congregation is a sort of *native* body in a town. It is not a body of foreign priests ⟨(*Yes*, says the Pregi)⟩ but at least in great measure, it is, as it were, the growth and fruit of the place. This peculiarity implies, so far forth, some kind of modification of a foregoing remark, that the members of the Congregation should more or less be men who have seen good society; for some towns do not supply good society, but are made up of the middle classes—but both peculiarities may be combined without much difficulty. However now I am speaking of relationship of an Oratory to the town to which it belongs. It ought in great measure to consist of priests, taken from the town. We ourselves have had the opportunity of seeing this and the effect of this at Naples. The Congregation there seems to be on the best understanding with the merchants and other respectable persons of the place, and to be a sort of ecclesiastical corporation or municipality, to which it sends members and in which the town takes interest and feels pride. We were present at the admission of a novice; he did not come by himself, but he was brought there by relations, who came to witness and take part in the ceremony. The Oratory is thus emphatically a local institution; it acts [on] and is influenced by the town in which it is found, it is the representative of no distant or foreign interest, but lives among and is contented with its own people.

5. It is but part of this same general character which I am describing, that it has little or nothing to do with religious or political controversy. I am speaking of individual Fathers, for Baronius may be considered in part a polemical writer, and Bozius is professedly so, and Gabrielli of Bologna, though it is

remarkable, in the way of literature, how little doctrinal teaching or controversy has been cultivated in the Italian Oratory. Rather its writers are historians, as Baronius, Ranaldus, Becillo, Marciano and Theiner, or ecclesiastical antiquaries as Aringhi, Bosius, Saccarelli, Severano and Laderchi of Rome, Piccolo of Messina, and Coppola of Naples; or local antiquaries as Antinori of Aquila, Baglioni and Crispolti of Perugia, Pietro of Sulmona, Grandis of Venice, Fioravanti of St Elpidio, Semeria of Turin, Calini of Brescià, and Gentili of San Severino; or critics as Bianchini and da Prato of Verona, Spada and Alberici and de Magistris of Rome; or oriental scholars as Valperga of Naples or Biblical Critics as Magri of Messina; or writers on Morals as Cadei of Brescia, and Chiericato of Padua; or writers on ascetics as Navarro of Fermo; or mathematicians as Valperga and others; or classical writers as Cesari of Verona; or writers of Collections, or Catalogues, as Gallandi of Venice, Mansi and Justiniani of Rome; or musical composers as Bartoli and Dentici of Naples and Pantaleone of Macerata.[5]

All these they were as writers, but it is remarkable they have written hardly anything strictly doctrinal; Gabrielli above mentioned makes nearly the sole exception; to which may be added a "defence of celibacy" by Adda of Rome.

This is a very remarkable fact, as showing how foreign the genius of the Oratory is from controversy, a point I will proceed to say more on presently. But there are two other remarks which the list of Oratorian writers suggests to us.

It is remarkable how many of them have engaged themselves in the local Antiquities of their own city. This is natural and might be expected; but it illustrates well the local character of the Institution.

But, besides this, I will remark on the general fact, which the list of writers I have read suggests, viz that the Oratory has been on the whole a learned institution. Made up, as a Congregation has been, in great measure, of highly educated men,

[5]Newman obviously compiled this list from a careful perusal of the exhaustive catalogue of Oratorian writers: *Memorie degli Scrittori Filippini o siano della Congregazione dell' Oratorio de S.Filippo Neri*, raccolte dal Marchese di Villarosa. (Naples, 1837–42).

lawyers and the like, it is not wonderful that even after they become members of the Congregation, they should have exercised themselves in their studies—and in fact the names I have read are no common names in literature, as in some instances, such as Baronius, Bozius, Aringhi and Gallandi will be plain to every one. The Catalogue of writers from which they are selected contains nearly 250 names.

But now we are speaking of the uncontroversial and undomatic character of the Oratory; a characteristic of it which is certain, and yet which needs explanation.

First, as I said before, I am speaking of the character of the Oratory as a whole, not of the case of individuals; next I am speaking of it in relation to the Church itself more than in relation to bodies not Catholic. It is very true that controversy has formed very little part of Oratorian literature at all; but then we must recollect that it is Italian literature, it is the literature of Italian Oratories, planted not among Protestants, but among Catholic populations. So far however is clear, that such controversy, as can fairly take place *among* Catholics, does not belong to the Oratory. I find a father at Naples ⟨Christoforo⟩ was attacked for a certain interpretation he gave to St Thomas; but when he was attacked by a Cistercian, he did not answer him. Another in the North of Italy actually burnt some remarks he had made on a critical subject in answer to learned persons of his day. To take part in disputed questions, however sacred and important, though a good and necessary work, is not the mission of the Oratorian. The Franciscan might contend for our Lady's Immaculate Conception; the Jesuit for the doctrine of grace or the prerogatives of St Peter; but the Oratorian has as little as possible to do with these necessary controversies; he takes the doctrine, which others defend, and uses it. His studies, if he must study, lie in the first place in these two directions, in morals, and in the ritual. The Confessional, as we know, was St Philip's great instrument of conversion; and, as to the Ritual, the Fathers of the Chiesa Nuova used to be accounted the authoritative rubricians of Rome. From the Ritual the Oratorian is led at once to history, as we see in the instance of Baronius; the Martyrology, the Lives of Saints, the history of the Church at large, of dioceses, the antiquities of

Churches, Catacombs and other holy places, these are subjects characteristic of the Oratory, and it is obvious how great a field of research they open. Hence it is that, as the Jesuits, for instance, might appropriate polemics, or ascetics as their own province of writing, so to the Oratorian history and antiquities belong, a line of research in which the Jesuits have done very little.

But this is all quite consistent with adopting a controversial tone in the Oratory exercises, when dealing with Protestants. There controversy seems to come in as one of the means of conversion, being as effective in our day, as the preaching of children, as used in the Roman Oratory, might be in the age of St Philip. And in taking this view surely our Holy Father, the Pope, is our sanction, when he sent us to England with the words, "Estote fortes in bello, et pugnate cum etc."[6]

But more may be said from the history of St Philip in illustration of the position which we are assigning to his Oratory. His institution is a bond of union between seculars and regulars, partaking of the character of both; and it has always stood well with religious the most jealous of each other, as St Philip stood in his own day. His history in this respect is remarkable; he is educated among the Dominicans at Florence, and is so intimate with them at Rome that they entrust their novices to him; ⟨They brought in the Oratory to Lucca, and the *ragionamenti*[7] were held in their chapter house, on which occasion the Annalist remarks, that the Dominicans "have never omitted to promote the glory of St Philip, who from them had drank [sic] the first milk of devotion and the spirit." Ann. t 2 p 60⟩ yet S. Felice the Capuchin, is not the less his friend. Hence there has always been a special alliance between the Oratorians and Capuchins, as if they divided the complete idea of sanctity between them, and could not interfere with each other, the one taking the rude and ascetic, the other the splendid and cheerful side of Catholicism, the one not allowed even to have stone⟨?⟩ altars or the precious metals in their Churches, the other carrying embellishment to the utmost point consistent with

---

[6] i.e. "Be strong in battle and fight" (part of an Antiphon for the Apostles in the Breviary).

[7] i.e. St Philip's practice of familiar discourses on sacred subjects.

15

propriety; the one dressing in coarse brown serge⟨?⟩ with a
beard on their chin and no shoes on their feet; the other, grave
indeed and decorous, but with the manners and habits of a
man of the world. It was a Capuchin, who introduced the
Oratory into Casale, collecting large sums of money for the
purpose; and here too Marciani observes that there had been
an interchange of friendly offices between the Oratorians and
Capuchins ever since the days of St Philip and St Felix. ⟨t 3.
p 552.⟩ Accordingly an interesting account is given us in the
history of the Oratory of Perugia of a yearly Easter visit which
the Oratorians made to the Capuchin convent some way from
the town. "These loving Fathers," says Marciani of the Oratorians, "by way of giving honorable and devout recreation
to the seculars of the Oratory, are wont to take them after
Easter in a large company to the noviciate of the Capuchin
Fathers, placed in a most delightful spot, three miles from the
city; whither arriving, all go to confession, and are fed with
the flesh of the Immaculate Lamb, and take part in a devout
procession, each bringing for that purpose a candle from the
city. The procession forms a circuit through the wood which
belongs to those Fathers, and Christ in the Sacrament is
conducted, so to say, in a silvan triumph, . . . A decent altar is
prepared in the same wood, on which is placed the Most
August Sacrament, and meanwhile the Priest, vested in a cope,
makes a short but devout sermon, Thence returning to the
Church in procession they all receive the benediction, and
each leaves his candle to the Capuchin Fathers. Then they sit
down to a frugal dinner, laid out for them in the wood, where
with the entertainment of modest music and other decorous
pastimes they pass that day, as cheerfully as virtuously. In the
evening they return to the city, chanting the Te Deum on
parting, and saying litanies and other prayers on their way."
⟨t 3 p 561⟩

Two religious bodies there were, which rose simultaneously
with the Oratorians, and which were in some sort rivals of each
other and not over cordial, but with both of them the Oratorians were friends, the Theatines and the Jesuits. It is not so
wonderful perhaps that they were friends with the Jesuits, for
St Philip was a personal friend of St Ignatius, and bodies so

different from each other had little chance of interfering, but one does not see what there was to attract the Theatines, themselves a rising Congregation, to the Oratorians, yet we have already found, in the history of the Naples Oratory, with what zeal the Theatines took up their cause, and extended the influence of St Philip in spite of himself. The Oratorians, though not so strict in their rule as the Theatines, yet in many respects resembled them, and their members were taken from the same rank of society (which we have considered as the nursery of the Oratory).[8] Yet while the Theatines by a great effort placed the Oratorians close by them at Naples, St Philip himself at any [sic] earlier date had refused the offer of a rich Genoese to introduce the Oratory into his native city, but had sent him and his money to the Theatines. And as to the Jesuits, Bellarmine speaks of "the mutual affection, which had ever existed between the fathers of the Blessed Philip and his own company of Jesus." ⟨Annal. Orat. ii p 43.⟩ A Jesuit suggested the foundation of the Oratory of Aquila; a Jesuit was the origin of the Oratory at Forlì; and when the new Oratorian Church at Trapani fell down, "the distressed fathers", we are told, "were comforted by the great love of the children of the holy patriarch Ignatius, who, mindful of the great friendship which existed between the two holy founders and had been continued always without interruption between their children, ran speedily all of them to the Church of the Oratorio, and with their loving voices and affectionate behaviour exerted themselves to give some comfort to the sad fathers." ⟨Ann. t 3. pp 532,3.⟩

These are but specimens of the popularity which the Oratorians have enjoyed with all classes and bodies in the Church. They have been friends of all, and have had no enemies. It has been their blessing, as St Philip before them, and as the Divine Prototype of all excellence in the beginning, "to grow in favor with God and man." At this day, when so many orders have dwindled away, when so many are violently oppressed, when so many have been spoiled of their property, they remain in vigor and in honor in most of the cities in Italy. At Turin, I have been told, all the secular clergy were accustomed to go

---

[8]Bracketed, perhaps for omission, in MS.

to confession to their Church; when the French plundered the
Churches of Naples, the Oratorian alone was spared. They
have in their spacious sacristy the accumulated treasures of
three centuries, and Murat's wife made them a present of a
splendid set of vestments. In Spain they seem to have taken the
place of the Jesuits on their suppression.

NEWMAN'S ORATORY PAPERS No. 6
9 FEBRUARY 1848

INTRODUCTORY NOTE

Summary

1. The inward characteristic of the Oratory—a return to
   the very first form of Christianity.
2. St Philip invites his followers back to primitive times, by
   moulding a special Christian character in them.
3. The Oratorian is without external Rule for his conduct—
   St Philip formed a community without vows.
4. The Oratory as contrasted with Regular religious life—
   the laws on which the community moves are not external,
   but within. A living principle takes the place of formal
   enactment.
5. An Oratorian is almost the reverse of a Jesuit—Obedience
   to the official Superior is the prominent principle of the
   Jesuit, personal influence is that of the Oratorian.
6. In order to be able to act for himself as one of a body, the
   Oratorian needs to have had a liberal education.
7. Influence as the mainspring of the Oratory.

This text speaks for itself: a description of the Oratorian
ethos, particularly as contrasted with that of Regulars, especially the Jesuits. For an assessment of Newman's treatment
of the Jesuits in this Address, cf. above pp. 80–81; 140–41. His

criticisms of the Jesuits in *A.W.*, pp. 270, 271 (30 August 1874) are in a different mood to those contained here.

This is the first transcription ever made of this MS—which indeed proved very difficult to transcribe, being full of erasures, re-writing and minute directions to cross-references. The end result is rewarding, since we have nowhere else in his hitherto published works, such a closely finished picture of Newman's Oratorian ideal.

Stæ Apolloniæ[1].

After the view we have been taking of the external aspect of the Oratory, it follows to turn our thoughts to its inward characteristics. Now here it will be at least convenient, if not in all respects exact, to trace its peculiar genius to the circumstance that in some sense it is a return to the very first form of Christianity, as it existed in the lifetime of the Apostles.

It was then a very bold and original undertaking on the part of St Philip, more original perhaps than any thing in the Rule of St Ignatius. Primitive Christianity had been without decrees of faith, a rule of life, and rites for worship; I don't mean that Christianity ever was without a creed, a decalogue, or a sacrificial rite, but that there was a plainness and simplicity in the external laws of the primitive Church, whether as to doctrine, ethics or worship, peculiar to itself. Now in the sixteenth century, after heresies and schisms innumerable, St Philip comes forward to bring back all who will listen to him to primitive times, not by undoing what the Church had grown into, but by cultivating those inward tempers and moulding that special character to which in the Apostolic age such especial and prominent attention was given and to which in the event those latter decrees and ordinances are attributable.

As to doctrine, so far the Oratory resembled the primitive Church that it did not prominently cultivate theology for its own sake. As to the ritual the resemblance of the Oratorian exercises to the worship of the primitive Church is noticed by

[1]*B. Or. Ar.*, B. 9.3.

Baronius in the first volume of his Annals. After quoting the
1 Cor xiv and speaking of the primitive assembly for worship, he
continues; "It has happened certainly by a divine providence,
that in our time, thirty years since, for the most⟨?⟩ part after
the form of that Apostolic meeting, there has been at Rome,
especially as regards the sermons on divine subjects, which, as
leading to the edification of hearers, the Apostle injoins for the
benefit of the Church, so much instituted by means first of the
Revd F. Philip Neri, of Florence, who, as a wise master builder,
placed the foundation, and then of his disciple in Christ the
Revd F. Fr. M. Tarugi of Monte Pulciano, who in conducting
them has been the dux verbi. For by their zeal and diligence it
was originally instituted, that almost daily, such as were cultivating the Christian life with special ardour, met at the
Oratory of San Girolamo, (whence is given to our College the
name of the congregation of the Oratory,) and held their
religious assembly in the following order." ⟨Annal. t l. p. 473⟩
and there follows an account of the exercises of the Oratory as
held at San Girolamo.

And what the Oratories were in worship, such were they still
more strikingly in social converse—instead of vows or forcible
impositions, they held it was enough to have Christian love,
and· they cultivated that love, towards God and man and each
other, in the spirit of that great Apostle to whose inspired
writings St Philip had so special a devotion.

As to vows, St Philip's peremptory prohibition of them in his
Congregation need not be more than referred to. One of the
two immutable decrees of the Institution is, that they shall
never be introduced; and should it occur, the property of the
Congregation is even to pass to a minority which opposes the
change.

After St Philip's death, there was, in spite of this, an attempt
to introduce them, but the Pope would not listen to it.

But not only are there no vows, but the rule itself is so light
and general that in one sense the Oratorian is without external
rule for his conduct. I do not mean to say that the rule, such
as it really is, must not be accurately kept—we shall have
another opportunity of considering this, but that St Philip at
the very time when he insisted on its strict observance, grounded

that observance on his rules being so few; indeed they are hardly more than is necessary for barely keeping the community together. And in his time they were fewer than they are now, for in the course of the 17 years which followed St Philip's death, at which time they were confirmed by the Holy See, they had naturally increased in number. Indeed an inspection of the Rule so confirmed reveals several curious circumstances concerning its composition. St Philip did not write Constitutions as St Ignatius might do; but he laid down a few which were suited to the moment; these were added to when the Congregation was set up in the Vallicella with consent of the Fathers, and they had been extended further in the interval before 1612 the date of the Pope's confirmation. At that time Consolini was called on to draw up an account of the Oratory for the Pope's object, and what he seems to have done was, to write down the observances of the Congregation, interspersing them with such actual decrees, not of St Philip, but of the body itself which had from time to time been passed. E.g. "Our customs as to festivals," he says, "are so and so, as you will see by the following Decrees—" then they follow—"Our customs about daily intercourse are of this kind, and under this head fall the following Decrees of the Congregation." The Oratorian Rule then, is not, for the most part, the Rule of St Philip, but it is the successive decrees of the Congregation for the first 30 or 40 years of its existence, put together, illustrated by its customs, and ratified by the Pope. And, though we are of course bound to them most strictly, yet the mode of their coming into existence may fairly be taken to illustrate the character of the Institution, and the subordination in it of leges to mores; for thus as a matter of history the Congregation is not built on the rule, but the rule is the creation of the Congregation. And this is in fact intimated in the Rule itself, which commences by a declaration that St Philip's Congregation is "moribus potius erudita, quam legibus astricta," and that "nullam, ad Religiosorum hominum consuetudinem, propriam sibi regulam habuit, ad quam consultationes dirigeret rerum gerendarum.[2]" F. Ricci says the same, when he speaks of the Congregation living for the most part "ex jure non scripto."

[2]*Instituta Congregationis Anglicae Oratorii S. Philippi Nerii*, Rome 1847, p. 3.

St Philip then formed a community, yet without vows and almost without rules; and he aimed at doing this as I have said by forming in his disciples a certain character instead. This was a far more difficult and delicate work; so much so, that to attempt it was like, according to the proverb, attempting to put salt on the bird's tail. It might be objected that it was impossible for any set of men, left to themselves, without vows or stringent rules, to fulfil so high a calling. Yet St Philip effected it. And what he did and the gift he exercised was continued to his followers after him. The Oratory has never degenerated, but is at this day faithful both to its traditions and its spirit. It is still conducted on the free spirit of St Paul, and walks forward to its work, with the law written on the heart, not so much by external precepts, as by the light and truth within it.[3] "Quicumque spiritu Dei aguntur," he says, "ii sunt filii Dei; non enim accepistis spiritum servitutis iterum in timore, sed accepistis spiritum adoptionis filiorum.[4]" This was the spirit of Oratorians; they presented their bodies "hostiam viventem, sanctam, Deo placentem, rationabile obsequium vestrum.[5]" They were filled omni gaudio et pace in credendo, abounding in spe et virtute Spiritus Sancti, pleni omni dilectione, repleti omni scientiâ.[6]

It was St Philip's object therefore, instead of imposing laws on his disciples, to mould them, as far as might be into living laws, or, in the words of Scripture, to write the law on their hearts. This is what the great philosopher of antiquity had considered the perfection of human nature; this is what is so frequently brought before us in Scripture, especially in St Paul's Epistles. It is what the holy Patriarchs of the Regulars, St Benedict, St Dominic, St Francis, St Ignatius, and the rest,

---

[3]The following text was erased by Newman: Yet he effected it; he was pre-eminently a guide of souls, he had penitents for years and years under his guidance; Baronius and Tarugi professed to be his novices all their days; and thus he was able to mould individuals . . . so that the Congregation went forward, self-moved, and throve and guided itself, not so much by external precept, as by the light and truth within it.

[4]*Rom.* 8:14.

[5]*Rom.* 12:1.

[6]*Rom.* 15:13,14.

had felt to be beyond them, (and which is, humanly speaking, impossible when any extended body is concerned; but) which in primitive times was possible in separate communities, and which St Philip revived, or rather reformed, reducing into something like system what in the case of the early monks silence and contemplation for the most part superseded.

But here we have touched upon a distinction which separates the Oratory from all monachism, early as well as late. In small congregations as well as large, in the monks of Egypt or Gaul as well as in those of the middle ages, monachism was a ceremonial, it was a lifelong function. In the habit and cowl, in the shorn crown, in the bare feet, there was the nature of a sacerdotal or ministerial habit; in their silence, in their nice adjustment of hours, in their chantings, in their fasts, in their disciplines, in their routine of observances, we have the majestic course of the great rite. And this applies, not only to the early and later monks, and the friars, but in modern times to those who have thrown off the name and in great measure the habit of monachism, such as the Jesuits. It is impossible to mistake the character of religious and regular discipline stamped on the exterior of the Jesuit by the influence of the long spiritual exercises and the almost military usages of their tradition. His look is imposing; his speech measured. Look at him as represented in a picture. You know by his staid and upright figure, his downcast or uplifted eyes, his abstracted countenance; and his high biretta. Contrast this with the picture of one of the first Oratorians and a contemporary of St Philip in the Borghese collection at Rome, by Andrea Sacchi. He sits in an easy chair, in a lounging posture, one hand stretched on a table, with bright sparkling eyes and a merry countenance. Here you have a type of the exterior of an Oratorian compared with a regular.

Of course it requires some limitation—the Oratorian dinner, and the Exercises of the Oratory themselves are of a regular character; and the very fact of there being an Oratorian Rule of course implies that in a certain point of view we may be considered regulars; for no body can be kept together without rules, and so far forth as we cease to be mere seculars by entering the Oratory, so far we begin to be regulars. This limitation however, does not interfere with the general truth

of the contrast presented by[7] a Regular and an Oratorian. I
conceive that an Oratorian Congregation[8] is in its external
aspect a Democracy. Enter into the house, join the community
in recreation, as for instance at Naples. The old and young are
present together, and talk together with ease and freedom.
The giovani[9] are pleasant, brightfaced, modest looking youths,
silent perhaps because they are young and backward in giving
their opinion, but they have nothing of the external gravity,
composed attitude, and reserve of a Jesuit novice. Every one
seems to be acting at his own discretion[10]—he acts from himself
—the laws on which the community moves are not external
but within—it is selfmoved. As is commonly observed the
Superior is never to say "I command", but always "I wish;"
and it is recorded even of St Philip that he never used the
words "I command" but once. It is the common sense, the
delicacy, the sharp observation, the tact of each which keeps
the whole in harmony. It is a living principle, call it (in human
language) judgment or wisdom or discretion or sense of propriety or moral perception, which takes the place of formal
enactment—according to the passage in the Psalms,[']I will
give thee understanding, and instruct thee in the way wherein
thou walkest; I will fix on thee Mine eyes[']. "Be ye not like to
horse and mule, which have no understanding; bind thou
their mouths with bit and bridle who come not nigh Thee."[11]
I may be rather exaggerating the contrast, but I will risk
doing so, in order to bring out at length what is substantially
true. An Oratorian as I have said is in a great measure a law
to himself, and is almost the reverse so far of a regular, for
instance a Jesuit. A Jesuit has a rule to fall back upon; when
he wants to know how to act, he recurs to it. He keeps it
before him, and therefore may be almost content with an
external view of others, with whom he has to act— He views
them in the light of the rule, he measures them by the rule, he
only knows them in the rule. The rule is to settle all disputes

[7]alternative in MS: existing between.
[8]original draft: House.
[9]original draft:novices
[10]original draft: pleasure.
[11]*Psalm* 31:9.

and difficulties between him and them—and obedience to a Superior is to complete whatever the rule may leave vague or obscure. Far different is the duty of an Oratorian: his rule does little for him—his community life is not determined by the rule; it will not remain in its perfection by a mere observance of it. He is not able to trust himself to it by a blind obedience, but he must be taught that the well-conduct of the house depends on each as a first spring of action. The course of things, to run smooth, is committed to the keeping of each member. Each in his place must stand with his eyes about him, and work independently of others, though in cooperation with them. Each is to be bound to each by a personal attachment; each must throw himself into the minds of the rest, and try to understand them, to consult for them, to take their hints, and to please them[12]. If we wish for an illustration, one is provided in the difference which existed between the Greek Phalanx and the Roman legion:—in the phalanx the soldiers were closely knit into each other, in the legion each stood and fought with free space for his weapons and his movements. "The legion," says Gibbon, "was usually drawn up eight deep; and the regular *distance of three feet* was left between the files as well as ranks. A body of troops, habituated to preserve this open order, in a long front and a rapid charge, found themselves prepared to execute every disposition, which the circumstances of war, or the skill of the leader, might suggest. The soldier possessed a free space for his arms and motions, and sufficient intervals were allowed through which seasonable reinforcements might be introduced to the relief of the exhausted combatants. The tactics of the Greeks and Macedonians were formed on very different principles. The strength of the phalanx depened on sixteen ranks of long pikes, wedged together in the closest array. But it was soon discovered by reflection, as well as by the event, that the strength of the phalanx was unable to contend with the activity of the legion."[13]

Thus to shift for oneself, to depend upon's own resources, consideration, fellow feeling, knowledge of character, tact, good

---

[12]erasure: Tact, not obedience to the Rule is the life of
[13]*The Decline and Fall of the Roman Empire,* Chapter I.

judgement are the characteristics of⟩ an Oratorian whereas the Jesuit does not know what tact is, cannot enter into the minds of others, and is apt to blunder in most important matters from this habit of mechanical obedience to a Superior and a system.

Of course I am not speaking of certain gifted men among the Jesuits, such as St Francis Xavier, or the China Missionaries, or the Fathers at Paraguay—but take the run of Jesuits at this day, and I can't help thinking you will find, among a hundred high qualities, a want of sagacity and mental dexterity in meeting the age, and the men and difficulties belonging to it. The great Saint, their founder, was a soldier—and they are in a certain sense a military body. They are the Knight Templars of modern history. They have excellence [sic] and the fault of soldiers; they are perfect as an organized bodies [sic], but, as individuals, they are often little more than mechanical instruments, and are least of all men able to deal with strangers or with enemies, not to say with friends. Let it not be supposed that I am extenuating the merits of the Company of Jesus. The debt which Catholics owe them is vast; they are a body of men, as hardworking as they are devout; their houses breathe the spirit of religion. Their renown is far higher than that of the humble Oratory. I am but speaking of them in a particular point of view and as contrasted with Oratorians; and so contrasted, I say, that Jesuit Fathers are part of a whole, but each Oratorian stands by himself and is a whole, promoting and effecting by his own proper acts the wellbeing of the community.

There is a comparison between Athenians and Spartans in the celebrated funeral oration of Pericles[14]; which illustrates what I would say: The point of the Orator's praise of the Athenians is this, that they, unlike the Spartans, have no need of laws, but perform from the force of inward character those great actions which others do from compulsion. Here the Oratorian stands for the Athenian, and the Spartan for the Jesuit. The mere allusion might be sufficient, but I will translate some sentences of it to recall to our memories what once we knew better than we do now.

[14] Cf. *L.D.*, XII, pp. 112–3, letter to T. F. Knox of 14 September 1847, where the comparisons between Athenians and Spartans, phalanx and legion, are also applied to the Oratorians and the Jesuits.

"Our form of government ⟨πολίτεια⟩ is one which needs not to borrow from ⟨ζηλούσῃ⟩ the institutions of others, being rather an example than a copy. (And in name indeed, it is called democracy, for that the power pertains to the) . . . And we carry on ⟨πολιτεύομεν⟩ our public matters on principles of liberty, so that, unsuspicious in our daily intercourse with each other, no resentment do we feel, if our neighbour acts to please himself, not even in our countenance bearing looks, which, though they harm not, yet annoy . . . And it is our wont to provide for our minds very frequent intermissions from our labours, having a custom of games and sacrifices, as the year goes on, and of the displays of private magnificence, whereof the daily enjoyment expels sadness. . . . As to education, they (the Lacedemonians), with a laborious exercise, ⟨ἄσκησις⟩ even from boyhood, follow after bravery ⟨ἄνδρειον⟩; but we, living (as we do,) at our ease, ⟨ἀνειμένως⟩ still sally forth with no inferior spirit to theirs, against perils when they come . . . And what though we choose to present ourselves to danger, after remissness rather than laborious discipline, and not so much by the schooling of laws as from a manly disposition? this gain we at least thereby, that we have no previous anxiety of coming sorrows, though when we come into them, we show equal prowess as those who are come toiling.

"And hence we cultivate the beautiful with frugality, and philosophy without effeminacy . . . And we have the power of being at once critical and original, not thinking that discipline is any detriment to action, but rather the want of previous information. It is our peculiarity at once to calculate yet to dare: but to others to be without instruction makes men rash, and to premeditate makes them backward . . . whereas we have individually the versatility to present ourselves to the most various kinds of action, and to be graceful in doing so[15]."

Now if we go on to inquire *how* the two Institutions, the Oratorian and the Jesuit, proceed in the formation of their respective characteristics, we shall find that each pursues a method different from that of the other, and necessary and congenial to itself. Obedience to the official Superior is the

---

[15]Thucydides, *Peloponnesian War*, II, 35–46. [Greek accents as in MS.]

prominent principle of the Jesuit; personal influence is that of the Oratorian. The Jesuit is formed chiefly by the celebrated Exercises which Our Lady[16] is said to have given to St Ignatius; the Oratorian is what he is, owing in no small measure to his existing place in society and his secular education. A few remarks shall be made on these points of contrast.

First, I think it, to say the least, a question, whether the wonderful Exercises, which are the characteristic and boast of the Jesuit, as the Rosary of the Dominican and the Scapular of the Carmelite are quite in keeping with the peculiar genius of the Oratory.[17] It will be observed that the daily Oratory is technically called "the Exercises" of St Philip—and it may be with some reason represented that the Saint intended them or at least daily exercises of some sort, to be his peculiar mode of disciplining the heart and strengthening the character. St Ignatius's process partakes of his own genius, it is high, powerful, tragic, and decisive—but it is more consistent with the gentle and amiable character of St Philip's rule to fear a process which, with all the prudence of the director, has a tendency to throw the subject of them into a state of excitement, and bids him to decide on momentous questions when it may be he is unable coolly to make the decision; more like St Philip to attempt a gradual and imperceptible change, and to invoke from heaven an influence which shall come "as the rain upon the tender herb and as the dew drops on the grass (Deut 32)." As far as I have searched, I do not find among the Oratorians of the 17th century traces of the use of the Exercises of St Ignatius in their retreats. Retreats they had, as all religious persons must have, but we read of Sozzini, for instance, that "every year he set apart some days for a stricter retirement, in order to attend in them with singular fervour to prayer and meditation on the things of God," ⟨p 222⟩ not a word being said about the Exercises of St Ignatius.

And there is a passage in the life of F. Magnanti of Aquila, which, though it relates to giving the Exercises to numbers, or

[16]original erased draft: St Mary

[17]original erased draft: I hope I am not making a hasty generalization, when I should say that the special Jesuit Spiritual Exercises form a part of the contrast between Jesuit and Oratorian.

Missions, as they are called, yet, as far as it goes, tends to discourage the adoption of such Exercises themselves. The account is long, but instructive, and I will translate parts of it.

"As F Magnanti was endowed with great talent and facility of ministering the divine word, his reputation was extended, not only into the neighbouring, but into distant cities, who eagerly desired to participate in that heavenly bread. He was even invited to this by the Bishops of these cities who were sometimes Cardinals, and by many Congregations of the Oratory . . . However, we must not omit to say that the Fathers of the Oratory, being customarily contented with their daily Exercises as instituted by their holy Founder, were with difficulty induced to embrace Spiritual exercises besides them, and foreign, so to say, to their institution. Accordingly, in his course through various cities to sow the divine word, the Servant of God received advice from various persons in his confidence, who, moved by zeal for the purity of the Institution, dissuaded him from giving these missions, and adopting spiritual Exercises other than its own . . . Being dissuaded then from leaving his own country for the aforesaid purpose, he set about justifying himself, bringing in his defence various reasons in certain letters, which he wrote on the subject to Fathers of the Roman Congregation." The annalist goes on to say that F Magnanti felt himself really called to this work, that he met with great success, that he acted with the approbation of spiritual persons whom he had consulted; moreover that he gave these Exercises in Churches of the Oratory, and not without the permission of his Superiors. "All this," continues our author, "should be considered by every member of the Oratory who is desirous to imitate him on this point; without the presence of these conditions he would be exposing himself to the evident risk of going wrong, not without detriment to the Institution which he has embraced." ⟨Annal t. 3 p 391⟩. So much on the question of the Exercises.

And as the absence of spontaneous action is the scope to which the Jesuit Exercises, as well as training, is directed, so the cultivation of those semi-ethical qualifications, above described, which enable the man to act for himself as one of a body, is the end of the training of the Oratory. Hence it is that its members are taken out of educated and more refined classes; for the virtues in question, I mean gentle demeanour, considera- tion, delicacy, elasticity of mind and the like are more commonly found among those classes than among others. There is a far greater tendency to misunderstandings, jealousies, irritation, resentment and contention, when the mind has not been cul- tivated or what is called enlarged, than when books and the intercourse of society and the knowledge of the world have served to put things in their true light, to guard the mind from exaggeration, to make it patient of differences, and to give it self command amid differences of opinion and conduct. I do not mean to say that the virtues I have mentioned are necessarily Christian—but they are Christian *in* a Christian—When a Christian mind takes them up into itself they cease to be secular, they are sanctified by their possessor, and become the instru- ments of spiritual good. And their advantage is undeniable; we have but to reflect upon the petty quarrels which are apt to divide religious houses, the rivalries, the punctilios and the misconceptions, and those again which exist in such very serious and aggravated forms in the world at large to appreciate the influence of a liberal education and the experience of life in enabling the mind to be at once calm yet observant and versatile⟨?⟩.

Here it may be worth while to mention that music is necessarily a study in the Oratory; and its softening effect is notorious— nay in some persons it operates, as it is described to do in Scripture in the case of Saul[18] and Eliseus, as a kind of medicine with a medicinal virtue in those who are subject to its sweet influence. ⟨Nay more tact etc. contrasted with drawing. On the other hand music is pointedly excluded from the occupations of the Jesuit.⟩

Of the same nature is the long noviceship longer by one half even than the Jesuit, and three times the length of the noviciate in the Orders in general. Such too are the traditionary spirit, the pattern of superiors, the superintendence of the Director[19], and the training of the Novicemaster.

[18]cf. 1 *Sam.* 16:16; 2 *Kings* 3:15.
[19]first draft (not erased): advice of the Confessor.

In this point of view the position of the Father Director Confessor is most important. He is at once Confessor and Director; and, since by the Rule there should be but one Director to the whole body, he is a silent influence exerted continually towards the cultivation of a real and inward love of member towards member, and a watchful and prompt observance and evasion of all the small hindrances which are likely to interrupt the equable course of the day.

It would seem indeed that influence, whether secret or open, is the mainspring of the Oratory, and here again is directly opposed to the Society of Jesus. By the latter personal influence is feared and instantly destroyed. It is not allowed a Father, of any talent or strength of mind, to remain in one and the same Community. If he gets power over others, he is at once sent away to another house. But the very primary constitution of the Oratory forces, were it necessary, a contrary discipline upon the Congregation—For where are such persons as I am speaking of to go? it would be worse than ostracism to send them out of the Congregation, and the very Congregation in which they are is the *whole* of the Oratory. It has not a multitude of provinces and houses as the Jesuits. The fewness of the numbers in an Oratory is another preparation for the exercise of influence. The Rule speaks of the notorum vultus[20]; the members are not to be so many as not to know each other; now mutual knowledge in beginning, is the parent of influence. Here again the Jesuits do not know the word "home"; they are emphatically strangers and pilgrims upon earth; whereas the very word "nido" is adapted to produce a soothing influence and to rouse a fraternal feeling in the heart of the Oratorian. The Oratorian, as we see in the touching address of Baronius, cited in my last lecture, lives in the hearts of his brethren; but the Jesuit meets and parts with Jesuit in resigned, mortified, I will add cold spirit, which becomes those who have emphatically put off all earthly feelings and ties.

Influence then may be said to do for the Oratorian, what Rules do for the Jesuit; and if we wish for an example, we cannot have one more apposite than that of St Philip himself,

[20]ed. 1847, Caput IV, Decretum XV, p. 13.

16

of whom personal anecdotes abound whether in books or in the traditions of Rome, whereas though St Ignatius lived so long there, it is, I conceive, just the portion of his life of which very little is preserved.

Lastly what the Oratory is within among its own members, such is it in its intercourse with the faithful outside its walls. It exercises, not power but influence; it dislikes whatever savours of pomp, pretence, or violence. It has a hidden life; it doth not cry, nor strive, neither is its voice heard in the streets; and this was one of the reasons of the objections to F. Magnanti's Exercises, that he was leaving home, and permitting a publicity which was unsuited to the character of the Oratory.

NEWMAN'S ORATORY PAPERS No. 7
17 JUNE 1848

INTRODUCTORY NOTE

The community was still in Maryvale at this period: 17 June 1848 was a Saturday (see *L.D.*, XII, p. 226).

The opening sentence of this Address can only refer to the 'Third Address' given above, of the *Early Chapter Addresses of 1848,* and confirms the fact that these hitherto unidentified MSS were, in fact, Chapter Addresses.

On the community life of the nascent Oratorian body, which this and the two following Addresses pre-suppose, see *Trevor* 1, p. 437–8, where she makes the point that it is difficult to reconstruct the atmosphere of this period in detail, since, as they were all together, there are few letters about it. See also above, p. 141.

For the underlying equation between the Oratory and life in an Oxford college, and the significance of this for Newman's concept of community life as a Catholic (in contrast to his more ascetical community life as an Anglican in Littlemore) see above pp. 23-5.

CHAPTER ADDRESS 17 JUNE 1848[1]

June 17/48 behaviour towards those who are without 2
Second[2].

I have in a former chapter, said that the Oratory is in many
respects like a College. So it is undeniably. The absence of vows,
of penitential discipline, of external subordination and submission, and the like give it very much the character of a body
of men who have come together of their own accord and may
part of their own accord, as if vocation had no place in such a
life, or rather as if it were not a life or state, but an accidental
position in which a person found himself. But still it is not really
this, as I have also observed, but has really a character of its
own, and is to be chosen as an end. If however it is externally
not exactly what it is, or if it seems to others to be what it
really is not, there is of course the danger that it should seem so
to ourselves—We may easily come to think it is so, and if we
do, we shall not only mistake our place and duties, but we may
really unawares offend others and become an additional party
in this country, when what we lament more than anything else
is the divisions and jealousies which exist among Catholics. I
will say a few words on this important subject.

Let it be considered then that any body of men is likely to
become an object of suspicion and jealousy to their equals,
who do not belong to them. for as being a body they seem to be
exclusive, and having privileges attached to them, they challenge the question whether they deserve them more than
others. Thus capitular and monastic bodies are disliked by
seculars, for this if for no other reason, that they are bodies, and
invest the individuals though individuals which compose them
with the power of the whole body. On the other hand there is a
natural temptation in the case of those individuals themselves,
to presume upon their being members of a body, to give themselves airs, and to make themselves disagreeable to those who
have not their special advantages.

The danger is mitigated in the case of monastic bodies by the

[1]*B. Or. Ar.* D. 4.9.
[2]This heading is pencilled in Newman's handwriting beside the date.

nature of their discipline. In the first place they lead a hard life, and so far are not objects of envy. It is true they have distinctions, but they are distinctions of discomforts as well as satisfaction—and it is a question whether the pleasures of the imagination make up for such sensible humiliations and sufferings as cold, hunger, sleeplessness, labour, silence and absolute submission to their superiors. They have given up their freedom, they are slaves—all this is adapted to disarm jealousy, while the discipline of mind which it implies ought to annihilate in the subjects of it that self-satisfied supercilious temper which in the case of other privileged bodies especially provokes it.

Now let it be observed, to go no further than this, that we have none of this bodily or personal mortification. We have nothing about us to lead men to feel sympathy in us, to compassionate us, to admire or revere us—nothing to subdue ourselves. We shall thus in both ways provoke the jealousy of the world, unless we are very much on our guard.

But further than this, it so happens, according to the good pleasure and kind providence of God, that we are, and apparently we shall be, better educated than the run of secular priests. We shall be, and it is to be hoped that we shall be, for such is the character of our Institution. But it must be recollected that this is one most serious cause of jealousy and distance on the part of others, and that, both from their fault and the fault of those who are the objects of these feelings.

We need only look at the Colleges of our Universities to see how this operates, how a particular name is given to particular Societies, and an especial aversion felt for them from the circumstance that their members have more talent or learning than ordinary. Now of course we are chiefly concerned with this disadvantage as far as in our own case it would be our own fault, and unless we pay anxious attention to it, we are sure to occasion it, through heedlessness and inattention, if in no other way.

It must be borne in mind that superior advantages of education are certain of producing a certain superciliousness or what looks like such, if it be not guarded against. I mean, persons of good taste cannot admire, cannot but be offended at, cannot but laugh at, the sayings and doings of persons of bad taste. Quite innocently, and without any intention of giving offence, they will give grievous offence by taking a high tone, by what seems like affecting superiority, by not entering into the reasonings or jokes of persons whose intellects are less refined, when they come into their society. It requires very little refinement of mind, to understand this. We all of us smile, or are offended e.g. at the advertisements and other things we see in the publications of our brother Catholics, such as the Tablet. Now as far as we really think those things injurious to the cause of religion or in other respects wrong, it is right to object to them—nor of course is there anything blameable, in a laugh among ourselves at things which we all feel to be absurd or vulgar. But I do think, and I speak from the experience which one has of years past, that there is the greatest need of caution, of recollecting always when we speak what we say, and before whom we say it, and to whom it may get who hear us not, through those who hear us.

But further. I have been speaking of the danger of thoughtlessness in our judgments and words, but the danger is greater than this. There is a very great danger I am persuaded of our body getting (and partly justly) a character of uppishness, flippancy, criticalness and the like, from neglect of mortifying those tendencies which lead to these odious results. Of course, my dear Brothers, you do not think I am speaking of an existing evil, but of tendencies and dangers, and those in the nature of things. It is in the nature of things as I have all along been saying, that you should tend to these results, if you are not on your guard. I am going to say things strongly and even abruptly, merely to teach you what to avoid. You will then infallibly look down on other people (not as moral beings but intellectually) if you do not take much pains to avoid it, you will have a sort of understanding and freemasonry one with another, you will put up your own standard of things as the right one, you will have a marked distinguishable character in the world, you will have almost your party tenets, your favourite doctrines, you will go against other people and bodies, and you will be a school, instead of a modest courteous Congregation of St Philip.

I have already hinted at the divisions in the Catholic body

in England[3]—*your* mission is to lessen them, to destroy them, to bind together in one, good men whom perverse circumstances or rather I suppose our Enemy is keeping separate from one another. But if you do not strive to do this, if you do not tend to do this, depend upon it, you will become the objects, and the subjects of similar jealousies yourselves. You know at this minute we have much to overcome, let us do our best to overcome it.

It is very difficult to draw the line, and far be it from me to weigh any one's words sentence by sentence—but I urge on you to repress, as far as may be, a critical *spirit*—be on your guard against it—do not be fond of finding fault—take everything in the best point of view—and, as far as you can, speak well of people. Not only be humble, but let your humility take such a form that, without your intending it, people may be moved by it. Do not put yourselves forward—do not talk much before others—do not argue much except in private, and when you are sure of people and never dispute and debate, *avoid* argument, when offered and be on your guard against saying strong things, or even sharp things. Meditate on the odiousness of smartness, flippancy, and overbearingness—till you are disgusted with them, and feel the bad taste, not to say the moral impropriety, of such exhibitions. Modesty, gravity, gentleness, cheerfulness, tranquillity, these are the tempers suitable to an Oratorian.

And lastly, let us recollect how much the honour and good repute of the body depends on every individual of us. Any one of you may (I was going to say) ruin the body. You may stamp it with a character from which it may but slowly and by great exertions recover. As then you are devoted to St Philip, as you love his sweetness and tenderness, as you are loyal to his Congregation, as you wish the Name of the Oratory to be blessed among us and the generations after us, as you love each other and feel an interest in each other, let each look to it seriously lest he bring discredit upon the fair fame of St Philip and his children. Let not that Institution which in Italy has

---

[3]At this very moment Newman was engaged in defending Faber against Pugin. See *L.D.*, XII, p. 435 "Newman on Gothic architecture." On the row about the *Lives of the Saints*, see ib. "Newman on saints."

been a bond of peace and a praise upon earth, suffer in England from you. Aim at being something more than mere University men, such as we all have been. Let grace perfect nature, and let us, as Catholics, not indeed cease to be what we were, but exalt what we were into something which we were not. Do not throw away those advantages, which God has given you, but perfect them for his service, and cherish, aim at having, a profound sense that these advantages are gifts not graces, talents to be improved, loans from the author of all good, for which we shall all have to give an account at the last day. And let us pray for each other, as well as for ourselves, that the gifts he has given us may not be squandered on ourselves, and used for our own gratification or our own reputation, but for His glory and the good of His Church.

——————

NEWMAN'S ORATORY PAPERS No. 8

30 JUNE 1848

INTRODUCTORY NOTE

The leading ideas of this Address on fraternal charity may be found already in the earlier Oratory Papers. Thus for the idea 'Love was to stand in the place of vows' see above p. 204 and in the appendices, the Santa Croce Papers, Final Draft, August/September 1848. For the assessment of this central theme of Newman's Oratorian spirituality (Obedience based on spontaneous love, not on vows) see above, pp. 115-8.

On St Philip Neri's devotion to the Epistles of St Paul, cf. the same Final Draft of the Santa Croce Papers, *On Obedience*. On the parallel which Newman often draws between St Philip and St Paul, see above Note 11 to Chapter 6, p. 91.

CHAPTER ADDRESS 30 JUNE 1848[1]

In commemor. Sti. Pauli. 1848

? *First*

behaviour towards each other

If I were to pursue the line of subjects which from time to time I have been putting down on paper, in illustration of the Oratorian character and mission I should now come to the subject of fraternal charity.

St Philip, we know, founded his Congregation in charity—making it the distinguishing mark by which his children were different from regulars, that what regulars did from observance of the sanctity of their vow, the Oratorian was to do from love. Love was to stand in the place of vows.

(I should, if I proceeded regularly with my subject, I should now come to charity, not as if I meant to pass over it, but because I feel that it is a subject too great for me to treat of, even in part. I do not therefore make any such profession, nor) shall I say any thing systematic or formal on so great a subject, but I will set down two or three remarks which may suggest something for our guidance in endeavouring to advance in this highest of Christian graces as well as essential characteristic of the Oratory.

And first I need hardly remind you how special a distinction it is of the Oratory. I have given some instances of the fraternal love of the Oratorians one to another in a former of these chapters. Thus I think I have given the following—(but I repeat them since they come into my mind.) We are told of one of the first fathers of the Chiesa Nuova, F Fideli that at the end of his life, his one exhortation to his brothers, was, like St John, "Brethren, love one another." And F. Velli, another, in his last moments, called all his brethren to take leave of him, and when one was still absent, who was (I think) saying Mass, he waited for him impatiently, as if he could not die in peace, till he had seen him. When he came, he folded him in his arms, and died;— as if fraternal love had been his ruling passion.[2]

[1]*B. Or. Ar.*, D. 4.9.
[2]See Santa Croce Papers Second Paper, 3 Genius of the Congregation: the same example resumed in *Remarks on the Oratorian Vocation*, below, p. 331.

But it must be confessed such instances *are* instances of a
passion or affection. and we cannot at a moment by willing or
by trying bring ourselves into such a state. We cannot have a
personal love towards individuals without going through
a course of discipline, in order to obtain it, without much care
and watchfulness, without knowing them well, without observing many minute rules. These rules may of course be multiplied:
—I will set down one or two which strike me.

1. It is our duty, as Oratorians, especially to look on ourselves as one body;—and ourselves individually as members of
that one body. Or, to throw this (what may be called) doctrinal
truth in to the form of precept, we ought, what St Paul calls,
to "bear one's [sic] another's burdens. The Apostle immediately
connects this duty with the essence (or rather the integrity)
of the law of charity. Alter alterius onera portate, he says, et
sic adimplebitis legem Xti; but, we know, the law of Christ is
love. What I mean by bearing each other's burdens is simply
this: that every one in his place should not only do his own
duty, but should try to support and cheer others in theirs.
The Superiors should do all in their power to make the duties
of those submitted to them light and pleasant, and they in
turn should be like Aaron and Hur (Ex 17) holding up Moses'
hands when he was tired. ⟨Do not be content with barely doing
your duty up to the necessary mark. but throw your heart in
it—nay more, do the duty of others, and when you help them
do it with that delicacy, genialness and goodnature that they
may feel it, not an encroachment, but a real kindness, and be
grateful to you.⟩ It is with great satisfaction and comfort that I
have observed instances of all this in your bearing towards
others. I have seen in you an eager offering of your services,
when any extra work pressed upon a father, a desire to make
yourselves in any way as useful as you can; nay I know it is
quite a habit of some of you, but it is still not without its use to
bring it distinctly, that you may aim at fulfilling the precept
more perfectly. Another part of the same excellent habit of
mind is that of hiding as far as it is right the imperfections or
deficiencies or mistakes of others, not drawing them into open
view, putting them aside from one's mind, and dwelling upon
their strong point or aimable points of character—so as to

depend upon, and make use of what is best in them, while we supply and assist what might be better[3].

It is part of the same excellent habit not to do things grudgingly, but, as far as we can, to rise and do at once what we are prompted or called to do for others: to avoid any unnecessary criticism ⟨observation⟩, knowing that any one can look on and see faults, but few persons can act without committing a great many: not to say a thing behind a person's back which we would not say to his face; and, though it be hard to practice [sic] it, to be mild and conceding in proportion as another is tempted to impetuosity or irritation.

It follows from one remark I have made, to state what I conceive to be our duty when we see any thing going wrong. I do not wish in this or any other respect to do more than give general rules, or to draw the line with rigour; but, as a rule, it would seem best, when we see or think we see any thing going wrong, great or small, not to talk of it, but to mention it privately to the person it concerns, the head of the department or the like. Thus if the lamp for the Blessed Sacrament was frequently extinguished, or if the brothers had too much their own way, or if the ceremonies are in any point wrong, it would be right to mention the circumstance to the F. Sacristan, or Father Minister, or Father Ceremonier, and to leave the matter there with him;—but not to be in the practice of talking of the mistake, opinion, view or whatever it is to others.

It is almost saying the same thing over again, yet perhaps it is a distinct view to place it in, to say that it is a duty, in a certain sense, for us to have all things common. There is a sense in which this is not true, for we know perfectly well that each of us *stipendiis militat propriis*. Our property, whatever it be, is our own, and there may be duties upon it external to the Congregation. But our persons, if I may so speak, are not our own—our time, our thought, our trouble, our abilities, are not our own. Thus it is a rule of the Congregation that no father can refuse an office put upon him. He may feel himself unfit for it, he may feel himself unrequited in it, it may involve relations to others who do not respond to his zeal and self-

[3]MS: next page.

denying kindness, as in the case of the Prefect of the Oratory, still the ultimate determination of his position and his duties, depends, not on him, but on the Congregation. When he became an Oratorian, he gave himself up, and became the property of others. And in like manner, as far as may be, there should be a common mind in the Congregation—each should profit by the advantages of the others—What proceeds from the Congregation of a theological, or literary kind, should be the work of all—I mean, that no one is to exhaust what he has of learning or resources on his own name, or should seek the aggrandiziment [sic] of his own name, but should freely give to others, be willing for others to have the credit, of his own labour, knowledge or ability.

Moreover, we should have a simple confidence in each other. Feeling that we love others and wish them well, we should in turn believe that they are in all things our best and kindest and truest friends. We should be very open with them; avoiding, as far as may be all suspicion or jealousy, and trying to give them no cause for any towards us. We should get rid of all reserve and distance towards each other—and we should try not to be afraid of each other. And, as not fearing them, we should feel we have no need to colour what we say, or to get round them, or manage them, having care the while that our simplicity does not degenerate into rudeness or indelicacy. We should have as few secrets as possible—taking care, that, when we have them, they are justifiable on some clear principles, and not from any spirit of exclusiveness or division.

And with a view to attain in some measure to these good feelings and practices, it would be well to follow St Philip's pattern in making much of the Epistles of the great Apostle, Mundi Magister atque Doctor Gentium, according to the Hymn we have just been using

Egregie Doctor Paule, *mores instrue*
Et nostra tecum *pectora* in caelum trahe.
Velata dum meridiem cernat fides,
Et, solis instar, *sola regnat charitas.*

His exhortations are more than any others perhaps calculated to rouse in us the spirit of brotherly love, and we may receive them as spoken to us Oratorians by St Philip. Rom 12 Sicut in uno corpore multa membra habemus, . . . ita multi unum corpus sumus in Christo, singuli autem alter *alterius* membra; . . . Dilectio sine simulatione—charitate fraternitatis invicem diligentes—honore invicem praevenientes—sollicitudine non pigri—spiritu ferventes. Domino servientes—spe gaudentes— . . . orationi instantes— . . . idipsum invicem sentientes— Rom 14 Nemó enim nostrum sibi vivit, et nemo sibi moritur—sive enim vivimus Domino vivimus, sive morimur Domino morimur . . . Quae pacis sunt sectemur—et quae aedificationis sunt, in invicem custodiamus . . . Rom 15 Unusquisque vestrum proximo suo placeat in bonum ad aedificationem . . . Eph 4 Loquimini veritatem unusquisque cum proximo suo; quoniam sumus invicem membra. Irascimini et nolite peccare. sol non occidat super iracundiam vestram . . . Omnis amaritudo, et ira, et indignatio, et clamor, et blasphemia tollatur a vobis . . . estote invicem benigni, misericordes, donantes invicem sicut et Deus in Christo donavit vobis . . . Eph 5 Loquentes vobismetipsis in psalmis, et hymnis, et canticis spiritualibus, cantantes et psallentes in cordibus vestris Domino; . . . subjecti invicem in timore Christi . . . Phil 2 Implete gaudium meum, ut idem sapiatis, eandem charitatem habentes, unanimes, idipsum sentientes, nihil per contentionem, neque per inanem gloriam, sed in humilitate superiores sibi invicem arbitrantes, non quae sua sunt singuli considerantes, sed ea quae aliorum. Hoc enim sentite in vobis, quod et in Christo Jesu; —Col 3 supportantes invicem, et donantes vobismetipsis si quis adversus aliquem habet querelam; sicut et Dominus donavit vobis, ita et vos. Super haec, charitatem habete, quod est vinculum perfectionis; et pax Christi exultet in cordibus vestris, in qua et vocati estis in uno corpore, et grati estote.

I will observe in conclusion, that, since this most heavenly temper of mind is on the one hand the special foundation of the Oratory (as taking the place of vows in its constitution,) yet on the other hand, as is evident, most difficult, should we be able to do nothing more in this whole year now passing but learn to live together, we shall have done, not a little thing, but the greatest which we could hope to do. I suppose all of you know that when we first gave ourselves to St Philip at Rome, we were cautioned that the one difficulty of the Oratory was the living together—community without vows—and for that reason it was especially injoined on us not to add to our existing number during our noviciate. We were told that we should succeed, if we could live together. or rather the great principle is Santa Comunità[,] that we ought to begin with a few so that our noviciate was precisely a trial whether we could, and we should have fininshed our noviciate, when we learned to live together—moreover that since we had already lived together both here, and at a former place, and thus had experience of each other, all that past period might be looked on in a way as part of our noviciate. We acted on this—we discouraged one, or rather several from joining us at Rome[4], referring them to our return to England. Here then we are at length in England carrying on that noviciate which we began in Rome, and in our secluded life we may in one sense be said all of us to be still in the state of novices learning to love each other and to live together—and, as God has been most gracious to us hitherto, we trust or rather are sure that He is still carrying on His work of mercy and will bring it to a good end.

NEWMAN'S ORATORY PAPERS No. 9
27 SEPTEMBER 1848

INTRODUCTORY NOTE

See above, p. 141 for a summary and an appraisal of this Address. Newman appeals to his own and his hearers' experience outside the Catholic Church in confirmation of his point that faith must be the basis for charity in community life, if this charity is to be lasting. These ideas are already to be found in his Anglican sermon "Faith and Love", *P.S.,* Vol. IV, Sermon XXI.

---

[4]See Newman's tactful refusal of George Talbot, 2 March 1847, *L.D.,* XII, p. 56.

CHAPTER ADDRESS 27 SEPTEMBER 1848[1]

Chapter of Faults. Wednesday Sept 27/48
Novice Chapter
Oct 30. 1850

The Christian life may be comprised in two words, faith and charity, as we all very well know. Faith is the foundation, charity is the building. Faith is the first and chief essential—charity the higher and more perfect—Faith is the essential—because no building can stand without something to stand upon—Our Lord describes the state of that man who built his house upon the sand—Descendit pluvia, et venerunt flumina, et flaverunt venti; et irruerunt in domum illam et cecidit—et fuit ruina illius magna—We see instances of this, alas, all around us in this country—instances surely without number of kind warm feelings, benevolent purposes, and pure intentions wasted and lost, because they are not founded and secured on the true faith. Hence they have no stability, no abidence—they come, they last awhile, and then fail. Men begin life with zeal and energy, wishing to give themselves with all their hearts to the good of their brethren; they join with others in works for the good of the world—but wait a little while, and you will see them dispirited and out of heart—they have had crosses and disappointments, and been unable to bear up against them. They give up their works, and what was once a vivid reality before them, was their thought day and night, and ruled their actions, becomes a dream. I am not speaking at random. I am describing what any one (like myself,) who has lived as many years, and has seen as much (as I have) of religion external to the Catholic pale, can abundantly testify from his own experience of life. This life is *wasted* in the case of so many, because they build their house on no foundation, because they begin with charity, or what seems like charity, when they should begin with faith.

I have said that any one like ourselves who have seen the workings and the issues of good purposes and benevolent plans and friendships and combinations external to the Church is in

[1]*B. Or. Ar.* D. 4. 9.

a situation to feel more vividly than another the absolute necessity of *faith* as a beginning of every charitable work. For the truth⟨?⟩ is [,] to be a Catholic⟨?⟩ to whom faith is habitual and familiar, its extreme necessity is not so distinctly perceptible. The Catholic takes faith for granted, and goes on to charity as the fulfilment of the law. With the Holy Apostle quae retro sunt obliviscit [sic][2], ad ea quae sunt priora se extendit. One and all are built on faith, not one and all are edified in charity—but we each of us have attained to different degrees of it—But as to faith, we take it for granted,—it is what we all start with—it is what we stand upon. And as we do not see what is under our feet, and we do not look at the ground as we walk, yet we cannot walk without the ground, so as to faith we exercise it, we use it, but we do not think of it.

Now all this, which is true in the largest consideration of faith and charity may be applied in particular to ourselves who are children of St Philip and members of this Congregation. Our great duty we know is charity—that is charity towards each other—a most perfect singleminded openhearted love—which in the words of the Apostle, patiens est, benigna est, non agit perperam, non inflatur, non quaerit quae sua sunt, non irritatur, non cogitat malum. And that of course particularly, in the shape of brotherly love, and affectionateness which tends to be like that of kindred. Much do we hear in our rule and the writings of our fathers of former years of this brotherly affection as taking the place of vows, as being the bond between Oratorian and Oratorian, as being the principle of unity and the life of the Congregation. Much is not said about faith—But of course when all this is said about charity, it implies faith as its foundation—and as faith in God is the ground of charity of God, so faith in the Congregation is the ground of charity towards the Congregation—and as we have no security that we shall continue to love God without true faith in Him, so there is no security that affection shall continue towards each other, if we do not start with a firm faith in the Congregation and in each other. We enter the Congregation in faith—we pass on, we take it for granted, and then we go on to something higher, to charity—and are enabled to go on to

[2]Cf. *Phil.*, 3:13.

that which is higher on account of that indispensable beginning, which we exercise indeed continually, but which we do not talk about, because it is so obvious.

This is what all of us, My dear Fathers and Brothers, feel, I know—and yet it is not superfluous to speak of it, and to pursue it into detail. I recommend then to you the serious cultivation of this habit of faith, and jealous watchfulness of it, as that which alone can serve you in stead in the many difficulties we may have to enter in our course. We all know and put before us the duty of mutual concession—of yielding one to another, of consulting for each other, of being tender to each other. We know the duty, we practise it—but be you sure that there is another duty without which such tenderness and consideration will not suffice, will fail of its end, and that is faith in each other. We are tender, we are considerate, towards many, in whom we have not faith and confidence—but if we are to bear the love of Oratorians one to another, of St Philip, of Baronius, of Tarugi, of Velli, of Licinio Pio, we must begin with faith, and the way by which we must gain faith in each other is, to have faith in St Philip and in the Pope. It is a great help to the performance of a duty to have a clear perception of its existence. We can indeed perform it implicitly, as we can receive Catholic doctrine implicitly—but it assists the exercise to realize and contemplate it. Therefore let us, while we give our confidence to the Congregation and to each other, do so by a direct act of the will and of a consciousness what we are doing.

Let us recollect then that the Vicar of Christ has sent us to England and has set us up here ⟨Infirm agencies he used⟩ so they are in all cases—still ⟨he called us to himself⟩ has sent us out again. He has founded the Oratory in England ⟨he gave us our motto "Estote fortes in bello" &c.⟩ He has sent us with his benediction—he does not forget us; he renews his benediction. Let us receive these gifts and present tokens of his interest with thankfulness—let us recollect from whom they come— recollect they come from him who sent over St Augustine to convert our ancestors—who chose in turn one among them, our Boniface, and sent him out to convert the Germans—who in a later age was the defence and stay of the glorious martyr

St Thomas—His benediction has done great things hitherto may we never forget the privilege we have and which we enjoy.

And then again into whose hands has he put [sic]—into the hands of that great saint, to whom every Bishop of the Holy City must bear a special devotion, as being the Apostle of that holy City itself, the Everblessed [sic] St Philip—We who are to do apostolic work in England, are sent hither under the banners of the Apostle of Rome. He who meditates on this, cannot fail, through the grace of God to carry in his heart a stability and a calm which put him above the external world. Let us aim, my dear Fathers and Brothers at this stability and serenity of mind. It will make us, with the Apostle think much of the charge and function given us. It will make each of us do his work in the body, whatever it be, not only cheerfully, not only lovingly, but with simplicity, with determination, with heavenly composure. He will not fear for the future—he will know that God's hand is on him—he knows that he is acting under the patronage, and in the strength, of the Most holy and Blessed Virgin, the Mother of God, and of the wonder-working St Philip, and with the prayers of our fathers past away from this scene and now in God's paradise, and, as sent by the Holy See to convert the erring population of this country, with the intercession and merits of all the English Saints, he will know this, and be at peace, and his love towards his fellow workers will be only the more fervent and tender because it springs up from so deep and true a source—charity will come of faith—it will be a heavenly stream springing up from the everlasting rock.

———

NEWMAN'S ORATORY PAPERS No. 10
11 DECEMBER 1850

INTRODUCTORY NOTE

The candidates for ordination (to the subdiaconate) mentioned at the opening of this Address were Stanislas Flanagan

17

and Edward Caswall (*L.D.*, XIV, p. 166). See the biographical notices in *L.D.*, XII, pp. 430, 431 (Flanagan) and p. 429 (Caswall).

The reference to bodily mortification may allude to the use of the discipline, introduced into both the Birmingham and London Oratories about this time (*Trevor*, I, pp. 538, 539). The reference to illusions in prayer is not quite so clear.

On the concluding passage "the constant aim to go through the ordinary day's work well" cf. above pp. 119, 120: "Is Newman's idea of Perfection theologically adequate?"

Dec 11/50[1]

At this moment, my dear Brethren, when some of you are on the point of going to retreat, in preparation for their taking that great step which for ever unites them to the ministry of the Catholic Church, and when their thoughts will be more especially turned to the consideration of that perfection which should be the object of all of us who have submitted to the rule and guidance of St Philip, there is one thought concerning the spiritual life, as it is called, not very recondite but very profitable to insist on, which I wish to bring before you.

It seems a mere truism to say that very few people are Saints—yet it is a most solemn and pregnant truth, which without mastering we cannot feel ourselves even in the way of sanctity. It lies at the foundation of the scientia sanctorum, and it is the lesson which all our experience of ourselves and of others who profess to aim at higher things than the common run of men forces upon us.

It is very easy to be religious up to a certain point—but when we pass that point, we get into a new region so utterly different from any thing which at present we are conscious of, and so far more perilous and terrible, that the temptations which beset, I do not mean the unformed Christian or the sinner, but which are the lot of ordinary dutiful and obedient servants of Christ, are nothing to those which are there encountered.

[1] *B. Or. Ar.* D. 4. 9.

The Church finds us on the tossing ocean—it brings us into harbour—but if we would be saints, it sends us out upon the ocean again. And though we go with far different appliances and hopes, though we are no longer without chart or compass or seaworthy vessel, yet we are exposed to the same variations of the sky, the same terrors of the deep, as before we came into port. It is easy to be a second rate Christian— many are called to nothing higher—they live in the pale of the Church and in the round of their prescribed duty, they do the precepts and wait on the sacraments, and they are comparatively safe—but those who are called to higher things, have temptations and trials, so fierce, so stifling, so opposite, that it is well indeed if they do not lose their election and fail. They are in their days like St Antony going out into the wilderness to meet the devils, or St Theresa, who found that if she relaxed or stopped in her course, a place in the eternal prison was ready for her.

This is so awful a fact that for our caution it should be impressed upon us when we enter the path of perfection, upon all of us who are to enter it—for their caution, not for their discouragement—yet so necessarily in the way of caution, that they will [be] sure of failing, if they do not weigh it well.

I will explain what I would mean by an illustration. Watch the bricklayer mounting a high ladder—as he gets up it sways, it is exposed to the wind, He needs to plant it fast at bottom— he needs to be proof against giddiness—he needs to be accustomed to bear his load well, on his head or his shoulder, that he may neither lose it or lose his balance. Watch him—his feet dance up and down—take your hod of bricks or your trencher of mortar on your own shoulder and follow him up the ladder— will you not fear to do so? In like manner, fear much to ascend up the rounds of perfection, fear much, yet shrink not, if you are called to it—fear because you need grace, shrink not for you are promised grace. But without grace, and abundant grace, ruin is certain—your head, your shoulders, your feet will betray you—you will be precipitated down.

And hence it is that those who aim at nothing great, often seem much better, sometimes are better, than those who aim at what is high—They are better, if those who aim at more are bold and fervent without caution—they seem better, because they attempt so much less. When St Peter said "Lord I will follow Thee to prison and to death," and then denied Christ, he aimed at more and in the event sinned more than those who professed nothing—He was right in attempting, but he was wrong in not watching and praying lest he should enter into temptation.

There is no duty of religion, but has its snares, and to go through them would be to write an ascetical treatise. Those who do more than others are in danger, at least, of getting attached to their own ways of acting. They find a pleasure in prayer, and in bodily mortification—but they are put out when they are obliged to intermit their prayer, or they are self-willed in their mortifications. A quiet censorious spirit grows up within them while they are but conscious to themselves of humility, selfrenunciation, and devotion. This state of mind matures into that stiff affectation and (as it may be called) priggishness, which is often the characteristic of heretical asceticism.

But its condition may be more serious still. In the science of the divine life nothing is more frequent than descriptions and discussions upon an evil which is to the common run of men unknown, and from which they may consider themselves almost secure, the illusions attendant on prayer. It is a frequent occurence in the lives of the Saints, and in all who attempt at all to resemble them to mistake or to be in danger of mistaking Satan for God—of worshipping him for God—of obeying his suggestions as divine precepts—again, of being elated by their apparent facility of meditating or intoxicated by a false sweetness, in prayer and meditation—of attempting to do presumptuous things, and of losing their souls in consequence of their gifts. And the heavenly ladder jumps up and down under their feet in proportion to the height they have ascended.

What then is to be done in these circumstances, in order to guard against a peril so great as to be appalling and discouraging to those who aim at perfection? Masters in the spiritual life, among other important rules, give the following two suggestions, as obvious yet as momentous as is the remark itself in which I suggested the danger when I began. The first is not to act of oneself—not to be one's own director—not to dare to aim at perfection without some definite individual to whom we really and in detail yield obedience. I cannot conceive any more fearful hazard than that to which a soul will be exposed than that of attempting to be a saint on its own capital, as it may be called, by its own management and its own wisdom. We shall float down the stream or drift in any direction, if we have nothing on the shore to steady our course by.

The other remark I would make is, that we need not go too fast. Unless you prune off the luxuriances of plants, they grow bare, thin, and shabby at the roots. The higher your building is the broader must be its base—So it is with sanctity—Acts, words, devotions, which are suitable in saints, are absurd in other men—The second precept then of the religious guides, to whom I have alluded, is this:— that, if we would aim at perfection, we must perform well the duties of the day. I do not know any thing more difficult, more sobering, so strengthening than [sic] the constant aim to go through the ordinary day's work well. To rise at the exact time, to give the due time to prayer, to meditate with devotion, to assist at mass with attention, to be recollected in conversation, these and similar observances carried duly through the day, make a man, as it is often said, half a saint, or almost a saint. It gives our aspirations too a definite scope. men often know not what to be at—they have fervent desires to serve God and advance towards heaven, but they choose strange ways of accomplishing them. Here is the true answer to the question—the practical tangible work to be set before the aspirant.

May St Philip bring us forward month by month, and year by year in the faith and the knowledge and the love of our Lord and Saviour and His Blessed Mother and all the Saints.

NEWMAN'S ORATORY PAPERS Nos. 11, 12 & 13
22 DECEMBER 1852 – 21 JAN 1853

INTRODUCTORY NOTE

This group of Papers, 22 December 1852 to 21 January 1853, all date from an anxious period preceding the climax of the

Achilli trial, when Newman was absent from the Birmingham Oratory, on a holiday in Scotland at Abbotsford (16 December 1852 to 25 January 1853, cf. *L.D.*, XV, pp. 221–275). There is a detailed treatment of the events in *Trevor* I, pp. 616–624: "Newman in Scotland: Crisis in Birmingham."

These Papers are best studied as a group, exemplifying as they do, what Newman himself has called a characteristic of the saints, his *calmness*. To quote a relevant passage from a later Oratory Paper, that of 31 August 1856 on the departure of Fr Bernard Dalgairns:

> One of the sure signs of the presence of the Spirit of God is peace. The Saints have gone through many fierce trials; I do not read that they were restless; or if they were even so, I do not find that it came into the *idea* or definition of their saintliness. No two saints can be so different from each other as St Philip and St Ignatius— one so unassuming, the other so imperial. They were both in different ways inexpressibly calm—the calmness of St Philip took the form of cheerfulness, that of St Ignatius the form of majesty. What men do calmly, has weight—but when they are restless, they seem to me to want the primary condition for inspiring confidence in others or claiming deference . . .

See above, pp. 141, 142 for an outline and appraisal of these Papers.

See also the fragmentary Chapter Address, below, 2 February 1854: "On the events of the last three Years."

CHAPTER ADDRESS: 22 DECEMBER 1852[1]

For the Chapter—December 22. 1852

We have many trials just now, my dear Fathers and Brothers; but this is so far from wonderful, that we might well be alarmed, if we had none. I want you, as well as myself, to understand this more and more; for things are much easier to bear, when they are not strange and unaccountable, but can be referred to the declared rule and will of Almighty God.

It is then the very *constitution*, as it may be called, of the

[1] *B. Or. Ar.* D. 4. 9.

Kingdom of Grace, that its children must all suffer. If they do not suffer here, they will suffer the more hereafter; and they suffer little hereafter, in proportion as they suffer much here. The Apostles have laid down the rule, that "through many tribulations we must enter into the kingdom of God." If then we have no trouble here, either we shall have a long purgatory, or, what is infinitely worse, we are not the children of grace at all, and are going straight for a worse place.

It is the children of this world who prosper. From youth to age they sometimes are without any trouble at all; they are what the world calls fortunate; every thing turns out well with them; they rise in the world, make fortunes, have a name with men, are treated with respect and deference by their fellows, and die. Such a history of life, which story books and tales set down as the perfection of happiness and the great object of desire, is terrible to the Christian; and he is frightened in pro–portion as he sees any fellow Christian approaching it. There was a great Pope, one of the greatest who ever lived, he was adorned with the gifts of nature, he had a wonderful prosperity, as Solomon before him, and he raised the temporal power of the Papacy to its highest point. He died, and no one has ever dreamed of calling him a Saint. Not that therefore he was not a holy man; not that therefore his name is excluded from the book of life; but merely because, having had good things here evil things remained for him afterwards. He left this life, with a good hope of heaven, but withal with a sure prospect of purgatory. All men sin; no one, except by a special privilege, can keep from venial sin; other Popes had sinned as well as he, but they had died and gone to heaven, and are invoked as Saints, and yet it is otherwise with him; for they satisfied, nay more than satisfied, divine justice here, by the sufferings they underwent for the Truth; whereas with him the Truth was a temporal crown as well as an everlasting.

This country has just lost a great man[2], a Protestant. What is it that makes one look with such special fear upon his pros-pects hereafter? The circumstance that he was so singularly fortunate from first to last; that he had a long life, overflowing

[2]The Duke of Wellington who died 14 September 1852.

glory, and almost a sovereign sway over the hearts and wills of his countrymen.

Here[3], on the contrary, I am just now on a spot which reminds me of a history strikingly in contrast to that of the great men I have spoken of. It is a Protestant's history too; the history of a man of letters[4], as famous in his way as that man of war; but it is the history of one whose temporal aspirations and ambitious hopes were frustrated, who attempted to gain his reward here, and was foiled, whose days became more and more evil as life advanced, whose years were shortened by toil of brain and anxiety of heart, and who met death with the Dies Irae on his mouth. Why do Catholics look so tenderly, nay even so hopefully on a history like this, compared with a history like that? Because it seems as if his Maker, Redeemer, and Judge had not abandoned him to the god of this world and to the glory thereof, but had been training him by disappointment for a future which is better.

It is the very rule then, my dear children, under which we live, if we are God's own, to sow in tears that we may reap in joy. When I was first a priest, and kissed the Cross on my maniple, and said, Merear, Domine, portare manipulam [sic] fletus et doloris, I used to say to myself, "Where is the sorrow? where the tears?"—and then I added "I suppose it will come." It is our very portion here. If we had no punishment, then, as St Paul says, we should be but spurious sons, not true heirs of the promise. But if we have trial and bear it well, then we have two proofs of God's love upon us: one in the trial itself, and another in the grace which has enabled us to sustain it.

For the Chapter Jan. 5 1853[5]
(read it *well* and *distinctly*, in Chapter)

On this our first chapter in the new year, My dear Fathers and Brothers, when we are reminded that time is going and that eternity is drawing near, I am naturally led to a practical

---

[3]Abbotsford.
[4]Sir Walter Scott.
[5]*B. Or. Ar.* D. 4. 9.

reflection, and one which admits of a personal application in the case of every one of us. Ever since we came here, I think, and for many weeks in Alcester Street, a Mass has been said week by week for the *sanctification* of our two Congregations; and in London too in like manner there has been a weekly Mass with the same intention. Here then is a subject, on which we cannot think too much.

Our only life, as a *body*, consists in our sanctification, as individuals. Do we wish St Philip's work and institution to continue? This is possible in no other way. Our sanctification is the life of the Congregation, not only in *God's* sight, but in the sight of the *world*. This would be true, even in a Catholic country; it is still more emphatically and anxiously true in an heretical. Amid a Catholic population, the sanctity of individuals might redeem and sustain the reputation of the rest who were in a state of relaxation and decay; but here the case is just reversed. What an individual can do abroad, by his own good repute, in covering the sins of the whole body, that, and more than that, in this jealous Protestant nation can one individual Father or Brother do by his failings or sins, in destroying the good name, the influence, the usefulness of all the rest. We are *all* of us at the mercy of *each* of us. A long life of saintliness cannot recommend Religion in the eyes of this people, as one scandalous act of sin can injure it.

I will tell you what seems to me a difficulty in the sanctification of a son of St Philip. When a soul has put off the world, has truly repented and turned from his sins, has been pierced with the love of God, and given himself up to him, (and this, I trust, has been fulfilled in the history of every one of us,) it is comparatively easy for such a one to manage with God's grace to keep in grace and to continue generally in his good resolutions. Such persons have taken a great step, and they are able to attain to a point, at which they guard against mortal sin, and strengthen themselves in such religious habits, which are a protection against any startling sin, or scandal, of any kind. It would indeed be a shame, if we, for instance, who are so shielded from temptation, did not keep clear of any mortal hatred, or revenge, or pride, or sloth, or intemperance, or sensuality. Not that we are out of *danger* of such, but we are preserved from the *commission*. A man who scales a precipice is in *danger* of falling, but he *does not* fall, if he is careful. If, however, he confides in his skill and grows careless, then, whatever be his skill, he *will* fall.

Such, my dear Fathers and Brothers, is the danger of those who keep generally from mortal sins and live in God's grace. They are in danger of falling from the very reason that a fall is not likely. While mortal sin was as yet evidently unsubdued, they had something to fight against; but directly that formidable struggle ceases, and they seem to have triumphed, and can go on from day to day and week to week, bringing nothing of a serious nature to the confessional, then they have a sort of holy day, they walk about at their ease, they have nothing definite to do, and, though they little suspect it, begin to be in *danger* though of a different kind from what it was before. While they were warring with *mortal* sin, they *fell* from time to time, but on the whole they made *progress;* now, they stand still. This is the problem always perplexing to conscientious persons; motion alone keeps us alive; but when the struggle is over, where is the motion?

This danger is mitigated in the case of all those who are obliged to hold intercourse with the world without, as (e.g.) of missionary priests, by the constant watchfulness which they are called on to exert throughout their various duties, in order to keep Satan from having an advantage over them, and to guard themselves from the shadow and breath, if not the actual presence of moral evil in one shape or other; still, after all allowances on this score, the danger I speak of, as besetting a religious body, remains.

Accordingly, Regulars meet it with their *Rule.* The Rule is a standard, over and above the Precepts of the Law, which *each* member vows to obey, which *no* member can exactly fulfil. It is a something continually pressing on them, and (so to say) harassing them, like a hair shirt, and keeping them from spiritual sloth. It keeps them awake all their life long. Hence you hear it said by holy men in regular bodies, that the sanctification, the perfection, the salvation of their brethren consists in *keeping their Rule.*

Here then is the peculiar anxiety of the Oratory. ⟨we have

no *Rule* like that of other bodies.⟩ I have not time to enlarge on it, but suggest it for your serious thought. I suggest it to each of you for the sake of each; I suggest it to those Fathers particularly, who in one way or other have others of the body under their spiritual care. *How* are we, Philippines, to keep from falling back? *How* are we to proceed in the work of our sanctification?

For the Chapter Wednesday January 19.[6]

Only this once, this one more, my dear Fathers and Brothers, have I as I trust, to address you in my absence, for our next Chapter falls on our own Feast of the Purification, when I hope to be with you. I shall then be with you for some weeks; and O that I could say that I was to be with you always; but St Philip does not think me worthy of him, and the loving will of God sees it good for me that I should have no home on earth[7], lest I should get too fond of it.

Five years are now finishing since the English Congregation of the Oratory was set up; four years, since our own Congregation was set up in Birmingham. On the Purification St Philip was first brought into England; on the Purification he was brought here. We are set up, indeed, under the invocation of the Immaculate Conception; but, historically speaking, we are under the patronage of the Purification. The Purification is the beginning of our history; and perhaps it may be its archtype and presage.

Most wonderfully have we been blessed, as all of us will bear witness to each other. We have given ourselves to our glorious saint, my dear Fathers and Brothers, and he has not failed us. When we were at Rome, we heard much of what he would do for us; but he has done far more than any thing, which we heard then, could lead us to anticipate. He has fulfilled to us our Lord's promise, that those who give up this world, its

---

[6]*B. Or. Ar.* D. 4. 9.

[7]The reference is to the possibility of being sent to prison, in the case of an adverse decision in the Achilli trial. See the Introductory Note for the Chapter Address of 2 February 1853, below.

interests, and its professions for Him, shall with Him find brethren, and friends, and houses, and lands, even on earth, in full compensation. We have prospered in whatever we attempted, and at times we have found in a singular way that what threatened evil has turned to good.

This is a time of year especially to remind us of this; but I say it here now, with reference to the special import to the feast of the Purification. Recollect then, that the Purification, on which we became a Congregation, is a day, which, excepting one, is the least festive of any of our Lady's festivals. The *saddest* and most sorrowful of them, if a feast can be sad, is the Feast of the Seven Dolours; that comes at the *end* of Lent; none of them of course is sorrowful as it is; but there is another of her Feasts, which comes before Lent, as if in anticipation of it; *preparing* for the penitential season, as the Feast of the Seven Dolours *consummates* it; and that is our own Feast of the Purification.

I say the Purification is a sort of penitential Feast, if a Feast may be so called, because it is then that Mary puts on a garb which is not hers; and, as in Passiontide she seems the mother of a public criminal, so now she is coming to us as the mother of a sinful child. She comes to be purified, as if she needed purification. She humbles herself in the Temple of God, with the Lord of that Temple in her arms, whom but just now, the Shepherds, the Sages from the East, and the Angels worshipped. And in that garb of humiliation she hears just Simeon prophesy her that the time is coming, when that glorious God, her own child, whom she holds so closely to her heart, shall be as a sword piercing through it with a pang corresponding to her overflowing privileges.

Let us not be surprised, let us not despond, let us not murmur, my dear children, if this be fulfilled in us, and so far as, and wherever it is fulfilled. St Philip himself is so bright, so happy from birth to death, his eighty years is such a long lapse of sunshine, that even other saints show nothing like it, and sinners, such as we, could not bear it. He comes to us therefore in the Purification; but not to make us less cheerful or peaceful, but that we may be cheerful and peaceful in the right way, with the love and in the spirit of penance.

Let us then at this season beg of him to gain us the love of penance, that we may embrace readily and cheerfully any sorrows he puts upon us. To do this the better, I propose to you to hold a novena before the Purification, in honour of Our Lady's first sorrow; and wish it to consist of the Veni Sancte Spiritus, verse and collect, of four stanzas of the Stabat Mater (the *Stabat, O quam tristis, Quis est homo,* and *Sancta Mater*) the *ora . . . dolorosissima* and the *Deus in cujus passione.*

NEWMAN'S ORATORY PAPERS No. 14
2 FEBRUARY 1853

INTRODUCTORY NOTE

See *L.D.,* XV, p. 280: "Tuesday 1 February 1853. F. Ambrose and I came down to Birmingham Wednesday 2 February distributed candles and sang High Mass."

The Achilli trial had ended (in London) on Monday 31 January 1853. The heading on this Chapter Address would seem to show that it had been written before the final judgment in the Achilli trial, since the sentence "£100 fine and imprisoned until the fine is paid" had been "paid there and then" (*L.D.,* XV, p. 278) and there was no further question of being sent to jail.

CHAPTER ADDRESS: 2 FEBRUARY 1853[1]

"To be read at the Chapter February 2, if I am in jail, or to go to jail."
for February 2.1853 at the Chapter.
My dear Fathers and Brothers: I do not suppose that either you or I feel able simply to rejoice and exult today in our secret hearts, yet reason tells us we ought to do so. It is *natural*

[1]*B. Or. Ar.* D. 4. 9.

we should be depressed; it is *reasonable* we should triumph. It is from human feeling that we are sad; it will be from grace, if we are satisfied and thankful. Human feeling is not wrong; but grace is better.

Nor need one exclude the other. Our Lord's soul was in heaviness in Gethsemani, though it was in personal union with His All-blissful Divinity; and in our best estate we cannot surpass the Apostles, who were "tristes, semper autem gaudentes," in sadness, yet in continual joy. I do not wonder that we feel pain just now; but I wish a supernatural consolation to consecrate that pain, and to raise it from earth to heaven.

Surely, the whole course of the trial which has come on me for the last year and a half, is nothing else than *God's* act and will. Every thing indeed which we do, is in one sense *our* act, and we are responsible for the consequences. And every thing we do is full of imperfection, and when we suffer, we suffer for our own infirmity and sin. I am not disputing this; of course I grant it in the present case. But still, I trust the trouble which has come upon me, and on you in me, is, in a true sense, God's act too.

I am at present under legal punishment for a step which I took with great deliberation. I denounced a very bad man; and, in doing so, I was perfectly aware that the consequences might *possibly* be most serious to me, though of course I had but a vague idea *how* serious. But I thought that, in *matter of* fact, nothing *would* follow from it; and I thought that, even though any thing *should* follow, I had *sufficient* proof of all the charges which I made against that person, and proof *close at hand*; and I considered that the mere *chance* of something following, inconvenient to myself, was no sufficient reason for *not* doing, what on other grounds I thought I ought to do. Nor did I do it, without trying to find out God's will, asking Him at the Altar and before the Tabernacle to teach me what it was, and offering up what I was doing to Him. Hence, though of course, had I then known what in fact has followed from what I did, (viz the expence and anxiety which have come upon me), I should not have done it, yet I never have been able to be sorry that I did it, considering I did *not* know what was to follow; because, supposing such ignorance was not my fault, then the act was not so much *my* act, as God's, and to be sorry at it would be to murmur against God's will.

And really, my dear Fathers and Brothers, the course which things have taken throughout, from the very time I put into execution the step on which I had so anxiously deliberated, seems fully to justify the feeling, that we have been all along under the operation of a divine dispensation, not simply of a mistake of mine—You recollect, how strangely and suddenly we seemed from the beginning given over (as it were) to some strong and furious wind, which took us off our legs, and hurried us here and there at its pleasure, and landed us, we did not know where; how, day by day, our best stays and confidences broke down, how an impenetrable darkness came over the scene, and we found ourselves, week after week, worse off and worse still, without being able to predict what was the worst to be; and then how that, after the prospect cleared, it got thick again, and promised and threatened by turns, promised and threatened without result, raising hopes merely to mock them; and how we were tossed and whirled to and fro, without or against our will, like nothing else than a ship in a storm, and how, when we were close to shore, we were carried off back into deep waters, till we gradually and irresistibly were drawn on into that settlement of our long conflict, which of all others had from the first seemed the most intolerable and the least likely, and I find myself in jail.

My Fathers and Brothers, can so extraordinary a Providence be for nothing? Must not something special come of it? One thing at least ought to come—which, alas, through my fault, is least likely of all, my own advancement in the spiritual life. When it broke upon me last August year, that I might have to go to prison, I involuntarily said, 'Well, if so, I ought to come out a Saint.'' Yet all that interval has passed, and, judging from it, never, never, was there less appearance of religious good accruing to a soul from an external trial than in this case. This is my real discouragement and trouble. At most I shall be doing some slight penance for sin past; to speak of more than this, is a romance or a dream. My children, what you are, depends much on what I am. You must pray for me, and you will be praying for yourselves.

NEWMAN'S ORATORY PAPERS No. 15

20/21 JANUARY 1853

INTRODUCTORY NOTE

See above p. 142 for a summary of this case of dismissal, and an appraisal of Newman's attitude to the delinquent Brother. It is instructive to contrast this case with that of Father Bernard Dalgairns, and Newman's very different attitude to Dalgairns' presence in the Birmingham community (in his second period, 1853–56) and his subsequent departure. See Oratory Papers, below, 31 August 1856. Full details of the Dalgairns case in *Trevor*, II, pp. 142–149: "Dalgairns leaves Newman;" and of Brother Bernard's case in *Trevor* I, pp. 616–624: "Newman in Scotland: Crisis in Birmingham."

By the fact of Newman's absence during this crisis, we have many letters of his dealing with it. They are to be found in *L.D.* XV, pp. 232–275 among the correspondence for December 1852 and January 1853. For a succinct summary of the facts of the case see *L.D.*, ib., p. 232, note 2.

It is useful to contrast these Memoranda with one of the earlier Chapter Addresses (9 February 1848) where Newman had seemed to draw an absolute antithesis between the Oratorian and Regular ethos. Here he appeals to the absolute need for 'form and authority' if the Congregation is to be saved from dissolution.

MEMORANDA[1]

January 20. 1853. Abbotsford.

In the observations which I am going to make on the distressing matter which has lately taken place among us, I must not be supposed as doing more than setting down my opinion. I am not ruling that what I say is right; but I think it my duty, being the Father of the Congregation, to make known what I

---

[1] *B. Or. Ar.* Oratory Letters, Jan.–Feb. 1853.

think, without of course hindering others from maintaining views on the subject contrary to my own.

Nor am I going to assume that my own conduct in the matter has been prudent and blameless; or that, when I was misunderstood, such misunderstanding was not my fault, instead of being the fault of others. On the contrary I am going to assume that I did what I was thought to do and did not mean to do.

Nor do I mean to say that anything has been done which would not have eventually been done, though the matter had been managed differently, or that any substantial injustice has been done to the person who has been the subject of the proceedings in question. I am only concerned with those proceedings themselves.

Those proceedings seem to me of so serious a character, that, were they to be of ordinary occurrence in any community, they would necessarily be its ruin. Authority and form are the life of a social body, it cannot exist without them; now the proceedings, of which I am to speak, seem to me to be grave breaches of both the one and the other, and therefore, if repeated, to be simply our dissolution. It is a most anxious sense of the danger we are running, which makes me remark upon it.

1. A Father of the Congregation heard a circumstance to the disadvantage of a Brother, as a natural secret. What ought he to have done? I can conceive his keeping the secret, and doing nothing. It would not have been the best course to adopt, but I can understand it. The best course, as I think, would have been to ask leave to tell that brother's Superiors; and then, if he could not get leave, he would be reduced to secrecy, but not before. But in the case before us, he neither did simply keep the secret to himself, nor ask leave to tell the Superiors of that brother, but he took a third course; he asked and gained leave to tell that brother and he exercised the office of a Superior towards him, by admonishing him on the fault alleged against him. He acted from the best of motives, (as every one did all through the proceedings;) still in fact though not intentionally. what he did was this; he made use of the communication he had received to place him in the situation of the Superiors of that Brother.

18

Here was a simple ignoring of the true authority, and a usurpation of jurisdiction, such, that, I say, no community could stand against it, if it became the rule of action. Were it freely adopted, every one might be exerting authority over any one else; every one, but the Superior, might know what was going on in the community, and endless confusion would ensue.

I have not the power to lay it down as a rule of action, but I make a prophecy against the omission of it as a rule:— if Fathers or Brothers, hearing charges brought on good authority against another Father or Brother, do not do their utmost to acquaint the Superiors of the person accused, and much more, if, instead of doing so, they do that themselves towards that person, which the Superiors naturally would do,—the Oratory is gone.

2. This was the first fault, aggravated by the circumstance that the course of action, which I have described, went on for five or six months. It would have been wrong to have entered on it for a day; but the length of time is more than increase of the impropriety; it makes it almost a specific impropriety of its own.

3. The next fault was, that, when at length it was divulged by the Father who was the trustee of the secret, it was divulged just at the worst of all possible times for making use properly of the information. It was made public when the two Superiors to whom the subject of it belonged, were just in the worst condition to hear it; viz when the Father was from home, and when the F. Minister was recovering from a severe illness. A secret, which had kept for above five months, might have kept a month longer.

4. However the Father was written to, and let us see what followed. As authority had been forgotten, so now was form. I am assuming the Father did, what he seemed to the Fathers in Birmingham to do. Three Fathers, the F Confessor, the F Minister, and the F Sacristan write to him on the subject, sending a statement *ex parte,* of the accuser. He at once, on this ex parte statement, writes back the next hour and sends by the first post a message to send down the Brother and to take immediate steps for his removal from the Congregation. He in fact judges, finally and unconditionally, that the Brother is to

go. Will any one say that this is just towards that Brother? Can any Society continue, when judicial acts are so conducted? Supposing the same informant had thus spoken about a Father, and supposing three other Fathers had written off in like manner about him to the Father Superior, and, in addition to that charge, accused him of malice against one of the three proved to be malice against that Father on the testimony of that Father and of another of the three, would the Father Superior have been justified, without waiting for the statement of the accused, to send off so peremptory and summary a message to the three Fathers in question? And what would be thought of these Fathers, if on receiving that summary judgment, they had at once acted upon it? and thought it obedience to the Father Superior so to act? Yet all this has been done. A brother has been convicted and dismissed by the Father Superior on ex parte evidence, and the Fathers to whom he wrote do not feel at all that it is a strange proceeding, or that any delay or explanation is necessary, but forthwith carry out his decision.

5. This, however, is not all. However strongly the Father might seem to speak, he had set down one condition before the matter was brought to an end. He had *not* absolutely judged upon ex parte evidence, but he had said that the Brother ought to be heard in his defence; and had requested to have without delay the Brother's own statement. So far is this injunction complied with, that about the very hour that the Father receives the first portion of that statement in Scotland, that brother is sent down for good in Birmingham. Here then is a simple act of negligence of the Father's wishes, and that in a matter of no less importance than sending away a member of the Congregation. What could be the good, was it not (though unintentionally) a mockery to send him the Brother's statement, when his supposed orders for his expulsion were acted on? What possible reason could he have for wishing to see the Brother's statement, except previously to the Brother being dismissed? But he had said expressly, "the Brother must be heard."

6. However, the Brother was sent away; about that there could be no mistake. The Father had spoken of his being sent to Liverpool, as synonymous with his dismissal—and to Liverpool

he was sent. Moreover he was sent to F. Lans, the Redemptorist; another act clinshing [sic] the dismissal, for a subject of the Congregation could not be sent to an extern Priest without the Father's approval. To do so, was to put that subject out of that Father's jurisdiction into the hands of a director with whom the Congregation had no relations. And the Brother took it as such; for after a while he wrote to say that, *previously to offering* himself to other congregations, he wished to offer himself for re-admission to the Oratory; clearly showing that he felt *himself offering* himself, or that he was no longer our subject.

7. Under these circumstances, the Father thought it best to leave matters as they had settled themselves; and he wrote to the Brother stating that the Congregation in general, including himself, had decided on his dismissal.

8. Such is an outline of the whole matter; and it comes to this,—that a Brother has been dismissed on a charge brought against him, without a hearing, and without any formal act of dismissal.

9. I confess I do not know in what terms to speak of these proceedings, which will sufficiently mark my sense of their injustice. Since we have been a Congregation, nothing has pained me so much. I think we have been unjust.

10. We cannot get rid of our members at pleasure. They have claims on us; their souls are committed to us. We have to answer for them. Again I conceive that open scandal committed is a reason for a summary removal; I am not able to see what else is a reason except formal contumacy in a very gross shape, e.g. deliberately striking a Father. In common cases contumacy ought to be the subject of warnings before dismissal.

I do not think that a sin of impurity as such are [sic] simple grounds of dismissal without warning, unless grave scandal occurs, or the sin is a frightful one. True contrition and the prospect of amendment being supposed, I hardly know what act of sin, not scandalous, is ipso facto punishable with dismissal. But, without saying what *one* sufficient causes ipso facto for dismissal, I can say more certainly what are not; viz sins of degree, sins of heart, not of overt act, that is, sins which it is very difficult to define and measure. Such, I conceive to be, a sin of malice, while it is substantially confined to thought or to words (unless the words become acts)—it being very difficult to ascertain what it is *worth* in a particular case. Now on the score of *malice* has the Brother been *in fact* dismissed. I mean, though the original charge was related to sensuality, yet the motive cause in fact of his dismissal, the feeling in the individual Fathers who were the instruments of his dismissal, the immediate energy of feeling under which he was dismissed was a feeling that he had been malicious to one of those three Fathers.

12. [sic] Nor is this all—surely if a member is dismissed by the Congregation, it should be for an *assignable offence*—Now the Fathers, whoever they were, for there was no formal act to show *who* dismissed him, *cannot assign the cause* of his dismissal. Three grounds have been assigned, and I have no reason to suppose that a majority can be got for any one of them. (1) The original ground was an offence against purity. It was this by which the Father originally was moved—yet the two acting Confessors of the Congregation declare their full belief there was no mortal sin in it. (2) The immediate motive cause was malice against a particular Father; but this ground at least the F Superior simply ignores, and puts out of the way. He cannot conceive an act, or a habit of malice, (*especially under* the circumstances, when it had for its object the particular Father who had exercised a jurisdiction over the Brother unwarrantably) is a ground of ipso facto dismissal. (3) A third ground is that of deceit, hypocrisy, intrigue, independence of action &c, which, whether a sufficient cause of ipso facto dismission [sic] or not, on its discovery, is not held, as far as I have heard, by more than the Father and another. I repeat my question, then, "*Why* was the Brother dismissed?"

13. How will it tell on the Lay brothers in general, nay or on the novices, to find that a Brother can be summarily dismissed, cause, not only not assigned, but not assignable, without any form act or process of dismissal?

14. Alas—we cannot afford to spend the birth-blood of the Congregation. It is said that the frame does not get over bleeding after 35—that is, the first blood is best. As time goes on, and we die, it will be a great thing to have those who remember our beginnings. They will be faithful and true to us after we are

gone. The Brother we have lost had to us, in the words of one of the Fathers, the fidelity of a dog. Is this nothing? was this no plea for extenuation, if possible?

15. Nor will the scandal, I fear, be little in Birmingham, and elsewhere, wherever our Oratory is known, to find that particular Brother gone.

Jan 21. 1853

As far as I know the facts they are these:—A female some months ago, say last July, told one of our Fathers that [paper torn here] at various times attempted to be rude to her. The Father in [paper torn here] of telling the Superiors of that Brother, among whom he was not, sent a letter of admonition to him. The Brother was angry at it, and destroyed it. During this time there has been an evident feud between the Father and Brother. It went so far that the F Minister revolted against the feelings expressed by that Brother against that Father, and then that Father thought the time had come to tell the cause of the feud.

On this those two Fathers declared him guilty of gross malice, and thought his dismissal unavoidable. The Father Dean (in the absence of the Father) did not feel either the ground of sensuality or malice, as decisive, and took the Brother's part.

When the Father Superior was informed of the facts, he did not feel the ground of malice, but he thought the original charge decisive—and he wrote back "He must be dismissed". In saying this he did not conceive that he was actually dismissing him—because he at the same time said "he must be suffered to give [paper torn here] own account of the matter, and send it me—" but he was [paper torn here] him by the 3 Fathers, on receipt of the letter, and was in fact dismissed [paper torn here] from Birmingham. Moreover, he was sent away before the first portion of his statement of the matter had reached the Father, or could have reached him, or rather just about the very hour when it did reach him or would reach him.

Meanwhile the Father, thinking over the circumstances, did not indeed think the brother's offence less, rather on receipt of the portion of his defence or statement sent him, he thought it greater, but he thought that the Brother had been sinned against as well as sinning, by the temptation to angry feeling suggested to the Brother by the particular Father, who first was informed of the matter, having exercised authority himself over the Brother instead of telling the Brother's Superiors. In consequence he wrote two letters to suggest keeping the Brother and punishing him as *possible*, but they came too late.

January 21, 1853

I shall not say any thing to the Congregation on this most painful of subjects. It will only give rise to warm and keen feelings. Mine own are such that I do not know how I could restrain them, if I once began—and if I so feel, others will too on their side. The thing is done—no record of it is on our books, so it cannot become a precedent. What at present I propose then is, for the sake of the future, to pass a decree in General Congregation, such as the following:

Decreed, that, following the precedent of the dismissal of Fathers of the Congregation in Decree . . . of the Rule, which prescribes a formal process for such a proceeding, no Novice or Lay brother shall be dismissed from the Congregation by the proper authorities except by the medium of some formal act or instruments presently to be determined by the Congregation and before which no proceedings with the object of dismissal shall be taken against him.

Then as to the nature of the formal act or instrument, I incline at present to a letter from the Superiors, who have the authority of dismissal, to the Congregatio Deputata, announcing the fact of the dismissal, the reason why, and the number of formal warnings, if any, the person in question has received from those Superiors. This letter, which in the *instrument* of dismissal, to be inserted, not in the Register, but in the book of *Annals* of the Congregation, which we have not as yet begun. There is an obvious reason for a letter to the Congr. Dep. for *how else* is the Community to know that a Novice or Brother is gone?

[Note by Ed.: In each case of a tear in this MS., only two or at most three words are missing.]

NEWMAN'S ORATORY PAPERS No. 16
6 JANUARY 1853

INTRODUCTORY NOTE

The main part of this text is available in *L.D.*, XV, p. 246. See above, p. 143 for an appreciation of the significance of this labour of love on Newman's part—of love at once towards St Philip, and to his own community, "the subjects of St Philip at Birmingham and that shall be." This Dedication should be studied in close connection with the *Fragment on the life of St Philip*, ORATORY PAPERS, below, Lent 1853.

For the importance which Newman himself attached to this service of community love, see *L.D.*, XV, p. 251, 254.

6 JANUARY 1853: DEDICATION FOR REFECTORY READING[1]

In majorem Dei gloriam
et B.M.V. et Sancti Philippi

Nulla Dies sine Linea
Lessons out of St Philip's Life
for every day of the year.
for the use of the Refectory
of the Birmingham Oratory.

———

To the subjects of St Philip at Birmingham
that are and that shall be.

My dear Fathers and Brothers,
St Philip's maxim, "Nulla Dies sine linea," cannot be better used by his children than in the inculcation of his own lessons

[1]Birmingham Oratory: Refectory Book.

and his own pattern upon their hearts. This I have attempted to do for them in the following pages; and it is a thought in which they may find an occasion for boasting and for thankfulness, that hardly a Saint can be named, whose recorded history admits of being separated into so many small wholes, for the year's course, as that of their own St Philip.

Charissimi, tum viventis, tum defuncti memineritis mei

Abbotsford

In festo Epiphaniae 1853

———

NEWMAN'S ORATORY PAPERS No. 17
LENT 1853

INTRODUCTORY NOTE

Newman's letter of 9 April 1854 to J. Spencer Northcote (*L.D.* XVI, pp. 100, 101), throws light on the origin of this fragment:

> I confess it is very disgraceful not to engage to write a life of St Philip—but what would you have? . . . I should like nothing better than to do it myself, for I want to see a life of him written which is *not* devotional, but historical . . . for which I think there are a certain quantum of materials, but how can I with a safe conscience promise, what I might not be able to do for ten years to come . . .?

The present draft antedates this letter by a year, and seems to have been intended for domestic rather than for public use. Having this draft by him, Newman could, of course, assure Northcote that "there are a certain quantum of materials."

Newman's distinction between the devotional and historical treatment of saint's lives is drawn out in further detail in his introduction to his sketch of St Chrysostom (*Historical Sketches,* 1872, Vol. 2, Essay 6). The value of the present Fragment on St Philip should be judged, not so much as a piece of original research, but as an interpretation, a 'view' (to use a favourite word of Newman's) of his own on St Philip's life and character. On his devotion to St Philip generally, and his 'preservation of type' in the English Oratory, see above, chapter 7. 'Newman did not "newmanize" St Philip Neri.'

For a recent study of St Philip on historical lines, the work of Meriol Trevor, *Apostle of Rome* (London, 1966) may be recommended. A survey of sources is provided there, pp. 354–8.

FRAGMENT OF A LIFE OF ST PHILIP[1]

Lent 1853

When I finished several months ago the arrangement of the Acts of St Philip into separate portions of meditations for each day in the year, I felt my dear children that there was another devotional offering which I would fain present to him, could I think there was any probability of my finding means or materials to accomplish it. There are two ways in which the life and actions of a Saint may be viewed, piecemeal and as a whole. When viewed in detail each portion has its own instruction independently of the rest, and has it as much, or nearly so, whether or not it can be referred to the particular agent to whom it belongs. Such separate passages of his history, or specimens of his virtues or miracles, may be indeed connected together in the mind of the reader or hearer, and combined into a whole, but in themselves they are materially parts of him, and are rather maxims than examples of sanctity. They are viewed apart from their formal existence in a particular person, and have almost the same weight as if they were parables or poems, or isolated facts of anonymous individuals as the good Samaritan, Lazarus, or the father of the prodigal son. Such is the shape in which Saints' lives are generally written, from the circumstance that they are naturally drawn up from the official processes themselves, which, being of a legal character are subject to certain technical rules and follow an artificial arrangement. But there is another mode of considering the

[1] *B. Or. Ar.* B. 9.3.

Saints and their doings, which is not only valuable in itself, but increases the value of the teaching conveyed in the details of their history, and that is the view of them as living and breathing men, as persons and invested with personal attributes and a character of their own, and peculiarities of habit and feeling and opinion such as belong to him and not to another. This mode of bringing a Saint before us, or (if I may use the word) realizing him, is parallel or cognate to the operations of the memory and reason practised in the Exercises of St Ignatius, and is not to be dismissed by the ascetical reader on the score of its being intellectual unless we are willing to find fault with those exercises which have never been considered deficient in spiritual excellence and strictly religious use. St Ignatius bids us bring before us the person or persons, the scene, the action, in which we meditate, by an act of pure reason, though sub-servient indeed, or rather because conducive to spiritual edification; and in like manner I should say that we gain a great deal in the way of intensity and stability of devotion towards a particular Saint, if we are able to bring him before us, as if he were present, to hang on his lips and to solace our-selves in his smile, a result to which we shall never arrive by the study of separate miracles, heroic deeds, and holy words, each taken by itself, and forbidden to tend to the illustrations and support of each other. And thus, while I freely and distinctly acknowledge the benefit of what may be called the dogmatic, or documentary, I think it is perfected, not thwarted, by the historical.

I would it were as easy to give an historical idea of St Philip, as to arrange the succession of separate incidents in his life. I would contemplate him, if I could, not merely in this action, or that, but as a man. I want so to bring him before me, that the most opposite or apparently irreconcileable points in his conduct, as detailed by his biographers, should at once by the very sight of him be understood and coalesce with each other. I wish to be in possession of that living view of him, which shall be a living key of all, of whatever kind, which has been com-mitted to tradition or writing concerning him. We have not the materials of it; who shall bring together or concentrate in one picture the watcher in the catacombs, the projector of the

Ecclesiastical Annals, and the founder of the Oratorio? While I dwell on particular paragraphs of his Process if he does rise out at all from the letter of the documents on our persevering meditation, he rises, according to the subject matter before us, a different man. He is four or five different persons at once to me, according as I am engaged in this or that detached incident of his life; or, in other words, I have not got the real man before me at all. Philip is away[,] lived three centuries ago; I have never seen him; I wish to be as though I had seen him; the spiritual reading to which I have given myself profitable as it is, does not tend to make us see him as a particular person or a living individual. Nor is this all. Let it be recollected that no acts have a definite value in themselves, but are estimated by their circumstances. A thing may be neither right nor wrong in itself, yet must be either the one or the other in the individual in whom we find it. Of few deeds comparatively out of the multitude that have been done, could we surely pronounce, a Saint did, or no Saint ever did this. And the deeds of one Saint are not the deeds of another Saint; and what is saintly in one might be a sin in another. There are acts certainly which in any one would be sins; but acts in general are to be praised or blamed by the occasion, the time, the person, the place, the manner, the object, and the bearing. To do justice to a Saint's acts, we must know the Saint himself. It is the absence commonly, often unavoidably, of this knowledge, which obliges us to resolve so many of their deeds into particular inspirations, a term which means (nothing else than to imply) that what in itself may be of a doubtful or invidious character is nevertheless right in the individual who does it. Nor do we merely lose the impressiveness and truthfulness of the particular passages of a life, by not realizing it as a whole. It may lose in edification. It is no human curiosity which makes us desire to know the age at which certain virtues were acquired, certain temptations overcome, certain gifts gained, certain works achieved, certain miracles wrought; all which are unaccounted for, if the mere facts are barely related as in the process[.] Spiritual readings are properly limited to spiritual subjects; but a Saint's life may often have in it things not directly and immediately spiritual. To find a Saint sitting down to cards, or reading a heathen author, or listening to music, or taking snuff, is often a relief and an encouragement to the reader, as convincing him that grace does not supersede nature, and that as he is reading of a child of Adam and his own brother; and he is drawn up to his pattern and guide while he sees that pattern can descend to him; whereas that shadowy paper-Saint, as I may call it, bloodless, ideality which may be set up in the mind from the exclusive perusal of a roll of unconnected details, may, from the weakness of our hearts, chill us unduly, lead [us] to shrink from the Saints and to despond about ourselves. And then what professes and promises to be the most edifying mode of studying them may in the event prove to be the least.

The lights and shades of the saintly character, of the individual saint are necessary for understanding what a Saint is. To enter into the meaning and the beauty of St Philip's life, I must compare together what he did when he was young and when he was old, when he was obscure and when he was an Apostle. I have to do with a very varied history, and I may make the most serious of mistakes, I may lose the most winning and instructive of lessons, if I confuse the Pippo Buono, the Solitary of St Sebastian, the lay preacher, the priest of St Girolamo, the confessor of all Rome, the founder of the Oratory with each other. He comes to Rome without a friend or acquaintance; he dies sixty years after in the arms of Cardinals. He starts with the saintliness of youth, he finishes with the saintliness of age. He lives long enough to live two lives, he has two sets of friends. He is reflected in his friends, as he passes along them, and to hear them is to hear him. He is interpreted by his friends, for what he says or does to one, he would not say or do to another. All these things are to be taken into account, if we would estimate him aright. His friends, his position, his age, his influence; and to all (of) them I would give attention, were the materials extant for doing so. As it is, very little can be done as it should be; and less than that little by one, who, like myself, have [sic] no time to attempt to do it thoroughly; and can but put down such things as occur to him, whatever be their worth for the object in question but it will be something to do even a very little, it will be something to show the way, for those who can do more and do it more exactly.

Chapter 2

Little could be known of Philip, before he left Florence, considering he was 18 at the time. The principal things about him are these: he was born in 1515 under Leo x—he was put out to nurse from home, and the house, I believe, is still shown to which he was taken. This might lead one to think whether he lost his mother when an infant and that he was the youngest of his family, and that his father's second wife is spoken of as old at the time of Philip's leaving Florence that is 18 after his birth. But she lived apparently till he was 5, yet might have been in delicate health for years. NB. Philip was *not* the youngest Antonio was 5 years younger. His mother seems to have died soon after. As he grew into boyhood, he simultaneously grew into fixed habits of piety, devotion, and obedience, so that it would appear he never committed a mortal sin his whole life. Two childish acts are recorded of him; one when he was 9 or 10, when he jumped upon an ass of his Father's laden with country fruits; the animal backed, fell down a cellar, and turned over upon him, though he almost miraculously suffered no harm. About the same time or soon after, when he and Elizabeth, his younger sister, were reading the Psalms together, the other girl, Catherine, interrupted him; in consequence he gave her a push, which caused his father to reprove him, and brought him at once to tears. He seems to have been by nature impetuous and sensitive; anger is nearly the only passion which we read of his feeling in after life, though never of his giving way to it. Bacci says "Whenever he felt momentary anger etc. To Gallonio, he said "Give me a kiss, Antonio etc". We read of his being angry with a penitent who called him a Saint. There is another act of his boyhood which shows impetuosity also; his tearing up his father's table of pedigree.

All this did not interfere with his having and constantly manifesting sweetness, gentleness, affectionateness and docility, which won all hearts, as is so well known. What he was abroad, he was at home. His stepmother bitterly lamented the loss of him, and he cherished the tender remembrance of her till her death.

His first confessors were the Dominicans of S. Marco, the

Convent of the celebrated Savonarola, who was burned in the unhappy days of Alexander vi,—years before Philip's birth. Owing so great a debt to that convent, as he always considered, he not unnaturally was through his life a . . .[1] champion of the aforesaid Reformer, and is said to have had his picture in his bedroom.

Two other incidents in his home life are related. When he was 16 he had a fever, which he bore without a word not only with patience but with a highspirited lightness and mirth till it was discovered by the women of the house. About the same time his home was almost burned down, and his father lost a great deal of property, a misfortune which Philip is said to have taken very lightly.

Whether this loss had anything to do with his leaving home for S. Germano does not appear; but of course it requires to be accounted for. He was an only son, and his stepmother's sorrow shows that there was an urgent cause for his going. It would seem as if his father had simply sent him out into the world, and so far as he was concerned left him to himself, as his own master; with no other ties to his uncle or rather cousin than those which grew out of a voluntary engagment with a rich principal. His cousin urges *Ph's family's need.* ⟨Italian Bacci p. 10.⟩ There was no coolness on the part of his father, he loved him tenderly to his death, and left him a life interest in his whole property. His father seems to have made an effort to get him back 2 years later. ⟨Squittrini p 21.⟩ His father's profession had been law; his uncle's was trade; he had a vocation to neither. As he went to S. Germano, which lies in the Kingdom of Naples, he must have passed through Rome, which will account for his mind [sic] thither and not to S. Marco at Florence, or any other place, when he determined to leave his uncle. It has sometimes struck me as singular that we hear nothing of any relation he formed with the famous Benedictine Abbey of Monte Cassino, [which] was close to him, and probably had property all about him. Instead of seeking for support and direction there, as he has sought the Dominicans of S. Marco, we find him frequenting a chapel of the Holy Trinity, belonging indeed

---

[1]Word illegible.

to the Benedictines in question, but on the other side of S. Germano from them and apparently not more than under their jurisdiction. This is remarkable. Benedictines not mentioned in his life? tho' other Orders are. Dominicans, Cistercians, Augustinians he used. In this lonely chapel in the neighbourhood of some awful memorials of Christ's passion, he found his vocation; and whether, because (as I suggested above) he found himself simply released from his father's authority, or whether he asked on unknown some divine motive that is, on a particular inspiration, he saw his way clear to leave his uncle and his wealth for the immediate service of God.

There are those who have their way clearly marked out for them from the first, who understand the work which God calls them to do, and perceive that each step they take leads to it; or if they do not see as clearly as this, yet are not in suspence above a certain time, or see their way in part. But Philip, who was now 18, did not find the specific place in the Church's history till AD 1575, forty years after this date; and as many as 22 years after it, he was questioning whether God called him to India. This seems to me a remarkable instance. Adhaesit anima mea post Te, me suscepit dextera Tua.

His cousin had as much as 22.000 gold crowns, which I believe are said to equal 10/ of our money or £11.000, a very considerable fortune. He came to him in 1533, when he was 18; he stayed with him two years, and then went to Rome being 20. He entered the city as a poor youth, without means or prospects. His father who heard of his plight, and sent him two shirts; afterwards his sister Elizabeth, who seems to have been his favourite? sent him two more, which never came to hand. ⟨vid *Italian* Bacci.⟩ He begged? no more might be sent.

Chapter 3

He got to Rome in the year 1535, as it would appear, when he was 20 years of age, and then he began a long and self imposed noviciate, which lasted 10 years. I say, "self imposed", because the Holy Ghost, who at the end of the time visited Himself in Person, seems to be his immediate guide; his, like St Paul's, was not taught of men or by men, by Dominicans or

Cistercians or Servites, Holy as they were. Of course I mean nothing to the prejudice of this direction of his confessor, whoever he was, though his name is not known.

Before proceeding it may be profitable to notice two or three other points of history, contemporary with Philip's coming to Rome. He had left Florence the very year Henry 8th had forsaken his wife Queen Catherine, and married Anne Boleyn, and had declared himself head of the Church in England; and the very year that St Philip came to Rome Cardinal Fisher and Sir Thomas More were beheaded for refusing to acknowledge him. There is a missionary[?] connexion of St Philip with England. In the latter years of his life he found himself close by the English College, which Gregory the 13th had founded almost opposite St Gerolamo; and this led to the especial interest he is known to have taken in the English missionary priests,—and their having sought his blessing before they returned to their country. It is a curious coincidence too that the Church of the Vallicella was dedicated to Pope St Gregory, the Apostle of England, and that St Philip's day of death and festival occurs on the day of St Eleutherius, the first christianized of the Britons, and of St Augustin the first missionary to the Anglosaxons.

To return, while these terrible events were taking place in England, events and persons of a different character were manifested in other parts of Christendom. St Theresa, who was born in the same year as St Philip, had made her profession, while he was at S. Germano. St Francis Borgia, as yet in the world as the Marquis of Lombay and master of horse to the Empress, being visited by a severe fever, was at the very time Philip came to Rome, commencing his life of piety by making a resolution to read none but works of piety and devotion. Moreover, while Philip was at S Germano, S. Ignatius had with his companions taken his famous vow in the crypt of Montmartre at Paris, which was [to] be considered the commencement of the Society of Jesus—and while Philip was travelling to Rome was travelling back to Spain, his native country, for the restoration of his health. St Carlo, the great Cardinal Archbishop of Milan was not born till five years afterwards.

19

For nine or ten years, Philip, as I have said, gave himself up to devotional exercises, and an almost solitary life. But while he advanced in the science of saints, his exterior life went through a succession of duties also. For two years he seems to have little more external engagement than the care of Caccia's two boys. The Florentines had a quarter in Rome, perhaps near their Church; and hence as his head quarters he went out, when his work of teaching was over, to visit the Churches and sacred places of the city. It was apparently during these two years that when he was coming out one day from a service at the Santi Apostoli, some bad fellows followed him and surrounded him for some wicked purpose. Finding them too many for him, he began so moving a discourse on religious subjects that he brought them to compunction, and so go[t] away.

He was engaged by Caccia to teach his children the humanities or litterae humaniores, which had been the subject matter of his own education in Florence. These consisted chiefly in the latin classics, for which and for literature in general his after history shows us he had a singular taste. He was fond of writing verse both Latin and Italian, and he was able to improvise in the latter. He had a great number of compositions of this nature up to the time of his death, when he burned all his papers, though several sonnets escaped and are still extant, and he had such a lively perception not only of classical literature but of the displays of genius and talent altogether, that, as is well known, when he would distract his mind from accesses of devotion in after years which threatened to incapacitate him for his sacred duties or even to affect his life, he could find nothing more effectual than books of wit or humour (qualche libro di facezie o di scherzo) which sometimes F Consolini (therefore when old) read to him, and he had Latin poets and books of philosophy, and *books* (as he confessed) "which he did not like", ready at hand, to divert his thoughts to subjects of the world.

However, he was not sent into the world to be a literary man or a promoter of literature; so, while he supported himself in Caccia's family by means of the education he had received, he at the same time followed the inspiration which carried him forward, by beginning at the end of two years to attend the schools of philosophy and theology, the second and third portion of the education of a priest. He attended the Lectures of the Sapienza, or Roman University, and he studied with the Augustinians. This course seems to have occupied not more than two years and a half; yet there is no doubt that in that space of time he had acquired such mastery over his subjects, that, unless we attribute it to a divine gift, his talents for abstract science must have been as remarkable as the sensibility to polite literature. Though he was no student from that time forward, yet he ever retained the freshness of his scientific knowledge. In his after life he sometimes would dispute with his spiritual children who were in the schools, either to exercise them, or to ingratiate himself with them, or to draw them to God's service, and he did this with the freedom of a practised theologian, so as to give them real matter for their thoughts and inquiries in their own.

He was no student, as I have said, from that time I have mentioned, that is, the end of 1538 or 1539; in fact he actually sold his books, and henceforth addressed himself simply to the spiritual life. Then began his special season of asceticism; he slept little, generally on the ground, disciplined himself with iron; and aimed at poverty,—lived by himself, ate sparingly, and passed sometimes as much as 10 hours in prayer. Now too he began his celebrated visits to the seven Basilicas, passing the whole night in one or other of them particularly the catacombs of St Sebastian. This remarkable devotion involved him in various praeternatural conflicts with the evil powers, some of which are recorded. He had already, while attending the schools, given himself to the active works of piety to attending the sick in the hospitals, and to catechising the poor in the porches of the Churches, Another office he undertook of a still more observable character, he had about a year before, when he was 23, commenced a more public duty of frequenting the Florentine quarter of the city, and talk[ing] on religious matters to the shop men and their hangers on who were to be found there;—and such seems to have been his life till he was 29 or 30; but we now lose sight of him for five or six years. And there we end the first stage of our review of his life.

Chapter 4

Let us suppose this 5 or 6 years over; Christendom has not slept the while, any more than Philip, tho' his life has been a secret one. In that interval good and evil have had their triumphs and their omens of triumph. King Henry of England had married his 5th wife and had been burning and hanging Catholics and Protestants alternatively. Also he had destroyed all the monasteries through England to the number of 645. He had desecrated many images, burned the bones of the great St Thomas of Canterbury and dispersed his ashes to the winds and water. He had seized on the treasures of the Martyr's shrine, and appropriate[d] the jewels, and was very near his end. St Carlo had been born and was a little child of 6 years old, just come to the years of reason, on the other hand the Council of Trent was on the eve of commencing its labours, and the Society of Jesus had been established by the Popes and St Ignatius was writing its constitutions. St Francis Xavier had commenced his labours in India for several years, and reformed Goa, and was preaching to the pagan populations of the East. St Francis Borgia, still in the world, had just lost his wife and was soon to give up the world too.

We have heard nothing of Philip since the age of 23 or 24. However, he had at that time begun a life, which in its general character continued for some years, so that we know the kind of life he led by the fact that nothing is told us about him. When he was 29 one of the most remarkable events in his life took place, and then there is silence again about him for 4 years. He was generally known as a most saintly man, of whom anything might be expected, and that the more prominently from the deplorable state in which Roman society lay at that time. The horrible sack of Rome by the German soldiery took place in the year 1527, eight years before Philip came there. It had prepared the soil for a reformation of manners, but the seed had not yet been sown, and as yet showed very little appearance of a harvest. The consciousness of existing evils and the wish of better days would naturally lead the minds of men even not especially religious in their own persons to look with interest and anxiety on one who recalled the image of past histories—and they said, "Philip here is a great saint, and among other wonderful things, he has dwelt for 10 years in the caves of St Sebastian by way of penance, and has lived on bread and the roots of herbs."

This, unlike many popular reports, was true almost in the very letter; he had sought His God in the ancient hiding places and sepulchres of His people, and had found Him. Especially had he addressed himself to the Third Person of the Blessed Trinity, and He had vouchsafed to him consolations more than ordinary, so surpassing that, as if in bodily pain, he used to writhe about the ground saying "No more, Lord, no more—"and hence in after life we find him crying out, on one occasion, "He who desires ecstasies and visions, does not know what he desires—O if every one did but know what an ecstasy is"—and then burst into tears. Another pain, the consequence of his gifts, was his exceeding longing to pass out of this world whence he was to continue still a good 50 years to the world unseen: "The true servant of God," he said, "takes life patiently, and death eagerly." It is the common belief that our Lord miraculously kept body and soul together in His agony when He said "My soul is sorrowful to death;" did He not exercise a similar miracle on a youth who lived almost without food, without sleep, and in the most fatiguing practice of charitable works, and in a divine exercise so high as to be a continual and acute pain? One would think that the body, like some feeble instrument overcharged, would break under what was put upon it; and so it did, and would have succumbed in consequence, but for the law of divine duty, which the early Fathers recognised in the physical world, that, when God puts forth his hand to create, He exerts a second virtue to enable the thing created to bear that Hand, lest it is perish again by the very act which brought it into being.[1]

I am alluding òf course to the famous visitation which came on him when he was 29 in the retreat of St Sebastian shortly before Pentecost 1544, which that year fell on [1 June]. While he was praying for the gifts of the Holy Ghost, he saw a ball of fire descend, it entered his mouth and lodged in his breast.

---

[1] Cf. *Select Treatises of St Athanasius* Vol. II. 1881, p. 142.

Immediately he began to experience those remarkable flutterings of heart and tremour of body which attended him through life, and on putting his hand to his side he found a tumour there of the size of a man's fist—It continued thus all his life, and never gave him any pain. After his death it was found that the heart had broken two of his ribs which thus showed itself.

Extraordinary as was this enlargement of his side, the tremblings I have referred to were more wonderful still. They are described by F. Bacci on various occasions. 'The palpitation of the heart only came on when he was performing some spiritual action, such as praying, saying Mass, communicating, giving absolution, talking on heavenly things, and the like. When ever he pressed any of his spiritual children to his breast, they found the motion of his heart so great, that their heads bounded off from him, as if they had received a short shock from something, while at other times the motion seemed like that of a hammer. The trembling which it caused was so vehement, that it seemed as if his heart would break from his breast, and his chair, his bed, and sometimes the whole room would shake. On one occasion in particular, he was at St Peter's kneeling on a large table, and he caused it to shake as if it had been of no weight at all—Sometimes when he was lying upon the bed, with his clothes on, his body was to float up into the air, through the vehemence of the palpitation.' Again, we are told, 'When he came to the Offertory the joyousness of his heart was so great, that his hand repeatedly leaped in such a way that he could not pour the wine into the chalice, yet he was quite young, and with nothing like palsy about him. In the memento he made extraordinary movements, even leaped, and was agitated all over. Occasionally after consecration, he had such spiritual exultation, that he raised himself on the tips of his toes, and seemed as if he was dancing, or he was lifted a span or more from the ground.' We are also told that when he was discoursing on religious subjects in a free and familiar way, 'he did it with so much fervour, that the usual palpitation of his heart came on, and made, not only the bed, but sometimes the whole room shake, and his whole body was occasionally lifted up into the air.'

An event like this, so miraculous in itself, so miraculous in its life long results and memorials, is of magnitude enough to fill the space of ten years and more although we have nothing else definite to record.

Chapter 5

We now commence the period of Philip's active life. It is told that ever since the year 1539 when at the age of 24 he sold his books and gave himself to God, he had addressed himself to work for the good of his neighbours, as I have already said—F Bacci tells us expressly that in the piazzas, and streets, and shops, and even in the rooms of the counting houses, he made attempts to gain souls to Xt. But we do not hear of any of his victories for 10 years, and [at] all events he formed no durable connexions with other people or brought about him any person whose names have come down to us till that date. The chief reason appears to be this that the class of persons whom he attempted. He ended as we know by being the guide and Confessor of Popes, Cardinals and the upper classes generally —but he began in the lowest of all, whose names are not likely to be recorded and who could not form a company round him, and gradually ascended in the scale of society. We hear first of his addressing the old women and beggars generally who congregated then as now in the porticos of the Basilicas— Then Bacci speaks of the Streets with the labouring men, and market women the shops with their journey men and apprentices ⟨the merchants with their warehouses⟩, and the bankers rooms with   [1] His first converts, as recorded are out of this class, but these do not occur till the 10 years was past, viz warehouse men etc.

There are two subjects here in the portion of his life between the Great Miracle in the catacombs and his ordination, (29–35,) the Pellegrini, his bearing on the Jesuits as a *bell*. St Ignatius came to Rome about 1539 (Philip aet. 24, when he had just sold his books) the Jesuits made a great noise in that year at Rome—the Society was established 1540—St Ignatius died about 1555—I suppose he sent subjects to the Jesuits between 29–35 aet. and so onwards. These are the subjects of ch V.[2]

[1] Space left blank by Newman.
[2] This is the end of the fragment.

NEWMAN'S ORATORY PAPERS No. 18

12 JANUARY 1854

INTRODUCTORY NOTE

This Address on virginity was delivered at the religious profession of Mary Anne Bowden (1831–67), elder daughter of Mrs J. W. Bowden, who entered the Visitation Convent at Westbury in 1852[1].

Mary Anne is mentioned more than thirty times in Newman's *Letters and Diaries,* vols. XI–XVII. She was 14 years of age at the time of Newman's reception as a Catholic; she herself became a Catholic the following year[2], and from the age of 17 began to think of entering a convent. It was five years before she eventually entered the Visitation Convent, Newman all along being in constant communication with her mother about the girl's vocation. As Newman saw it, the main difficulties in the Visitation Convent were:

> . . . inclosure, want of practical object, company of invalids, and prohibition of music. I wish dear M. [Mary Anne] were led to a religion of a more practical character—but if she is really led to the above, she will be blessed in it[3].

Shrewd remarks of this nature occur frequently in his letters on Mary Anne's vocation; while Newman himself spared no trouble in seeing the Bowdens—he even had an interview with them on the very day of the fifth Lecture in the Corn Exchange "the Achilli one."[4]

What a contrast in tone when we turn to the text of his sermon on the occasion of her profession. Here we have an almost lyrical treatment of virginity as a marriage with Christ. What could have been a commonplace theme on virginity as the "better part", Newman makes all the more telling by linking virginity *with*, rather than opposing it *to*, the fulfilment

[1] cf. *L.D.,* XI, p. 333.
[2] cf. *L.D.,* XI, p. 205 (12 July 1846)
[3] *L.D.,* XV, p. 12
[4] *L.D.,* XIV, p. 320.

of human love in marriage. Rather than say that all human affection is sacrificed, he shows that it is transferred to Christ himself.

Celibacy, both religious and sacerdotal, was under constant fire from non-Catholics in England at the time, as can be seen from the frequent references in Newman's *Letters and Diaries*— even the crude calumnies of *Maria Monk* were subjects of the day. In this sermon, Newman gives a serene and ennobling view of Christian virginity, which scorns these vulgar attacks, and goes back to patristic and New Testament values. It is this serenity, combined with his full appreciation of the role of human love in marriage, which can make this sermon relevant to our modern *problématique* on celibacy and marriage.

Although not strictly speaking an Oratorian paper (since it does not concern his own Oratorian community) it is included in the present collection as illustrating Newman's thought on an important aspect of religious life in the Catholic Church.

12 JANUARY 1854[1]

Let us be glad and rejoice and give glory to Him; for the marriage of the Lamb is come, and His wife hath prepared herself. *Apoc.* xix, 7.

There is but one God and he has been from the beginning. He is all perfect, all sufficient, all in all—He has all things in Himself, and there is no power, goodness, or any other excellence external to Him. And therefore, when He created the visible and invisible worlds, they could have no excellence of any kind but what He gave them, for He was the one Fount, and abiding centre and Sovereign Lord and Owner of all that was good and true, strong or beautiful. It was impossible even for the Almighty to create a being who should be independent of Himself; for, because He was Almighty, all things besides Him from the nature of the case depended on Him.

This is the second fundamental truth of all religion. The

[1] *B. Or. Ar.* B. 3. 2. ii.

first is that God is all sufficient—the second that nothing is sufficient but He. The first that He is His own good and his own bliss; the second that the blessedness of every creature lies in resting in Him. Without this the highest of holiest Archangel [sic] would suddenly droop, and collapse and shrivel up—or rather without this no Archangel would have height of place or sanctity of person to forfeit.

This it is which the good Angels understood so well, this was it which the rebel hosts forgot to their own destruction in the beginning. Satan fell from heaven like lightning before any formal condemnation on the part of the Most High; he was condemned already in his ambition[—]to attempt a rival throne to God, was in itself to build upon the great deep. The creation can but build itself upon God: He is the only possible foundation. as well might men imagine leaving the solid ground to tread on air or water, as the creature to leave the God of Ages and yet to plant himself upon a basis of his own. And who would wish to do so, if he could, but spirits so perverted and unnatural, that, unless there are such, unless in our own hearts we have vestiges[,] a sad witness of its possibility, we should have thought it could not be. The Gifts of God within us, the grace which comes from Him, witnesses to its Author, extols Him, draws the spirit towards Him from whom it comes, makes it His child while it makes it acceptable to Him, and preaches devotion while it imparts sanctity. An intense self renunciation, a profound self surrender to Him is, I will not say the duty, but the very law of all created beings.

And therefore in simple love to us, for the very love wherewith He created us, is He necessarily led to proclaim to us this elementary truth, that if we would live we must look to Him for life, if we would be happy, we must make Him our glory. He asks us compassionately, "Why *will ye* die?" Quare moriemini. I am not imposing on you any positive law, which I could dispense with, I am not simply proving your obedience, by the conditions of an arbitrary command, I am but stating what is involved in the very fact of my being the living God, that if you would live, you must live by Me.

However Angels fell, and man disobeyed, and a world of sinners was the consequence; but the Eternal Truth remained, and not thousands upon thousands could reverse it. The will of nations might say "It shall not be". but it was as true as before. The wit of sages, the fiat of monarchs, the decree of states could not do that which was impossible even to God. The tender mercy of the Creator might look out mournfully and yearn over the work of His hands—but if He was to create, unless He was to annihilate, even He could not reverse it; He could not deny His own being and attributes; He could not make a second God; He could not bring it about that man should be happy, yet should rebel against Him. And therefore His love was exercised, not in allowing an impossibility, not in recognizing a rebellion, but in calling back the rebels to the sweetness of paternal forgiveness and the tenderness of paternal affection. Destructio tua Israel &c. O Israel thy destruction is thine own—in me only is thy help—Convertimini, filii revertentes, et sanabo aversiones vestras, Jer 3, He does not say go on, He says return—He cannot change His own nature: He cannot compromise His power and sanctity, He can but enlarge His mercy[2].

How He enlarged it, my Brethren, you know full well. He would not be outdone by man—Man had done great exploits in the way of sinning, but the Creator resolved on greater in the way of love. He determined to win man's heart back to him; in spite, if I may say so, of himself. Therefore He veiled His glory and His high estate—He came in disguise, He put on Him a created nature, He made Himself our equal, He came to the world which He made, as a man; and He ate and drank, and conversed and mixed with us, as the brother of this nature. He condescended to what would seem impossible in God, but the idea of which to God only was possible, He condescended to come and all for the sake of the poor sinful soul, to ask its love, to display to it His own celestial excellence, to win it, and to join it to Himself in an eternal marriage. Nay, and when He determined to give a proof of how much He loved and how much He would sacrifice for the object of His choice, for, lest He the Creator should not come with a sufficient recommendation, or bid high enough for His beloved, He went out to fight

---

[2]Newman is quoting here the Vulgate text of *Jer*. 3:22.

the tyrant who enslaved it, and He rescued it from captivity at the price of His own blood.

And thus in a far more endearing way, according to our need, has He brought before us the momentous doctrine of our dependence on Him. It is an eternal truth that without Him we cannot do any thing good—and that in His presence is our blessedness. But He insists not on this—in the bare form of doctrine He summons us not to Him—rather He goes out to win us and to meet us. He manifests Himself not as the Judge of the spirits of all flesh, but as the Lover of souls—Convertimini, filii revertentes, dicit Dominus, quia ego vir vester[3]. He has married Himself to His Church, and to every elect soul in it, giving Himself for it, ut illam sanctificaret, mundans lavacro aquae in verbo vitae, ut exhiberet ipse sibi gloriosam Ecclesiam, non habentem maculam, aut rugam, aut aliquid hujusmodi, sed ut sit sancta et immaculata[4]. Such is the mode He has so graciously adopted to win us back to Him; such is the great event which lies before us after the resurrection according to the text, the marriage feast: "Let us be glad and rejoice and give glory to Him; for the marriage of the Lamb is come, and His wife hath prepared herself." (*Apoc.* xix. 7).

Now to enter into the full force of this condescension, we must consider more attentively what man is, and what is his condition. Recollect then, my dear Brethren, that man is, not a pure spirit, not an Angel, but is far differently constituted, having a compounded nature, made up of soul and body. He is a creature of the elements, and is subject to their power. He is weak, wayward, irritable, irrepressible, wavering, capricious; he is carried off in various directions; and, in order to fulfil his mission at all, he must first be directed to one object and fixed in one course. His Creator, who knew what He had created, and saw his need, even in the time of his innocence, and while he was elevated above himself by supernatural grace, even in Paradise itself anticipated and supplied it. The only human way to bringing him into harmony with himself and preparing him to discharge the duties which were incumbent on him,

---

[3]*Jer.* 3:14 (Vulgate).
[4]*Eph.* 5:26, 27 (Vulgate).

was to withdraw him from the numberless influences which surrounded him and to fix his mind upon one object. It was not good for him to be alone, and a helper was created for him. Such is the perfection of human nature, viewed in itself, divinely ordained, and recognised as such by Christianity which has raised matrimony to the dignity of a Sacrament.

Man has great capacities; he has an intellect, and a heart for many things; his nature is expansive, nor can you say how many things he can know, how many things he can love, but he must begin from some fixed points. It is by the law of our nature, the happiness of everyone, man and woman, to have one central and supreme attachment, to which none other can be compared. An affection, one, mutual, sovereign, unalterable, is earthly happiness and his earthly strength. Two mortal creatures of God, placed in this rough world, exposed to its many fortunes, destined to suffering and death, join hands, and give the faith to each other that each of them will love the other wholly until death. Henceforth each is made for the other—each has possession of the affections of the other in a transcendent way; each loves the other better than any thing else in the way; each is all in all to the other; each can confide in the other unreservedly, each is the others irreversibly. There is but one mind, one aim, one course, one happiness, between two. Each is reflected in the other; each reads his own thought in the other's face; each feels for the other more than for himself. Such is the fountain head of human society and the continual provision of the human race: such is the beginning of civilization, the guardian of religion, and the norm of philanthropy, and the sanctification(?) of mankind. There is no such union elsewhere in this natural world; even the tie which binds mother and child may be broken—Ineffable as was the interchange of love, and close the union which bound Mary and Jesus—Thirty years it lasted, but then He had to go to preach and suffer; and, as far as this world went, He had little more to do with His Mother. But conjugal duty is indestructible: and in its ardour and its security it may seem (if I may speak the word with reverence) to recall to us the everlasting ineffable love with which the Father loves the Son who is in His bosom and the Son the Father who has from all eternity begotten Him.

Such is the blessedness of man viewed in his own nature, and without reference to grace. And now considering what shall we say of the dispensation of grace? [Grace] you know my Brethren, has innovated upon nature, not destroying or suspending it, but bringing in a higher order. Under the Gospel not marriage, but virginity, has been in honor, and that because the kingdom of Christ is the Kingdom of heaven, and its luminaries, as becomes such a kingdom, neither marry nor are given in marriage but are as the Angels of God. Under the Jewish Law marriage was in honor even according to the standard of the religion itself. Moses the Lawgiver was married—Aaron was married—the priests and levites generally were married—the prophets were married—so too were the prophetesses as Debora and Olda[?]; there are a few exceptions, as Josue, Elias and Eliseus, the anticipation of what was one day to be. But when the fulness of time came, and the Gospel was preached, and the· Catholic Church set up, then forthwith virginity became honorable as the higher state. Our Lord Himself, the Crown of Virgins, His everblessed Virgin Mother, St John Baptist, set the pattern to the new disciples. The Apostles followed, never married, or separating from their wives; the rulers of the Church; the priests and other sacred ministers, and then lay persons, men and women, who aimed at perfection. Henceforth a system of grace came in, which raised man above himself, and without repealing the laws by which he was naturally governed, or making that wrong which was God's ordinance regarding him, put before his eyes a nobler state of life and counselled him to do that which came to him on no obligation.

Now I ask, Has the Almighty God deprived us of any blessing of man innocent when He has thus set before us a higher life. Not so. Observe this then, my brethren. The Gospel recommends celibacy, but observe how it draws around it the choicest blessings of human nature, while it seems to be giving them up. There is a state of celibacy recommended by philosophers, exemplified in religious teaching, which does but harden the heart, which is of that forlorn, haughty and repulsive nature—as it has been imaged and extolled in the pages of heathen writers or in the teaching of false religions. There

have been those among the philosophers of antiquity who have
been led to praise of a life of asceticism and self-denial almost
Christian. There have been those among false religions who
have actually observed the state of celibacy, and that on the
ground that it was higher than the common life of man. To
make a single life its own end, to adopt it simply and solely
for its own sake, I do not know whether such a state of life is
more melancholy or more unamiable, melancholy from its unrequited desolateness and unamiable from the pride and self-
esteem on which it is based[5].

This is not the Virginity of the Gospel—it is not a state of
independence or isolation, or dreary pride, or barren indolence,
or crushed affections; man is made for sympathy, for the
interchange of love, for self-denial for the sake of another
dearer to him than himself. The Virginity of the Christian soul
is a marriage with Christ. Hence the words, "I have espoused
you to one husband, that I may present you as a chaste virgin
to Christ[6]." O surprising love and wisdom, that has thus
allowed us to aim at being Angels without ceasing to be men.
O transcending condescension that He should stoop to be ours
in the tenderest and most endearing way—ours to love, ours to
consult, ours to minister to, ours to converse with, ours to joy[?]
in [?][7]. Ours so fully that it is as if He had none to think of but
each of us personally. The very idea of matrimony is possession
—whole possession—the husband is the wife's and no other's,
and the wife is the husband's and none but his. This is to enter
into the marriage bond, this is the force of the marriage vow,
this is the lesson of the marriage ring. And this it is to be
married to Jesus. It is to have Him ours wholly, henceforth, and
for ever—it is to be united to Him by an indissoluble tie—it is
to be His, while He is ours—it is to partake of that wonderful
sacrament which unites Him to His Blessed Mother on high
—Dilectus meus mihi, et ego illi, qui pascitur inter lilia[8]. Such

---

[5] later addition by Newman: Like a Mahometan's god, who from eternity has
had no exercise of love.

[6] *2 Cor.* 11:2.

[7] doubtful reading, perhaps: gaze [?] on [?]

[8] Vulgate text of *Song of Solomon*, 6:2 (=RSV, 6:3): 'I am my beloved's and my
beloved is mine; he pastures his flock among the lilies.'

has the Highest deigned to be to His elect; to all of them in the world to come, as the text tells us, and to those of them in their degree by earnest or by anticipation who are called to follow the Lamb whithersoever He goes, to those who are called to the holy orders or to the monastic state—to those especially the Spouses of Christ, those dear children of grace, who leave the earth and its allurements and its enjoyments, for Him alone, all of them ineffably united to Him, (you know it far better than I can tell you my sisters) some of them ascending so high along the ladder of mystical devotion as actually already to forestall that perfect solemnity which will be the portion of all the saints in the world to come.

Such were the innocent and beautiful saints, in past ages of the Church, martyrs or confessors, who are your patterns, my Sisters, and your guardians and your intercessors and your intimate friends. Such was St Agnes, who when offered for husband a Roman nobleman, answered that she had found a better spouse—such St Domitilla, the emperor's niece, who,⁹ when offered a high marriage, answered "If a maiden were offered the choice of a monarch or a peasant, which would she prefer?" Such St Susanna, such St Agatha, who were martyred rather than lose Christ. Such your own heroic St Frances who was ever pining for the presence of her Spouse. Such the blessed Margaret Mary, who would have nothing short of his sacred heart, and could speak of it alone.

You, my Sisters, who form this holy community, you, too, my sisters, who are the subject of the present solemn rite and the occasion of our present meeting, you know all these things far better than I can speak of them—and, were you not as charitable as you are, would smile at my rude wordy attempt to describe blindly and vaguely what you have so long experienced, or have so anxiously expected. Anxiously, with many beatings of heart, and holy aspirations, you have been waiting for this day, my dear Sisters, who are now before the Bishop who has the charge of you, anxiously waiting for this day, and now it has come. The joyful, the solemn day is come, (when some of you are to begin your trial, and others to receive its reward—) O

⁹Note by Newman in text: St Alfonso—Nun sanctified.

joyful, solemn day, the remembrance of which will be sweet through all eternity—that day of your espousals to Him whom you have chosen. He has chosen you, and you have chosen Him. He loves you with a love incomparable. He yearns over you in tenderness, He has drawn you with the cords of Adam[10]—He has come to you in all His sanctity and all His divine beauty, and you have yielded yourselves to Him, to love and serve Him, and to love none other but Him except in Him for ever and ever.

Each of you has her own wonderful history known to herself —each has been drawn to Him in a way more wonderful than all the rest—for God can do these blessed things, each most wonderful. Each has had most mercies shown it, and most sins forgiven, and most graces bestowed. Each has the greatest cause of gratitude and affection —each is visited with the most special marks of His loving remembrance—I know it— I thank God for it—but there is one here, whom I cannot help singling out, not as having more of mercy shown her my sisters that you the rest, but because I know her better, and because in contemplating Our Lord's exceeding mercy upon her, I am able to imagine, without knowing, His surpassing mercies to you all.

You, then, my dear Child, I have known almost from your very birth. There is one, now no more, who was my earliest and truest friend, almost from my boyhood. To you he had more claim than anyone—for he was your father[11].Well do I remember in your earliest infancy what you do not recollect the day of your baptism—well do I recollect that day, the 15th of April 1831 so many years ago, and the great anxiety that dear father showed that in every the least particular of ceremony you should be baptized rightly. I baptized you—thus, it was, long before I was a Catholic, that according to the Anglican rite, I took you in my arms[12], and baptized you with water in

---

[10]*Hosea* 11:4. a favourite text of Newman's, to illustrate God's compassionate dealings with mankind.

[11]John William Bowden (1799-1844), Newman's close friend from undergraduate days at Trinity College (Oxford). See *L.D.*, XI, p. 333.

[12]cf. the rubric in the *Book of Common Prayer:* "Then the Priest shall take the child into his hands, and shall say" &c.

20

the name of the Three Divine Persons, and signed you with
the sign of the cross. That baptism, though administered in
ignorance, I believe to be fully valid—wisely and· mercifully
has the Church given you conditional baptism on coming to her,
lest there should be any chance of mistake; but the form was
right and the matter right, and I had the fullest wish and
purpose to do what the Church does, and I fully believe that
from that moment you were rescued from the power of Satan,
and made the subject of God's supernatural promises and
supernatural graces. From your very infancy then God has
chosen you, and claimed you as His own. From your infancy
has your dear Lord put His seal upon you, and drawn you
towards Him out of the world, nay out of the multitude of
faithful, to be with you more intimately than with others, to
inhabit your heart, to fill you with heaven, and to preserve
you in innocence and peace. Ah my child, I am not unmindful,
nor are you, that whatever be His graces to you hitherto, they
constitute no claim on Him to continue you to the end—I am
not unmindful, that peaceful as your course has hitherto been,
trials may come before life is over—rather the more you have
received the more you may pray and tremble lest you should
have to answer for the forfeiting of such manifold mercies. I
know no one is safe till he has finished his course, but, not
forgetting this, I return thanks to God for what he has been to
you from the first. I tenderly and thankfully look back on those
past years, when, while you were all unconscious, I was narrowly
watching you from the love I bore your parents. Your image
is before me, as you were a child, and as you were a girl—I
recollect your manners and your ways—Well do I recollect
your dear Father, when you were a child, predicting that you
would be a nun, so early gently and perseveringly has God
drawn you. And so, as time went on, God's purpose towards
you became plainer—and then, when he was about to be taken
from you he[13] passed his last days in this very vicinity, as if
with his last breath to commend you to the tender care of a
Father and Master even kinder and more powerful than your
· own, the glorious St Francis and St Frances Chantal. He

---

[13]Note in pencil by Newman: your earthly guardian

brought you as if to the very door of this sacred house, and then he left you.

This is a world of separation and of bereavement—but the day will come fulfilling that which this begins, the day of the solemnity of the eternal marriage between God and His elect. Here we are variously called in His service, to the right and on the left—we go abroad or we sit at home—we remain in retirement or we go forth into the world. But that Day will reassemble us, when the voice goes forth, Behold the Bridegroom cometh —and then the wise Virgins will take their lamps and go forth to meet him—and He will take them up to the everlasting banquet—and there will be the mother of Jesus, with the flagons of celestial wine—and the Angels will sing joyfully Blessed are they who are called to the wedding supper of the Lamb. *Apoc.* 19.

NEWMAN'S ORATORY PAPERS No. 19
2 FEBRUARY 1854

INTRODUCTORY NOTE

Although only a bare list of points, this Chapter Address is a valuable record, showing us as it does Newman reviewing a "very eventful three years" 1851–1854, dominated by the Achilli trial indeed, but accompanied by many other crosses (the greatest of these being the death of Joseph Gordon in February 1853). Two other major events had taken place, viz. the installation of the community at Hagley Road, and Newman's acceptance of the Rectorship of the Catholic University. A hidden source of trouble lay under the surface of the life in community—the disturbing presence of Fr Bernard Dalgairns. On this see below, Oratory Papers, 31 August 1856. The whole difference with the London Oratory was also in the offing. On this latter see above, pp. 100, 102, and the outline supplied on pp. XIII–XVII of *L.D.* XVII.

The following Annotations (corresponding to the sub-divisions in Newman's text) will help to elucidate what might be obscure in this outline Address.

St Wilfrid's: A property at Cheadle, whither Newman and the first group of Oratorians went from Maryvale, after Faber had joined them. On the implications of all this, see above, pp. 96–99.

Lady O. A.: Lady Olivia Acheson (1816?–1852). See *L.D.*, XIII, p. 509.

F John Cooke: see below, Oratory Papers, 1 February 1878 for Newman's comments on the death of Fr Cooke.

My sermon at St Chad's: Sunday 27 October 1850, *Christ upon the Waters*, O.S. pp. 121–62. See *L.D.*, XIV, p. 114.

Alcester Street mission: Newman's first mission in the city of Birmingham. Full references in *L.D.*, XIII, p. 509.

New House: The (present) Oratory at Hagley Road, Edgbaston. See Oratory Papers, below, *The House*.

ii 1851.

Aloysius: Laybrother at the Oratory, Robert Boland (1825–52), see *L.D.*, XII, p. 427.

F Joseph: John Joseph Gordon (1811–53), Oratorian in Newman's community at Alcester Street. cf. *L.D.*, XII, pp. 431, 432. Newman's tribute to him is printed in H. Tristram, *Newman and His Friends*, London, 1933, pp. 111–16 and is included as Oratory Paper No. 29, below, p. 361. In 1865 Newman dedicated *The Dream of Gerontius* to him.

Leeds: See Oratory Papers, below, Decree Book of the Birmingham Oratory (Paper of 25 January 1869) under the date: April 14, 1851: "A prospect of an Oratory at Leeds is opened on us (in consequence of our having received into the Church the Anglican community there of St Saviour's)." See *L.D.*, XIV, p. 246.

F. Wm: William Paine Neville (1824–1905) received into the Church by Newman at Leeds, on 3 April 1851; became an Oratorian at Birmingham. See *L.D.*, XIV, p. 549. Alternatively, since Neville did not become a priest until 1861, the reference here may be to Father William Penny, for whom see the entry in Oratory Papers (25 January 1869), Decree Book, under the date 30 January 1851.

F Philip Molloy: Philip Butler Molloy (1827–55), at the Birmingham Oratory 1852–4. See *L.D.,* XIV, p. 548.

May 26—Father Robert: See *L.D.,* XV, p. 91: "Wednesday 26 May 1852 . . . Mr Tillotson must have arrived from America this day, and soon after began his probation as Fr Robert"; see further, *L.D.,* XVIII, p. 519.

The Synod: The first Synod of the new Province of Westminster, 6–17 July 1852, at which Newman preached 'The Second Spring' on Tuesday 13 July. See *L.D.,* XV, pp. 122–6.

Father Bernard (Dalgairns), 1818–76. See *L.D.,* XI, p. 338. See also Oratory Papers, below, 31 August 1856.

Bishop in partibus (infidelium): Titular bishopric in lands formerly but no longer Christian. The reference is to a proposed bishopric for Newman, on which see *L.D.,* XV, p. 338; *L.D.,* XVI, p. 99, note 3; ib. p. 121, note 1.

misericordiam &c: A quotation from the Vulgate text of the Psalm: 22(23):6. RSV 23(22): Surely goodness and mercy shall follow me all the days of my life; and I shall dwell in the house of the Lord for ever.

CHAPTER ADDRESS 2 FEBRUARY 1854

Address to the Fathers on the events of the last three years Purification 1854.

A very eventful three years
Existing State
i Lately—
    1. St Wilfrid's given us. 2. we collected together *all.* 3 I lately received the Doctorate. 4 We had lost F John Cooke. 5. Lady O.A.[1] had come for the winter. 6. The Hierarchy.
−7. My sermon at St Chad's.
    Converts flocking in. Alcester Street mission flourishing. The foundation of the new House laid.

[1]Lady Olivia Acheson (1816?–1852). See *L.D.,* XIII, p. 509.

1851

ii My forebodings of Crosses.

1. Aloysius taken ill—F. Joseph sickening
2. Still this did not strike us—Our house went on
3. another portent *Leeds.*—F Wm.[2]
4. Hierarchy agitation.
5. My Sermons in the Corn Exchange.
6. F Joseph still getting ill.
7. I getting ill.
8. My engagement to go to Ireland.
9. the Achilli business.

1852

ii [sic] A dismal time.

how dreary—*not* haec olim.

nothing but running about—F Joseph here, F Ambrose there &c. I hurried up to Town.

The strange *unexpected* sort of thing—the event so uncertain My Midnight Mass at Xtmas 51–52.

2. immediately after that mass Lady O.A. taken to her bed.
3. New house getting finished—Lady Olivia anointed 16 February the day I first said mass here.
4. Meanwhile F Joseph had gone abroad and returned.
5. Aloysius had taken to his bed in September his death but the same day F Philip Molloy a compensation.
6. May 26—Anniversary[?] —Father Robert, a compensation.
7. The Synod.
8. November 22 called up to judgment—F Joseph took to his bed.
9. then this new year the bubble or gathered [gathering] broken.

[ref to Brother Bernard, *Or.P.* No. 15.]

---

[2]Fr William Neville [the only fruit of the Leeds conversions]. See *L.D.*, XI, p. 351. Novices were called Father, so he could be Fr Wm. The portent was the conversion of a group.

1853

iii Since, a sort of reaction or calm.

　1. Last year only building Church Father Bernard.

　2. My being called to Ireland

　3. Bishop in partibus.

Survey of whole

　1. Just includes our settlement in House and Church here—

　2. the loss of John, Aloysius &c.

　3. The Achilli matter.

　4. stretching from my doctorate to the Episcopate.

———————

misericordia subsequetur me omnibus diebus &c
et ut inhabitem &c.
our many mercies

———————

NEWMAN'S ORATORY PAPERS Nos. 20 & 21
FEBRUARY 1854

INTRODUCTORY NOTE

On these two Addresses, see above. p. 143. There is no date given for either of these Discourses, but they must be among those Newman sent from Ireland in February 1854, when he went there to begin his work of founding the Catholic University. See the Introduction to Newman's Oratory Paper No. 22, and Henry Bittleston's letter, Oratory Paper No. 23, which explains why the Discourses were not continued. *L.D.*, XVI, pp. 57–60, and 175–6. In the Discourse on the House Newman shows his affection for Joseph Gordon by addressing him as if still living, 'though not here.' Bernard Dalgairns, who is also addressed, did not rejoin the Birmingham Oratory until 5 October 1853, and in the first draft, after the reference to Ambrose St John in the final paragraph as 'Father Minister,' Newman continued 'who are adding my duties to your own in my absence.' St John only took on these duties when Newman left for Ireland on 7 February 1854.

As to the Hagley Road House, the following entries in *L.D.*, XV, give the stages in which they moved in:—p. 38: Monday 16 February 1852 sung First Mass (Missa Cantata) in Edgbaston House—and took up my abode there

p. 62:—Saturday 3 April finished getting in all my books and papers into my room at Edgbaston. (*all the time thinking I might have to leave them for prison!*)

p. 68: Thursday 15 April 1852 went up to Edgbaston, leaving Alcester Street for good.

As to the importance of the "House" in the Oratorian ethos, see above, pp. 97-99.

As to the Discourse on the Refectory, cf. *L.D.*, XV, p. 506: "Tuesday 20 December The French painters went after finishing the Refectory." [The year was 1853]. Also, *L.D.*, XVI, 3: "Sunday 1 January 1854 we got in to the Refectory at last, after the decorations etc—having been two months out of it. *The decorators having been 2 months in it.*"

CHAPTER ADDRESS: THE HOUSE[1]
FEBRUARY 1854

There is one point, my dear Fathers and Brothers, which has naturally pressed a good deal on my mind, ever since we came to Edgbaston, and which I only wish I had more vigorously acted on myself, and more consistently carried out in the Congregation.

You recollect I often used to say, before we came here, in answer to suggestions made to me on house matters, particularly to dear Fr Joseph, our then Fr Minister, "Let us wait till

[1]*B. Or. Ar.* D. 4. 9.

we go to the new House." It was indeed true, that, while we were in our first dwelling, in many respects we did not fulfil the idea of St Philip's Institution, nay, nor the spirit or letter of our Rule. It is true perhaps that, even now, in this country, and at least with a Mission still so little formed, we cannot exactly and severely fulfil it, or while we are, as now, so short of hands; still, we are in a condition for aiming at it now, which we did not enjoy before we came here and at least we may begin by making the House itself, in which we dwell, a subject matter for the exercise of our devotion to St Philip, and of our attention to order and rule.

This large House is in some sense a *subject* of the Oratory, and has to go through its noviciate, before it can be said really to belong to us. And again, since the Congregation has to grow *into* the House as into its outward covering or shell, almost a corresponding process must be undergone by ourselves, before we can be considered to be established on the spot of ground, to which our dear and Holy Father has conducted us.

As then St Philip himself used to say to his children one by one, Nulla dies sine linea, "No day without its touch," so at this time I would urge on you and on myself a continual progress in the work of bringing into shape both this House and the Congregation which inhabits it, into that shape which he has chosen for the Oratory. It is still our trial to have the duties of our pastoral charge undetermined or inchoate; nay it is a trial to have but a temporary Church; a more serious trial to be short of hands, and heads, and hearts, for St Philip's work;— but after all we can do much, and must do all we can.

Let it be our aim then, my Fathers and Brothers, that every fresh month, that every chapter, as it comes, may find us more and more in our place, more and more at home, more and more in possession of our true relations to things about us, and a good understanding with our duties. Emigrants take up their abode in the wilderness or the forest; they rough it; they clear the wood, drain the swamp, dig for water, plough the soil, stake out, fortify their homestead, and build their dwelling. Our occupation is not so toilsome, so hazardous; we are not quite like the medieval Cistercian or Camaldolese; still we have to bring things into order, as they, we have to find a place for every one, and every thing, and to get into our own. We have to set in order the public and private rooms, the Library, the Refectory, the Sacristy, the Oratory, the Recreation and Congregation Rooms, the corridors, the cellars. We have had to sort what is miscellaneous, to dispose of what is littering, to get rid of what is useless, and to put aside what is occasional. And so again, to go to higher matters, the state of our accounts, the arrangement of our property, and the calculation of our prospects, the distribution of our offices, the work of each of us, the routine of the day, the principles, the maxims, the usages, by which our Oratorian life is to be governed, our tone of thought, our going out and coming in, our religious exercises, our prayers and meditations, all may form matter for the undertaking to which I am exhorting you. To us is intrusted the high and onerous office, of forming the character, of starting the traditions, of an infant Institution; and, while St Philip's own idea is our only pattern, so his glorious intercession on high, and our own anxious prayers and jealous diligence, and the blessing of Almighty God and His dear Mother are our only means.

I charge you then, my dear Fathers and Brothers, for His greater glory and the honor of His Church, for the love of our supreme Patron, the Blessed Mary, and for duty's sake to our own Father Philip, I charge each of you in his place,—you, Father Minister [Ambrose St John] by your zeal for the Congregation, you Fr Bernard [Dalgairns] by your gentleness, you, Fr Frederic [Bowles] by your fidelity to your friendships, you, Austin [Mills], by your habit of contentment, you, Nicholas [Darnell], by your earnestness, you, Stanislas [Flanagan], by your conscientiousness, you, Edward [Caswall], by your unassuming temper, you, Henry [Bittleston], by your cheerfulness, and you, dear Father Joseph [Gordon], though not here, by your loyalty to me,—and you, my dear Novices and my dear Brothers, by the love I bear you, do each of you your own part in prayer or in work, co-operate in the work of others, make up the defects of mine, give to the whole body the benefit of your best thoughts, and, as St Philip has given you a good house, do all of you your best to provide it with good tenants, and to adorn it with a visible attractiveness and a moral beauty.

THE REFECTORY, FEBRUARY 1854[1]

My dear Fathers and Brothers, I do not like our Refectory to be finished and us to return to it, without some notice; and I should have made mention of it at the time, had I not expected to have a more suitable opportunity of doing so now.

In one respect it is an event of more intimate interest to us than the opening of our Church; for our Church belongs to our work, but our Refectory to ourselves. It belongs to us as a Congregation, and has a special recognition in our Rule. It is not too much to say that it has a religious character, and may be called a sort of domestic chapel, and claims, as it is provided with, a ceremonial.

This is the reason of the careful regulations which are given us for our behaviour at the times when we assemble in it. The punctuality of attendance, the bowing to the Cross, the grace, the reading, the waiting, the theological questions proposed, bring before us emphatically that our meal is not as the meal of others, not an indulgence of our animal nature, but a true *Coena Domini*, and one of the chief religious acts of the day.

As, when He vouchsafes us celestial food, He feeds us with His own hand, and we do but present ourselves for the gift, so here too we bear witness before we sit down to table, that the supply of our bodily necessities comes from Him who feeds all flesh. *Aperis tu manum tuam.* We receive from His tender provision and his recurring solicitude that daily bread for which He has taught us to pray.

It is our solemn time of meeting day by day. Only at rare intervals does our Rule bring us together in Church; we do not keep choir; we seldom have high mass, vespers or other functions; our own masses one by one, our attendance in the Confessional, our instructions, our whole work, is necessarily personal and isolated, or nearly so; but twice a day, besides the stated Oratory meeting, does our Holy Father bring us together, to take part, each in his own place, in that great Sacrament of nature, which is recognized by the Patriarchal Dispensation, by the Mosaic Law, and by the Gospel. He teaches us to renew

[1] *B. Or. Ar.* D. 4. 9.

in our own age Abraham's feast in thanksgiving for Isaac, the Jewish Feast of Tabernacles, and the Apostolic Agape, or feast of charity.

Edent pauperes et saturabuntur, et laudabunt Dominum qui requirunt Eum. We assemble together, not to make provision for the flesh in its concupiscences, but as the redeemed of Christ, who eat and drink before Him to recruit our strength with Elias for His strenuous service—as those who are consecrated to Him, and hate every impulse of soul or body which is incongruous with this high state,—as those who would keep back nothing from Him, but "whether they eat or drink or whatever else they do, would do all things for the glory of God."

These are some of the considerations which naturally suggested themselves on our getting back into the Refectory. But I confess, my Fathers and Brothers, a further feeling rose in my soul, and I dare say in yours also; for the time has been ere now, when all of us, though some of us more than others, but in one way or another almost all of us, have found ourselves simply thrown upon God's mercies for the future, without prospects, not knowing what was to become of us, or how we were to live. For myself, when I look back eight or nine years, and bring before my memory the changes that took place in my life, how little could I fancy that in the course of so short a time I should find myself in a house like this, so truly a home in every sense of the word, spiritual and temporal! How little had I reason to expect, except that the word of promise was sure, that by giving up I should so soon receive back, and by losing I should gain! And what is true of me, is true of you too, my dear Fathers and Brothers, of each his in own way.

When then Our Lord has so signally blessed us, when He has so speedily silenced the jeers and falsified the predictions of those who hated us because they hated the Catholic Church, when He has reared over us a building so noble as this, when He has lodged us in such ample rooms, and conducted us to and fro through such spacious corridors, when He has given us our corn and oil and wine so abundantly, and seems to promise us a provision for the future, what could I do but write up in that apartment, which is the special seat of His bounty to us, a memorial for future times of the sense deeply imprinted on our hearts, on yours and mine (though the deepest imprint we can receive is but a faint acknowledgement,) of His truth and faithfulness, the fufilment of His promise to those who through His grace have trusted Him? "Dominus regit me, et nihil mihi deerit." The Lord guides me, and I shall want nothing. He has set me in a place of pasture. Thou hast prepared a table before me against them that trouble me, and Thy mercy shall follow me all the days of my life in the House of the Lord.

———

NEWMAN'S ORATORY PAPERS No. 22
8 APRIL 1854

INTRODUCTORY NOTE

During his absence in Ireland for the preliminary work connected with the founding of the Catholic University, Newman wished to keep in close contact with the Birmingham Oratory of which he remained Superior though frequently absent. He drew up a paper of points on the observance of the Rule, asking for reports along these lines after the fortnightly Chapter, where faults against the Rule were publicly acknowledged.

The community took him up wrongly, understanding him to require private reports on each other's observance of the Rule—which would obviously have been an odious imposition. Their unfavourable reactions to this supposed command were given vent to in the *Congregatio Deputata*, the body of four priests who have spent ten years in the Oratory and who are elected as the Superior's Council, according to Decree XXVII of the Rule. This action, in Newman's view, was equivalent to a formal act of contempt of the Superior by his council. Hence this Memorandum, which was doubtless delivered as an Address, since Newman was at Edgbaston at this date (*L.D.*, XVI, p. 100). The 'Decennials' are those who have been members of the Oratory for ten years. See further on this incident, *Trevor*, II, pp. 39–41; *L.D.*, XVI, pp. 57–9.

MEMORANDUM FOR THE DECENNIAL FATHERS
APRIL 8 1854[1]

1. I have something to say to the Decennial Fathers, which I consider it would be a want of moral courage in me not to say. I have waited in vain till we should be all together. I have put it down on paper, that I may know what I am saying, and may keep it.

2. I have not to complain of any one of the Fathers. What has been done is past and over, as far as I am concerned— but I am looking on to the future. The past casts its light upon it.

3. I shall pain myself, I shall pain you, I shall pain some of you a good deal in what I have to say. You must bear it, and I must bear it, by the affection which we bear each other. Something has been done publicly—which ought not to have been done; what has been done publicly, must be publicly undone.

4. I must go back to my first appointment to the Rectorship of the University, 2½ years ago. I did not take the initiative in it. The utmost I proposed for myself was to be Prefect of Studies. Other Fathers persuaded me to consent to be Rector. If it be a great anomaly, as it is, for the Father to be absent from the Congregation, others share with me the responsibility of bringing it about.

5. However, when it was to be, the great problem was how the ruling authority was to be morally present, though I was away. I saw only two ways of meeting the difficulty.

6. The first was, the appointment from out of the Fathers, of a Rector chosen by the Fathers, an appointment to be renewed every six months, whether in behalf of the preceding Rector or of a new one, with the whole power of the Fr Superior, whether the Fr Superior was present or absent; the prerogatives of honor, and nothing else, remaining to the Fr Superior.

7. The objection of this expedient, is, that it divides the honor and the claim of loyalty and love from the power; which is unfair both to ruler and subject. The advantage would be the gradual habituation of the Congregation to do without me.

[1] *B. Or. Ar.* Oratory Letters March–June 1854.

8. The other plan was, for me, though away, to take special means of my own accord, and at my own discretion, to keep myself continually before the congregation, as if present; e.g. by incessant letters, questions, messages, addresses, and the like, as well as by frequently coming over from Ireland, though but for a day or two, that I might not be felt to be really absent.

9. The difficulty in this plan, I do not feel it can be called an objection, was, that it was formally, absolutely essential to it, to commit congregational matters to writing, and to correspond in minute matters instead of conversing. This correspondence indeed was involved in the very idea of a non-resident Superior.

10. As my absence would be an anomaly, every thing which necessarily flowed from it would be anomalous too—and could only be sustained and carried on by the sympathy, the indulgence of the whole body for the absent Fr Superior.

11. I chose the latter of these expedients, as involving less immediate change and risk; and, when I went to the North last winter year, did my best to fulfil my own view of its requisitions. I need not recount the various things I did to keep myself before you.

12. When I went to Ireland two months ago, I proceeded to do the same.

13. In both cases, in the North and in Ireland, the very first start has been a swerve and a miss—and on the latter occasion more so than on the former.

14. I left this place in February last with the greatest reluctance, and with nothing but affection for the Congregation. I might have dwelt in my mind upon the prospect, but it did not occur to me to doubt, of the tenderest assistance from the whole Congregation, when, in a difficulty which was theirs as well as mine, I proceeded to act in the way I thought necessary for the government of the Community in my absence. Whether I had ever given any one a hint what I was doing, I do not know—most likely not, for I could not do so, without some kind of ostentation. It is a poor love which demands reasons and explanations at every step.

15. My very first act a few days after I had left, was met on the part of the Fathers, promptly, instantaneously, spontaneously met, not merely with coldness and criticism, but with (to say

the least) surprise and disapprobation. I have traced these feelings to as many as six decennial Fathers out of eight— (alas! that it should take the form of a secret to be found out). It was met on the part of one of them by a protest. The lightest thing that was said of it, was, that it could not be carried out, and would die of itself. Sympathy with me there was none, at least expressed.

16. The general ground of this dissatisfaction was that the returns for which I asked could not be made to me in Ireland without the risk of divulging the secrets of the Congregation to the Post-Office. The sigillum Congregationis was spoken of. That was felt to be a hardship, which was involved in the very fact of my being in Ireland.

17. It was further urged that my call for returns by letter would be a precedent; that is to say, an absent Fr Superior could not constitute a precedent, but that which necessarily followed on an absent Fr Superior might be a bad precedent.

18. Further, the *nature* of the details about which I inquired seems to have been felt as an additional hardship—as if any one in the Congregation will soberly maintain, that it is not the Fr Superior's duty to enforce the Rule and the bye laws of the Congregation.

19. This was not all. I wish to speak of the Congregatio Deputata in particular. This is especially the intimate Council of the Fr Superior, to support and advise him in carrying out the management of the House. If there is a place in the Congregation, where he is ever present, it is the Congregatio Deputata. He cannot depart from it.

20. Now on the other hand, what is a protest? No two persons can differ as to its nature. It is an hostile act, it is the act of an adversary. We never protest till we have tried other means. When it is our part to advise, we never protest without first advising.

21. Once more, what is the Oratory? It is a body bound together, not by stipulations, or rights or engagements, but by love. Love is its uniting principle. A breach of love in the Oratory is like an act of·contempt in other congregations, and we know what an act of contempt is.

22. If a subject of the Oratory protests against his Superior,

there must be, from the nature of the case, a breach of love on one side or on the other. If the protest is justified, the Superior must have been very wrong—if it is not, the subject who makes it is very wrong. There is no medium.

23. Yet in the Congregatio Deputata of the Oratory of St Philip, the Father's first act, when he was away, was abruptly protested against.

24. What certainly does not diminish the force of this protest, is, that the only excuse offered for it, is, that it was a sudden burst, a spontaneous movement. That is, the natural unstudied expression of feeling of one of the subjects of the Oratory, on a message coming from the Fr Superior took the shape, not of a question, of a complaint, of a representation, of an expostulation, but of a protest.

25. I will not quarrel about the details of what passed; it is sufficient that the word "protest" was uttered.

26. Moreover, no one seems to have remonstrated in behalf of the absent Fr Superior or cordially to have taken his part. He in Ireland was having his own very different thoughts about the Fathers, and was bringing them before his mind while he was among strangers. Meanwhile the force of the feelings in the Congregatio Deputata which his message roused was such, that it carried away one member of it to think that act strong in the Fr Superior what [sic] at first and left to himself he had not thought strong—while another Father, who said a great deal for himself satisfactorily, was so far from feeling that any disloyalty had been manifested, that he said he really had forgotten the whole matter from the moment of the protest till my letters from Ireland recalled the subject to him.

27. Nor is this all—the Father who mentioned the word "protest" was surprised that some faint hint had been given to the Fr Superior of the dissatisfaction of the Congregatio Deputata—though no word or sentiment of his had been mentioned to the Fr Superior, and he wrote to him that, if any thing he had said had to be told him, he should wish it told by himself.

28. As if we were a boy's school, and the Fr Superior head-master of it—as if the error lay, not in another speaking, but in his not speaking—as if the Fr Superior were not ever present in

21

his own Congregatio Deputata—as if any thing whatever that was said there might lawfully be kept from him—as if St Philip recognized any democratic meeting in his Congregatio, in which his subjects might come together to talk about the Father Superior behind his back.

29. My dear Fathers, I am very much perplexed what I am to do. You will perhaps tell me I am making much of a little thing; and I tell you that you are making little of a great thing. Perfect openess on the part of the subjects of the Oratory with its Fr Superior, is the fundamental, the vital principle of the Congregation. I have no right to ask your thoughts; I have no wish to know what *one Father says to another* for the sake of advice or to relieve his mind. But, what is said about me by more than one Father to another, what is said of me in formal Congregation, this I claim to be distinctly told. Nothing that is said about me or what I do, except in that strict privacy and confidence I have mentioned, can be obliterated, as if it had not been said. The walls ought to have ears.

30. What am I to think of you, when I am away, when my very first act on going, done amid many masses said for you, done on principle and after long deliberation, most light and most necessary, is received by you, at best with coldness, at worst with warmth, first is met with surprise, and then is followed by concealment? When the first use you make of my absence is to talk without me about me?

31. How easy would it have been for a Father to submit to me in Congregation, and to send me a private letter expressing his opinion! How easy for the other Fathers, to remind him, if in Congregation he began to say any thing which he ought to say privately out of it!

32. And last of all, the very painful thought comes upon me, if you show so little consideration for me, for whom else of your number will you show any consideration, if he is Fr Superior instead of me!

(Fr Darnell, as far as I recollect, was the Protester)

NEWMAN'S ORATORY PAPERS No. 23
27 JUNE 1854

INTRODUCTORY NOTE

This letter (already available in *L.D.*, XVI, pp. 175–6) shows that the situation referred to in the Memorandum of 8 April 1854 (Oratory Paper No. 22, above) still prevails, and inhibits Newman from writing, as he would have liked to, Papers for the community on their Oratorian life. This is a regrettable loss since it makes our task all the harder when we attempt to bring out in detail his view of the Oratory. On this point see above pp. 91, 133.

On Henry Bittleston (1818–86) see *L.D.*, XIII, p. 510.

[Letter to Henry Bittleston]

16 Harcourt Street,
June 27/54

My dear Henry

As to your reference to my Chapter Papers, you must know, that, though when younger I could write off things, now I suppose from declining vigour, I feel it very hard to get up the steam. I am like an old horse, who, when warm, goes well, but stumbles at starting. It has cost me, for instance, a deal of labour to begin the Gazette—now I am in the work and at present write very fast, am well in advance, and have a great many subjects in petto. Did I leave off for a few weeks, I could do nothing. Now I *had* got up the steam for the Chapter Papers, and I think they would have gone off swimmingly—a number of subjects seemed to open—I hoped it would have been, on the part both of yourselves and me, a constant intercourse of affection—and I thought to myself, that, when I was gone, it would have been a memento after me in the Oratory to have left such a series of papers behind me, interesting both historically, as showing our state, and for their own worth—such as they were. As far as I see, this is quite at an end. How can I get up the steam with my present engagements? and where are the coals and the fire to get it up withal? It was in a simple confidence in the *sympathy* of the *whole* community for me, that I wrote to them. I did not expect, that hardly would my back be turned when a *spontaneous* exhibition of a different feeling would take place. You may *tell* me that every one now wishes for the papers—but how am I to realize it? how is a feeling, which hitherto I freely indulged, the grounds for which I took for granted, to be restored? I may speak with the utmost confidence to a or b —but how am I to speak confidently to all together, which is the very thing you ask, when you want a paper for the Chapter?

Ever Yrs affly J H N

P.S. I think you had better delay the further question of the Middle School, till you see me.

REMARKS ON THE ORATORIAN VOCATION
Nos. 24 and 25: 5–9 MARCH 1856

INTRODUCTORY NOTE

A succinct account of the background to these *Remarks* has been provided above, pp. 144, 145; see also *Trevor*, II, pp. 142, 143. The full correspondence is now available in *L.D.*, XVI and XVII.

As regards the texts, we must distinguish the following:
1. A Rough Draft of 24 pp. in Newman's hand. This is reproduced here in full, as Oratory Paper No. 24, except for p. 17 and one-half of p. 18 of the MS which are sufficiently covered, in equivalent terms in the printed *Remarks*, which figure in this edition as Oratory Paper No. 25. An editor is always liable to attach more importance to unpublished material than to

existing editions. In Newman's case this preference is not always justified, since Newman himself often selected the matter for publication in preference to what he left unpublished. In this particular case, however, we may be pardoned for succumbing to the bait of the *inédit* if this Rough Draft seems more interesting to us now than the *Remarks*. These latter work out a thesis, on historical precedent, while the Rough Draft gives us a close-up of Newman, as Superior, trying to re-vitalize and re-orientate the undertakings of his community in the challenge provoked by a crisis. Together with the Chapter Address on Father Bernard Dalgairns of 31 August 1856 (Oratory Paper No. 27, below) they form his *Apologia pro vitâ suâ . . . Oratoriana,* Many of the projects adumbrated here are those which Newman laid before the Pope during his visit to Rome in connection with the quarrel with the London House which occasioned these *Remarks.*[1]

2. The version printed privately by Newman (1861 or later) as pp. 13–65 of the booklet *Sanctus Philippus Birminghamiensis.* This version is that reproduced here as Oratory Paper No. 25, although it differs in some minor details from the fair copy in Newman's hand inscribed 'Original, sent from Dublin.' There exist two Italian translations of this printed version.[2]

3. An earlier draft in Newman's hand, of which the letters dated 28 February and 1 March 1856 (ante-dating therefore the letters printed in the *Remarks,* which are dated 5–9 March 1856) are reproduced here in Appendix 5 on account of the fuller treatment they offer on the subject of obedience.

REMARKS ON THE ORATORIAN VOCATION
(1856): ROUGH DRAFT[3]

The Congregation of the Oratory then is a community of secular Priests living together without vows for the fulfilment of their ministry under a Rule and with privileges given them

---

[1]See especially *L.D.,* XVII, p. 137.

[2]*Note sulla Vocazione dei Filippini.* Tipografia *Cuggiani,* Rome. 1918; *Lettere sulla Vocazione dei Filippini.* Quaderni dell'Oratorio. No. 1. Rome. 1962.

[3]*B. Or. Ar. B. 9. 2.*

by the Holy See. The Oratory is this, and nothing more or less than this, and in being as much as this it has various characteristics, some of which I will now draw out.

In the first place, being no more than this, it is not a religion or a religious body. St Philip disowned the idea; he said there were already many such in the church of God without his adding to the number. A religious body must be under vows to deserve the name; or at least under the counsels of perfection to which those vows relate. The Oratory is no such state, we are nothing else than secular priests with the addition of community life, but not made over and consecrated to that life. We are in no state and under no profession of perfection, which is the characteristic of regulars or religious, except so far as it belongs to all secular priests.

In the next place, although the Oratory is only a congregation of secular priests, and does not profess the perfection of regulars, yet it must be recollected on the other hand that there are other modes of attaining perfection, nay, I may say other types of perfection, than the method and the type of religious perfection. I define perfection to be a perfect obedience. If this be so, it consists mainly in the performance of our duties, and in the precepts of the New Law, in a life of faith, hope and charity according to the calls of every day and every occupation. He is perfect, in substance, who does the duties of the day perfectly. It has to do with counsels only individually or secondarily, viz. in as much as no one can fulfil the precepts perfectly who aims at nothing more, and that without that courage and generosity of obedience which counsels imply, we shall not be exact or complete even in those things which are directly required of us.

But, whether this be true or not, which I leave to theologians, so far I think is plain that the observance of all counsels is not necessary to perfection, nay not of the three great counsels, but only of some counsel or other, without determining which, which depends on the particular case. It follows from this, that two persons may be both perfect and their perfection of a very different character. St Gregory the First could not fast;— yet might he not be as perfect as St Basil, who wore himself out by selfimposed austerities before he was fifty? St Theresa reproaches herself for her frivolities, at the time she was a nun; yet was St Basil, or St Gregory Nazianzen astray from the perfect path, because they had their memory, and even their eyes possessed by the writings of heathen authors? St Philip stayed in one place, St Francis Xavier travelled over the East, St Philip had property, St Antony had none. All self-denials are not necessary for the soul's perfection, but a resolution in a person to do the divine will, whatever it may be in its own particular case. And therefore though technically speaking the three vows may be necessary for perfection, yet to say so is not to grant that secular priests may not be perfect, or that the Oratory, without making a profession of perfection, may possess the means of leading on its subjects to perfection. And, is one and the same life is not necessary for perfection, neither as one and the same external occupation. So that it is this occupation to which a man is called, it is consistent with his perfection. And in matter of fact these external occupations are still more distinct from each other than the methods of inward obedience. St Thomas and the Blessed Fra Angelico were both Dominicans; they were both in the way of perfection; but St Thomas wrote theology and metaphysics, and Fra Angelico painted pictures. St Chrysostom and St Gregory Nazianzen were both Archbishops, and both in the way of perfection, but the one wrote comments on St Paul, and the other wrote hexameters and pentameters.

And, as being a community it has particular advantages—the members have the example, the restraint, the encouragement, the advice of each other. They are kept out of the reach of the world, in a circle of their own whence temptation is excluded. Moreover besides the vow of chastity, which they live under as secular priests they are under the counsel though not the vow of obedience, which is quite a sufficient matter for perfection.

This, however, goes only a certain way in describing our vocation, as in plain; but what I have hitherto said applies to any community which exists without vows. Various other circumstances go to make up our vocation: adaptation to our Rule, a particular education, a relation to particular classes in society, and the like; but that which is least to be expected and most undeniable peculiarity of our vocation is that it is founded on human affection; or that it is a drawing towards (and a vocation for) a given set of men. The carità, which we are taught is to be to us instead of vows, is not a mere supernatural grace, else it would not have for its object one Christian more than another but the sort of mixed or twofold love which St Paul, for instance, felt for his converts, whom he loved not simply as the regenerate sons of God, but as having certain associations with his own history. Hence the vocation of the the Oratory has for its object not simply the institution of St Philip, but a certain specific congregation.

On this point, which most requires distinct statement, the Rule especially gives it. First, it insists, as a necessity, on the members of a community having the image of each other before their mind's eye, and gives this necessity as a reason against their multiplicity or their separation from each other; in order that they may be more closely bound together by that bond of love which is created by daily intimacy, and may possess that knowledge of individual character which such intimacy supplies, and may all of them feel the influence of well known countenances. And, while giving directions how to proceed in the choice of members, it lays especially stress on having known well and long the community they come to join, and on their having been themselves careful[ly] tried in turn by its individual Fathers.

Such is the general type and the vocation of the Oratory, and these last remarks I have made lead naturally to the consideration how to set up an Oratory and how to regard and treat candidates for the Oratory. It will be observed then that the great object on the side both of him who offers himself and those who have to take or decline is to determine the point of congeniality of character, and to ascertain whether he can comfortably live with them. Mental similarity and sympathy is the substitute for vows. Hence there is more force than appears on the surface of the words in its being said that the candidate must be 'idoneus and *natus* ad institutum.' Again he must be over 18 years of age that he may have a formed character and not over 45 that he may be capable of further assimilation. He must not have been a regular of any kind, lest a wrong character should have been impressed upon him: he must have been a frequenter of our services, a penitent of our Fathers; he must have already made trial of our Institute. Moreover (if these conditions are fulfilled, next) two of the Fathers are to find out all they can about him, about his life, and his turn of mind and habits. They are to hold repeated conversation with him, to live with him, to make inquiries of his neighbours in the country, concerning him, his connexion and associates. Other Fathers are to employ themselves in the same business, and to bring home to him that it is useless to come unless he is resolved to remain in it till death, and with the sole object of serving God and keeping the Rule.[4]

See how this applies to setting up an Oratory. The first step is to find two or three Priests who can from experience declare that they are able to live together. Accordingly when we were at Propaganda and told the Jesuits there of our intention, they asked, can you live together have you experience of it; and when they were told it was the case, they said that very little time would be necessary to be under a Father of Chiesa Nuova —and in matter of fact we were only a few months under Fr Rossi at Santa Croce, not so much as the five months from June to December. In like manner, when a foundation is made of those who know each other, new members are very slowly[?] added and taken up.

When this living together is yet future, a very long probation is necessary. In spite of all which has already been said about the pre-existing connexion of the candidate with the community, a period of three years is laid down; for the trial. They begin with a month in which they can live as guests in the house without the habit, "that they may know all our ways" says the Rule, "and may act with the riper deliberation," and on the other hand that the trial may be made of their readiness to obey in all things even in what is humble and severe, of their love of meditation and the Sacraments, of their freedom from quarrelsomeness, pertinacity, and pride whether towards high or low.

---

[4]Newman added after this: vid paper O p. 6. [See below, p. 419, the 'Santa Croce Papers', in which a summary of Paper O is provided. P. 6 contains the relevant extracts from the Rule (in Latin) concerning the tyrones.]

It is observable moreover that they are not called novices but tyrones, and the novice master Tyronum Praefectus. Indeed Van Espen says expressly that they are not novices, but only probationers, and in Italy, or at least in Rome they are called simply giovani.

As to the mode of treating them, this differs in different houses. At Naples, there is a sort of approximation to Jesuit discipline. They are made over to their Prefect, they are kept separate from every one else even ⟨?⟩ the Fr Superior, and thus are treated all together as one body. We found lately,[5] as you know, the Superior at Verona strongly opposed to such a course. In other Oratories they are allowed more or less to form an intimacy with the other Fathers; at Florence they are dealt with by their master not as a body, but one by one. I confess such a mode of treatment approves itself to me; I do not like recognizing them as one body considering how individual each may be in character, turn of mind, age, and history, and how various and multiform is the character of the subject of the Oratory. They are not to be brought up on any one precise model, as a Jesuit or Dominican. It must be considered too that the difference of age especially, and of state, e.g. in orders already or not, will make it very difficult to throw them together. And as to separating them from the other Fathers, such a course seems to contradict the very idea of probationship, which is to see if they can live with the existing body, and to draw them in closer and closer love to its individual members.

Speaking under correction then, the course I should propose to the Bm [Birmingham] Oratory as regards the tyrones or beginners would be this: to direct their Prefect or Master to see them and talk to them, not as a body, but one by one, according to the wants of each, and to give them hints and directions according as each required it, with an absence as much as possible of form;—moreover, to give them leave, though with the discretion of doing so in his own hands, to mix freely with the other Fathers, and to put them almost on a level with the Fathers as to work of the House, that is, to employ them in and for the *House* according to their respective

[5]In January 1856. See conclusion of letter of 8 January 1856 to Nicholas Darnell, *L.D.*, XVII, p. 115; and *Trevor* II, p. 101.

capacities: letting them, if priests, do the work of priests, and so on:—in sanction of this view we found when lately at Rome[6] that they could even hold offices, as that of the custos sacrarii[7]; in short to treat them as companions and friends, not as inferiors, except so far forth as youth, or want of education or experience or the like made them so.

I will make one more remark about them: they do not abound in the Italian Oratories, and this has sometimes been taken as a proof that those Oratories are in a state of declension. This seems a mistake. They have none at Florence; yet, when we asked them on the subject, they seemed in no way annoyed at the fact, but said "We shall have them when we want them." The truth is the Oratory is not an order of religious, which can expand itself. The Jesuits, for instance, may go all over the earth, cannot have too many members, and will ever look out for fresh ones. The Oratory is a local body, consisting of a small and definite number of priests: it is forbidden, in the words of the Rule I have quoted, to increase its numbers, and to be ever looking out for new ones, except when there was a call for them, would be a greediness, the same fault as wishing ever to be eating for eating sake. The rule forbids "dissipating the Congregation under pretext of increasing it," and introducing that "confusion which comes from a multitude." and I very much doubt if the Holy See would allow of an Oratory increasing beyond a certain number of subjects.

The next subject I shall come to consider is the work of the Oratory. I observe then that every institution gradually forms its objects and duties as it grows, and it would appear that not even St Philip knew at first what the Oratory was to be. On looking back at its history through several centuries, as far as we have the opportunity of contemplating it, we see what it has become; and in those traditions of the past we might at first sight have been disposed to rest. But there have been indications at various times of the desire of the Holy See to expand and to accommodate the uses of the Oratory according to circumstances and the change of times, and I think I shall

[6]For Newman's journey to Rome, January 1856, to settle the point of the Oratorian Rule controverted by the London Oratory, see *Trevor*, II, pp. 99–107.
[7]Sacristan.

be employing my thoughts usefully, if I lay down some canons or principles upon the subject.

(First, looking at the past we see so great a diversity of work that it would seem as if no change or addition now, servatis servandis, need surprise us.) And here I shall lay down the canon that it is any work which does not infringe on the principle of continuous residence, that is any work suitable to the priesthood, which is town work. There can be no doubt at all, for instance, that my own present position in Dublin is distinctly incompatible with the Oratory, nor should I ever have taken it if left to myself. At first I wished to be mere Prefect of Studies, and at the very time of my appointment at Rome I was writing to Dr Cullen to see that I was made nothing more than Pro-Rector. And I felt, as you know, that I could not be absent from the Oratory at all, even after my appointment without an express permission from the Holy See to that effect. What I have observed in my own case, I wish to apply to others. For this reason I consider that any occupation which carries a Father often or for a considerable time from the Oratory, is inconsistent with its spirit; but of course some latitude of view is necessary in this matter, and Oratories will differ in their judgment on the point. The brief of Leo xii declares that to give missions is not contrary to the Institution of St Philip; yet it might easily happen that a difference of opinion might exist how far or in what cases such exercises involved accidentally a breach of the great principle I have laid down: or whether this or that house, as the Brescian, availed itself too freely of what was in itself (permissible or) compatible with Oratorian work.

I know of no other condition restrictive of our labours; though there is one recommendation contained in the Brief, not of a prohibitory but of a directive nature, which we must observe, if we can,—viz that the Pope wishes us especially to direct our exertions towards the benefit of the upper classes; a recommendation, which, with whatever incidental inconveniences, I myself am certainly following out by my own engagements in Dublin. The Brief says Laudamus etc. (quote)[8].

---

[8]See below, Appendix 2, note 4. Marginal note by Newman: a great wish at Rome to develop according to the *need*, and to make the Oratory *useful*.

That is the recommendation given us in our Brief, and though it refers to a purpose of mine, as if communicated to the Holy See, the Brief [puts] its own sense on the words in which that supposed purpose was conveyed, and I have ever accepted that sense as if I ought to have meant what I cannot say I did exactly mean. However, the remark which is to the point here is the duty it throws upon us as regards the inhabitants of Edgbaston. It is not a little remarkable that almost against our will we have been thrown among that class of persons here who most exactly answer in this place to the classes mentioned in the Brief. In the years 1848, 1849 our views of buildings were limited to the localities of Derritend, Alcester Street, Smithfield, Carr's Lane, and the Moseley and Bristol Roads. In spring 1850 Mr Tarlton, without our seeking it, found out the ground, which still remains unpurchased, at the corner of Francis Street, Hagley Road. We bought it with a misgiving that it was too far out of Birmingham, yet many months had not passed before the Fathers were dissatisfied with the ground, as not large enough for their purpose, and went out further still to our present site. There is no doubt we should have absolutely rejected our present site, if offered us while we were speculating about the piece of ground near Smithfield. Unless then we have acted without religious consideration, St Philip has put us here, and has had a meaning in so doing. I conceive then both from the Brief and from the circumstances of our location, we are sent to the rich manufacturers of Birmm in a way which we have never fully realised; and, much as I desire to encourage plans of conversion among the Protestant poor of Smethwick, I think distinctly we have prior duties to the Protestant rich of Edgbaston.

Before going on further, I wish this point carefully considered. If the Fathers say that it is an hopeless undertaking, that is another matter: we must tell St Philip so, and the Holy See. This does not make it less true that we are appointed for this hopeless undertaking, that its being hopeless (if so) does not alter the fact of the appointment, that the appointment does not depend on the hopefulness of it, and that in consequence we must be quite sure that it is hopeless, if we are to stand excused for not acting upon it. For myself, I confess that, however hopeless Edgn [Edgbaston] may be as regards the success of any immediate exertions, still there is one aspect in which I have not sufficiently considered it is open to us, and not hopeless—and that is as an object of intercession. I see clearly that the Holy See has at least put that duty upon us, and I confess I have not considered it as much as I ought. Mere general prayers for the conversion of our neighbourhood do not seem enough for the exigencies and the claims of the case. We have a mission to Edgbaston; and we ought to be straitened till it is accomplished[9]; and whether it can be accomplished or not, a dispensation of the Gospel towards it has been committed to us. I know great discretion is necessary, and that we must not take the words of Scripture too literally, but still it will do us no harm to recollect that, when the prophet was sent[10] "ad gentes apostatrices", and to men "durâ facie et indomabili corde," who at least were as iron breasted as the poor people about us, he was told to "speak God's words to them," "si forte vel ipsi audiant, et si forte quiescant, quoniam domus exasperans est." And he was cautioned against being "exasperans" himself "sicut domus exasperans est," for, whether they heard or not, "scient quia propheta fuerit in medio eorum." Truly the Catholic Church is in the midst of them, as a light shining in the darkness; let us take care that its want of illumination is owing merely to the grossness of the atmosphere, and not to our neglect to light up, trim, and set aloft the flame. So much at least I do think imperative upon us, that we should consider with an earnestness which perhaps will be new to most of us, that to them we are sent, and we shall have to account hereafter for the failure of our mission if it fails. At least we can pray individually and in a body in a very pointed manner for those openings in the absence of which may be an excuse at present for doing no more.[11]

However I have no wish to throw away labour upon a soil

[9]cf. *Luke,* 12:50.

[10]Newman is embroidering here on *Ezek.* 2:1–7. The text may have been suggested to him by its current use in the liturgy (as when he mentions the Life of St Ignatius, at that time being read in the community refectory in his paper of 31 August 1856 on Fr Bernard Dalgairns).

[11]Marginal note by Newman: development of Oratory it must be useful in such ways as it can.

which will make no return. This is the very principle I have been laying down concerning the duties of the Oratory.

The characteristic of the Oratory, as such, has been its care of young men, for whom especially the Oratorium Parvum has been instituted. Having mentioned then the peculiarity of the English Congregation, I take this general characteristic of all Oratories next. Here again we have been able to do very little hitherto, and here again I say, that, while we lay out ourselves for work in this light, we must not waste time and labour upon, profess more than we can do, and possess men's minds with the idea that we have failed. What has stood in our way in forming the Oratorium Parvum, is the circumstance that there are so few Catholic families, comparatively speaking, in our mission. Families imply hereditary Catholicism, steadiness, perseverance, and organization in the Catholic body; but the Catholicism which we have to do with is irregular and shifting; it is made up chiefly of individuals, gathered here and there, of parents whose families are Protestant, or at a distance, of single women of Protestant parents, and of paupers. Nor do we need young men alone, but we ought to have persons of a higher class, who will set them an example, guide them, and keep them together. We neither have done much here, nor, since the fact is that much cannot be done just now, have we wasted strength here. The Prefect of the Oratory, however, at this minute has some hopes of making progress.

However, on the cultivation of two studies we have lately obtained the direct approbation of the Holy See, which are peculiarly congenial to the spirit of St Philip and the history of the Oratory, viz on schools of painting and music. If we succeed in these, we shall be doing a benefit to English Catholicism in general, while we advance the Oratorium parvum in our own place. These arts are naturally congenial to young minds, and to Birmingham especially. Music is one of the special characteristics of the Oratory, and it is the art for which Birmingham is famous. A school of painting, on the other hand, is a great *desideratum* in England; we have about us various youths who have a talent in that line, and there are various arts in Birmingham, which would naturally group themselves under a school of ecclesiastical painting and decoration.

It has been from the wish to do something for young men, and for the upper classes, that ever since we have been a congregation I have tried to form a school or college (of youths) in our house. Of such a College I am told the Oratory at Palermo gives us a precedent, nor do I think one needed under the clear wishes of the Holy See on the subject. We first attempted this object at St Wilfrid's, lately at Edgbaston; in neither case with success. However, we have now the Pope's distinct sanction upon keeping School; so, without wasting time upon an unfeasible scheme, we may perhaps look towards it once more. I prefer the care of youths to that of boys, as more Oratorian, and as more compatible with our other duties and mode of life.

Now on this whole matter of the *care* of youths, I think I gained an instructive lesson the other day, from what Mr Nugent[12] mentioned to me. He has been as you know some years working there with a kind of Oratorium Parvum. I was suprised to hear him say that he had only lately, within the last year, had any success with them, plan after plan failed—nothing solid was done, and his success began, as I understood him, by getting a retreat or mission given to them. He is repeating it, Fr Suffield being the preacher, at the very time I am writing. I mention this both as a consolation and perhaps a suggestion. He is still unable to form them into a choir, though he has taken a good deal of pains about it.

Hitherto I have mentioned those departments of work which are most distinctly Oratorian, but then at the same time in which, we cannot conceal from ourselves, we have had least success. I do not wish to continue exertions without a fair chance of success; I should like to limit the exertion to the prospect, and while we hope to have in future success which has not yet been granted to us, to be cautious of wasting strength and to be prepared to throw our exertions into directions which promise more. If the wealthy, and the educated class, and the youths of Bm [Birmingham] cannot be got, we have still classes enough to act upon there, and must turn to them.

[12]James Nugent, (1822–1905): see brief biography in *L.D.*, XV, p. 563. A priest whose life was devoted to charitable work in Liverpool. In 1853 he founded the Catholic Institute for young men under the patronage of St Philip.

From the first we have been more successful from several causes with women than men; that is a sufficient reason for turning the work of the Oratory in that direction. It is this consideration which has induced me in my visit to Rome[13] to gain from the Holy See an express encouragement of pious women who are disposed to co-operate in our missionary labours. The large sums bestowed upon our Oratory have come nearly entirely from women[14]. The schools, our sick, our poor, our popular music, owe a special debt to the services of women in various ranks of life. Accordingly after the pattern of a similar institution now or formally [sic] attached to the Naples Oratory, we have got leave to set up a Little Oratory for women, with Indulgences similar to those which belong to the Confratres of St Philip already. I think we have a right to expect a great deal under God's blessing for this new Institution: it may be turned to a great many persons: especially will it subserve a project, which has been at the heart of various pious ladies and penitents of the Oratory almost from the time we came to Birmingham, viz. the creation of a Catholic hospital.[15] How best to conduct it will be a question of some anxiety whether to form a body or to run the undertaking[?] without any association. At first sight it would appear well, that we should proceed on the plan which the Father Prefect intends to adopt for the Oratory of men. viz a select or small number of tried persons to be the real members, who are in possession of the Indulgences and to have a large number of various ages who will be improprié[16] called Sisters of the Oratory. This arrangement would answer in some measure to the double Oratorium Parvum of various Congregations in Italy.

The Union Workhouse comes next to be mentioned; and the care of it is just one of those works, which, historically belong to the Oratory. Not only did St Philip send the Brothers of the

---

[13]January 1856; *Trevor* II, pp. 99–107; *L.D.*, XVII, p. 138.

[14]This may be verified from the Decree Book (see Appendix No. 6, 25 January 1869), v.g. 9 January 1851, 18 April 1853.

[15]Two ladies went to Paris to train for this hospital, it was opened in December 1856, but the two ladies died almost at once, and it had to be closed. See *L.D.*, XVII, p. 492.

[16]broadly speaking.

22

Oratory, to the hospitals, as their distinct work on feast days; but Baronius, when a priest and as a priest, attended them. The Blessed Sebastian is said to have preached, among other places, in poor houses, prisons, and hospitals. "I myself have seen" says one witness "the great labours of the servant of God in our hospital 'della Carità' wherein at that time more than 1500 poor were assembled." And, to say no more, we have reason to know that it is one of the works which the present Pope has especial satisfaction in hearing that we are engaged.

The care of the prison is another of those works; we may trust that, as time goes on, we may be able to do more there that [sic] the law of the land allows us at present.

It has been very common for Oratories to have the parish attached to them in which they are situated, and it is our case ever since we have been in Birmingham. Hitherto our charge at Edgbaston has rather been a mission than a parochial cure. We are in the midst of Protestants, we are in some sense in the country and the scattered Catholics are not very near us. It would be a great thing if we were able to do anything permanent in and for Smethwick. They [sic] are difficulties in the way; but they have been the lot of flourishing Oratories before us. Fr Ambrose and I were told at Turin[17] that St Eusebio, the parish of the Oratory which is now in the best part of the town, was in the Blessed Sebastian's time, in the country. Accordingly we read in his life of its extending "four miles beyond the gates of the city," and of his going into the country in the district of the parish of St Eusebio, and preaching to the country people. He sought them out and collected them into a small chapel ⟨p. 41⟩ On the discouragements at Turin vid B. Sebastian ⟨p. 137⟩[18] I should propose to throw the force of the Congregation in that direction if there was a fair prospect of doing something; not, if it seemed to be a waste of strength.

Lastly for the same reason I consider we should not open our Church for services oftener than we get fair Congregations. To preach with none or few to hear is to put ourselves at disadvantage, as far as appearances are concerned, and would be a

---

[17] January 1856; see *Trevor*, II, pp. 99–100; *L.D.*, XVII, pp. 105–108.

[18] *The Lives of the Blessed Sebastian Valfré of the Oratory of Turin . . . and Others*, London 1849, in the 'Oratorian Lives of the Saints' series.

neglect to economise strength. *We know, from the variety of customs abroad, that we are not bound to open our Church daily*[19], and I am disposed to recommend to suspend at present, the sermons of Monday and Tuesday; for the same reason, if I could avoid it, I would not let the hearers, when a sermon there was, be in such a place as was too large for them.

The one principle in all exertion is keeping near *home.*

————

NEWMAN'S ORATORY PAPERS No. 25
18 AUGUST 1856

REMARKS ON THE ORATORIAN VOCATION

1856.
CONGREGATIO GENERALIS.
August 18.

DECREED UNANIMOUSLY:
  That the remarks of the Father on the Oratorian Vocation, brought before the Congregation in March last, be printed at our expense, for the use of the Fathers.

I.

DUBLIN, *March 5, 1856.*

MY DEAR FATHERS,—When the Oratory of St Philip was first set up in England eight years ago, I put on paper, and from time to time read to the Fathers, various sketches of what I conceived to be its scope and spirit; but so many changes have taken place among us since, so few of those who belonged to our

———

[19]Marginal note by Newman: This "every day" service is doubtless the formal substitute for fastings etc., but still *when* it is of use. If something else is not substituted elsewhere, we sacrifice spirit to letter.

Congregation at Maryvale are members of it now, that there
is more reason than I can at once realise myself for bringing
before the present body of Fathers, as if for the first time, views
and explanations which are familiar, not only to my mind, but
to my very ears. And there is a propriety in my repeating them
now, when I am so lately returned from the presence of the
Holy Father at Rome; and there is even a call to do so, in
consequence of the circumstances which took me to him.

That in the main I shall be saying nothing that I have not
said before, will be plain from my quotations, which at present
I have neither time nor books to collect for the first time. It
will, I trust, be equally plain that I shall be only saying what is
received already by the Congregation in its substance, even
though in form and language there may be something of my
own.

The Congregation of the Oratory, then, is a community of
secular priests, living together without vows, for the fulfilment
of their ministry, under a rule and with privileges given them
by the Holy See. First, Its members are "secular priests;"
Secondly, "Living in community." The Oratory is this and
nothing more or less than this; but, being as much as this, it has
various characteristics, some of which I will now draw out.

In the first place, being no more than this, it is in consequence no Religion, or religious body. St Philip disowned the
idea of framing a Religion; he said, that there were enough already in the Church without his adding a new one. He said, that,
"If a man, desirous of a higher state, proposed to take vows,
various Religions were at hand; for himself, he wished that in
his own Congregation men should serve God without bond, as
he had no intention to introduce a new Religion, but meant
charity to be his bond of union." Indeed, a congregation must
be under *vows*, or at least under the *counsels* to which the three
vows are attached, if it is to be called a *Religion*. Now the Oratory is no such body; we are considered by our Rule, as we are
considered by St Philip, as secular priests, and in the state of
secular priests. In the introduction to the Rule, for instance,
where St Philip's "way," or "discipline," is spoken of, he is said
to have shown to secular priests, "viam à religiosorum institutis
distantem." And he himself used to say, more explicitly, that

"he purposed that those who entered his Congregation should be in the state of secular priests and clerks, to whom he wished them to be conformed in all externals."

A regular and a secular priest differ in idea from each other, though a given individual may happen to be both at once. A regular need not be in Orders, and a priest need not be under the three vows; a woman may be a regular, and a Lord Chancellor may be a priest. Thus they differ; into which of the two classes, regulars or seculars, are we to place the Fathers of the Oratory? I repeat, among seculars. Thus they differ from Dominicans or Benedictines. Melchior Canus, for instance, was a Dominican, who was *also* a priest; Baronius was a priest, who was *also* an Oratorian. We are neither religious, nor have the perfection proper to religious.

However, true as this is, still it is true also, that, by a certain improper use of language, the Oratory may be called a Religion. For instance, when the Theatines at Naples hesitated to lend to the Oratory a preacher for some festival, on the plea that they never preached abroad, St Philip wrote to them, as Father Marciano tells us, "not to feel a scruple on the point, inasmuch as it was not a house of seculars that was in question, but a *religious house,* like their own, for the churches of the Oratory were like those of the Theatines." Again, Father Tarugi, in a memorial presented to the Pope in behalf of the House of Naples, speaks of it as "consisting of clerks, though secular, that is, without vows, still *regular in their observances,* and not inferior in their life to *other* observant Religious." In like manner the author of the "Pregi" speaks of the Oratory, "though not a Religion, because without any sort of vow," yet "*almost after the manner of a Religion.*" And so again, as to perfection, St Philip said that his subjects should "seek all of them to *imitate the religious in perfection,* though they did not imitate them in taking vows."

To reconcile these opposite statements of the Oratory being a community of secular priests, and yet a sort of Religion—of its members aiming at perfection, yet not being under vows, we must bear in mind that there are various modes, nay types, or at least species, of perfection, and that the perfection of regulars is only one of these. What is meant by perfection? I suppose it is the power or faculty of doing our duty exactly, naturally, and completely, whatever it is, in opposition to a performance which is partial, slovenly, languid, awkward, clumsy, and with effort. It is a life of faith, hope, and charity, elicited in successive acts according to the calls of the moment and to the vocation of the individual. It does not consist in any specially heroic deeds; it does not demand any fervour of devotion; but it implies regularity, precision, facility, and perseverance in a given sphere of duties. He is perfect who does the duties of the day perfectly. The idea is a familiar one in matters of the world. We talk of a man being *equal to* his work, *fitted* to his situation, and being *master* of his position; of a lawyer being *well up* with his brief, of a lecturer being *perfectly at home* with his subject, of a leader of the House of Commons being a capital *debater;* and so, again, of passing a *brilliant* examination, or of turning work of art *neatly out of hand;* of fencing, or skating, or playing at billiards *beautifully*. In all these encomiums one and the same idea is contemplated, viz., that of your being *master* of your work, or having your work in *your hand*. Such, too, is Christian perfection; and if so, it consists, in its substance, in the observance of precept, not of counsel; and it immediately depends upon *acquired habits* formed in the soul by means of past supernatural acts, or contemporaneously with their exercise.

But, again, to be master of one's work is to be superior to one's work. Superiority is involved in the very idea of mastery. Hence the exact performance of precept, or a state of perfection, accidentally, but of necessity, includes some observance of counsel. So it is in matters of this world. A candidate for an examination has to read a great deal which he does not present; a Cicero will tell us how many collateral studies are necessary for a great orator. In like manner there can be no perfection without the observance of counsel. He who attempts nothing more than his duty will be certain to fall short of it; and apart from that generosity and courage of obedience, which works of supererogation imply, there will be no satisfactory obedience at all.

So far the pursuit and the practice of perfection are common to all Christians, whether laymen, priests, or regulars. The observance of counsel is necessary in every case. But then, be it observed, there are many Counsels, and not *all* are necessary for perfection, but the observance of *one* or *other*; and as counsels are very different from each other in themselves, and still more in the mode of fulfilling them there will be very different modes of pursuing and practising perfection, and men may be all going on to perfection, though they look very different from each other. And if we do not carefully take this into consideration, and admit it in the fulness of its consequences, we shall run the risk of becoming narrow-minded, and of making rash judgments.

One man may observe one counsel, and another another, and yet each may be perfect. St Gregory the First was perfect, though he did not fast like St Basil; St Basil was perfect, though he did not abstain from secular literature like St Theresa; St Theresa was perfect, though she was not allowed to go to the heathen, like St Francis Xavier; St Francis was perfect, though he did not confine himself to one place, like a hermit of the desert, or like St Philip. Nay, even when the perfection is of the same kind, it may differ in its several specimens. St Thomas and the blessed Fra Angelico were both Dominicans; they were both in the way of perfection; but St Thomas wrote theology and metaphysics; and Fra Angelico painted the Madonna. St Chrysostom and St Gregory Nazianzen were both consecrated to the episcopal office; they were both in the way of perfection; but St Chrysostom commented on St Paul, and St Gregory wrote hexameters and pentameters.

It does not follow, then, that the Fathers of the Oratory are not to aim at perfection because they are not under the Three Vows; but it does follow thence that the Oratory is not a Religion. It is, then, a quasi-religion, or a sort of Religion. That it professes perfection indeed is quite plain from the history and lives of its first Fathers; nay, of its succession of Fathers in every part of Italy. As many as eighteen of the first Fathers of the Chiesa Nuova have received the title of venerable. The founders of the Oratories of Macerata, Jesi, Florence, Padua, Forli, Camerino, and various other Fathers, either wrought miracles, or gained graces, or died in the odour of sanctity, or appeared in visions, or left their bodies incorrupt after them, or are under process of canonisation. The missionary labours of

Father Santi of Padua and of Father Magnenti of Aquila were unbounded. The Oratory of Fermo has had a succession of saintly men down to this time. On the whole, the Oratory has been a pattern and a stay to the secular clergy, wherever it has been established. It has fully answered, then, the idea of a quasi-religion; but still, in spite of all this, and especially because it is not fixed in one certain direction by vows, it may not answer, whether as a whole or in its individual members, to the idea of perfection necessary for a hermit, or a Cistercian, or a Carmelite, or a Jesuit; and the question recurs to us, and has yet to be answered, What is the perfection of a Father of the Oratory, and what is, and what is not, inconsistent with it?—I am, &c.,   J.H.N.

II.

MY DEAR FATHERS,—Having said that the Oratory is not a religious body, and yet is like one, that its members aim at perfection, yet at a perfection different in its circumstances and peculiarities from that of regulars, I have next to consider what those distinguishing marks or characteristics of its perfection are. To do this, I must go back to the original description which I have given of its Fathers. Now, they are secular priests, living in community. Here are two peculiarities in which they differ from regulars as such:—1. They are secular priests. 2. They live in community. Regulars, indeed, may be priests, and they may live together in one house; but neither of these points is more than a circumstance at the most, and often an accident, and nothing else, of regular life. Though they may be priests, anyhow they are not seculars; though they live in community, that community is not necessarily a congregation. In these points, on the other hand, lies our essence, and the character of that perfection which is required of us.

First, I shall enlarge on our being secular priests, and consider how we stand, so regarded.

All secular priests are called to perfection, but they are very variously situated. It is a great principle, I believe, adopted by the Church with reference to them, that, since they have to minister to all ranks of society, from all ranks they should be taken. The lower ranks are the more populous, and therefore the bulk of the priesthood will always be taken from the lower ranks, elevated above them only by spiritual training and theological knowledge. But, as it would be a want of consideration towards the humble and unlearned to send them priests who had no knowledge of their feelings or sympathy with their state, it would surely be equally unfair to the upper classes, perhaps far more so, to submit them to the pastoral care and spiritual direction of those who were much inferior to them in cultivation and refinement of mind. It has been one of the uses of certain portions of the regular clergy, to supply this necessity towards the educated class. Such have been the Benedictines in certain times and places, and such especially have been the Jesuits. Here is one characteristic of the Oratory: its Fathers are secular priests, but they have commonly been superior to the run of secular priests; they are unlike, indeed, both Benedictines and Jesuits, as those regulars are unlike each other; but so far they are similar to both, that they are sent to the upper classes, and therefore must be of the upper class themselves.

That they are not of the lower class almost follows, if nothing else could be said to show it, from the circumstance that they are ordained on their patrimony, and live on their own means; for the lower classes and the bulk of secular priests will have no patrimony; and, in the next place, they who have a patrimony to show when they come for ordination, are likely to have had it actually or virtually already, and accordingly to have been sent to superior schools, and to have had the advantage of a liberal education.

Is not this peculiarity of the Oratory brought home to us by its history and its actual condition? Go back to the time of St Philip, and to the foundation of his first Italian Congregations, and you have abundant illustrations in point. The Saint's first disciples were men of rank, or members of the liberal professions, or devoted to literature or to the fine arts, or in some way or other superior to the mass of secular priests, and on a level with those who rose to the prelacy, or had a place in courts. In this respect the Oratory contrasts with the Community of the Pellegrini, which was St Philip's first foundation, and which is said by Bacci to have consisted of "about fifteen companions, simple persons and poor, but full of spirit and devotion." This was his work while he was yet a layman; but when he became a priest, and commenced his special mission, he drew about him, says Bacci, "many of the principal men of the court." There was a brother of Cardinal Salviati, a near relation of Catherine of Medici; Tarugi, a relation of two Popes; Tassone, nephew of the Cardinal of Fano; Altieri, a Roman noble; and one of the house of Massimi. Others, well born or not, had situations about the court. Others were lawyers or physicians, as Baronio, Bordini, Modio, and Fucci.

In like manner, among the first Fathers of the Chiesa Nuova, we find Tarugi, already mentioned, Savioli, and Ricci, men of noble families. Gabrielli, the founder of the Oratory at Fano, Santi of that at Padua, Nardi of that at Aquila, and D'Aste of that at Forli, were such also. Paccaroni, one of the original Fathers at Fermo, was attached to the Cardinal d'Este; two of of the first Fathers at Perugia had been in the service of the Spanish Government; one at Fossombrone came from the Court of Rome,—another from a Nunciatura. Three out of the four first Fathers at Naples were lawyers, the fourth held property. The founder of the Oratory of Bologna was a young man of wealth, and, as we now speak, of fashion. The founder of Lodi, too, had property of his own; the founder of Cesena, Chiaramonti, was a man of family, and a celebrated writer.

Did we pursue the inquiry, I think we should find, on the whole, the case the same now. The Oratory of Palermo is said to consist almost exclusively of men of family. At Brescia, we found the other day that the Father Superior was noble, and the Fathers come of gentlemen's families round about. The late Superior at Naples was of a ducal house. There, too, Caracciolo is a Filippine name, as Colloredo is at the Chiesa Nuova. The late Superior there, Father Cesarini, was also of noble family; and another Father of the last generation was uncle to the present Pope. So, too, the Oratory at Florence has many noble names: at Turin, its Church is, or was, the Court Church.

Now, here I have to make two remarks in explanation:—
First, I do not say, —nor is it necessary for my point, nor is it at all what I wish to advocate,— that all the Fathers of the Ora-

tory must be of the class I have mentioned, or that more than
a minority have in fact been either noble or highly educated.
In a community like the Oratory, the higher or more cultivated
class would set the tone, and the rest would fall into it. We see
this in society in general; a few are cultivated, accomplished,
refined, large-minded; but these become a standard, and
insensibly form the rest upon their model; and that, first,
because the qualities in question are attractive, and have a
natural gift of setting the fashion;—next, because they are
positive; whereas the absence of mental culture, being negative,
is not equally influential and effective. Accordingly, even a
few men of intellect, correct feeling, and good manners will be
sufficient to leaven and transform a community; yet at the
same time, in matter of fact, the rest, even though not exactly
geniuses or nobles, have commonly been, in some way or other,
superior to the average of secular priests.

My second remark is this: it may be asked, whether, if men
of good family are necessary for the Oratory, we shall not have
to wait some considerable time before we get them? True; but
times have altered since St Philip lived. Whole classes of society
have come into existence of late centuries; whereas there
was no medium formerly between the very high and the very
low, the peer and the tradesman or farmer. In those times there
were no middle classes; not to be high was to be low, and to be
low was to be ignorant and rude. Therefore I conceive that, as
in St Philip's time, the Oratory belonged to the *higher* class, so
it belongs now *not to the* lower. Certainly, if it was the case even
now, that the upper class, that persons of family, would not
make friends of any priests but such as were themselves of good
family,—if they considered none but such to be their equals.—
if they would not look for their directors and instructors except
among priests of their own rank in society,—then I should even
now be forced of necessity to draw the line of an Oratorian
vocation very high. But since the case is otherwise, since by
"upper classes" Englishmen do not simply mean the well-born
and no others, but account "birth" as merely one element in
the notion of "a gentleman;" since men of noble family will
use the services of priests who are not such, provided they are
gentlemen; since whole classes, having the education without

the ancestry of a gentleman, have sprung into being since St Philip's day, and want priests to instruct and direct them, it follows that, provided a priest rises above the level of his brethren in liberal education and refinement of mind, he answers to the vocation of the Oratory in this day, even though he is as little above them, as the blessed Sebastian Valfri was, in the antiquity or lustre of his family.

So much on the rank of gentlemen, as being the ordinary condition of Fathers of the Oratory. Next, I come to speak of their literary qualifications and liberal knowledge; but this being a large subject, I think it best to postpone for another letter.—I am, &c.,   J. H. N.

III.

MY DEAR FATHERS,—I spoke in my foregoing letter of certain qualifications attaching historically to Fathers of the Oratory, by which they are distinguished from ordinary secular priests, —viz., the breeding of a gentleman, the mental elevation and culture which learning gives, the accomplishments of literature, the fine arts, and similar studies. But now the question naturally arises,—Are we quite sure that such endowments, excellent as they are in a human point of view, and highly prized by the world, were not simply laid aside and disowned by their possessors on joining the Oratory? Are we sure that it was not the special merit of the first Philippines that they did discard them, and the very condition and means of what may be called Philippine perfection? so that we might as well argue that monks must show themselves to be gentlemen, because they often come of high birth and from the schools of wordly knowledge, as insist on cultivation and refinement of mind being the mark of the Oratory, merely because its Fathers, before they were such, had been conspicuous for such secular advantages.

In answer to this objection, it would be enough to observe that a secular priest *cannot* put off himself, for the reason that he does not live under a rule stringent enough for the purpose. A religious, indeed, of a severe Order, by the discipline of silence, by being absorbed into the action of his community, by words and deeds prescribed in mode and measure, and according to a necessary ritual, may break from his former self, and destroy his personal characteristics and the manifestations of his identity; but if his vocation be short of this strictness, in spite of its obliging him to put aside his friends, his books, and his pursuits, the effect of having been conversant with them will remain upon him, will give a character to his thoughts, language, and manner, and will be a means of his influence; so that, even were it the case that a priest, on becoming a Philippine, or a youth on leaving his secular instructions for our noviciate, did put aside his former studies and occupations, he would still inevitably be different from those who never had had them; and, therefore, the past tastes, past knowledge of the world, past intercourse in good society, and the like, of the Fathers of the first Oratories, would be their permanent attributes in their new vocation to the end of their lives. Even if they professed to despise them, they would not the less profit by them, as being human instruments of doing their work and of promoting the divine glory in their new calling; and therefore they are deserving of mention when we would describe the qualifications of a member of the Congregation of St Philip.

This, I say, would be the case, though it were our duty to put aside for ever the pursuits and studies which once engaged us; but such a renunciation, which is the peculiar merit of a monk, is not a counsel specially recommended to us, or a means of our perfection, as a very few references to the history of the Oratory will show. It is indeed its very characteristic, on the contrary, to admit distinctly and freely of the cultivation of art, learning, and science, in those members whose gifts lead that way, provided of course that that cultivation be directed solely to the glory of God and the salvation of souls, which are the ends of the Christian ministry. As our perfection is the perfection of secular priests, so whatever is allowable in a secular priest is (*exceptis excipiendis*) allowable in us.

I say, that learned studies and literary pursuits and the fine arts, far from being proscribed in the Oratory, have had a distinct place there from the first. The instance of Baronius is decisive; it was St Philip who made him, against his own will, write his Annals. Nor let any one hastily suppose that, because those Annals are ecclesiastical, the reading necessary for writing them was simply of a religious character. The text of them shows that, at least during the early volumes, the author could not have got forward page by page without a careful examination and a profound knowledge of the contemporary classics, which, considering his other occupations, is most surprising.

Nor is the great Cardinal a solitary instance of Oratorian learning, even in St Philip's day. Bozio and Gallonio, both penitents of the Saint, and members of his community, gave their minds and their time, by his orders, to historical research.

Another remarkable instance in an early Father of the Chiesa Nuova is Father Justiniani. His work bears date of 1612, only seventeen years after St Philip's death. Its title is the exponent of a phenomenon which, after all, I should not have expected in the Oratory. I should have thought that reading was allowable with us, not for the *sake* of reading, that is, with the general object of turning it to religious account, but only for some definite assignable religious end, as in the works of Baronius and Bozius. But, on the contrary, Justiniani's work is a mere commonplace book of a student who rummaged libraries, and turned over the pages of books, without any immediate aim before him, or prospect of utility. It is entitled an "Index Universalis Alphebeticus," referring to the authors who have professedly treated subjects in *every* faculty, "materias in omni facultate consulto pertractatas designans." You see, it has no subject-matter of its own, but is a mere literary work. The author commences his preface by saying, "Taken up, as I am, by the various public and private exercises of my congregation, I have undertaken to put this Index into shape in *my spare hours,* by way of assisting my own studies and those of my brother-priests." Those other priests, then, had their studies too, and he also *other* studies in hours which were *not* his spare hours. "And I will confess," he proceeds, "that I have found it undeniably more laborious to collect together the works of others than to write works of my own." So his studies were not only without definite and immediate scope, but were more severe than they would have been, supposing they had had one.

Well, I turn over the pages of his folio, and I find the fruits of a reading simply miscellaneous. The following are some of the headings:—"Academiæ, Aër, Acies, Africa, Agesilaus,

Alcestis, Alchimia, Anglia, Astronomia, Aragonia, Bucolica, Cato, Cæsares, Chirurgia, Cicero, Circulus, Civitas, Classis, Color, Cometa, Computum, Consules, Convivium, Critica, Cutis, and so on. Among the authors whom he quotes, I catch the names of Delrio, Eunapius, Moscopulus, Manutius, Aristotle, Demosthenes, Pausanias, Ælian, Virgil, Hippocrates, Dio, Columbus, Heliodorus, Bembo, Petrarch, Hanno, Xenophon, and Plutarch.

Again, the first Custos (as I think he is called) of the Vatican Library, I think soon after St Philip's time, was a Father of his Oratory. So was the second, in the time of Pallavicino. If there be any office which implies the possession of multifarious knowledge, it is that of a librarian.

The tradition is carried down to this day; if there be an ecclesiastic now in Rome who represents literary, at least historical, learning, as distinct from theology, it is Father Theiner of the Chiesa Nuova. And he, too, is, or is to be, closely connected with the Vatican Library.

To add one more general instance:—I have read, and I think taken a note of it, though I cannot find my paper, that in the middle of last century Benedict xiv set up a literary *academia* in the Chiesa Nuova.

Historians who view the matter impartially, say the same thing. No one denies that at least the French Oratory, whatever were its faults, was a learned body. Now, Schlegel places Italian and French in this respect under one description. He says, "Both agree in this, that *they devote themselves* to learning; but the Italians pursue especially Church History, while the French pursue all branches of learning." Mosheim says of the Italian Oratory, "They have had not a few men distinguished for their erudition and talents." Surely this is something distinctive. I do not think it would be said of the Ministri degli Infermi of St Camillus, the Benfate Fratelli, the Sommaschini, the Lazarists, or the Redemptorists, though they may have writers among them. It might, on the other hand, be said of the Theatines and Barnabites.

In like manner, had I materials here, I might draw out, I am sure, the historical connection of the Oratory with the fine arts, and especially with music. The highest application of the musical art began with St Philip,—the Oratorio,—and retains in its name the memory of its origin. Bartoli and Dentici of Naples, and Pantaleone of Macerata, were musical composers. As to painting and architecture, there is a church in Piedmont, unless my memory fails me, built by a Genoese Father, who is recorded to have devoted himself to the art; and this, I think, is far from the only instance which the records of the Oratory furnish of the devotion of its members to architecture. In this connection, it may be worth remarking, that two out of St Philip's first companions were goldsmiths, whose profession at that day, as we see in the instance of Cellini, was a branch of the fine arts.

Now, observe how remarkably the present Pope has taken up the feature of the Oratory, on which I have been enlarging, in establishing the English Congregation. I have not a copy of our Brief here, but I think he contemplates in it, as a desirable object, that it should be formed or recruited by means of converts from the English Universities. And he goes out of his way to tell us for what class of Catholics we are especially intended: "Hominum cœtus doctioris, honestioris, et splendidioris ordinis;" and recognising it as the intention of those who brought the subject of the English Oratory before him, he says, "Laudamus plurimum consilium," &c.

It is but in keeping with this purpose that, while distinctly recognising the other duties and employments of our Fathers, he has just now, on my solicitation, given us a special indulgence, if we employ ourselves in publishing books, in liberal education, and in promoting the arts of music and painting.

Here I should leave the subject of literary pursuits and the fine arts, viewed as a characteristic of the Oratory, were it not that by pursuing it a little further we should gain some collateral information into the genius and mission of our Congregation. Let us investigate, then, to what studies our Fathers have principally given themselves, and from what they have abstained,—a subject touched on by Schlegel above.

I find, then, in the literary history of the Oratory, very few doctrinal, or moral and ascetic writers. I do not know of one doctrinal writer, unless Fr. Cristoforo of Naples were such, who was attacked by a Cistercian for an interpretation he gave to a

certain passage of St Thomas. However, he showed his un-
polemical spirit by not answering him, as did a Father in the
North of Italy by burning an attack which he had been induced
to write on some critical observations put forward by a learned
person of the day. Bozius has written controversy in his two
folio volumes, "De Signis Ecclesiæ;" and Baronius's great work,
though not in form, in design was controversial, St Philip
putting him upon it *apropos* of the Protestant Centuriators.
However, it is in substance as well as form historical. Fr. Adda
of Rome has written a defence of celibacy; Father Marchese,
whose work is in our library, has written a defence of Pope
Honorius; and Gabrielli of Bologna is also a controversialist.
In morals, I find Cadei of Brescia, and Chericato of Padua,
whose folios we have got; in ascetics, Navarro of Fermo.

Fr. Cesari of Verona is an editor of the Italian classics; Fr.
Valperga and others are mathematicians, especially the celebrated Fr. Conti of Venice, of whom we hear so much in the
Life of Newton, though he afterwards left the Oratory. Justiniani
of Rome, of whom I have already spoken, is emphatically a
man of letters; such, I believe, is Mansi. Again, Valperga of
Naples is an oriental scholar, and Magri of Messina, a Biblical
critic.

Critics, indeed, are more common, such as Bianchini and
De Prato of Verona, Spada, Albini, and De Magistris of Rome;
here too should be mentioned Gallandi, the editor of the
"Bibliotheca Patrum."

But history, antiquities, and topography, supply the principal
fields of Oratorian research. St Philip set Baronius upon the
Ecclesiastical Annals, and Raynaldus, Laderchi, and now Fr.
Theiner, have carried on the work, and made the province
almost our property. The subject of primitive antiquities was
once ours also. St Philip betook himself to the Catacombs, and,
while Baronius and Gallonio, at his bidding, wrote upon the
martyrs, Aringhi and Bosius investigated the wonderful sub-
terranean galleries where they were buried. Antiquities have
also been pursued by Saccarelli, Severano, and Laderchi of
Rome, by Piccolo of Messina, and by Copola of Naples.

Lastly, local antiquities, a subject which singularly becomes
the genius of the Oratory, have been pursued by Antinori of

23

Aquila, by Baglione and Crispolti of Perugia, by Pietro of Salmona, by Grandis of Venice, by Fioravanti of St Elpidio, by Semeria of Turin, by Calini of Brescia, and by Gentili of San Severino.

It is not necessary to suppose that all of these are first-rate authors; but that a list has been published of about two hundred and fifty Oratorian writers of one kind or other, with few doctrinal and so many historical, is a sufficient evidence that the Oratory encourages literature, and a sufficient indication also of the province of literature which it prefers.—I am, etc.,

J.H.N.

NOTE *on p.* 33.—I suppose my allusion in the last lines of that page is to Fr. Haffner. In the *Biographie Universelle,* we read, "Antoine Haffner, né à Bologna, et peintre de perspective, en 1704, fut chargé de peindre la chapelle de St François de Sales dans l'église de St Philippe-Néri [à Gènes]. Il conçut bientôt du goût pour la vie tranquille de ces frères; il demanda l'habit avec instance, et l'obtint, mais avec l'exemption de tous les emplois qu'on donnait aux autres religieux. De ce moment, Antoine ne pensa plus qu'à embellir l'église de St Philippe. L'élégance et la vérité du dessin, l'harmonie et la suavité des teintes, la fraîcheur des compositions, lui attirèrent un grand nombre d'admirateurs." *Vide* also Lanzi's "History of Painting," vol. iii., pp. 175, 285 (Bohn's translation). [see p. 326 Ed.]

IV.

MY DEAR FATHERS,—I am considering what pursuits and occupations are, and what are not, inconsistent with the vocation and perfection of a Father of the Oratory. Perfection involves some mortification, which is of counsel, not of precept. What is that mortification in our case? It is not that of renouncing literature and literary occupations, or the refinement of mind consequent upon them; it is not that of ceasing to be gentlemen and scholars: on the contrary, a certain moral and intellectual standard, higher than is necessary for secular priests in general, is one of the qualifications of the Oratory, as being an institution intended (the English Oratory expressly so) for the service of the upper classes. We must be priests; and to do the work of priests, we have the special and the obvious functions of priests upon us, as being ministers of the Word and Sacraments,—in the main, as other priests have, for the difference is one of detail here; but while we have the same sacred office and spiritual duties of other priests, still, in our own persons, we are such as I have described, and our mortification does not lie in the direction of literature and art.

Let me pursue the enumeration of negatives, since I have commenced it.

2. In the second place then, our perfection is not wrought out either by the sacrifice of human affection or personal attachments. On the contrary, a love for each other, a love of the Oratory as a home, is one of the chief characteristics, bonds, and duties of its Fathers.

E.g., First of all, their vocation is to a *fixed place,* and, I may say, to a particular body. Regulars may consider themselves wanderers upon the face of the earth; such is not a Father of the Oratory. In spite of that detachment, which St Philip esteemed so highly, he bids us, in his rule, "bind ourselves more closely to each other in love," by "daily intercourse," and "daily knowledge of one another's ways," and even by the very look of "familiar countenances." Accordingly, each house is said to be a "family," and the Superior is "the Father."

This is the reason, says the Rule, why the community must not be large; for then this distinct knowledge and loving intimacy of one with another cannot be. Brockie enlarges on this point. "The type of the Italian Oratory," he says, "according to the mind of St Philip, was a sort of holy family, having its own private house, and made up of just so many brothers as might be able to know and love each other well. The custom of years, known faces, similarity of character, all that creates human love, becomes that bond of union and perseverance, which the founders of Orders and Religions place in the vow of absolute and perpetual obedience. Accordingly, it is a local, nay a domestic institution; simply without outshoots; observing an almost sacred seclusion within its own walls so that even the bishop, whom it serves in all things, instead of being admitted into it, rules it as a whole, and not in its individual members. It is diametrically opposite to the Jesuit type, which St Philip, it may be, did not like to rival, being so great a friend of its originator." Such is Brockie's account of the Oratory.

Residence has in consequence ever been enforced as a cardinal point in the Oratory. Fr. Sozzini mentions four causes which alone excuse from it. Of these the first is, "When the Pope would employ some member at a distance from the Oratory, as in the instances of Fathers Tarugi, Velli, Scarampi, and others." And this residence, I say, is treated, not simply as a duty, but as a necessary bond of the community in the absence of vows, promoting, as it does, a triple attachment, to the *place and neighbourhood,* to the *Fathers,* and to one's own *room.*

The last of these is spoken of by the same great authority, whose words I have just quoted. "The love of our own room," he says, "is always to be commended, and carries with it the best effects; since there spirituality may be cultivated, and interior peace preserved, and a sweet school of perfection found," St Philip himself was a remarkable instance of this attachment. Not only did he not quit Rome for more than fifty years, but he lived in St Gerolamo itself for thirty. Even when his subjects were established by Papal Bull in the Vallicella, and he was their Father Superior, he did not leave his old habitation. He remained there for six years more; he did not move even at last (if I recollect aright) till the Pope obliged him; and then his remembrance of the cat he left behind him for six years more, which he made his penitents keep, was at once a symbol of the affection he felt for his old home, and perhaps the expression of a playful malice towards those who brought the Pope down upon him. St Gerolamo was his old long-possessed *nido* or nest, in which he had experienced summer's heat and winter's cold, the jealousy and spite of enemies, and the throng and affection of generations of happy penitents.

An attachment like this became a tradition of the Oratory; and the word *nido* is the term expressing it. Fr. Manari of Reggio, and Fr. Grossi of Fermo, both cry out: "Hæc requies mea". When Father Sensi of the Chiesa Nuova was obliged, for his recovery from illness, to betake himself to his mother air, still "so dear to him," we are told, "were the walls of his beloved *nest,* that, nothing moved by his bishop, he desired to return to Rome, with the hope that that climate would perchance suit him better than before." When Amadei, a lay brother of the Oratory of Perugia, had finished some business he had in his own country, "without even seeing his relations, he returned to his beloved *nest.*" When Fr. Morico was driven from his Oratory at Fermo by a family law-suit, his only thought, on gaining it, was "to return to his beloved *nest*." Fr. Licinio Pio, the founder of the Oratory of Bologna, was attacked by his last illness, and had been away for change of air; but he intreated he might be taken back in order to die "in his *nest*." When Cardinal Baronius was permitted, after his public life, to return to the Chiesa Nuova, the reading one day in the Refectory happened to be at the beautiful passage in the Book of Job, "Dicebam, in nidulo meo moriar,"—"I used to say, I shall die in my dear nest." On this he broke out into a series of touching reflections too long to quote here. "Certainly, my dearest Fathers," he cried, "with reason can I apply these words to myself, while I reflect on past years, and those most happy days, when I dwelt in these domestic walls, when God dwelt in my tabernacle, and the Omnipotent was with me, and you, my brothers, round about me. Drawn thence by force, like the dove from the ark, I have ever longed to return, that I might die in my *nest*." Lastly, when Fr. Velli was dying, the love of his brothers, and of their familiar faces, was of human attachments the only one he had, and that, not superseded, but sanctified by that supernatural grace of which he was so bright a creation. He sent for the Fathers to be round him; one was absent saying Mass. He waited with impatience till he came; folded him in his arms, and gave up his spirit to his Maker and Judge.

3. So much on the permission or duty of *personal attachment* and *love of our nest* in the case of members of the Oratory, the mortification of which is so chief a feature in the discipline of Regulars. Nor have we those other mortifications ordinary with religious bodies. Our perfection, for instance, as we well know, does not consist in the counsel of *poverty*. "Habeant possideant," were the words of St Philip, when some persons were anxious to introduce it into his Congregation.

4. Nor in unusual *fastings*. Fr. Manni, one of St Philip's spiritual children, tells us, that the Saint wished that "the hearing daily the Word of God should be the compensation for fastings, vigils, silence, and psalmody; for the Divine Word heard with attention was equal to any such exercise."

Accordingly, when the Monastery della Pace at Brescia wished to put themselves under the rule of St Philip, some of the Fathers there were very unwilling to give up their fasts; but the Chiesa Nuova persuaded them "to embrace with cheerfulness the constitutions of the Oratory, without diminishing or altering anything."

And when Grande, a saintly man, who had joined the Oratory of Camarino, introduced fastings three days in the week, Fr. Velli, the then Superior of Chiesa Nuova, interfered, and told him and his brethren that, though they might abstain if they would, "they might observe no fasts but such as were of precept, experience having shown that, in an Oratory, additional fasting was destructive of what was more important."

5. Nor, in fact, does the perfection of the Oratory lie in *anything external*. The show of sanctity, the profession of strictness, was altogether foreign to St Philip's teaching. His Fathers were to seem to be secular priests, as they were; and, whatever they might be more, this they were to carry about with them on their front. Their dress was to be that of secular priests; and this is so strongly felt by some of the Oratories in the North of Italy, that they have altered the Philippine collar into something very like to the Roman, following the changes which time has introduced into the customs of the priesthood. Hence St Philip disliked slovenliness of dress and dirt of person; nothing was to be fine or costly, but nothing, again which savoured of unusual austerity. Hence, too, it was that, much as he insisted on obedience, as we shall see in a future passage of these Letters, he never made a show of it. He is said never to have used the word "command" but once.

6. Lastly, there being *no* vows in the Oratory, *vows*, of course, are not the instrument of its perfection. The rule is especially precise and decided on this subject. It makes their absence one of the two "altogether immutable points in the form of the Congregation." The Decree on the subject declares that St Philip has forbidden vow, oath, or promise of any such sort "by divine inspiration," and that it was the unanimous mind both of himself and of all his Fathers so absolutely, that, even though the majority of the subjects of the Congregation should at any time think of changing its condition in this respect, that majority is free to go, and the whole property of the Congregation falls to the small minority.

An attempt is recorded as having taken place soon after St Philip's death to introduce vows; but the Pope stopped it.

V.

MY DEAR FATHERS,—I have now enumerated various characteristics of a Father of the Oratory, both in describing how he differs from the ordinary run of secular priests, and how he differs from the type of a Regular. And I have made some progress in describing the line which his perfection will take; and now that I proceed to point out what I conceive to be the precise *instrument* of his perfection, or that counsel which is the especial means of it, I shall be adding one more characteristic, and that a remarkable one, in which he differs both from the secular priest and from the regular.

I have noticed various counsels which he does *not* pursue; such as those of poverty, fasting, external observances, and vows. There is indeed one very high and principal counsel, which I might notice, and which he observes on vow, in common with both regulars and seculars—viz., that of chastity—a counsel and a vow which necessarily impart a special character and colour both to his duties and to his perfection. But this I do not dwell upon here, for the very reason that it belongs to him in common with *all* secular priests, and by virtue of his *being* a priest. But the question to be asked here, is,—What is his perfection as a Father of the Oratory? And what that perfection is, is plain at once from the last words of the description which I have from the first given of him. He is "a secular priest;" but not only so, but a secular priest "*living in community.*"

Consider what is implied in the word "community." To live in community is not to be simply in one house; else the guests in an hotel form a community. Nor is it to live and board together; else a boarding-house is a community. Priests living in a chapel-house or presbytery, with each his own room, and a common table, and common duties in one church and parish, do not therefore live in community. To live in community is to form *one body*, in such sense as to admit of acting and being acted upon as one. You may recollect that Brockie, in a passage

I have already quoted, observes that "the Bishop rules the Oratory as a whole, not in its individual members;" whereas he contemplates and acts towards his own priests, though they live in one house, as separate individuals. An Oratory is an individuality. It has one will and one action, and in that sense it is one community. But it is obvious that such a union of wills and minds and opinions and conduct cannot be attained without considerable concessions of private judgment on the part of every individual so united. It is a conformity, then, not of accident or of nature, but of supernatural purpose and self-mastery. It is the exhibition and the exercise of a great counsel, carrying with it a great sanctification, according to the maxim, which has almost become a proverb in the Oratory: "Vita communis, mortificatio maxima."

Now, I say, this conformity of will and action, based indeed on human affection, limited to place and person, yet rising within its limits to the full dignity of that self-denying religious obedience which is the matter of one of the three vows of regulars, while it constitutes the bond of the members of the Oratory with each other, and converts a lodging-house into a community, is also the special index of its vocation, and the special instrument of its perfection. And this is *why* I say it:—

It is not every one who has the gift of living with others. Not every holy soul, not every good secular priest, *can* live in community. Perhaps very few men can do so. Seculars do not, nor do regulars. At first you will say that regulars do. No; for consider, in the first place, that regulars are commonly members of a large extended body, not of a local household or family. They have no home. To-day they are here; to-morrow they are there; they are sent about; sometimes it is the very principle of their Order *not* to let its subjects be for any great time in one place. At least, for long intervals of time they go out on missionary work, and at length come back to what is a retreat rather than a home. Sometimes their house is even called a "retreat." They are, of course, under superiors; they are under rules; but they are not subject to one unchangeable community. Again, even suppose regulars to be *bonâ fide* in a community, as is the case often with women; well, but it is because they cannot help it. They conform, they obey, because they are under a *vow*.

There is nothing to show that they have the gift of living together as such, and for its own sake. They obey, not for the sake of obedience, but from a past act which binds them. There is, then, as distinct a difference of vocation and of perfection, between us and regulars in this respect, as there is between us and secular priests.

Conformity to the Congregation, and a loving submission to its will and spirit, is all in all to a Father of the Oratory, and stands in the place of all other counsels. He may, indeed, personally and privately live under other counsels also, which are not discountenanced by the Rule, as are poverty and fasting, but, as an Oratorian, he has this badge. Father Consolini says, "Chi vuol vivere a suo modo, non è buono per la Congregazione."—"He who would live in his own way, is not the man for the Congregation." The author of the "Pregi" says the same. Quoting the same Father as saying, "All members ought to accommodate themselves to holy community," he adds, "This Father was very energetic on this point, for, when it is understood, it brings with it a store of merit." The same writer quotes also St Philip's saying, that sanctity lies in three-fingers'-breadth; "for perfection," he continues, "consists in bringing one's own will into captivity, and acting in accordance with the governing power." "Whoso walks in the way of obedience," says the blessed Sebastian, "goes securely to Paradise." "In the service of God," says the venerable Fabrizio dell' Aste, "it is not well to be too ready to invent new things, but rather to accommodate ourselves to the usage of others." Father Sozzini says, "Though thy vocation of secular priest does not admit of a life in community in what regards the exterior, such as clothes, furniture, and property, yet it does admit, nay, it demands of thee, the living in thy interior altogether in community; that is, thou oughtest in everything to strip thyself of thy own will, thy own opinion, thy inclinations, and thy ease, and to make them over by a perpetual renouncement for the use and benefit of thy Community."

Now how peculiar is the vocation, how special is the perfection, of which community life, thus explained, is the characteristic! Even granting the existence of mutual attachment, how rare is the fact of an enduring domestic union without a vow!

Take the case of the marriage-tie:—though woman is inferior to man, and depends on him, though man and wife are attracted in the first instance by mutual liking, and have the pledge of children to keep them together, yet a vow is necessary for the security of the union; it is sealed by a sacrament. Human affection, then, though the initiative principle, though the abiding support, of the Oratorian vocation, is after all not its life. Its life is a supernatural grace. As faith is preceded and sustained by human reasonings, yet is really a divinely-imparted assent to the Divine Word, so, were there not a real vocation, the work of a divine influence, in the Oratory, its members would not keep together.

Hence it is that, in the evening exercise of the Brothers, we pray so earnestly for perseverance, which becomes our special grace for the very reason of the voluntariness of our obedience. On entering the Congregation, the candidate is carefully examined whether he comes to it "animo permanendi semper in Congregatione usque ad vitæ obitum."

Hence one of the old Fathers of the Oratory said, "The true sons of St Philip are known at their burial."

Hence Father Grassi of Fermo, who had been used to say, "Hæc requies mea in sæculum sæculi, hic habitabo, quoniam elegi eam," exclaimed in his last agony, "O che bella cosa, morir figli di S. Filippo!"—"O what a happy thing to die sons of St Philip!"

Hence the pain excited in the minds of Baronius and Tarugi, when the venerable Giovanni G. Ancina, on St Philip's death, talked of passing from the Oratory to a religious order. "Quid fecisti? What have you done?" wrote Baronius, at that time Father Superior. "May God forgive you! This is not the sort of lesson which our Father has left us, to desert from his ranks, and to consult for yourself; he, who lived eighty years, yet never lived for himself, but ever, day and night, even to his last hour, was studying the convenience of every one else." Tarugi, too, at that time Archbishop of Avignon, writes: "If I can advise, if I can beseech, if, in the thought and the mind of your reverence, I have credit for being able to distinguish temptations from good inspirations, I supplicate you, and I conjure you, to lay aside this new thought, and to believe most absolutely that it is a temptation, and so much the more dangerous in that it comes in the guise of justice and greater perfection."

In truth, those holy men felt, that to remain firm in a good resolve without a vow had a merit of its own, and was as acceptable an offering as could be made to the Most High; and was as sure a means of drawing down a blessing on the offerer; and was as efficacious an instrument as could be selected for raising the general standard of his obedience, and for leading him to that perfection, which is the fulness of charity and the happy way to heaven.—I am, &c.,

J. H. N.

VI.

My Dear Fathers,—I should prefer to treat the subject of Obedience, which is the counsel of perfection incumbent on us, more as a matter of loving conformity to the will of the Congregation, to considering it as a necessary duty to be paid to Rule and to Superiors. And in this higher, more comprehensive, and more generous way of viewing it, it has sometimes been compared to that voluntary and loving obedience which the Eternal Son rendered to the Father in our flesh, when He came to do His will. "Oblatus est, quia ipse voluit," says the author of the "Pregi," "He suffered through zeal for the glory of the Father and for the salvation of souls; 'zelus domus tuæ comedit Me.' Observe the exemplar of the sons of St Philip, who, after the pattern of the Redeemer, do spontaneously what they do for the service of God in congregation, of their full free-will, so that they can say, 'Voluntarie sacrificabo Tibi.'" Elsewhere the same writer says, "We obey when we might disobey, obedience being free; which is the very praise given by Ecclesiasticus to those who *can* transgress and transgress not, 'Qui potuit transgredi, et non est transgressus.'"—However, it is necessary for me to treat of Obedience also in the light of a duty toward particular Rules or Persons: and that I proceed to do.

1. Obedience was due to the Community, even before there was a Rule to be the object of obedience; nevertheless, rules began in the Oratory very early still. St Philip gave his subjects

some "poche costituzioni" twenty years before his death, while they were at S. Giovanni. They went to the Vallicella soon after; and there they seem to have wished their Father to *draw up* a Rule, which he did not do. Some years afterwards, however, nine years before his death, we read of some sort of Rule as existing. He was most strenuous in enforcing it, such as it was. On one occasion he said, "My Fathers, I am most fixed in my resolution to forbid the House to any who do not observe those few orders which are given to them." On occasion of the Naples House, he speaks of the "Capitoli." However, they were not yet formally imposed upon the Congregation as essential to it; they were on their trial, and after St Philip's death depended, I suppose, on the will of the Father Superior and the Congregation. They had at that time one remarkable sanction given to them by the glorified Saint. He appeared to a Capuchin of holy life, and, among other things, said to him, that "the Congregation was pleasing to God," and "così sono le Regole tutte, e se ne tenesse conto, e non s' innovasse minima cosa." So says the author of the "Pregi," though Fr. Bacci seems to state the matter rather differently, referring St Philip's words to the Little Oratory. The latter writer also tells us, that the Saint made many of his Constitutions with the advice of Cardinal della Rovere, Archbishop of Turin, confirming them by the unanimous consent of his Fathers.

However, he did not write a Rule, as St Ignatius might write one; and he left what he had laid down for the experiment and judgment of the future. After his death, other decrees were gradually added; and by the year 1612, seventeen years after it, and nearly thirty from the time when he left S. Girolamo for the Vallicella, Fr. Consolini was called upon to draw up our existing Rule, with a view to obtaining the Pope's confirmation of it. What he seems to have done was, to write out the existing Decrees, as successively passed by St Philip, and by the Fathers after his death, embodying them in a sort of running account of his own of the genius, character, and customs of the Congregation. Such at least seems to have been the case, judging by the internal evidence of the work, by the change of style, tense, form of expression, and the like. I mean, he seems to say, "Our usages as to festivals, daily intercourse, &c., &c.,

are so and so, as may be seen by the Decrees which follow." This will account for the want of system with which his statement is drawn up, which would not be the case if the work had proceeded from a lawgiver. Such as it was, however, Paul V. confirmed it as the Rule of the Congregation; and Gregory XV. did the like ten years afterwards, about the time of St Philip's canonisation. From the time of the first confirmation, no Congregation out of Rome might profess to belong to St Philip Neri which made or published any other Constitutions; and this seems to have been the reason why Cardinal Berulle, when he introduced the Oratory into France with certain modifications, could not call it St Philip's Oratory, and therefore gave it the title of the Oratory of our Lord Jesus Christ.

For ourselves, when I had the matter in my hands nine years ago, I considered that the lapse of three hundred years, changing external circumstances, made changes necessary in the religious instruments which are their correlatives. I found that, in fact, the Fathers at Chiesa Nuova felt it difficult to observe portions of the Rule; and then I reflected, too, how gradually the Rule had grown up, how time had been made the test, and, as it were, the measure of its usefulness, and how, as a matter of history, the Congregation has not been established upon the Rule, but the Rule established by the Congregation. I considered that what had been made since the Founder's time could equitably be unmade; that St Philip, too, was most averse to rigid forms and burdensome externals; moreover, that the Rule itself begins by saying that his Congregation is "moribus potius erudita quam legibus astricta;" and that Fr. Ricci speaks of it as being carried on, for the most part, "ex jure, non scripto." Further, on looking into the Rule, with that view of it in my mind which I have already noticed (viz., that it might be distinguished into two portions, as consisting partly of real Decrees, partly of a mere relation of practices which were historical and existing facts), I thought I saw that the former were of a nature far more permanent than the latter, and such that we might obey them in this age, as three centuries ago, with very slight changes. Accordingly, making those slight changes, with the permission of the Holy See, I got the further permission to print these Decrees separately from the rest of the

Rule in which they are embodied, with the understanding that
the Decrees alone should be binding on us as Fathers of the
Oratory; and the rest, printed in a different type, should only
be recommendations, to be followed or not at our discretion.

I have said thus much as introductory to the question of
obedience to the Rule. Our obedience, as a *principle* and a *duty*,
is, I conceive, what it ever has been in the Oratory; though
that which is the *subject-matter* of our obedience is not precisely
the same. And now, having shown what liberty has been
granted to us as regards the *matter*, I proceed to show, from one
or two instances from the history of the early Fathers of the
Oratory, what strictness there ought to be, in order to please
St Philip, in the *obedience* itself.

"Father Tarugi," we are told, "scrupulously observed the
most minute rules of the Congregation, according to the spirit
of St Philip;" and even when he became Archbishop and
Cardinal, he continued to observe them as far as was possible
in his position. Fr Francesco Bozio, in the decrepitude of old
age, was most exact in the observances of the Oratory, and
refused particular indulgences. Fr. Consolini's singular prerogative was "to have perfectly inherited St Philip's spirit, to be
zealous for the purity of the Institution, and for the perfect
observance of the Rule." The blessed Sebastian of Turin caught
his death by coming in hot from walking to the Oratory exercise
—then held in a damp and cold place—and baring his shoulders
for the discipline. Fr. dell' Aste observed, "before all things,
with the greatest diligence and the most exact perseverance,
all the Constitutions left by St Philip to his children." "Let the
Father of the Oratory," says the venerable Mariano Sozzini,
"ever have the Rules of the Congregation in his hands;" and
he observed his own exhortation. Fr. Grassi of Fermo made a
point of "an exact observance of every Rule, even the least;"
and had a maxim, "that nothing but necessity excused an
observance of the letter." Fr. Oblioni of Casale accounted
nothing light which the Rule prescribed, which was never to be
transgressed. When Fr. Morico of Fermo refounded the Oratory
of Macerata, his first object was "to introduce that strict
observance of the Rules for which his own Oratory was so
conspicuous." And Father Borello of Naples was remarkable

for the "custody and observance of the Constitutions and the laudable customs of the Oratory."

Such instances may be multiplied without limit. It must be recollected, indeed, that the Rule does not bind under sin; but observance of it is the condition of our obtaining and securing the love and protection of St Philip. If we wish to interest him in us individually, we must keep his Rule, as the Holy See gives it to us. It is in this sense I understand Fr. Matteo Ancina to say, "that we should have to answer for the observance of it at the judgment-seat of God."—I am, &c.,

J. H. N.

VII.

MY DEAR FATHERS,—Having spoken of the duty of obedience to the Rule, I have next to speak of obedience to the Superiors. And first, I shall, as before, direct your attention to the obedience itself, and then to the Superiors who are to be obeyed.

As to the duty itself, it is difficult to insist upon it in stronger terms than are used in the books which are of authority with us.

"Let all things be done under the seal of holy obedience," said Father Ancina. Fr. Airoli looked for this principal comfort in the "tremendo punto" of death, that he had "acted with an entire dependence on holy obedience." "Christus factus est pro nobis obediens *usque ad mortem*," even unto death, said Fr. Tarugi, "et exemplum dedit nobis." "Be like a stick," he says to his nephew, " in the hands of your Superiors; have no feeling or will or your own. Above all, beware of those who possess not this spirit, and who consequently have little or no sincere devotion." "Though the Fathers and the Brothers," says the author of the "Pregi," "make no vow of obedience, as Religious do, nevertheless they do not yield one whit, for all that, in the perfection and delicacy of this virtue, supplying the want of vow by love and voluntary promptitude and perfection." Elsewhere he says, "Whether the Superior or Director who commands be a saint, as St Philip, or of small or no virtue, the obedience will be always the same." Where this is not recognised, the obedience of a Father is as suspicious as would be his faith, if he prostrated himself before a gold crucifix, not before a wooden one. The Father Airoli, above spoken of, "showed to his superiors, whoever they were, the highest esteem and reverence, and obeyed them with the greatest cheerfulness and promptitude."

So much for the obedience itself. When we come to consider the Superiors in detail, to whom obedience is to be shown, first we have to mention:—

1. The Congregation itself, that is, I suppose, in its legislative capacity. This is the highest of all authorities, which the Father Superior, as the rest, has to obey. "Not even the Provost for the time being," says the author of the "Pregi," "is exempt from obedience; for even he must obey the greater Council, which is composed of Decennial Fathers, and the lesser also, which consists of none but the Deputies; and when these bodies, by a majority of votes, have determined anything (unless it belongs to the Superior by himself), he is bound to obey, and to enforce their decrees, without having power to change them, though they are against his own judgment."

2. Next, as to the Father Superior:—

His power is rather limited than created by the Rule; by which, I mean, he is in possession from his situation; and all that rule and custom have to do, is to determine the cases, in which the prescription, which goes with his office, is restrained and cannot be appealed to. This limit is given in the "Pregi," viz., when the Superior wishes to introduce "novelties directly opposed to the rules, or destructive of them."

With this reserve, which may be necessary where men are Superiors who are inferior to a Saint like St Philip in sagacity and discretion, we may allow the forcible language of Tarugi, that "all the respect and submission showed towards St Philip when alive, ought to be transferred to the Superior who takes his place."

The same sentiment was professed by Fr. Consolini: "The obedience," says Marciano of him, "which he cherished towards the Saint when alive, he transferred to his successors who governed the Congregation after his death."

There is a remarkable instance recorded of the obedience of the Blessed Sebastian. In the Jubilee of 1675, he proposed to visit Rome, and got leave for the purpose of the Father Superior and Deputies. On parting, the Father gave him a note, which he was to read before he embarked. He got to the vessel; his luggage was put on board before he opened it. It ran thus: "Father Valfrè will return home at once." He returned: perhaps it is more wonderful that he should have been commanded, than that he should have obeyed; yet the Father Superior was not considered to have exceeded his *power.*

3. But there are others who, in their place, are to be considered Superiors also, and who must be obeyed in those matters, where they have the right to give the law, as unhesitatingly as the Father himself, and by him as well as by others.

Thus we read of Fr. Consolini, that, "not only towards St Philip and his successors did he exhibit a prompt obedience, but equally towards inferior officials of the Congregation, down to the last of the Brothers. It was his maxim, many times repeated, "that that God who has placed the one in the Office of Provost has placed the other in charge of the door or the kitchen." He called the Porter's bell "the voice of God." Marciano tells us the same of St Philip himself, both as regards his enjoining and exemplifying the Rule, and that, from obedience to the Sacristan to obedience to the Porter. "One official is subject to another," says the author of the "Pregi," "so that the first Deputy, the Secretary, the Minister, the Prefect of youths, and so the rest, even the Superior himself, all ought, when the occasion requires, to obey the Prefect of Sermons, the Sacristan, the Porter, and the Cook."

"Voluntary obedience," says Fr. Sozzini, "extends not only to the Father, but to all the officials of the Congregation, each in his proper sphere, requiring indiscriminately from all, not merely obedience, but also humility and fraternal charity."

Marciano gives an apposite description of Father Grassi of Fermo. "In respect of obedience," he says, "though, from being so long a time Superior, he appeared to have no opportunity for its exercise, yet he knew how to follow in its track. First, he placed his private will in the hand of his Confessor, as if he were a child. Next, though Superior, he used to render a most exact obedience to the officials of the Congregation. Called by the Porter or Sacristan, he never was heard to say, "I cannot."

24

And, whereas in the last years of his life a Brother was assigned him for his attendance, he called him his guardian-angel, and recognised him as his Superior, and obeyed him in such sort as not even to change his place without his leave. In his journeys, he so depended upon his companion, to whom he then gave the name of governor, that his intimations were for him inviolable precepts." The same is related of Father Consolini.

And now, my dear Fathers, I have said all that I can say for perhaps some weeks, though I have hardly got into my subject. By which I mean, that, instead of as yet having delineated a Father of the Oratory, and given him a substance and a form, I have done little more than set down certain observances, or provisions, or aims, which belong to him, certain circumstances in which he finds himself, certain points which are personal to him, certain limits within which he moves, certain permissions which are granted to him, and certain prohibitions which are laws to him. To illustrate what I mean, I would observe, that I have only cursorily mentioned his duties as a priest, as saying Mass, as attending the Confessional, as discoursing to the people,—that is, I have taken for granted all that was involved in the sacerdotal office, after I had once said that he was a secular priest; and I have given greater prominence to what was not more important, but less obvious.

However, I will sum up what I have done, as far as it goes.

It appears, then, that a Father of the Oratory is a secular priest under certain peculiar conditions. As a secular priest, he has the duties of a secular priest, and is bound to aim at perfection in the exercise of those duties. And in those duties, and in the endeavour after perfection in these duties, his week, his month, his year, his life goes.

Next, the duties of a secular priest are *various,* and all do not attach to one and the same person. One may be a missioner, another a preacher, another attend to schools, another be a theologian and lecturer, another write books, another have the charge of convents, another give retreats and missions. Now, the ordinary duties of a Father of the Oratory are the ministry of the Word and Sacraments,—that is, attendance at the altar, the confessional, and the pulpit. These duties are not such, however, as to take up more than a *portion* of his time, as is evident from the great stress which is laid, in the lives of various Fathers, on their living so much in their room. Nor, again, are they more than the *rule* of his duties, in the sense in which they are the rule of a *priest's* duties. I mean, you may have priests, who, after saying Mass, do nothing more of a directly religious character (in public) through the day, but give themselves to literature or science, to classics, or astronomy, or chemistry, or antiquities. And in like manner, I conceive there have always been Fathers in the Oratory who have been exempt, in a great measure at least, from those directly sacerdotal duties which belong to them as priests, even independently of their being sons of St Philip. This caution only must be observed, that they do not so devote themselves to secular occupations as to forget that they are supremely dedicated to a life of religion; St Philip having been "very particular," as Fr. Bacci tells us, "in seeing that his subjects did not engulph [sic] themselves in study, and take too much affection in it."

And in the third place, I have observed that, as the duties, so the temporal position of secular priests is various and manifold. Some are for the higher classes, some for the lower; some are gentlemen, others are not; some are delicately brought up, others are hardy; some have cultivated minds, and others have not; some are literary men, and others are not. And I said that the Oratory on the whole was composed of priests who belonged to the upper classes, and who addressed themselves to the upper classes, not confining the word "upper" in this country to any very strict sense.

However, whatever be their personal qualifications and peculiarities, anyhow the Fathers of the Oratory pursue perfection; and whereas perfection cannot be attained without the observance of some counsel or other, the question arises what is *that* counsel on which the perfection of the Oratory depends? I have answered—Not in poverty, not in bodily mortifications, not in externals at all, not in the renunciation of a home, not in vows, but in community life. For, though to live in a family has great advantages, and human affection is a great stay of supernatural charity, yet, after all, this kind of community life, sustained and persevered in without vows, involves a great mortification, according to the saying already quoted, "Vita

communis, mortificatio maxima;" and has, when encountered
and undergone well, a special effect upon the character and
perfection of our obedience; for it is conformity to the spirit of
a body, and it is a volùntary act continually repeated.—I am,
&c.,   J. H. N.

March 9, 1856. [See Appendix 5, p. 444. Ed.]

NEWMAN'S ORATORY PAPERS No. 26
2 & 16 AUGUST 1856

INTRODUCTORY NOTE

These two Addresses need to be studied in conjunction with
the second half of the 'Undated Fragment' which follows. In
the *Remarks on the Oratorian Vocation* p. 344 Newman had pointed
out that the priestly ministry takes up only a portion of the
Oratorian's time. In these two Addresses (2 and 16 August
1856) he draws the inference that some further work, some
tangible object is necessary, in order to avoid 'the largest and
most elementary waste, to which we are liable, the waste of
time . . .'

The Oratory School had not yet begun at this time. The
drafts of the *Remarks on the Oratorian Vocation* contain many
concrete hints as to possible works to be undertaken by the
Oratory. On the background to these two Addresses see above,
p. 145.

CHAPTER ADDRESS

August 2. 1856[1]

I.

The Blessed Sebastian Valfre used to say, with respect to
our Congregation of St Philip, that there were two ways of

[1]*B. Or. Ar.* D. 4. 9.

living in it;—that he who chose could do much, and he who chose could do little. He said, that, if a person would, he could do much for God and for his neighbour, and rise to a high perfection; Again he said, that, on the contrary, if a person wished it, he might content himself with living without sins, with fulfilling ordinary duties in a matter of fact way, without heart and spirit, and so would pass his days without profit, and perhaps at last get tired of his lot.

These are words, my dear Fathers and Brothers, which we ever should have in our minds. Let us ever ask ourselves why we have come to the Oratory? We came, I suppose, in order to save our souls, to please God, to have safeguards and a shelter against sin, and to be able to do what other[wise] we should not find ourselves equal to doing. The very fact that we belong to the Congregation is a sort of promise made to God—it is our seal put to the engagement that we will serve him with our heart. We have given ourselves to Him. We are not under vows, but still we have made ourselves peculiarly His. Let us day by day, let us, when we rise in the morning, make an offering of ourselves to Him. We make the offering through St Philip, but it is a whole offering or holocaust. And be sure of this, that it is the only way in which we can promise ourselves perseverance. We may be very happy here at present —it may please us that we are out of the way of any great temptation—but all this may be so, and yet carry with it no promise of perseverance. To persevere we must daily say to ourselves "How can I serve God in this blessed state of life to which He has called me?"

August 16. 1856

2.

I consider, my dear Fathers and Brothers, that when we once have apprehended that distinction on which I insisted last Chapter, I mean, the difference of living here to ourselves and living to St Philip, we shall see our duties in a new light. As Christians, we have given ourselves to Christ; to make this more sure and definite, we have, as Oratorians, given ourselves to St Philip—we are not our own property, but his, and we must please, not ourselves, but him.

Now the first and the vaguest consequence which follows from this, contains a great deal, on which I think I might say things profitable to us all. I mean on the duty of not wasting ourselves or things committed to us. By wasting I suppose is generally meant using things in such a way that they answer no good purpose. *Our* purpose is to use things for Almighty God, our Lord Jesus, for our Blessed Mother, and for St Philip. Now, the largest and most elementary waste, to which we are liable, is waste of *time* or what is called *idleness*. And this I think will be one of the characteristic existing [sic] between those who, as the Blessed Sebastian says, do much, and those who do little for God in the congregation, that the one will think their time their own, the other will think their time St Philip's. Now this is a very serious thought for us all. I am far from deciding what is to be considered a waste of time, and what not, for this will be various with every individual. What is waste in one, is not waste in another. What are the duties of one, are not the duties of another. Nor have we any call to judge each other. Nor can we lay down boldly what occupations come into the vocation of the Oratory, and what do not. Nor are we to fancy, or to distress ourselves with the idea, that fair and proper recreation or rest is waste of time— but still without deciding these points, as to what is idleness or waste of time, and what not, we may very profitably, and we ought, at the commencement of each day, if we are to be good children of St Philip, to set before us, that our time is not our own, that it is his—and, in our usual offering of ourselves and all we are through the day to God, to recollect that our time comes first, and the most obvious gift we have to offer.

FRAGMENT:

Subjects for Addresses

1. on the way we are watched—therefore we should be very circumspect.

1. persons in Chapel. who watch us so closely—a
   . . . . .[1] our very dress.
2. on things getting outside the house from gossipping
2. on our each having a work.
   1. it may be an external object
   2. it may be to save our soul

but any how, shocking if we come to the Oratory to be idle.
especially if we are young
an object-less life.
a mere harmless life may do very little for us in the day of
account.

———

NEWMAN'S ORATORY PAPERS No. 27
31 AUGUST 1856

INTRODUCTORY NOTE

The general public are aware of the contrast between
Newman and Faber—one insisted on, perhaps too much,
throughout *Trevor I* and *II*. In a sense the difference between
Newman and Dalgairns was even more serious, particularly
from the point of view of the Oratory. See above, p. 77
(original choice of vocation), pp. 109–112 (on the place of
intellectual work within the Oratory). For the details, see
Trevor II, pp. 142–149: 'Dalgairns leaves Newman,' and *L.D.*
XVII, pp. 15, 33–4, 349–62.

This Address is an open statement by Newman of his conviction that the London Oratory meant to reform his (Birmingham) community by having Dalgairns live among them.

As was suggested above, in the Introductory Note to the
Remarks on the Oratorian Vocation, here Newman deals with the
personal angle omitted from his minor 'Apologia pro vitâ suâ
—Oratoriana'.

---

[1]Three words illegible here.

31 August 1856[1]

My dear Frs

I cannot propose for your acceptance the decree which Fr B.D's departure from us has rendered necessary, without saying a few words on the subject of the time he passed with us and the circumstances of his leaving. I am for many reasons unwilling to do so—and it is nothing else than the duty of doing so which overcomes that unwillingness. He was a man of various unusual endowments, and I suppose we all feel, (I certainly do myself) that there are points in which he may well be a pattern to us all, and that, under other circumstances, his general example, his advice, his influence would have been great and constant service to us. I trust we all have in various ways gained good from his being here—so that, whatever painful thoughts accompany his sojourn and his departure, we may have cause to bless God for his coming here, and reason to remember him in our Masses and our prayers.

I have a very personal reason besides, for not liking to make the remarks which are to follow. I know he has the kindest, tenderest feelings towards myself; and, though I cannot accuse myself, I trust not, of not valuing and admiring him, yet I shall be obliged to seem, at least to myself, to be making an unsuitable return for words which he has addressed to me. Moreover, I feel very much how sadly and mysteriously dear F Bernard have [sic] been sent about (if I may use the word) from one House to another—a trial which it is impossible to duly estimate, impossible not deeply to sorrow for.

But I have duties towards the Congregation—the Congregation both now, and as a matter of record, should have a clear view of its own actions and its own conduct. It is bound to contemplate what it does—when it thinks it is right, it should bring before it the reasons which have actuated it; when it is led to think it has been wrong, it should state distinctly such mistakes, both in order to right itself with its own conscience, if I may so express it, and for the advantage of posterity.

[1]*B. Or. Ar.* Oratory Letters July–August 1856.

In this particular case one or the other side—we or Fr Bernard must be wrong. And as he has implied blame of us, so we are bound to bring before us our own side of the question, for the tranquillizing of our own minds, and for the removal of all scruple, doubt and misgiving.

I say he has implied blame of us, in the formal letter which he sent me, recording his wish to leave us. He says, "As you wish me to announce to you formally my intention of quitting the Birmingham Oratory," (here was a slip in expression which I record, merely lest it should be misunderstood in time to come—what I desired was a request from him to be allowed to leave the Congregation.) "I write to beg you to have the kindness to communicate it to the Fathers. The *only* reason which I can assign for this step, is my not *having the spirit* of the Birmingham Oratory, and, therefore, having no vocation to it." What he has stated here formally, he has in conversation stated freely, and in such a way as he leaves no doubt as to his meaning. He distinctly thinks that *he has* the spirit of St Philip—and wishes to remain one of his children—he as distinctly says that he has not *our* spirit—from which it follows as a matter of necessity that he considers that we have not the Spirit of St Philip. He has a right to his opinion. I am not going to prove the contrary here—but, putting proof aside, some weight at first sight may attach to his opinion *because* it *is his* opinion, because *he* holds it who has so many high qualities and gifts. It is incumbent on me then, as Fr Superior of the Congregation, to remind you or to inform you of various circumstances which deprive him of authority in this matter, and make his opinion about us no more than the opinion of any one else. I am obliged to show that there have been certain infirmities in him, which allow us to put his judgment, his parting judgment, of us on one side, and to go forward on our own way without anxiety.

And here I will say first of all, that I can fancy a case in which he would have remained [with] us, and been again and an ornament to our community, and nothing else. And that is, if, he had been under another kind of Father Superior. I know, my dear Fathers, I am quite deficient in what the life of St Ignatius, (which we are now reading in Refectory,)

ascribes to that great saint so justly, the art of government—
one branch of which is, what I do not mean to speak invidiously
about, when I call it, the art of management. I think another
person *could* have managed Fr Bernard. A person so amiable,
so affectionate, so gentle, could have been led by the hand, I
know perfectly, into all that he *should* have done, and led away
from all he should *not* have done, by one who had the gift of
doing it. It was a very delicate matter to have a Father from
another Congregation suddenly plunged into ours. We could
not give him a *noviciate*—yet every community necessarily
differs from every other, a [sic] putting aside whether here there
is a right and a wrong in that difference, and again who is right
and who is wrong, it was impossible but that a collision, or a
convulsion, must have taken place any how, on this sudden
introduction of a new element, definite in its kind and powerful
in its influence, and free in its action, into a constituted community. The more valuable he might be in himself, the worse
for our tranquillity. Even had he been a saint, it would have
been the case of the new cloth in the old garment—and, in
proportion as there was error or infirmity in him, and some
truth and grace in us, so would be the gravity of the disturbance
which his presence occasioned.

But I think I must admit, that, far from considering these
serious risks, we went into an access [excess?] of generosity
towards him. From respect for him, from desire to make him at
home, not only did we not give him "the lowest place," but we
call[ed] him up to some of the highest of our offices. Not only
did we place him according to the precedence which he had,
before he left us originally, but we showed him an unwise, an
unkind confidence. Two of our most momentous offices are those
of Confessor and [Master] of novices—we felt they ought not to
be united in *any* case; yet in *his* case, we not only gave him
the one *or* the other, but we gave him both. We went out of our
way to show him an extraordinary, an excess of confidence,
by giving him offices, as if he could exercise both duly, which
never can be otherwise than incompatible with each other.

It is not wonderful that, under these circumstances, humanum
aliquid passus est—that such sudden elevation in a Congregation which he had just entered, was too much for him.

No paradox is truer than this, that the higher we are in
holiness, the more are we in danger of going wrong. I have
been accustomed to compare the ascent to perfection to the
mounting a high ladder[2]. As the climber gets higher, the ladder
dances under him—behold the state of a soul mounting towards
heaven. I thus account for the wonderful falls of holy men—
the utter shipwreck of ascetics—the heresies of grave and
learned teachers—the delusions in which Satan enwraps souls
which he cannot on the whole separate from God. This is why
Saints are so few—they drop off as they get more likely to be
Saints.

If then I proceed to say that there were certain great defects
in the Father we loved so well, and defects which tell in the
question which has divided us, I am implying praise while I
blame—for not every one is in such a state that he can be so
deluded, as I verily believe he has been.

The Apostle says, "Nihil per contentionem, per inanem
gloriam—sed in humilitate, superiores sibi invicem arbitrantes."[3]

And, applying this to the subjects of the Oratory, one of its
Fathers tells us to do our own work and look to ourselves
with[out] criticizing others.

If there was one member of the Congregation above another,
who, for *personal* reasons, should have been content with his
own work, and abstained from finding fault with others, it
was one who had just been received into the Congregation,
and had to learn what it was, before he *formed* a judgment,
and to remember the claims of delicacy, before he *pronounced* it.

Again, if there was a member of the Congregation who was
bound by considerations of his *office* to abstain from external
interference with its proceedings and with the conduct of
individuals, it was he who held the office of Confessor—an
office, as I told him, which necessarily must be kept detached
from the administration of the House, to be performed well, as
is shown in its incompatibility, according to our Rule, with a
seat in the Congregatio Deputata.

Do what I will, I cannot get myself to fancy that Father

[2] See above, Chapter Address, 11 December 1850, p. 233.
[3] *Phil* 2:3.

Bernard thinks *us* better than himself. Do what I will, I cannot convince my intellect but that, in all that relates to an Oratorian life, he despises and has ever despised us. I have seen what seem to me continual instances of this defect. I have *told* him that he despised us; I am but saying what I have said to *him;* I do not recollect his offering me any reasons to convince me otherwise. For myself I say I cannot wipe this deep impression out of my mind. This impression of mine is quite consistent with my fully allowing and believing that he has a deep sense of his own imperfections, without which of course he could not be what he is. My impression which I speak of is as to his *comparative* view of *us* relatively to himself. It is plain how such an impression must interfere with my having any deference to his judgment, as the judgment of one who had a right to decide the questions between us. He alone has really the grace to judge in such questions, who *shrinks* from judging.

Though so lately one of us, though the Confessor, no long time passed before he began to give out his opinion that the Congregation was in a very unsatisfactory state spiritually. And he began by a quiet course of agitation to get various things altered, and the more was done, the more he wished done besides, and this, I may say, from the first. He had not been in office a year when he went out of his way, without any one asking him, to write me letters of advice, and to expostulate with me. I have no delicacy in saying this for this plain reason—that he professed to speak not in his own name, but in behalf of the other Fathers, as if heading them and presenting their complaints. And this very circumstance of his speaking *for* others was an aggravation of the impropriety which I have noticed, of a Confessor mixing himself up in external questions at all.

I have been searching for the letters, but they are in some place by themselves, and I cannot put my hand upon them. But, as I read portions of the longer and more urgent of them to the Fathers about this time year, they will bear me out, that I state their contents correctly in substance, or correct me, if I am wrong. He wrote then, as of course he would write, very kindly—but he said that it was right I should know the feelings of the Congregation—that Fathers did not like to speak—that it was possible to get unwell from having too little to do, as well from having too much; that there were souls burning for opportunities of usefulness which were not allowed them; and that the Congregation was doing nothing compared with what it might do—and similar statements which would naturally grow out of these. And he spoke warmly.

Speaking as he did in behalf of the Fathers with reference to matters which necessarily touched my conscience very closely, I spoke to them on the subject, I think in Chapter—and I conjured them to tell me, if it were so—for there is nothing of course I want more than they should do for God all they can do, whether it be more or less, which is in *His* hands, not in ours. They assured me, it was not the case—they did not feel what Fr Bernard ascribed to them. This is what you told me, my Fathers. It relieved me; but, in proportion as you re-assured me, you necessarily made me dissatisfied with Father Bernard.

But his conduct involved a further inconsistency. He was asking others to do what he had no wish at all to do himself. Take the duties of the Fathers of the Congregation in their length and breadth, and how little of them did he wish to take part in! He ever seemed to forget, and I am saying nothing which I have not urged upon himself, that there were a variety of duties incumbent on the Fathers, quite as necessary as those of a lay brother who cooks the dinner or sweeps the corridor, and quite as unspiritual. He seemed to ignore the office of Father Minister and Father Treasurer, and seemed to grudge their existence. The whole circle of duties connected with a mission, he ignored too. No one was to do a hundred things which were absolutely necessary, they were to be done, or the day could not be got through. But he was not to hear of them— he was to hear of nothing but of Confessions, and other directly religious occupations—and these he undertook himself. Fathers were idle, if they were not engaged in these. Now it became him who thought the Congregation moved so slowly to put his shoulder to the wheel. Accordingly I proposed to him to take Smethwick—thinking that he who criticizes ought to be set to do—the project languished on for months, and then, as I had foreseen, almost silently died. It is one test of sanctity given in spiritual books, not to care being put out of one's way. I am sure *I* do not like being put out of my way, but *I* am not accusing other persons' way[s]—but I must say that Father Bernard, while wishing others to do more than they did, did not like himself to go one step out of his way to relieve them of burdens which hindered them from doing more. He even murmured at his duties as guest master. He even complained of the uninterestingness of routine confessions in Church.

I do not wish every one to do the same thing—rather I am insisting on the very opposite. He could not live without excitement. I do not sympathise with him—but I do not condemn him on that account. Fr Sozzini says "As our Congregation is not bound by religious bonds, a holy liberty of spirit should shine amongst us. It is the will of God that one person should be more favoured in contemplation, another in active graces; one in works of temporal mercy, another in spiritual words; one in sacred studies, another in holy simplicity; that one should excel in one virtue, another in another. This variety of spirits will render the Congregation supremely beautiful, and that no one may err by canonizing his own spirit, it must be discerned by holy obedience, under the guidance of the Father. This due liberty of spirit being presupposed, it will follow, that every one must esteem and be edified by the spirit of his brethren, and sincerely prefer them to himself; avoiding a subtle error of such as are little spiritual, who only esteem those who follow their own spirit, censuring, or little esteeming, and perhaps trying the spirits, of those who do not walk with them." I never should have thought of wishing Fr Bernard to engage in works which did not suit him—but I wished him to allow others the liberty which he received. If I offered him Smethwick, it was to show that it was easier to criticize than to perform.

I must go on to make one more remark, which perhaps I have not had an opportunity of making to himself; but it bears on what I have to say in the sequel. One of the sure signs of the presence of the Spirit of God is peace. The Saints have gone through many fierce trials; I do not read that they were restless; or if they were ever so, I do not find that it came into the *idea* or definition of their saintliness. No two saints can be so different from each other as St Philip and St Ignatius—one so unassuming, the other so imperial. They are both in different ways inexpressibly calm—the calmness of St Philip took the form of cheerfulness, that of St Ignatius the form of majesty. What men do calmly, has weight—but when they are restless, they seem to me to want the primary condition for inspiring confidence in others or claiming deference. Now really I do not know any single person who saw any thing of Fr Bernard, but would allow that he was all through this matter, nay always at all times, restless. There is, there has been a want of rest in every Sermon he preaches, in every letter he wrote; and in this whole matter pre-eminently. This simply to my mind invalidates his testimony about our want of St Philip's spirit, altogether. The first element in St Philip's spirit is rest and peace.

But I mention it for another reason.

It made him unconsciously, (for I do not impute any thing to him,) the instrument of others, outside the Congregation, in working on those who were within it. When he implied that *we* had not St Philip's spirit, he meant that we had not the spirit of the London Oratory—and he has been used by the London Oratory to new-make us after the pattern of the London Oratory.

It is not to the purpose to go into the evidence, of what in various ways has been brought home clearly to my own mind and the minds of other Fathers. I never should be surprised to hear the London Fathers say, that the Congregation of the Oratory wanted a Reform *generally*—that the Oratories on the *Continent* needed reform—that the Pope's view of the Oratory was not St Philip's view—(this indeed *has* been said to me almost in terms,) that the Birmingham Oratory held the relaxed view of the Continental Oratories—and that the London Oratory was going to be towards the General Congregation of St Philip, (mutatis mutandis) what St Bernard and Citeaux were to the Benedictine Order; and that with this view one of themselves, Fr Bernard, was intended (and this, if I have not heard said, I think I have heard implied) that *he* was providentially sent here to infuse into us the spirit, (may I say the spirituality?) of the London Fathers.

Well, if all this be so, then I can only think it providential on the other hand and from God, that St Philip has taken him away from us—He might have been of incalculable value to us, if he had been one of us; but if, without meaning it himself, he was one of another House acting upon us, then against his nature he would have been constrained to be a mere element of division in us, and a principle of party in a community which was one. He would, with all his endowments, have been in a false position, and an originator of nothing else than what Fr Sozzini calls "antipathies or sympathies—" which, he continues, "destroy communities, since antipathies occasion ill-will and ruptures; and sympathies, under special appearances, are the cause of great evils, since, not content with gnawing their own bones, persons begin to gnaw the bones of their friends, and are in *continual disquiet;* besides which, to 'form a Congregation within a Congregation' is its destruction, and in as far as we cling to some, we necessarily withdraw from others." [4]

But I have said as much as I need on this part of the subject, nay on the subject generally which calls us together. Nothing I have said can interfere with the love which we have, and ever shall have, for dear Father Bernard—I am sure we shall ever have an affectionate memory of him. Whether St Philip meant this to be his place or not, he has not had a fair chance—for the London House have done their best, it seems clear to me, that he should not have a fair chance. And now they will say that it was St Philip did not wish him here. Still, painful as the circumstances are under which he leaves us, he has done us two benefits, for which we must be thankful to St Philip. I will mention them, and so conclude.

1. It is undeniable he has brought out the latent genius or spirit of our own Congregation. Others have looked on us, perhaps, he himself has looked on us, as a number of priests, brought together by human motives, who had no view of the Oratorian vocation. Certainly, it has *not* been our way, it has been part of our idea of that vocation not to make it our way, to bring out importunately and officiously any scientific definition of what an Oratorian should be. But I think no one can deny, from the unanimity with which we have expressed

---

[4] This quotation and that on p. 356 are from pp. 383 and 285 respectively of *The Lives of the Venerable Servant of God, Fabrizio dall'Aste and Father Mariano Soggini,* London 1850.

our dissent from him, that we have a very definite idea of our vocation for all that, and that that idea is one and the same too in all of us, and that this idea is not his.

2. and lastly I should not do justice to my own feelings about this troubled history, now closed, if I did not remind you, that, though we may not agree with him, we may gain benefit from his view of us. It is never a bad thing to be criticized, it must do us good, if we take it rightly. I trust his remarks will be of use to us, though we cannot simply accept them. I trust we shall remember them. All things are good, if we take them, as St Philip means them and without any wish except to get good from them.

NEWMAN'S ORATORY PAPERS No. 28
27 SEPTEMBER 1856

INTRODUCTORY NOTE

On the background to this Address, see above, p. 146, and on its theology see ib. pp. 119–20: §iv. "Is Newman's idea of Perfection theologically adequate?". This address was found by the editor in a box of unclassified Newman MSS. on 13 July, 1962. It had already been printed substantially in *Meditations and Devotions* pp. 379–383 but with some omissions and inexplicable alterations.

CHAPTER ADDRESS

Sept 27. 1856[1]

3

It is the saying of holy men that, if we wish to be perfect, we have nothing more to do than to perform the ordinary duties of the day well. ⟨A short rule to perfection. Short, not

[1] *B. Or. Ar.* D. 4. 9.

25

because easy, but because pertinent and intelligible [.] There
are no *short* ways to perfection, but there are *sure* ones.⟩

I think this is an instruction which may be of great practical
use to persons like ourselves who make a profession of aiming
at perfection. It is easy to have vague ideas what perfection
is, which serve well enough to talk about it, when we do not
intend to aim at it—but as soon as a person really desires and
sets about seeking it himself, he is dissatisfied with any thing
but what is tangible and clear, and constitutes some sort of
direction towards the practice of it.

We must bear in mind what is meant by perfection—it does
not mean any extraordinary service, anything out of the way,
or especially heroic in our obedience ⟨not all have the opportunity of heroic acts, sufferings⟩ but it means what the word
perfection ordinarily means. By perfect we mean that which
has no flaw in it, that which is complete, that which is consistent, that which is sound. We mean the opposite to imperfect.
As we know well what imperfection in religious service means,
we know by the contrast what is meant by perfection.

He then is perfect who does the work of the day perfectly—
and we need not go beyond this to seek for perfection. ⟨You need
not go out of the *round* of the day [.] ⟩We are perfect, if we do
perfectly our duties as members of the Oratory.

I insist on this, because I think it will simplify our views,
and fix our exertions on a definite aim. If you ask me what
you are to do in order to be perfect, I say—first—Do not lie
in bed beyond the due time of rising—give your first thoughts
to God—make a good meditation—say or hear Mass and
communicate with devotion—make a good thanksgiving—say
carefully all the prayers which you are bound to say—say
Office attentively, do the work of the day, whatever it is, diligently and for God—make a good visit to the Blessed Sacrament.
Say the Angelus devoutly—eat and drink to God's glory—say
the Rosary well, be recollected—keep out bad thoughts. Make
your evening meditation well—examine yourself duly. Go to
ded in good time, and you are already perfect.

NEWMAN'S ORATORY PAPERS No. 29
29 SEPTEMBER 1856

INTRODUCTORY NOTE

On the subject of this fragment, Father Joseph Gordon (1811–53), see the full biographical note in *L.D.*, XII, pp. 431, 432 and numerous references throughout volumes XII–XVI of *L.D.* In 1855 Newman began a custom which lasted several years, of presenting, on the feast of St Michael, to the Oratorian community and the congregation around them, an annual review of events. In 1855 Caswall gave a history of the Oratory in England from its inception, together with biographical accounts of Aloysius Boland and Joseph Gordon, 'who had died in 1852 and 1853.'[1] The last pages of the memoir on Joseph Gordon were written by Newman himself,[2] speaking of himself in the third person as 'the Father' (i.e. the Superior). These pages have appeared already in H. Tristram, *Newman and his Friends*, London 1933, pp. 111–16. They have been included here (transcribed from the autograph) in order to complete this *corpus* of Newman's Oratory Papers.

MEMOIR ON FATHER JOSEPH GORDON
29 SEPTEMBER 1856[3]

The Father is accustomed to say that there is nothing which has touched him more, or has remained more deeply engraven on his mind, than the generous confidence with which Father Gordon committed himself to him, without as yet having any personal knowledge of him. At the time that Father Gordon was received, our Father was at Rome, where he had gone to present himself before the Pope, and afterwards to ask leave of His Holiness to set up the Congregation of St Philip in England.

[1] *L.D.*, XVI, p. 541, note 1.
[2] *L.D.*, XII, pp. 432.
[3] *B. Or. Ar.* A. 51. 8.

Immediately on his return Fr Gordon hastened to him, and put himself into the Father's hands without reserve. The love he felt for the Father did but increase the mortification of this act. From the nature of a religious Congregation two persons, who wished to be intimate with each other, could not be so without an intervening delay. Accustomed from the singular clearness of his perceptions, the keenness of his intellect, and the persuasiveness of his conversation, to make friends rapidly, and soon to be among the foremost, wherever he was, he now at once had to subside into the position of a novice, who has to be silent, and do nothing which is not pointed out to him. The first had to become last, and to take the lowest seat. He had to postpone the gratification of wishes, which had led him to be where he was. And so it was, that, not even when the Oratory Fathers had left their country homes and came to Birmingham, had Father Gordon had the opportunity of familiar intercourse either with the Father himself or others who had come with him from Rome. A second time then he was obliged to give a proof of an affection which had not been visibly returned, and of a magnanimity, to which many would have been unequal. He promptly and unreservedly put himself afresh into the Father's hands, and at the Father's service, and was one of the chief of those who began the Mission in Alcester Street.

With what success, with what a blessing, he there laboured, it needs not me to tell. In some departments of Missionary and Oratorian work he stood by himself with an excellence of his own. We all recollect what animation he imparted to any undertaking which he began; how interesting was his conversation; how impressive were his instructions; how his remarks struck home; how he could bring people together, mark out their work for them, and keep them up to it; how skilfully and efficiently he managed the schools; how forcible he was in discussion, how happy in making converts. [And then besides, how very mild and courteous was his manner, or what the world calls, gentlemanlike, tempering the impetuosity of his reasonings by the sweetness and gentleness of his bearing.][4]

---

[4] The passage shown in square brackets was erased by Newman.

To him, as much as to any one, under Divine Providence and and the patronage of St Philip, the establishment of our Mission in Alcester Street was owing. It is a great mercy, when a man's work endures. There are those who are active, and create a sensation, who are brilliant and winning, but the effect of whose exertions soon ceases, and is forgotten. They begin well, and end poorly. The grace of Him, to whose supreme service Father Gordon had devoted himself, dealt otherwise with him. *He* has been taken away early, but not his work; his work remains.

But, alas, that work was almost limited to Alcester Street; he was not allowed to serve St Philip and assist us here. He had taken a foremost part in choosing our site, but he did not live to see us do much more than take possession of it. The building of this house had not long commenced, when he showed symptoms of the feebleness, which brought him to the grave. The house was begun in December 1850. On the 14th of February after, just two years before his death within a day, we felt it right to send him on a short visit to St Leonard's in Sussex for change of air and a milder climate. He returned by the 1st of March the Saturday before Ash Wednesday, and remained in Birmingham for Lent and Easter till St Philip's day. Immediately after, on May 29th[5] he set off to Brighton for two months, till the 4th of August. He still was not well; indeed fresh symptoms there showed themselves of an alarming character, as the event bore out. In the autumn, when our Father had need of the presence of friends in Italy, in order to collect evidence for the serious trial in which he was engaged, Father Joseph was one of the two Fathers deputed by the Congregation for that purpose. He was selected, among other reasons, because of his state of health, which, it was hoped, a southern climate would benefit.

I say "among other reasons", because that loving zeal, which had ever actuated him in our Father's behalf, manifested itself on this occasion; and he exerted himself, beyond his strength, for the attainment of the object, which was the direct cause of his journey. He was absent for three months; and, when

[5]See *L.D.*, XIV, p. 292.

he returned, his appearance was not satisfactory. This was on the 10th of February 1852. It was a most exciting, trying year. He returned only to see the last month, and the death, of our dear Brother Aloysius. The death of Lady Olivia Acheson followed. The trial, in which he was so interested, took place in June; but the suspence and the anxieties of the process continued after it, and, to the end of the year, he was harassed by anxieties which certainly preyed upon his health, which still declined.

On St Cecilia's day, November 22, our Father was called up to London for judgment. It was too much for Father Gordon; faithful to his own loyal heart, on that very day he was seized with a pleurisy; and, when our Father returned from London on the morrow, with his process still delayed, he found him in bed. It was the beginning of the end. He languished and sank; got worse and worse; and at the end of nearly three months, on 13th of February 1853, he died at Bath. He is in the arms of his God. We all loved him with a deep affection; we lamented him with all our hearts; we keenly feel his loss to this day. But the Father's bereavement is of a special kind, and his sorrow is ever new.

We are warned by the Apostle "not to be sorrowful as others who have not hope". For dear Father Joseph the change is gain; nor to us, in spite of the appearance of things, is it really loss. He who takes away can compensate; and our Holy Father, St Philip, himself reminds us that "God has no need of men". His mercies abound and continue. Every year brings with it fresh instances of them. In our *degree*, we may humbly use the same Apostle's words, and bless "the Father of mercies and the God of all comfort, who comforteth us in all our tribulation; for, as the sufferings of Christ abound in us, so also by Christ doth our comfort abound".[6]

---

[6] *2 Cor.* 1: 3–5.

NEWMAN'S ORATORY PAPERS No. 30
APRIL 1857

INTRODUCTORY NOTE

This Memorandum is valuable as an example of Newman's power of 'discerning spirits'. On Ryder, see *Trevor*, II, p. 177, and *L.D.* XI, p. 355. According to *L.D.*, XVIII, p. 9 and p. 10, note 1, Ryder went to the English College, Rome, at the wish of his father, (who had quarrelled with Newman) for the year 1855–6. On 7 December, 1856, Ryder was admitted as a novice in Birmingham, and by April 1857 was in an unsettled state (as witness this Memorandum), but persevered. Newman addresses him by name in the Chapter Address of 20 February 1858 (Oratory Papers, below).

Ryder was just twenty years old, and his trouble arose from the fact that he thought his attachment to the Oratory was a merely human loyalty. Newman skilfully traces out the legitimate place that human loyalty (and affection) may rightly hold in a vocation to the Oratory.

[MEMORANDUM]

April/57[1]

N.B.

There are one or two things, to which his attention should be drawn, by way of being fair to him, and lest we should hereafter have to say to ourselves that we have not brought out things to him which he ought to be told.

It is probable then, that either he has been told, or will be told, that his human feelings indeed lead him to *us*, but his supernatural motives *elsewhere*. He will have to consider, whether he has any better proof urged on him that grace leads him *elsewhere,* than the fact that nature leads him *here*. But this

---

[1] *B. Or. Ar.* Oratory Letters: January–June 1857.

is no proof, for it may easily happen that grace and nature lead the same way. This our Rule especially recognises, when it puts before us as an object, "*ut* arctius inter se, qui sunt e Congregatione, amoris vinculo colligentur, quem quotidiana *consuetudo* conciliat, ac *mores cujuslibet* ipsorum ex hoc cognosci possint, et *notorum vultus cunctis revereantur*".[2] If then he feels an habitual affection for us, a love of our ways, and a fear of annoying or displeasing us, or of losing our good opinion, all which in themselves are natural feelings, such a circumstance does not prove they are not St Philip's instruments for protecting supernatural charity. Any how they are not inconsistent with it, unless human nature and divine grace are essentially opposed to each other.

Then again, he should remember that his love for his Father is a human motive; and, while I allow, according to what I said above, that the human motive *may* possibly run with a supernatural motive to take him away from this Oratory, yet it is not so certain that grace is not leading him to *us* and a human affection leading him *away*.

Moreover there is a *natural principle*, to the influence of which he is necessarily and especially exposed, which may easily be taken for the operation of grace, and deceive him into the notion that God calls him elsewhere. Familiarity increases attachment, but decreases reverence. This is expressed in the proverb "Familiarity breeds contempt". On the other hand we admire what is strange and unusual to us; according to the saying, "Omne ignotum pro magnifico." We cannot feel romantic notions towards what we know well. Any drawing he may think he has in another direction, so far from supernatural, may come of human romance.

Nor must he for an instance suppose that we are bent on keeping him. He hardly can. The one thing we wish to know for him and for us is what is God's will. It is said that when thoughts about a particular vocation first present themselves to the mind, they are to be repressed and dismissed, under the certainty that, if they are from God, they will return. When we sent him from us last Summer year, and his Father sent him to Rome, we

[2] *Instituta Congregationis Anglicae Oratorii S. Philippi Nerii*. Rome 1847, Caput IV Decretum XV, p. 13.

took this course in order to see whether it was a human motive or a supernatural which drew him to us. The strength of the feeling which brought him back from Rome to us, seemed to us to show that it was more than human, and justified us in receiving him. If, however, he thinks he has not sufficiently tried himself, and if, by showing want of faith in us, he leads us to think the same, by all means let him go away again, and settle his mind once for all. We will allow him this last trial, and, if he returns, the only inconvenience which it will have been to him is that he will begin his noviciate again.

He may go for what length of time he likes. But, if he returns, we make this stipulation; that henceforth he does not read any thing from any one, and closes his ears to any suggestion, against us: and suppresses, as sin in his case, any such thought or feeling rising up within him.

NEWMAN'S ORATORY PAPERS No. 31
20 FEBRUARY & 8 MARCH 1858

INTRODUCTORY NOTE

On the background to these two Addresses to Novices see above, p. 146, and on the idea of "Santa Comunità" which they insist on, see ib. pp. 118–20. 'Santa Comunità'—the second basic principle of the Oratory.

On Stanislas Flanagan, the novice Master (absent at this moment through illness) see *L.D.*, LVIII, p. 259.

Reading between the lines of these Addresses, especially that of 8 March, the sympathetic reader can only become involved in Newman's anguish, how best to preserve a house spirit, without narrowness, and yet with firmness to force an opposing spirit to be its own catalyst and to remove itself, ". . . St Bernard must go forth from St Benedict, and set up a dwelling for himself, before Benedict and Bernard can each abound in his own sense and his own spirit . . ."

CHAPTER ADDRESS 20 FEBRUARY 1858[1]

Febry 20. 1858

    to Novices [i.e. George Crawley and Ignatius Ryder]

1.

If there is any one of whom it may be said that in the performance of the duties which he finds placed upon him he has to turn, not to natural or spiritual qualifications, but to the will of God and the vocation in which he stands, it is, my dear sons, myself. At various times of my life, and now as then, I have to do many things to which I feel myself quite unequal. I have been chosen in matter of fact to bring the Oratory to England; and, as head of this Oratory in Birmingham, I have upon me the responsibility of all the offices and functions necessary for or implied in the existence of the Congregation any of which revert to me, when there is no one else to fulfil them. And hence it is that now, in the absence of dear Fr Stanislas, I have to exercise certain duties towards you; yet little as I may do, it is more than I am able; and I can only act under the simple feeling that I am doing St Philip's work and obeying him, for, if we go to the question of merit and claim, I solemnly declare, in the presence of my Guardian Angel, my absolute and distinct conviction, my dear Sons, that, considering my years, and my opportunities and my advantages of various kinds, I am very far inferior to each of you.

Every one in this world has to play a part, the part which the great Lord and Master of all assigns him. This is my consolation; I must take my part whether it is high or low; as in the casting of characters in a drama. If He gives me that part which in fact He has given me; and made me Superior, and you my subjects, I must take mine, and you must take yours, without any concern what each of us may be in his own personal qualifications and his private spiritual history, in his own individuality in the sight of his Maker. We must each of us submit himself to God's will, and in each case that resignation, as it will gain for us His approval, so will it be attended doubtless with self mortification.

[1] *B. Or. Ar.* D. 4. 9. [See *L.D.* XVIII on Crawley and Ryder.]

Each of you has his own trials. You come to be assimilated
to a body which was once external to you. Every institution
which has life has its proper mode of life, its spirit and character; something which is its own, and which does not belong to
others. You come then, as on the one hand to belong to that
body, so on the other to gain a participation of its life and
spirit, and this necessarily implies a process, and in some way
or other a trial, from the nature of the case. The elder of you
has a great merit, to which the younger cannot attain, the
merit of having, with a resolute will submitted himself in mature
age and with the renunciation of a position which his own energy
and perseverance had made for himself, submitted himself
(I say) to take the lowest place and to become a learner in a
new school, whereas he had been for years a teacher. My dear
Ignatius, you cannot rival this, but you may take it as a pattern,
you may derive encouragement and a lesson from it, and, if
you understand it as well as I do, you will admire and love it.
Putting this aside, and looking at you both in yourselves, each
has his trial, and I do not know which is the great[er] of them.
It is a task on the one hand to submit formed habits, and on
the other hand to submit the unformed natural character to
an existing standard. In both cases there is especial need of
attending to the apostolic exhortation, "Lift up the hands
which hang down, and the feeble knees; and make strait steps
with your feet, that no one may halt and go astray, but rather
may be healed." [*Hebr.* 12: 12, 13]

I propose in these Chapters at present to set down what
occurs to me about our Congregation and our relation individually towards it, and I will begin by recurring to a remark
which I have already made, that every body that has life must
have a character and spirit proper to itself. This is the case
preeminently with Christianity itself, viewed as a Religion. The
heathen understood this, as far as they had experience of the
Religion, unmistakeably. Putting aside the question of truth
and falsehood, and looking at the fact only as a point of history,
we see that Christianity appeared to them sui generis, and
different from every other religious body. St Paul exhorts us
to the cultivation and attainment of this one spirit, properly
Christian, on various occasions, as when he speaks of our "all

meeting together in the unity of faith and of the knowledge of the Son of God unto a perfect man, unto the measure of the age of the fulness of Christ." And when he bids us "Whereunto we are already arrived, to be of the same mind, and continue in the same rule;" and to "be perfect in the same mind and in the same judgment," "in eodem sensu, et in eâdem sententiâ."[2]

At another time, however, he says, "Unusquisque in *suo* sensu abundet;" "let every man abound in *his own* sense." [*Rom.* 14:5] And hence it is that while the spirit of the Church is as truly one as the Church itself, nevertheless within that comprehensive and most real unity, there are a number of separate unities, each of which is made separate and one by some particular sense and spirit of its own, as is especially illustrated in the instance of religious bodies. The great families of the Benedictines, the Bernardines, the Carthusians, the Franciscans, the Minims, the Dominicans, the Fathers of the Mission, the Jesuits, the Redemptorists, has each a sense and spirit of its own, which, I will add, is necessary for its life. That one characteristic sense or spirit is seated of course in the governing body of the Order, and is partaken in by each individual according as he has, what St Paul calls, arrived or attained— but whatever want of assimilation there may be in particular members, at least rival spirit there is none—and if any contrary spirit gained a footing in the body, though it were in itself a good spirit, for, [sic], for instance, the spirit of another order, it would tend to the dissolution of the body. If the Jesuit sense got an introduction among the Dominicans, or the Benedictine among the Bernardines, we should have the case of a house divided against itself; and it could not stand. Two families of religious may indeed divide from each other, and each take to itself its own spirit; or one may go out from the order, as St Stephen and St Bernard from the Benedictines, and form itself upon a separate spirit—but go out it must. St Bernard must go forth from St Benedict, and set up a dwelling for himself, before Benedict and Bernard can each abound in his own sense and his own spirit.

But if this homogeneity of spirit is necessary where vows

---

[2]The quotations are: *Eph.* 4:13, *Phil.* 3:16, 1 *Cor.* 1:10.

exist, much more necessary is it where there are no vows; for vows secure a certain profession from one and all the members of a body, under and by means of which its spirit is created and perfected; and their absence throws the body at once upon its homogeneity as the immediate bond of its unity. And secondly, if this particular spirit is in all cases the principle of corporate unity, it follows that there will always be as many distinct senses or spirits as there are distinct body.[3] This remark, it is obvious applies immediately to the Oratory, which differs critically from Religious Congregations in these two points, as they are laid down in the 4th Chapter of our Rule, first that its members are not under vows, next that its Houses are independent of each other. I say, it follows from this of necessity, what we see indeed before our eyes; first, because of the separation of House from House, that each House has its particular sense or spirit; and secondly, because of the absence of vows, that that sense or spirit which is peculiar to a House must more or less, but still must extend with a force and substance unnecessary in bodies which are under vows, to every one of its members.

But this subject is too large to be exhausted in one of these Chapters—so I propose to continue it this day fortnight:

March 8. 1858

2.

I said in the last Chapter, that every ecclesiastical body must have a sense or spirit of its own, strongly marked or not, but still such as to be proper to itself. And it matters not whether the body be large or small, an extended order, or a local community, or whether its particular sense or spirit be original, and operative or ordinary and little worth, just as individual men have each his private judgment, whether that judgment be good or bad. And as two individual men may, though independent in their minds, agree together—so in like manner bodies may be like each other—but this will be an accident— and I think it will be found that such accidental congeniality between body and body is not to be relied on. Any how, it has

---

[3]This is clearly a slip. A rough draft of this Address has 'bodies'.

nothing to do with size—the independence of thought and spirit goes with the fact of its being a body as such—and small communities may differ from each other as much as large.

If the Oratories are separate bodies, they have each its own separate sense or spirit. And this is seen to be the case in matter of fact. Though the Rule is one and the same to all Congregations of St Philip, I think it impossible for any one to have seen ever so little the Oratories of Rome, of Naples, of Turin, of Florence, of Brescia, of Verona without allowing that one could not mistake them for each other—though the difference between them one by one varies.

In proportion then as the members of a body have it incumbent on them as a duty, or as a matter of religious expedience, to partake in the spirit of their one body, in the same degree does the period, first of inquiry, then of postulancy, then of the novitiate, become a time of experiment, trial, attempt, and success in the assimilation of the new member to the body to which he is to belong. And applying this to the Oratory, it is plain, from what has been said that the object or standard of assimilation is not simply the Rule, or any abstract idea of an Oratory, but the definite local present body, hic et nunc, to which he comes to be assimilated.

I am stating this in a dry scientific way to bring out my meaning, but do not fancy, my dear Sons, I mean any thing magisterial or severe in thus speaking. Those who come to us must have liked us before they came, or they would not have come. They must have been drawn to us, to have tried. They must already be in good measure of that spirit, which is ours, before they became one with us, unless before they came, they were greatly wanting to themselves in caution—if they took fair time about an important step, and acted with prayer and deliberation, they were half ours before they came to us. On the other hand, do not suppose I am setting up any one in the body as so identical in spirit with the body itself, that he has not himself to submit to the spirit of the body more or less, and from time to time. As you will see as I go on, I am but exalting Santa Communità. I wish to urge and inculcate, that the only security and principle of permanence in an Oratory, is the submission of all of us one to another *ever and at all times,* and till death, to the mortification, whenever necessary, of private judgments.

What the process is by which the spirit of a particular Oratory is formed, may not be easy to trace out in fact, though it may be imagined. Those persons who begin it carry their own tastes with them; and those tastes must be one and the same, or the chance is that they never would have coalesced to carry out one undertaking. The particular locality, the people with which they are surrounded, the circumstances of their country, the age of the world, all exert their separate influences— and time is generally necessary before this mixture of separate elements, if I may use the term, works clear. There is often a time of unsettlement and internal commotion—which results either in the destruction of the infant body, (answering in our physical history the sharp maladies of children) or in its consolidation. The history of Oratories proves this—The instance that rests most clearly on my mind is that of the Oratory of Camerino, which was founded by a holy man, whose process was commenced in the Sacred ῾Congregation after his death, named Matteucci. He was blind and only in minor orders, and entered into communication with the Roman Oratory, two years before his commencement, which was in 1591—Fr Ancina, a most holy man, a penitent of St Philip and a member of his Oratory, yet after all not quite an Oratorian in spirit, as his life shows, (and who on St Philip's death, elicited the grave remonstrances of Baronius and Tarugi for his wish to become a Capuchin)[4] assisted Matteucci at Camerino. Then came a priest named Grandi, who apparently followed in the same line with Ancina, and on him what I have to say turns. It was the introduction of a new, and as it turned out, impossible element. The infant Community, however, seemed to grow and thrive—its members mounted up to 14, though as yet they were very poor. Next we hear of their beginning to fast rigorously three times in the week. The Roman Oratory interfered and set them right, telling them that they must observe no fasts but such as are of precept, for that experience showed that it was incompatible with the Oratorian duties.

[4]This is inaccurate. Ancina wished to be a Carthusian, not a Capuchin. Cf. Trevor, *Apostle of Rome* (1966), p. 211.

Grandi ⟨a man apparently of decided character⟩ got the management of the congregation into his hands. Matteucci, being blind and only in minor orders, though still Rector, naturally gave up to him the care of priests and novices—and at last the place of superior. Their prospects still continue to advance: they have one, two, and at length a third Church and a house within the walls of Camerino. A papal bull establishes them—After eleven years Mateucci becomes superior again, and they relinquish two of their Churches as contrary to their Rule. This led to Grandi's leaving them, after a residence among them for 20 years. Of course in such accounts as we have left us of the Italian Oratories, scandals are hushed up—so it is difficult to speak positively—but it would seem, from what is told us that, till Grandi's leaving the House of Camerino there were two spirits struggling in it, one far more impetuous and energetic (for good or bad) than the other—each might be good, ⟨even for an Oratory⟩ but they could not both be in one body—nor was there peace established in it, till one of the two was eliminated.

And now secondly if this homogeneity of the constituent members of a body be always necessary, how much more in a body such as ours! and that for two reasons—

First because there are no vows, as I have already said. Wherever there are vows, there is the means of the peremptory setting down and crushing of any spirit contrary to that which actuates the governing body. Private judgment is unknown. But there is no such means with us to hinder internal dissention. Men of vigorous energetic minds spontaneously develop into opinion and action, and into opinion and action marked by their own personal characteristics. Among Regulars, I say, if this spontaneous vigour is not in accordance with the spirit of the body, it is summarily and immediately put down by throwing the parties who show it upon the duty of that implicit obedience which they have vowed. But supposing an earnest conscientious able man, say like Grandi, to be in a community without any motive so strong as the duty of vowed obedience to restrain his agitating in behalf of certain views which are contrary to those of the body and which seem to him better, what is to hinder his introducing great confusion into it? The truth is, if his views are much opposed to the body he has joined, he should never have joined it—If they are such, that he cannot yield to santa comunità, if they do not so nearly approximate to those of the rest, that, without sacrifice of conscience, he can do as they do, and influence them only in those indirect loving ways in which they are to influence him, and in which he can consent that they *should* influence him, his place is not there. Unless, from previous deliberation, he has that faith, that loyal trust in the body, that love of its members, that he is willing to throw in his lot with them, and to go along with them leaving the future to itself, he has not exercise[d] proper precaution and prudence.

The absence of vows then, the unarmed weaponless state [of] an Oratorian body, involves the necessity of our *all* being one in spirit. It is a call on every one of us, not as simply the better way, but as a matter of life and death to our body, to cherish a personal affection for its [sic] other, and to show each other all kind, attentive, and humble service; and in this our great duty the difference between Superior and subjects, young and old, simply vanishes—for we live then only if we submit ourselves to each other, think others better than ourselves and are ever willing to take the lowest place, forgetting self.

———

NEWMAN'S ORATORY PAPERS No. 32
7 JUNE 1858

INTRODUCTORY NOTE

When Newman had adapted the Oratorian Rule to English conditions, he had omitted one passage on reserve in dealing with boys, which he now (1858) felt obliged to restore. At this time, since vocations to the lay brothers were not successful, the domestic work was being more and more confided to men servants. Hence the present note. As alterations in the church were in progress (see Decree Book, under the dates April 21 and June 2, 1858), many strangers were in about the house and

26

Church, and any indiscretion on the part of one of the community, even when quite innocent, might easily be misinterpreted by unfriendly observers. The first version of this Address was torn up by Newman, and the bits were collected from the fender by a servant. See *Trevor*, II pp. 182–3. Newman describes this in a letter of 8 June 1858 to St John. See *L.D.* XVIII under this date, p. 370.

CHAPTER ADDRESS 7 JUNE 1858[1]

I am sorry, my dear Fathers, to have to say, that we must just now consult for the weakness or bad feeling of people, in a way which it never occurred to me would be necessary.

It has been reported to me that scandal has been taken at a very simple and natural action of [sic] the part of one of the Fathers; so simple and natural, as to show that the scandal arises from a previous suspicion or misgiving about us in the mind of the parties scandalized. And, on asking the question, I am told that, in matter of fact, there was such a previous feeling.

I fear I must say that we have a number of sharp, not to say unfriendly, eyes upon us; and we have not now the protection of lay brothers, who would take our actions on faith, if in any respect they did not understand them.

At present, it seems as if there were nothing, however private, but might be known abroad.

I fear you will be surprised, or even think it a scruple, when I express a wish you would observe the following rules.

1. Never to put your arm round a boy's neck, or to show any other familiarity towards boys.

2. To observe the rule of the Roman Oratory, which I got leave, not wisely, as I now see, to omit from our body of Rules. I say, "not wisely", because people so weakly take offence at innocent practices. The rule is this: "Nec sinat quis pueros ingredi cubiculum suum, nisi ducantur ab aliis, qui testes

[1]*B. Or. Ar.* D. 4. 9.

intersint; reliquos parcè admittant, sed vocati deorsum ad illos se conferant."[2]

I take this opportunity, my dear Fathers, of reminding you that at this moment we need especial caution; first because we are likely to be in some disorder and confusion in the weeks now to follow, next because we shall have strangers about us, Protestant as well as Catholic.

There is something solemn in this suspension of our work. I cannot forget the trial[3], which attended the suspension of it when we came up here.

May St Philip be merciful to us, and may we have grace to invoke his aid—for we need it.

                                               J H N

June 7. 1858

NEWMAN'S ORATORY PAPERS No. 33
1857-8

INTRODUCTORY NOTE

From the beginning of his Oratorian career, Newman had singled out the confessional as one of the characteristic works of the Oratory (see above, Oratory Papers, 17 January 1848), and one of his reproaches against Father Dalgairns had been his complaints of "the uninterestingness of routine confessions in the Church" (Oratory Papers, above, 31 August 1856).

Now in 1857-8, he had to consider whether, in his own case, he should devote the time and energy necessary for such routine confessions. The following Memorandum weighs the pros and cons. He finally decided to resume his duties as regular confessor (which had lapsed owing to his work in Ireland). See *Trevor* II, pp. 177, 178, where the touching phrase has been

[2]i.e. Let no one allow boys to enter his bedroom, unless they are conducted there by other persons, who remain as witnesses; let them admit other persons only sparingly, rather, when called, let them see them downstairs.

[3]See above, p. 286.

preserved: "Old Mrs Brennan has found me out." See also pp. 121–2 'Newman and the Care of Souls.'

In our image of Newman the Priest, we must not forget to fill in these unrecorded long hours spent in his "box" in the Church. At times he was the only priest so occupied in the Oratory, when numbers were low, and the others were absent. For a busy day in the Confessional see v.g. *L.D.* XVIII, p. 361.

[MEMORANDUM]¹

1857–8 whether I should go again into the Confessional, which I had left since 1852–3.

Affirmative

1. because is according to the idea of a Father of the Oratory and I should be in my place.

2 because there is a question whether on my deathbed I shall not look back on my last years with more satisfaction, if I have than if I have not.

3 because it would be an assistance and relief to the other Fathers.

4. because, whatever difficulties I might have in it, the special grace of ordination would go with it and overcome them

5. because the very repugnance I feel to it may be a reason for it.

Negative

1. because I should have to give considerable time to get up sufficient knowledge

2 because I have a repugnance to it which operates in making the study more difficult.

3 because my memory is so untrustworthy, that to keep up the knowledge, I must ever be in the practice, and can't take it up now and then, or in [?] emergencies when the Congregation wants it.

4. because the many mistakes I am conscious of having made in the former time, gives me a want of confidence in myself almost amounting for a disqualification for the office.

5 because, if I took up this, I must abandon other pursuits

---

¹*B. Or. Ar.* Oratory Letters, Jan–June 1857; *init.* [See *L.D.* XVIII, p. 259.]

and labours for which I am more adapted; e.g. I am unlikely
ever to write any thing more.

6. because the time the learning and practice would take is
hardly consistent with my existing engagements—e.g. the
University—and much more the translation of Scripture.

————

NEWMAN'S ORATORY PAPERS No. 34
20 DECEMBER 1858

INTRODUCTORY NOTE

Newman returned for good to the Birmingham Oratory
following his resignation of the Rectorship of the Catholic
University. The idea of opening a school for boys, which had
recurred from time to time almost since the beginning of the
English Oratory, now began to take definite shape.[1] The delays
and disappointments in the preparatory stages of this undertaking are described in *Trevor*, II, pp. 178–80, and pp. 185–6.
The present address reflects Newman's anxiety in face of these
difficulties and his fears lest the proposed Oratory school prove
a failure. In the event, the school 'while remaining small, proved
a real success, and its example and competition raised the
standard of the other Catholic schools.'[2]

CHAPTER ADDRESS[3]

Dec 20. 1858

I wish to ask you to hold a Novena to St Philip for an intention which before now has employed us in a very special way,
I mean for divine light on the subject of our proposed boys'

[1]See below, Appendix 6, the Decree Book of the Birmingham Oratory, the
entry under the date 21 April 1858.

[2]C. S. Dessain, *John Henry Newman*, Nelson, London, 1966, p. 110.

[3]*B. Or. Ar.* Oratory Letters Sept–Dec 1858. [See *L.D.* XVIII, p. 316.]

school. And I beg two things first, what perhaps is scarcely necessary to say, except that I feel it necessary for me, that you would consider the formal prayers which we use only the token and memento that we are holding a novena, and not really the novena itself, which is rather a space of nine days during which the intention which is the reason is especially before our minds. And my second request is that the intention should be conceived as nearly as possible in these words, so that they may form the burden of our supplications 'O St Philip, give us no new mortification—but either prevent the school, or prosper it.'

And now I must explain to you what I mean by mortification, and how I exemplify it in our own case. A common sense of the word is that of humiliation, that is, of bringing shame on a person from and in the presence of others. Thus St Philip, when Baronius gave himself to him, 'set to work training him in a disregard and contempt of himself and men's opinion of him; and for this purpose he used to send him to the public house with a huge bottle to ask for half a pint of wine with, and the like.' Such instances, as you know abound, and are contemplated in his great maxim that is duty of his children 'spernere se sperni.' I never wish to pray to St Philip to save us from such mortifications either from himself or from others, or, to use our own word, snubs. He had plenty of them himself —he took care to bring such mortifications on him. I put only one limit to my free acceptance of such wholesome penances— and that is this that, as in the case of bodily penances, we must have a care of life and strength, so I wish these snubs, and humiliations, and taunts, and scorn, and slander on the part of the world, only not to go so far as to hurt us as an Oratory. Should the effect of them be such, that the continual dripping of water, to [sic] injure us with the Holy See, of course we must bear it—but I should pray for their removal, or rather alleviation, so far as to prevent any serious harm coming on us thereupon from the august source and centre of ecclesiastical power.

By mortification then I do not mean humiliation, but I mean disappointment—I mean the giving time, thought, anxiety, labour, prayer to an object, and failing it in [sic]. I mean such trials, as tend grievously to discourage, or rather to perplex, under the feeling that we really did not know how to find out what St Philip wished, because we had tried our best, and had failed to do so. I do not say we have ever so failed, because I never say, I cannot say, that we have done our best at any time. I am far too conscious how very much more prayer and careful deliberation ought to have preceded all that we have done not to feel that when we *have* been prospered, it has been simply beyond our deserts, and when we have failed, we have been served right. Still St Philip is too tender a father to exact all that might be exacted—and I do not think it wrong, considering we pray daily not be led into temptation, to be saved what is above our strength in that sort of trial which the Prophet describes when he says, 'Et ego dixi, In vacuum laboravi, sine causa, et vanè fortitudinem meam consumpsi; ergo judicium meum cum Domino, et opus meum cum Deo meo.'[4]

I [am] sure we cannot complain of the want of fatherly care in St Philip in the main matters. See how wonderfully we have been brought together, knit into one, carried on, enriched, and established. See in how many specific plans we have had success. I consider the establishment of the mission in Alcester Street a great success. We went to it as a sort of desert as far as Catholics were concerned—in three years we formed a flourishing mission —and what was wanting to complete it, the Bishop took it off our hands. Else it would have dropped—our work would have been undone—we should have left no memorial there of our labours. But we were prospered here in a very difficult matter, considering the want of Priests in the Diocese. And I don't think we are thankful enough for it—and, if ever by adverse circumstances the mission were thrown back upon us, as the alternative of its extinction, I should say that it was a punishment for our want of acknowledging the mercy shown to us. In like manner I consider that our establishment at the work house is a great success—and I could mention other similar ones.

But now lately we have certainly had several great mortifications, at least as I feel them, which have given me a good deal of anxiety. One has been the remarkable blighting of the hopes of a hospital, when we had just begun it. In the first week, after a long time of preparation for the start, the two good ladies

who began it were taken off, and it was suddenly extinguished.
The waves went over it. Now such a startling occurrence must
have a divine meaning, yet it was difficult to read it—what did
St Philip mean by it? Then again our efforts to found a Reform-
atory have broken under us, as if something were at work
against us; and the question again is, What does St Philip mean
by it. And then again as to myself, I personally considered Mr
Crawley's conduct to us, to me, a considerable discouragement
—not for its own sake, not as if I had any special desire that he
should be with us, but on the contrary, because it took place
in spite of a great wish to be prudent and to know God's will,
and yet it would seem as if St Philip had not taught us on this
point God's will. As many of you know he came to me to my
surprise something like a year and a half before his actual
coming as a novice. I did not encourage him—some of you said
that I did not encourage him enough—indeed, I may say, he
said so, for he himself reported the saying. I promised to say
mass for him weekly, and did so for a considerable time; again
and again he wrote stating his extreme desire to get rid of his
existing engagements in the north. When above a year was
passed, he changed and said he thought of joining other body
—and I gave up the thought of his coming—then suddenly
about this time year he went into retreat with the Jesuits, and
wrote to me that he had in retreat made up his mind to offer
himself, and without giving me time to answer his letter he
presented himself for admission. We gave him more than the
usual month's probation—I think six weeks—and admitted
him—before those weeks were out, in the midst of our great
trouble about our two fathers who were so ill, he began to speak
to his director about going and he went before Easter came. I say
one member more or less in the Congregation is not the point—
nor had we known him long enough to have any personal
feelings of attachment to him—but I myself felt it as if St Philip
was discouraging me, and I could not tell why.

Then at the same time he gave us a very great encouragement, let us never forget it, in the recovery of Father Henry,
when it seemed hopeless—a far greater encouragement than
the other was a mortification—not to say that he evidently
has heard us already to a great extent as regards Stanislas.

Still now that we are beginning a great external work, or at least when I am beginning it with one of the Fathers, I feel somewhat sad and discouraged, not because St Philip's will is this way or that—but because I find it so difficult to be sure that I know his will and wish. For my own personal comfort I would much rather give up the plan altogether—I very much want to be at peace—but there comes the question, is that St Philip's wish too. We have certainly very great difficulties in our way; besides we have difficulties from those who have not especial connexion with us. But our great difficulty lies in a quarter where we might have expected neutrality, if not sympathy for in our case are fulfilled in their degree our Lord's words, 'Et inimici hominis, domestici ejus.'[5]

I should like the Novena to begin today, so that it will end on St Thomas of Canterbury. The prayers and Pater Noster, Ave, and Gloria—and not said by us together.

NEWMAN'S ORATORY PAPERS No 35.

1 FEBRUARY 1878

INTRODUCTORY NOTE

On this (last extant) Chapter Address, see above, p. 146. On the background to the Address see *Trevor* II, p. 547.

The two deaths referred to are those of Ambrose St John (1815–75) and Edward Caswall (1814–78). See the biographical notices in *L.D.* XI, p. 355 and *L.D.* XII, p. 429, respectively.

[5] *Matt.* 10:36.

CHAPTER ADDRESS[1]

Febr 1 1878
First Vespers of
the Purification.

It is many years since I availed myself of this opportunity of speaking to you, my dear Fathers, on matters connected with the Oratory. If I do so now, it is because a retrospect of the last three years, with what has happened in them, seems to call for it, suggesting to us, as it must do; that we have now at length entered for the first time, into what may be called the normal state of the Congregation, a state not to be contemplated without seriousness.

A congregation like this, in the intention of the Church, and of those who set it up, is in its idea everlasting, one and the same through all time, until the end of all things comes. Its members change, but it remains; to be ever one and the same, to be ever changing, both together, one as much as the other, is its normal state. But at first it has not experience of the latter of these two conditions of its life. While it is of recent formation, it remains identical in its constituent parts, as well as in its whole. It is commonly founded by persons, some in the prime, some in the springtide, of their lives; they live on; of them it consists. A time passes before they are made to understand that, of necessity, it is by change, that it perpetuates its identity; that succession is the principle and the law of its being; and that, when once it has experience of that second element of its identity, it can never be loose of it again. This is that state of our Congregation, my dear Fathers, on which we have now entered; henceforth change is an element of our existence.

Thirty years have now passed of our recognized position as a Congregation in the Catholic Church. On the first Vespers of the Purification in 1848 I set up the first Congregation of the Oratory in England according to the Brief I had obtained from the Holy See empowering me to set up Oratorian Houses there. It was at the Old College at Marivale [sic], which Bishop Walsh had given to us two years before, and which the Papal

[1] *B. Or. Ar.* D. 4. 9

Brief named, as constituting with our prospective house and church in Birmingham by special privilege one Oratory. During the long 27 years which followed we have had here only one loss by death. There was indeed Fr Cooke's death in 1850, but one can hardly call his death properly one of our losses. He was a religious, well educated Priest, as his books in our Library show; a theologian and a good Ritualist, but a stranger to us, and a friend of Dr Wiseman's, he was in a consumption and came to die in the Oratory. He was with us 14 months from first to last. We shortened his noviceship, and he died a Triennial. He was buried at St Wilfrid's near Alton Towers, then our property, which has long passed out of our hands.

I can hardly then put down Fr Cooke's death as a bereavement. The loss I speak of in our first years is of course that of Fr Joseph Gordon. It was great and permanent; and felt, not only in itself, but in its direct consequences, which it is not to my purpose to speak of here. Just about that time this house was building, and it was not the only trial which, according to God's good will, went with it. I grant Father Joseph's death was a blow; we have had many trials since, but they have served to served [sic] to strengthen us; this death was to human eyes a real loss. But I am mentioning it, with great thankfulness, as an instance of the saying "Exceptio probat regulam." We have had an extraordinarily long exemption, in this Congregation, from the common destiny of man. We provided a Church yard 24 years ago, but till lately it has almost remained unoccupied. We have had then abundant cause of thankfulness to Almighty God and to St Philip.

This thought is especially suggested to us by the contrast presented in the London Oratory. The selection of the Fathers of that Oratory was by all the members of what was then one House left to me; and out of our existing body, I determined, as a religious duty to St Philip and the Holy See, for so important a mission to make the new Oratory as effective, strong, and permanent in provision as I could. I gave it nine members, some the youngest and some [the] most brilliant of our body; knowing how much depended on the union of hearts and mind [sic], I gave it those who were most likely to rally round the Father who went as my representative and their Rector. Nay

I let them change some of those I had named for some whom
I had not named, with, I fear, almost an injustice to the Mother
Oratory, to which I belonged myself. I left for Birmingham
the older, and, those who, as being older, had less of unitive
capability than those whom I sent to London; and my choice
for the London Oratory has been prospered as far as this, that,
thus formed, it has been abundantly able to recruit itself and
supply its loss.

But it is its losses that has led me to speak of it. Compared
with it, what a respite has been given to us! We in 30 years
have lost three Fathers, while they have lost six; and out of
that six, five are their original Fathers, whom I chose for them.
And, three of these being their most prominent, best, and of
these two in the first half of the 30 years; whereas, though we
have lost three of our most prominent in 30 years two out of
our three losses have been at the end of the second half. So
much for the past, for which, I say, we must be deeply thankful; but, I say also, we must [not] shut our eyes to the truth
that the three decades which have now run out are no sample
of the decades which are to follow, and that among the sacred
solemnities which will from time to time have a call upon us,
that sad rite has a normal place on which we have been lately
engaged.

We cannot speculate on the future; nothing is more deceptive
than the scientific calculation of average lives; one man dies
before his time, another after it. We shall have one Father
outliving another against all rule. But, supposing tables are
interrogated for an illustration of the solemn prospect as it
stands for each us [sic] at our several ages just now, the answer
for this date, though it alters year by year, would be, that, out
of us twelve, who now are here, *one* will go during the decade
ending 1890, *four* in [sic] the decade ending 1900, *five* in the
decade, ending with 1910, and *two* in the decade ending
1920 (Unless we live beyond our present average, which of
course is continually varying. none of us will see 1920.) But
I have pursued this subject farther than I had intended—the
moral I wish to draw from it is this:—

Succession, I have said, is the law of our being. Hence we
cannot really lament when those who have worked hard for

God, and borne the heat of the day, are taken to their rest. We may be sure that St Philip will provide successors to them, that "instead of our fathers we shall have children", as he has done lately, according to our need. So far we have nothing to be anxious about, but there is one thing which ought to make us anxious, because, whatever St Philip may do for us, the issue depends upon our own co-operation with him, not on him solely. Succession implies change, and it is for us to take care, each of us in his own place, both Fathers and Novices, that that inevitable change does not become so great as virtually to annul that succession which involves it.

That is no real succession which is not a continuation of what was before it; that is no identity, of which the elements are heterogeneous and discordant. It is for this reason that I have never wished, I have never liked, a large Oratory. Twelve working Priests has been the limit of my ambition. One cannot love many at one time; one cannot really have many friends. An Oratory is a family and a home; a domestic circle, as the words imply, is bounded and rounded. A family can be counted; there only, in the natural order are to be found the "noti vultus" of which our Rule speaks. A large body can hardly help breaking from its own weight. The continuity of the succession is snapped, not strengthened by its numerousness. We become unable to carry out the duties of the Oratorian vocation. We ought, for instance, as far as possible, to have one sentiment, one interest; we have, as far as possible, to suppress all serious conflict of opinion; we should be slow to introduce our own notions; we ought to be sensitive of the feelings of others; we should be very jealous of, what is so difficult to avoid in a large body, the spirit and existence of party. We should in all Congregational matters strive to move as one mind; avoid, if possible, going by majorities; be tender of the Fathers who form a minority, while on the other hand single Fathers should not inconsiderately take advantage of the tenderness exercised towards them. Only by a tradition such as this, only by a happy gift of healing in those lacerations of heart which the law of bereavements necessarily involves, only by a moral constitution in its members thus healthy and elastic, that our Oratory will thrive.

Thus only, my dear Novices, I repeat it, can a body like ours, which is without vows, with the right of personal property, and with fixity of place be maintained in that unity, identity, and integrity which is essential to it. Don't suppose while I address you, that I fancy that your own sense of what is delicate, gentle and kind does not teach you this without any one's preaching it to you. But I wish you to enforce it as an essential Oratorian tradition, one of prime necessity to our wellbeing. I am not content that you should have good instincts and nothing more. I wish you to go by what is reasonable; nay and much more, I wish you to go by authority, by tradition— tradition is the voice of authority—I wish you to go, not in what I have mentioned only, but in all things by the traditions of the House.

The tradition of our authorities is the continuity and strength of our body. We are all naturally prone to question and criticise; criticism is the compensation which persons under obedience make to themselves for the necessity of obeying. Thus it was when I was young, thus in my own case; and I don't think human nature has changed in the course of fifty years. You will think of this, my dear children, some time hence, when you have to inculcate the lesson on younger men.

And now God bless you. May St Philip be with us all, authorities and subjects, may he be in some sense a personal life, a principle of continuity and of identity to our Congregation. As for me, if I meet you again at our next elections, I shall then be eighty years old.

NEWMAN'S ORATORY PAPERS No. 36
10 MAY 1878

INTRODUCTORY NOTE

On Newman's choice of vocation see above, Chapter 5: 'Newman in Quest of a Priestly Vocation (1845–47)', and on his examination of the Jesuits in particular (the point covered by this paper of 10 May 1878) see pp. 79–81 ib. See also Oratory Papers, above, Chapter Address 9 February 1848, which is a long-drawn out contrast between the Jesuit and Oratorian ethos.

I have, unfortunately, not been able to trace the Address of 14 February 1848 here alluded to, on the occasion of his admitting the 'Wilfridians' (i.e. Faber and his group) to the Oratory.

[MEMORANDUM][1]

(The following is far too laboured. Qui s'excuse, s'accuse)

May 10 1878. Some time back an Article in the Quarterly Review said that I had once offered myself to the Jesuits and been refused admission. I wrote to deny it with great surprise, and the statement was withdawn. Writing to (I think) the Echo I said that the report must have arisen out of the circumstance that the College of Propaganda at which I was for 6 or 7 months, was at that time under the supervision of Jesuits, and that for those Fathers I had felt much respect and admiration. And indeed how was there time for application and rejection, seeing that I came to Rome in October 1846, went to Propaganda not till November, and on January the 18th following began prayers to determine whether or not I had a vocation to the Oratory? a question which I decided in the affirmative (under advice of my Jesuit confessor) by the beginning of February.

However, I find on turning over the leaves of the Letters to me of my friends in England in this January, that they imply that I had said something in mine to them in favour of the Jesuits, which it is necessary here to explain. When I have distinctly read their letters, doubtless I shall be able to quote further passages from them in illustration, but even without this advantage I have no difficulty in explaining myself here.

The truth is that (as was natural) up to this date (January 1847), from the time of my reception I have [sic] been engaged

[1] *B. Or. Ar.* A. 32. 6.

all along in determining my vocation. First of all, as I have intimated in my Apologia, was the question whether I was to go off to some lay profession or employment—then whether I should determine to enter the ecclesiastical state afresh. So far I had settled before I left England, since I had received minor orders and acquiesced in Dr Wiseman's sending me to Propaganda. I had gone somewhat farther in England, for I had inquired about the *Lazarists,* and in passing through Paris, I had made it a point to go to the Church of St Vincent of Paul, from the interest I felt for his people, whose establishment near Dublin I had heard of from Dr Whitty. Also Dr Wiseman had already spoken to me about *St Philip Neri,* whose Congregation he earnestly recommended to me, as desirous of its introduction into England, since he considered it specially suited to the state of the country. Also of course I had a profound reverence for the Jesuits, though I had seen no more of them than a short visit to Stonyhurst, uninvited, when I was passing round with Ambrose St John, from Durham and York to Manchester, Bath &c immediately on my conversion.

When I got to Rome, my first (and very crude) thought was to form and devote myself to the establishment of a theological College in England of secular priests. Then I said "Shall I be a Jesuit?" and I mentioned the idea to my friends out of Rome as to Stanton, Dalgairns, A. Christie etc., and then, after other inquiries and speculations, I said (in words which I have elsewhere used, perhaps in my address to the Wilfridians on admitting them into the Oratory on Febr. 14. 1848) "Dear me! I have forgotten St Philip," and then at once I began acquaintance with him, finding out his Church as the first step. ⟨I should add I was choosing *for my friends,* if possible, as well as for myself, and had to consult them with this purpose.⟩

In the sense then that I could not say for certain that I should *not* be a Jesuit, I certainly approximated to them about Christmas 1846-7, but in the same sense I approximated to the Vincentians or Lazarists, to the Dominicans, to the Rosminians, and to others.

I have fallen upon a passage in a letter of Dalgairns, (evidently, though undated of January 1847 from Langres) (I have found the date "In festo S. Nominis Jesu", which that year fell on January 17) which confirms and illustrates what I have been saying. I subjoin extracts from it "I will first talk about myself. Since my ordination, I have felt an increasing desire of a missionary line . . . There is one field open in England . . . preaching for educated people . . . among lawyers &c . . . This, I believe, is really the origin of my liking for the Dominicans . . . Your arguments do not touch the point which took my fancy in the French Dominicans . . . What does influence me in what you say is that Lacordaire is a new start for himself. Again, I agree with what you say about the Jesuits. I must say that, much as I venerate them, I do not feel drawn towards them . . . As for you, I do think that it would weaken your influence in England, if you were a Jesuit."[2]

Again, on January 31, he says, "Do you know any thing of the Theatines? Would they suit us? The thought was suggested to me by &c. . ."

And Stanton, under the same date, says, "I shall be anxious to know what you think of the Oratorians. Lately I have begun to think more of them than I used to do . . . You now mention *Redemptorists* . . . Do you hear much of them in Rome?"

These extracts bear me out in affirming that this interval, my first months at Rome, was devoted to a survey of the various religious bodies, there to be found, with reference not to my own vocation solely, but for one common vocation, if possible for me and the friends I had left behind me, ⟨and among, and only as among, these bodies, of the Jesuits⟩.

As soon as we decided on the Oratory, A. Christie, one of my chief correspondents at once declared for the Jesuits ⟨left Maryvale and us,⟩ and joined them in England. Thus I account for the impression existing with some Jesuits, that I had once offered myself to their body. Christie, on going to them, knowing I had written home in their praise, and had not simply put aside the thought of joining them, would be sure to say, on going to them, "I should not wonder, if you had Newman;" which would be quite a sufficient basis for the report that I had proposed and been declined.   J H N

---

[2] Cf. *L.D.*, XI, p. 306.

27

APPENDICES

Appendices

Appendix No. 1

THE SANTA CROCE PAPERS
AUGUST/SEPTEMBER 1847

INTRODUCTORY NOTE

In a letter of 19 September 1850 Newman himself speaks of
the 'Santa Croce Paper' (in the singular, not in the plural):
   'I will send you the Santa Croce Paper, but it is nothing
   out of the way—it is at Birmingham[1].'
The present editor in the course of research in the Birmingham Oratory Archives for Oratorian materials connected with
Newman, had already unearthed this Paper, together with its
accompanying notes, and had named the bundle, the 'Santa
Croce Papers', before he was aware of any reference of Newman's to these documents.

On the importance of these Papers for our understanding of
Newman's vocation, see above pp. 90–3 and 135–8.

There are four Papers in all, of which I have named the
first 'Final Draft', the second 'Second Paper', while Newman
himself had headed the third and fourth respectively 'Paper n'
and 'Paper O'.

In the present edition, the first paper—the 'Final Draft'—is
reproduced in full, followed by a summary of the 'Second
Paper', 'Paper n' and 'Paper O' (made by the editor from
the MSS).

[1]*L.D.*, XIV, p. 73 and cf. ib. Note 3.

FINAL DRAFT[1]

INTRODUCTORY NOTE

This represents Newman's analysis of Oratorian authorities made during his novitiate at Santa Croce in Rome (1847), and is an attempt to define the nature of the Oratory of St Philip Neri as a Congregation compared with a "religion", i.e. a religious order. Having established that it is not a "religion" in the canonical sense, but nevertheless resembles one, he then proceeds to show that the specific characteristic of the Oratory considered as a body consists in community life voluntarily undertaken without vows. He then examines three great ascetical implications of such a life: Mortification of self, Obedience and Perseverance.

He makes no reference here to contemporary observance in the Roman or Naples Oratories; he is concerned with Oratorian origins and precedents. In spite of the deprecatory note in the right-hand corner of page 1:

> "This has no authority, beyond what comes of its having been drawn up by the Father and assented to by the rest at Santa Croce in August or September 1847. JHN. Jan 15/52"

we must look on it as a most important step in Newman's Oratorian vocation. It is not too much to say that he never wavered from the view of the Oratory which he has crystallized here.

The full titles of the authorities quoted are given above, under Abbreviations, p.XVIII. They are mainly three: "Marciano" (or "Annals") with 30 quotations, the "Pregi" with 23, then 7 from the Rule (of the Roman Oratory), and 2 from "Bacci". On these sources see above p. 91.

In the Annotations which follow, the original Italian and Latin texts have been given in English, either from an existing English translation where available, or else in a translation made directly from the originals.

[1] *B. Or. Ar.* B. 9. 3.

FINAL DRAFT

(This has no authority, beyond what comes of its having been drawn up by the Father and assented to by the rest at Santa Croce in August or September 1847.
JHN. Jan 15/52)

[§ 1.] Whether the Congregation of the Oratory can be called a religion, and what its relation is to religion.

Simply speaking of course the Congregation of the Oratory is not a religion—for St Philip distinctly contrasted it with religions. He says 'if you want a religion, go elsewhere. There are plenty already. I have no mission to found one.'

In saying this, he seems principally and especially to have meant that his Congregation had no *vows*—as is plain from the passage in Bacci i.19[1] dicendo, che, se qualcheduno bramoso da più alto stato, desiderava far *voti*, non mancanavano diverse religioni, . . . *ma* che egli nella sua Congregazione voleva persone che . . . *senza legame* sacrissero a Dio, non volendo introdurre nuova *religione,* perchè intendeva che la carità fosse vincolo e legame.

⟨vid the strong Decree against vows. After his death there was an attempt to introduce vows, but the Pope would not grant it. ⟨Annal t 2 p. 55⟩[2]⟩

How, moreover, *love* is contrasted to *vows*.

Presently we read, diceva, che cercassero tutti d'imitare i religiosi nella *perfezione*, sebbene non l'imitavano nel fare i voti.[3] Since then religion is reckoned in its very idea as a more

---

[1] Bacci (Eng.). Vol. 1, p. 114: "for he said that if any one was desirous of a more perfect state, and wished to take *vows*, there were plenty of religious orders . . . *but* that he wished his Congregation to be composed of persons who would serve God freely and *without bond* . . . He protested that he had never had any idea of introducing a new order . . . mutual charity . . . was to be the sole bond of his disciples."

[2] *Annals,* Tome 1, Lib. 1, Cap. XV, p. 55.

[3] Bacci (Eng.), Vol. 1, p. 115.

perfect way than a secular life, St Philip here seems to enjoin that more perfect way all but the vows; or to say that his institution is not a religion *because* it has not vows.

The same contrast is found in a letter which he writes to Naples to Father Giovanni Battista through Bordini the Secretary, Che nelle religione, formate e legate con voti, vi si trovano ben spesso tanti intoppi, . . . che sarà, dove non sono voti, ma con libera voluntà siano insieme legati gli uomini? ⟨Annal t. 2 p. 13.⟩[4]

But it differs from a religion in another and further respect viz because externally its members are to look like secular priests—esser la mente sua, che coloro che entravano in essa, dovessero mantenersi in istato di Preti e chierice secolari, ai quali voleva che fossero in tutte le cosi conformi quanto all' esterno.[5]

This external difference from a religious order shows itself in various ways.

First there is to be no poverty, and no appearance of it—habeant, possideant, were St Philip's words, when one of his subjects wished to decree poverty.

They are to have their own rooms, and to make themselves comfortable in them. A remarkable stress is laid upon their rooms as their *nido*, which would not apply to a monastic house, and still less to an order like the Jesuits or Dominicans. When Baronius got leave at the end of his life to return to the Vallicella, this verse was read by chance in the Refectory, Dicebam in nidulo meo moriar,[6] which gave him the occasion of a most touching speech. Haec requies mea, cried F. Manari of Reggio and F. Grassi of Fermo. And St Philip himself was loth to leave S. Girolamo, where he had lived 30 years, for the Vallicella.

There were to be no fastings over and above what the Church prescribed, nor other austerities (except the discipline). When Grandi, a saintly man, had joined the Oratory of Camerino and introduced fastings three day in the week, Velli, the

---

[4]*Annals*, Tome 2, Lib. 1, Cap. III, p. 13: This text is available as translated by Newman, above, p. 168.

[5]Bacci (Eng.), Vol. 1, p. 114.

[6]Vulgate text of *Job* 29:18 ("I used to say, I shall die in my nest.")

Superior at Rome, interfered; and told the Congregation that though they might abstain, they were not allowed to keep any fasts but such as were of precept, as harm had come of it. When the Brescian Monastery della Pace wished to become Oratorian, some of the Fathers were very unwilling to give up their fasts; but the Roman House persuaded them abbraciare con allegrezza le costituzioni senza diminuire nè alterare cose alcune. St Philip contrasted with these austerities what he wishes to be the peculiarities of his Congregation, according to F. Manni. Praecipue hoc instituto voluit consulere viris Congregationis suae, ut per quotidianum auditum verborum Dei, haberent *quod jejuniis,* vigiliis, silentiis [sic] psalmodiis contraponerent, divinum enim verbum attente auditum instar omnium exercitiorum est. ⟨Ann, t 1 p. 27⟩[7] It is remarkable how strongly this is insisted on at various times in the history of the Oratory.

Another external difference between his Congregation and Religious was the absence of the appearance of government. At first there were no Rules or Constitutions at all. This seems to be the meaning of Cardinal Carraciolo of Naples that St Philip ruled his subjects with a filo di seta.[8]

The Superior was to have no show of power. St Philip only on one occasion used the words "I command". He said that the best means of having power was to command seldom. ⟨Annal t 1 p. 563.⟩[9] It comes under this head to observe that in the Oratory there is no connexion of house with house, i.e. such government as exists in a religious order. In short the whole action of the community was to be, as it were, spontaneous and natural, as if things went on of themselves.

From all this I conclude that St Philip's wish and aim was, that his Congregation should be in one sense a religion, i.e. *taking away* externals, vow, rule, poverty, bodily mortifications and the like;—that is, it was to have the internal perfection of a religion, whatever that may be said to consist in.

[7] This Latin phrase of Manni's ("He wished especially to offer to the men of his Congregation the daily hearing of the Word of God as something to be preferred to fasting, vigils, silence and psalmody, for the devout hearing of the Word of God is as good as all exercises"), is contained in the Italian passage of the Annals referred to above. Cf. pp. 331–2.

[8] *Pregi* (Eng.), p. 144 "with a thread of silk."

[9] *Annals,* Tome 1, Lib. VI Cap. II, p. 563.

It is remarkable that on one occasion St Philip seems to call it "a religion *like the Theatines;*" for, when the Theatines objected at Naples to lend the Oratory a preacher on the plea that they did not preach in other Churches, be answered, che non dove[v]ano avere scrupolo dio ciò fare, poichè non sarebbe andato in casa di secolari, ma in *casa religiosa,* e come sua propria, essendo le Chiese dell' Oratorio come loro proprie. ⟨Annal. t 2 p. 16.⟩[10]

The foregoing view of the nature of the Congregation of the Oratory, deduced from the words of St Philip, is confirmed by other authorities.

For instance Marciano, the author of the Annals, quotes the words of Tarugi,—a memorial given in to the Pope in behalf of the House of Naples, which speaks of La Casa di Napoli di chierici, seben secolari, *cioè senza voti,* però di *osservanza regolari,* e non inferiori di vita ad altri religiosi osservanti. ⟨Annal. ii, p. 60.⟩[11]

In like manner the author of the Pregi speaks of the Congregation, benchè non sia religiosa, *non avendo alcuna sorta di voti.* ⟨part i. p. 15⟩ and therefore calls it only 'quasi a modo di religione. ibid.'[12]

He compares moreover the Congregation to volunteers as contrasted to regular troops; ⟨p. 19.⟩ And, as no one supposes that volunteers have not substantially th⁃ same life as regulars, therefore Oratorians are substantially, though not in form, a religion.

F. Fabrio in his comment on the rule, makes a remark to the same effect, which is important both as being his view of the Oratory and as being a comment on the Rule. Quoting the words of the Introduction 'et hanc viam merito saecularibus Presbyteris ille monstravit, *licet a Religiosorum institutis distantem,*' ⟨Pregi part 2, p. 304,⟩ he observes 'Via dolce, e di santa ed

---

[10]i.e. "that they should have no scruple in doing so, because they would be going, not to a secular but a religious house, and one like their own, since the Churches of the Oratory resembled their own."

[11]i.e. "the Naples House of clerics, that is to say without vows, but nevertheless of regular observance, and no whit inferior to other observant religious."

[12]*Pregi* (Eng.), p. 1: "although it is not a religious Order, since it has no vows . . . almost after the manner of a religious Order." ["volunteers" ib. p. 4.]

amorosa *libertà*; *perciò* differente da quella degli *altri* religiosi istituti. Il Comando e l'Obbedienza non si chiamano con questi vocaboli, ma con quelli di Preghiera e di condiscenza. Quì non ha luogo il terror del Peccato, ma l'allettamento del dovere e del buono.' ⟨Pregi part 2. p 304.⟩[13]

[§ 2.] On the characteristic of the Oratory considered as a Congregation.

Its characteristic is that it is a *sort* of religion, though not properly a religion, to determine then *in what* its characteristic consists, it is only necessary to determine *in what* it is a religion.

The answer to this, as far as words go, has already been given; —it is a religion, or the same as a religion, not externally, but *in its perfection*. Whatever then is meant by the word 'perfection' in its ordinary sense, and that is intelligible enough, such is the characteristic attribute of the Congregation of the Oratory.

But to be more particular (i.e. Proof that the particular perfection of the Oratory is that of yielding one's will to that of the rest):— the nature of the case suggests what must be the characteristic attribute of the members of any community whatever, viz. their perfection, as members of a community is to act as such or as *parts of a whole*.

Here then is the characteristic and the perfection of the Congregation of the Oratory, that its members act *as* members, that they do not act in an independent isolated way, but in and for and by and from the body, as having no distinct interest and no private will.

This is a most momentous principle, and must be dwelt upon.

F. Consolini, who was for 40 years novice-master, and is called the Benjamin as last born and perhaps dearest of St Philip, finding that a father of the Congregation neglected answering the Porter's call, because he was in prayer, reproved

[13]This part of the *Pregi* has been omitted in the English translation. It reads as follows: "A gentle way, and one of holy and loving *liberty*; *therefore* different from that of the *other* religious institutes. Orders and Obedience are not called by these names, but by those of Request and Compliance. There is no place here for the terror of sin, but for the attractiveness of Duty and of Goodness."

him with the following maxim, which however difficult it may be of application in particulars, is the cardinal principle of the Oratory:— chi vuol vivere a suo modo, non è buono per la Congregazione. Tutti devono accomodarsi alla santa Comunità. ⟨Preg. p. 228⟩[14]

A voluntary submission of the will to the Congregation is, as it were, the definition of good membership. In religious, properly so called, it consists in a scrupulous fulfilment of the vows, which includes obedience; but, there being no vows here to protect the life of the Society, to be an Oratorian is directly to consult *for* that life, to postpone one's own wishes and will to its welfare.

Consolini was most earnest in pressing this point on his brethren:—we ought, says the author of the Pregi ⟨p. 228⟩, seguire in tutto e per tutto la Comunità, studiando di accomodarsi a quella in ogni cosa, senza cercare singolarità. Qui è, he proceeds, dove il P. Pietro Consolini fermeva tanto, e replicava sovente con tutta l'energia, che tutti dovevano accomodarsi alla santa Comunità, la quali, chi ben l'intende, racchiude in se tesori di meriti.[15]

He himself was an instance of what he taught, for though he was very abstinent in his mode of living, he managed to sit at table and to seem to eat as others, lest he should seem singular.

Other and more familiar instances of this same living for the community are given by the author of the Pregi. Avrà uno in disegno di andar fuori di Città, o di far qualche passegiata per prendere un poco d'aria, o uscire di casa per qualche affare; e gli converrà stare in casa per qualche servizio della Congregazione, o per assistere alle consulte, o per supplire all'Uffizio d'un altro che manca, o per servire o leggere alla tavola, o per proporre i soliti dubbj a mensa, o per altri consimili casi, che arrivano totalmente impensati. Sarà applicato

---

[14]*Pregi* (Eng.), p. 130.

[15]*Pregi* (Eng.), p. 130 "following the community in all things, accommodating ourselves to it in everything without singularity. This it is on which Father Pietro Consolini insisted so much and which he repeated so often and with so much energy, saying that all should adapt themselves to holy community life, for he who understands how to do this well may obtain great treasures of merit." [See p. 335.]

a comporre il sermone, o a scrivere una lettera; e gli converrà interrompere la sua applicazione quattro, sei, dieci volte in una sola mattina, perchè vien chiamato al Confessionario, o alla Porta. Gli sarebbe comodo di dire la sua Messa ad'un'ora; e gli converrà aspettare di dirla ad'un'altra molto per lui incomoda. ⟨t 1 p 53⟩[16]

It is then the fundamental principle of the Oratory, that no one is his own master, no one can live for himself alone. To live and let live, in this sense of the words, to say 'I will not interfere with you and you shall not interfere with me,' is the ruin of the Congregation—and a person who so speaks has not in him the first element of an Oratorian.

[§ 3.] On Mortification of Self.

The subject is involved, or rather has been treated of, in what already has been said concerning the characteristic peculiarity of Oratorian life. *External* mortification, as has been already said, is *not* the mark of an Oratorian, but *internal;* or in other words, mortification of his private judgment, and his own will. And the necessity of internal mortification arises out of the simple fact that he lives in a community. For a community, if it be really such, and not a mere lodging or boarding house, if it be really a body or corporation, has a will of its own, to which the wills of individuals must be subordinate. Hence the celebrated saying, which we must ever keep in mind, if we would be real Oratorians, Vita communis, mortificatio maxima.

It is scarcely necessary to refer to the life of St Philip, to show the place which mortification of the will holds in his ethical system. "Mille imperscrutabiles artes", says Manni,

---

[16]"He may intend to go out of the city, or to take a walk to get some fresh air, or to do some business, and he will have to remain at home for some service of the community—to assist at a Congregation, or to supply the place of someone who is absent, to serve, or read, or propose the accustomed doubts at table, or similar things which are quite unforeseen. He may be occupied in composing a sermon, or in writing a letter, and he will perhaps be interrupted four, six, nay ten times in one morning by being called to the confessional or to the parlours. Some one hour may suit him for saying Mass, and he will be put down at another very inconvenient one." p. 44.

"mille habebat adinventiones, ut propria voluntate ex animo eradicata, divinis eam virtutibus habitaculum praepararet." "Sanctity" he said "consists in three fingers' breadth" touching his forehead as he spoke, adding by way of explanation, that "the important thing was to mortify the Razionale, " (a familiar word with him, meaning every superfluous or undue exercise of the intellect, soverchio discorso dell' intellecto,) and not to aim to be wise and rational, non voler far il prudente e ragionare, in every matter, since Perfection, (perfection being the characteristic of the Oratory as a quasi religion) Perfection consists in bringing one's own will into captivity, and acting in accordance with the governing power. ⟨Preg. p. 209⟩[17]

Many instances in the Saint's life in inculcation of self-mortification will present themselves without effort to our memories—how he was suspicious of ascetic persons till he had proved their humility, or if they acted without a director, how he put on his penitents arbitrary or what seemed capricious commands, how he kept them from saying mass, how he made them do what in itself was ridiculous,—all in order to break their selfwill, and so prepare them simply to submit themselves to the will of God.

[§ 4.] On Obedience

As *mortification of selfwill* is the vital principle of the Oratory, so *obedience* is the essential and necessary means by which it is exercised. We are to mortify ourselves *by* obedience, that is, by submitting our own will to that of another. "Non sarà mai Santo chi non è ubbidiente," says Consolini, and Valpi "chi cammina per l'obbedienza, va sicuro al Paradiso."[18]

St Philip's demand upon his own penitents and sons in this respect was most absolute and unmeasured. Aut pareat aut abeat, he said of Baronius himself, when he contended for a. point when he had a great show of justice on his side. And there

---

[17]*Pregi* (Eng.), pp. 112–3. Newman's exact reference to *Annal* for Manni's text is illegible.

[18]The man who is not obedient will never be a saint . . . To walk by obedience is to go straight to Paradise. [See p. 335.]

are his famous written words, Pıdri miei, io sono risolutissimo di non volere in casa uomini, chi non siano osservatori di quei pochi ordini che sono stati loro assignati. ⟨Bacc. i. 19. § 15.⟩[19] (It may be added that this is probably what is meant by St Philip's special love for St Paul's Epistles—for, if there be one aspect of Christianity which the Apostle delineates beyond others, it is that of *voluntary obedience* after the pattern of Christ.) Non si contentava già il Santo, says the author of the Pregi, di qualunque ubbidienza, ma la voleva pronta, cieca, interna ed esterna; e diceva che, per essere vero ubbidiente, non basta l'eseguire ciò che l'Ubbidienza comanda, ma che bisogna farle senza discorso. ⟨Preg p 242.⟩[20] Cardinal Tarugi compares it to the obedience of the monks of Egypt. ⟨Bacc. i. 20.⟩[21]

Nor was this obedience to cease with St Philip's death, if we listen to Cardinal Tarugi. Discorrendo, says the same author, intorno alla materia (di Ubbidienza) con alcuni discorse, per esortarli a *conservare l'antica* ubbidienza, ebbe a dire, che niun capo di religione, per quanto egli sapesse, ancor delle antiche, fu più ubbidito dai suoi religiosi, che Filippo da' suoi figliuoli. ⟨ibid.⟩[22] Now in so saying, I am not determining on the moment who since St Philip's death that other is:— whether one individual, or several together, or all members of the body in various relations, or the rules and customs of the body.

This obedience, to whomsoever it is now due (which is a further question) is enforced in the strongest terms by writers who are authorities on the subject, the difference between the obedience of the Oratorian and that of a religious differing only in this, that the one is voluntary, and the other is vowed.

Questo Pregio dell' Ubbidienza, says the author of the Pregi, "di tanto merito e necessità, lo gode pur anche la nostra Congregazione dell 'Oratorio; e lo gode in modo tanto speciale e distinto, che si guadagna tutti gli stupori del mondo. Imper-

---

[19]"I am fully resolved, my fathers not to keep any in the house who are not observers of the few orders which are given them." Bacci (Eng.), Vol. 1, p. 122.

[20]*Pregi* (Eng.), p. 138: "The Saint was not contented with any kind of obedience, but he required it to be prompt, blind, interior and exterior; and he used to say, that to be truly obedient, it did not suffice to do the thing commanded, but it must be done without reply."

[21]Bacci (Eng.), Vol. 1, p. 125.

[22]Bacci (Eng.), Vol. 1, p. 125.

ciocchè tutti i Padri e Fratelli laici, che vivono in essa, non fanno alcun voto di Ubbidienza, come i religiosi, appure *non cedono punto* per questo, nella perfezione e finezza di questa virtù,che la professano ne' chiostri con voto solenne, supplendo alla mancanza del voto coll' amore e colla voluntaria prontezza e perfezione nell' ubbidire ai cenni del Superiore." ⟨p. 240.⟩[23] vid. the same in Consolini ⟨Annal t. 1 p 582⟩

The same author founds this voluntary, yet perfect obedience upon the example of our Lord. Gesù Cristo ha dato esempio ai Padri dell' Oratorio, perchè servissero a Dio da liberi, e sempre voluntarj, quando, per incontrare la volontà dell' Eterno Padre, qual era di redimere il mondo, egli si offersi pronto di farlo a qualunque suo costo, 'Ecce Ego, mitte me;' e quando si mostrò disposto di sofferire la designata tormentosa passione,' Oblatus est quia ipse voluit,' . . . Patì per lo zelo della gloria di suo Padre, e della salvezza delle anime, come si era già fatto intendere per bocca del Reale Profeta, Zelus domûs tuae comedit me . . . Ecco l'esemplare de' Figliuoli di S. Filippo, i quali ad imitazione del Redentore, ciò che fanno per servizio di Dio in Congregazione, lo fanno spontaneamente, di lor piena libera volontà, e possono dire col medesimo, Voluntarie sacrificabo tibi &c. ⟨p 221-3.⟩[24] And again, È bella la nostra ubbidienza, perchè non mossa o forzata da nessun timore, ma sol dall' amore, che a Dio si porta; e perchè si ubbidisce, quando si può dissubbedire, essendo essa libera; che è appunto l'elogio fatto

[23]*Pregi* (Eng.), p. 137: "Our Congregation also enjoys this Excellence of obedience, which is of so great merit and necessity; and it enjoys it in such a special manner as to excite the admiration of the world. Although our fathers and lay-brothers make no vow of obedience, as do religious, they are nevertheless no way inferior in the perfection of this virtue to those who profess it in the cloister with solemn vows. They supply the want of vows with love, with voluntary promptitude, and perfection in obeying every wish of the Superior."

[24]*Pregi* (Eng.), 351-3: "Jesus Christ has given an example to the Fathers of the Oratory, that they should serve God freely and voluntarily, when to comply with the will of the Eternal Father, namely to redeem the world, He offered Himself readily to do it at any cost: 'Lo, here am I, send Me' (*Is.* 6:8) and when He showed himself willing to suffer the pre-ordained torments of His Passion: He was offered up because it was His own will. . . . He suffered for zeal for the glory of His Father and the salvation of souls, as He had already made known by the mouth of the royal prophet: "For the zeal of Thy House hath eaten me up . . . Behold the model of the sons of St Philip who, in imitation of their Saviour, do what they do in the service of God spontaneously and of their own free will, and say with Him, *Voluntarie sacrificabo tibi*." [See p. 337].

dall' Ecclesiastico a chi può trasgredire e non trasgredisce: Qui potuit transgredi et non est transgressus. ⟨p 290.⟩[25]

And, since it is obedience to *God*, therefore it is, that the absence or presence of a Saint, such as St Philip, has no weight in the measure of the duty. L'Ubbidienza è lo stesso che la voluntà di Dio—says the same author. Qui vos audit, me audit . . . ⟨vid also Annal t l. p 459⟩ Qui potestatem resistit, Dei ordinationi resistit. E così, o sia Santo il Superiore o Direttore che comanda, com'era Filippo, o sia Superiore o Direttore di poca o di minima virtù, l'Ubbidienza sarà sempre la stessa, dello stesso valore e merito, e produrrà i medesimi ottimi effetti. ⟨p 245⟩[26]. (In like manner he writes to his Nephew who belonged to the Congregation of Naples, Se ve ne andate a Roma, siate come un bastone in mano de'Superiori; p 252 lasciatevi elevare, abassare, portare, e gettare, e non abbiate senso e volere proprio).[27]

It may be added that one main reason of the long noviciate of three years is to break the will of the novices. Periculum fiat, says the Rule, si prompti sint in omnibus parere, vel in humillimis ac durissimis. Omnia sub sigillo sanctae obedientiae fiant, said Ancina. ⟨Ann. t l. p 364.⟩[28] F. Mateo would not be let off any thing when old, and said that we should have to answer for the observance at the judgment seat of God. ⟨Ann t. l p 544.5⟩. F. Airoli looked for this principal comfort in the "tremendo punto" of death, "to have acted with entire dependance [sic] on holy obedience". ibid. t ⟨l. p 603.⟩ F. Fr. Bozius strictly observed the rule at 80. ⟨ibid. p 498,9.⟩ F. Grassi at Fermo observed un'esatta custodia di ogni, benche minima,

---

[25]*Pregi* (Eng.), p. 185: "Our obedience is therefore beautiful, because it is not moved nor compelled by any fear, but purely by the love we bear to God, and because we obey when we might disobey, being free. This is precisely what is praised by Ecclesiasticus in him who might transgress and did not."

[26]*Pregi* (Eng.), p. 141: "Obedience is identical with the will of God . . . He that heareth you, heareth Me (*Luke* 10:16) . . . He that resisteth the power, resisteth the ordinance of God (*Rom.* 13:2). Whether the Superior or director be a saint, as was St Philip, or a man of little or no virtue, obedience will always have the same merit, and will produce the same excellent effects."

[27]*ib.* p. 147: "If you go to Rome, let yourself be as a stick in the hands of your Superiors; let them raise, lower, carry or throw you away; have no opinion or will of your own." [The reference is to Tarugi. See p. 341.]

[28]Let all be done under the seal of holy obedience.

28

regola, and had a maxim that nothing but necessity excused from observance of the letter. ⟨t 2 p 338.⟩ F. Oblioni of Casale accounted nothing light which the Rule prescribed, which was never to be transgressed ⟨t 3. p 553.⟩ When F. Morico of Fermo refounded the Oratory of Macerata, his first object was to introduce that strict observance of the Rules for which his own Oratory was most conspicuous ⟨t 4. p 394,⟩ he himself having, on his first admittance at Fermo, applied himself with all his might ⟨earnestness⟩ to imbue himself with the Rules and Constitutions of the Oratory and faithfully to practise them; quindi è, continues Marciano, che, regolando tutte le sue attioni [sic] giusta la breve, ma santa idea lasciata dal santo Padre a suoi figliuoli, erano quelle irreprensibili. ⟨p. 399.⟩[29]

[§ 5.] *On the persons to whom obedience is to be paid.*
Rule. The Constitutions.

The highest authority is the body of Constitutions or the Rule, for that in fact is the voice of the Pope himself who has confirmed it; and moreover, short of him, it is the traditional voice and authentic bidding, not only of the whole living Congregation, but of the whole body of members from the beginning to this time.

To this high authority even the Superior is subordinate, as is evident from the nature of the case.

And it is to be observed that obedience here, as in all other cases, is to proceed from love; the founder expressly laying down that his Constitutions do not bind under penalty of sin, either mortal or venial.

But, under whatever sanction or motive obedience is to be enforced, it is certain, if we listen to the authoritative writers on the subject, that obedience to the rule is to be so exact as to be almost fearful. Christus obediens *usque ad mortem,* is made the model for the Oratorian. ⟨vid end of Tarugi's life.⟩[30]

[29] therefore, basing all his actions on the pithy but holy idea left by the holy Father to his sons, these actions were irreproachable.

[30] The reference is to Tarugi's retirement to the Vallicella at the end of his life, and living there in obedience to the Superior, although he himself was a Cardinal. *Annals,* Tome 1, Lib. III, Cap. VI, p. 260.

The Congregation, whether of Deputies, of Decennials, or of members generally.

Next to the Rule it is necessary to mention the *Congregation*, in whatever form it exerts the function of a Superior, whether in its collective capacity or by deputies. The reason for mentioning the Congregation before the Superior is this, that for the most part the Congregation acts *through* the *rules* which it passes, or is *legislative;* as the idea of legislation is prior to that of execution, and as the Superior is mainly executive, therefore the Congregation is prior to the Superior.

And in fact the Superior obeys the Congregation i.e. as a legislative power, as he obeys the Rule;—on which point there is the following clear passage in the Pregi.

Neppure quegli, che è attualmente Preposito, può avere questa esenzione, mentre egli stesso deve ubbidire alle Consulte Maggiori, in cui entrano i Padri Decennali, e alle Minori ancora, ove sono i soli Deputati; e quando queste con la maggior parte de' voti abbiano determinato qualche cosa, (se non è di quelle che spettino al solo Superiore) è tenuto ad ubbidire, e a far osservare i decreti fatti delle medesime Consulte, senza poterli mutare, ancorchè siano contro il suo proprio sentimento; perchè la Congregazione, canonicamente radunta a Consulta, è sopra il Preposto, in maniera che la di deporlo del suo uffizio. ⟨p 253⟩[31]

In the lives of the Fathers of the Oratory there is frequent mention of their obedience to their "Superiors", the plural being used as well as the singular, which in some places at least must mean the Deputies. For instance of Father Airoli; Era somma la stima e riverenza, che egli portava a' suoi superiori, qualunque essi fossero; e somma era l'allegrezza e prontezza, colla quale si esercitava in ubbidire. Se alle volte non finivano i superiori

---

[31]*Pregi* (Eng.), p. 149: "Not even the father who is actually Provost can be exempt, since he himself must obey the General Congregations, in which the decennial fathers take part, and also the smaller ones composed only of the Deputies; and when these by the majority of votes have determined anything (if it is not of those things which belong to the Superior alone), he is bound to obey and to put in force the decrees made by these Congregations, without being able to alter them, even supposing them to be contrary to his own judgment; because the community, canonically united in a Congregation, is above the Provost, in such a way that it has the power to depose him from his office."

di dichiarare la loro volontà, bastava, che congetturasse la loro mente per fare &c ⟨Annal t l. p 603⟩.[32]

The Superior

As several opportunities have occurred· already to show in what or when the Superior is to obey instead of commanding, and as after all, as we shall see presently, he is the principal instrument of the obedience of the individual members of the Oratory, it may be well to add this also, (though it is partly to forestall what will come presently), that he has to submit himself to certain other officials *in* their office.

Of this submission F. Grassi of Fermo gives us a striking example.

"In respect of obedience", says Marciano, "though being for so long a time superior, he appeared to have no opportunity for its exercise, yet he knew how to pursue ⟨?⟩ the track of it. First he placed his private will in the hands of his Confessor . . . as if he were a child. Next, though Superior, he used to render a most exact obedience to the officials of the Congregation. Called by the Porter or Sacristan, he never was heard to say 'I cannot', or 'I am busy.'.... And, whereas in the last years of his life . . . a Fratello was assigned to him for his attendance, he called him his Guardian Angel, and recognized ⟨?⟩ him as his superior, and obeyed him in such sort, as not even to change his place without his leave. In his journeys, he so depended upon his companion, to whom on such occasion ⟨?⟩ [sic] he gave the title of Governor, that his intimations were for him inviolable precepts &c." ⟨t. 2. p 380⟩. The same is related of Consolini. ⟨t l. p 555⟩. [See above p. 343.]

The superior then is in his place subordinate to the Rule, to the decisions of the Congregation, and to the officials of the Congregation acting in their own department, but, after all these deductions, still it would appear that he is more than any

---

[32]"The esteem and reverence which he showed to his superiors, whoever they might be, was extreme; and he exercised obedience with the greatest promptness and cheerfulness. If at times, superiors did not declare their wishes, it was enough for him to guess what they wished to proceed to action." [See p. 342.]

one or any thing else the governing power and the instrument of obedience in the Congregation.

1. First because rules cannot *govern,* strictly speaking. They cannot enforce themselves—whereas the Superior is the *enforcer* of the laws; in the words of the Rule[33], ad ipsum solum pertinebit rite constituta perficienda curare, (exigere rationem actorum vel agendorum a singulis nostrorum) et videre ut singula recte expediantur [*Rule,* Caput V, Decretum XXIV].

2. And next, because he is specially elected ad Congregationis rerumque ad ipsam spectantium gubernationem et curam.[34]

There are a multitude of minute matters, which laws cannot determine, and which must be determined in some way or other, these are in the disposition of the Superior.

Moreover the other officials act together with him and under his supervision;[35] ad ipsum solum pertinebit exigere rationem actorum vel agendorum à singulis nostrorum, quibus est aliquod munus vel onus quomodolibet ubique locorum mandatum [*Rule,* Caput V, Decretum XXIV]. Hence we find in one place that he has a concurrent power with the Father Minister, qui rebus domesticis administrandis, Praepositi sententia consulta et explorata, det operam. ⟨p. 17⟩[36] "Legitur Italice, quandoque inter caenandum, arbitratu *Praepositi vel Ministri.* Again, nihil preaterea exposcentes, vel per se ipsi deferentes, nisi *Praepositi vel Ministri* fruantur licentiâ &c."[37] With the Prefect of the Oratory; de rebus praesertim gravibus ad Oratorium spectantibus quibuscumque *Praepositum* Congregationis nostrae consulat, penes quem rerum

---

[33]He alone is to see that decisions are carried out (demand an account of things done or to be done by our members) and to see that everything is properly carried out.

[34]for the government and care of the Congregation and the things pertaining to it.

[35]He alone is to demand an account of things done or to be done by each of our members, to whom any task or burden is ordered anywhere.

[36]who takes charge of domestic matters having consulted with the Provost.

[37]The reading at dinner shall be sometimes in Italian, at the good pleasure of *Provost or Minister;* again, Asking for nothing more, nor bringing anything themselves except with permission of the Provost or Minister.

Oratorii eadem est gubernatio.[38] And with the Confessor as
Director of meditations:— praeter hortatorem Praepositum,
quem audiant, etiam Sacerdotem sacris familiae nostrae
Confessionibus audiendis Praefectum [*Rule,* Caput I, Decretum
II].

The Superior then is *practically* and *proximately* the supreme
authority in the Congregation, and the particular laws and
statutes of the Congregation do not specify and prescribe his
power, but regulate and limit it. He may enjoin what is not
commanded in the Statutes, but not what is forbidden in them.
And hence the reason assigned by the author of the Pregi for
deposing the Superior, is, se commettesse delitti gravi, o volesse
introdurre cose nuove, *direttamente opposte* alle *Regole,* o distruttivi
delle medesime. ⟨p. 254.⟩[39]

That this is not an exaggeration of his power, seems to follow
from the following passages which exemplify it.

It seems allowed that the obedience paid to St Philip is due
to Superiors after him. One passage to this effect has been
quoted. O sia santo il Superiore o Direttor che comanda,
com'era Filippo, says the author of the Pregi, o sia Superiore o
Direttore di poca o di niuna virtù, l'Ubbidienza sarà sempre
la stessa . . . Chi ubbidisce con più facilità all'uno, che all'altro,
sogettandosi all'uno e non all'altro, è sospetto nella Ubbidienza,
come il sarebbe nella fede, chi si prostrasse ad adorare un
Cristo di oro, e non un altro di legno. ⟨p. 246.⟩[40]

Tarugi's obedience to St Philip was notoriously unbounded,
but he exercised it towards the Superiors after him. Nè sola-
mente sì contentò, says the author of the Pregi, di esercitare la
sua sì perfetta ubbidienza a S. Filippo; ma con lo stesso tenore
la esercitò con tutti gli altri Superiori che furono poi eletti

---

[38]He should consult the Provost of the Congregation especially about more
serious matters, since the Provost has the same power over the matters of the
Oratory.

[39]*Pregi* (Eng.), p. 149: "If he should commit grave sins, or should wish to
introduce novelties *directly opposed* to the rules, or destructive of the same."

[40]*Pregi* (Eng.), p. 141: "Whether the Superior or director be a saint, as was St
Philip, or a man of little or no virtue, obedience will always have the same merit
. . . He who obeys the one more readily than the other lays himself open to suspicion
in the matter of obedience; just as the faith would be doubtful of one who should
prostrate himself before a crucifix of gold and not before one of wood."

dopo la morte del Santo ⟨p. 251⟩ Nay even when a Cardianl, retiring at the end of his life into the Chiesa Nuova, in tutto e per tutto si regolava colla direzione del Preposto, anche in quelle cose che erano contrari al suo proprio sentimento, &c. ibid.[41]

The same is told us of Consolini—L'Ubbidienza, che al Santo portava mentre fu vivo, trasferì poi ne' suoi successori che governarono la Congregazione. ⟨Annal t l. p 555 vid. also p 582.⟩[42] These instances are remarkable, for if any persons were likely to make a distinction between obedience to St Philip and to his successors, it was they who had known the former.

An instance of a later date is found in the history of the Blessed Valfrè of Turin—In the Jubilee of 1675 he proposed to visit Rome, and got leave for that purpose of the Superior, and the Congregation of Deputies, since the journey would take up more than a month. The Superior on parting gave him a note which he was to read before he embarked. He got to the vessel, his luggage was put on board—then he read the note; it ran thus:—Il P. Valfrè tornerà subito a Casa.[43] He returned.— There is an additional circumstance to be remarked here— The Superior counterorders the leave of the Congregatio Deputata. How is he able to do so? because they are not *legislating,* but dealing *towards an individual.* He is only bound to act with them in quod spectat ad *universalem* gubernationem Domûs.[44] Hence the leave of absence is required, not only of the Deputies, but of the Superior as a separate act. The Superior did but withdraw his permission.

Other Officials

It would appear that various officials are in this department, in their place and during the time of their office, as absolute as the Superior, and to be obeyed by him and all others.

[41]"He did not content himself with practising this perfect obedience to St Philip alone, but was equally submissive to all the other Superiors who were elected after the death of the Saint . . . in all things and everywhere he guided himself by the direction of the Provost, even when it was at variance with his own judgment." *Pregi* (Eng.), p. 147.

[42]The obedience which he showed to the Saint during his lifetime, he transferred afterwards to his successors who governed the Congregation.

[43]Father Valfrè will return home immediately.

[44]In anything that concerns the *general* running of the house.

Thus we are told of Consolini, ⟨vid also Annal t l. p 479.
481⟩ Non solo verso Filippo, ed i suoi successori esibiva pronta
la sua ubbidienza; ma l'istessa rendeva egualmente agli
officiali inferiori di Congregazione sino all'ultimo de'Fratelli,
e era la sua massima, spesso da lui replicata, che quel Dio, che
ha posto quello all'uffizio di Preposto, ha posto quell'altro
nell'uffizio della Porta, e della cucina. Thus he called the
Porter's bell voce di Dio. ⟨Annal. t l p 555.⟩[45]

And Marciano tells us expressly of St Philip himself, voleva,
che non solo si ubbidisce all'imperio del Preposto, ma anche
agli altri ufficiali minori, come al Sagrestano, al Portinaio in
quel che concerne il loro uffizio. ⟨ibid p 71⟩ a rule which he
exemplified most strictly in his own person. ⟨vid also p. 59⟩[46]

The author of the Pregi expresses this more in detail: Un
Uffiziale è soggetto all'altro, in maniera che per fino il primo
Deputato, il Segretario, il Ministro, il Prefetto de' Giovanni, e
così gli altri, anzi il Superiore stesso, tutti devono ubbidire,
quando porta l'occasione, al Prefetto de' Sermoneggiante, al
Sagrestano, al Portinajo, al Cuoco. ⟨p. 49⟩[47]

And in like manner the Ministro, the Prefect of the Oratory
&c. have their own department.

What has just been said gives us a means of illustrating the
power of the Superior—for what these particular officials are
in some particular department, *such* is the Superior in the
general conduct of the House. The author of the Pregi expresses this in one place:—He speaks of le mortificazioni, che
il Superior estudia talora di dare a' suoi sudditi per loro bene,

[45]Not only to Philip and to his successors did he show a ready obedience; but
he rendered the same equally to the lower officials of the Congregation, down to the
last of the Brothers, and it was his maxim, which he often repeated, that the same
God who had placed one man in the position of Provost, had placed the other in
the office of Porter and of Kitchener. Thus he called the Porter's bell the voice of
God.

[46]He wished that they should obey not only the order of the Provost, but also
to the minor officials, such as the Sacristan, the Porter in what concerned their
offices.

[47]One official is subject to the other, in such a way that even the first Deputy
the Secretary, the Minister, the Prefect of the youth, and so the others, nay even
the Superior himself, all should obey, when the occasion calls for it to the Prefect
of sermons, the Sacristan, the Porter, the Cook. *Pregi* (Eng.), pp. 40, 41.

il Prefetto a' suoi Novizj, il Ministro a' Fratelli. ⟨p 53.⟩⁴⁸ F. Borello of Naples was remarkable for la custodia e l'osservanza delle costitutizioni e delle lodevoli consuetudini dell'Oratorio.⁴⁹ ⟨t 2. p 22.⟩ And, to take a particular instance, F. D'Aste of Forlì was most rigid in enforcing the rule of silence at dinner. ⟨t 4 p 295.⟩ vid observance of Velli ⟨Annal t 1 p 487⟩.

It is well too to bear in mind the circumstances under which the Rule has been formed and imposed, which implies a deliberation and distinct treatment and view of the case so remarkable, as almost to suggest the presence of a divine direction, and to warn us against altering them except as places and times change.

E.g. St Philip gave his sons some poche costituzioni ⟨Annal t l. p. 210⟩ twenty years before his death at S. Giovanni's. After they came to the Vallicella, which was not very long afterwards, they seemed to wish St Philip formally to draw up a sort of rule. Nine years before St Philip's death it existed in two MSS books. ⟨Annal t 2 p 316.⟩ The saint himself, as we have seen, was "most resolute" that they should be observed. He refers on the [sic] one occasion the Naples House to the Capitoli.

After it had been tried for thirty years, and not till then, the Rule received the approbation of the Holy See.

Moreover it is said that St Philip appeared to a Cappucin of holy life, and among other things said that "the Congregation was pleasing to God" e così le Regole tutte, e se ne tenesse conto, e non' s'innovasse minima cosa.⁵⁰ ⟨Pregi part 2 p 272⟩.

[§ 6.] On perseverance
⟨cases of leaving the Oratory
paper n p 8⁵¹⟩

One subject remains to be mentioned in the contrast or comparison between the Oratory and religious bodies. The

⁴⁸The mortifications which the Superior studies to give his subjects from time to time, as well as the Prefect to his novices and the Minister to the brothers. *Pregi* (Eng.), p. 44.

⁴⁹For the custody and the observance of the Constitutions and of the laudable customs of the Oratory.

⁵⁰And also all its Rules; and that they were to hold them in esteem, and not to make the slightest innovation. (*Pregi* Eng.), p. 369. [See above p. 338.]

⁵¹Note by Newman (Ed.)

solemn vow administered to the latter precludes any change of state—on the other hand it is distinctly permitted to the Oratorian to return to a merely secular life. This is true in the abstract—but, when we view the case practically, there is not so much difference between them.

First, no one can *enter* the Oratory without the *intention* of remaining in it to the end of his life. *Diligenter* exquirent Patres, says the Rule, num (candidati) animo veniant *permanendi semper* in Congregatione usque *ad vitae obitum*.[52]

Hence one of the old fathers of the Oratory ⟨Pregi p. 271 part 2⟩ said, I veri figliuoli di S. Filippo si conoscono alla sepoltura.[53]

Father Lanzi reminds us that the five Paters and Aves said of an evening in the Oratory, are for perseverance nel divino servizio, that is perseverance in the Congregation. ⟨Pregi part 2 p 271⟩

Father Grassi of Fermo, who had been used to say, Haec requies mea in saeculum saeculi, hic habitabo, quoniam elegi eam, exclaimed in his last agony, O che bella cosa, morir figli di S. Filippo. ⟨ibid p 273.⟩[54]

The Venerable F. Ancina's instance is remarkable. When at Naples he had thoughts for a time of leaving the Oratory for a religious order, and mentioned the subject to Baronius at that time Superior. This was immediately after St Philip's death. Baronius writes to him thus: ⟨vid Marcian. t. l p 394⟩ "Quid fecisti? parcat tibi Deus. Veluti improviso tonitruo perculsus contremui totus, ubi tuas legi litteras. Siccine tui, tuorumque fratrum oblitus, ea meditaris, quae et tibi levitatis, et nobis crudelitatis notam inurant? ... Hoc non Pater noster reliquit exemplum, ut recedas è castris, et tibi prosis qui octogenarius numquam sibi vixit, sed omnium semper utilitati noctu diuque usque ad extremam horam ... Si qua charitas, si quae viscera misericordiae, rogo, obtestorque, ut tuis me litteris consoleris, ne penitus consternatus nimio maerore obruar atque deficiam.

---

[52]Let the Fathers carefully examine whether the candidates come with the desire of remaining *for ever* in the Congregation, *until death*.

[53]The true sons of St Philip are known at their burial. *Pregi* (Eng.), p. 368.

[54]*Ps*. 131:14 [Vulgate]: 'This is my resting place for ever, here have I chosen to live.' 'Oh, what a glorious thing to die sons of St Philip.' *Pregi* (Eng), pp. 369, 370.

Rursus dico, Nos vivimus, si vos statis &c."[55] And so he proceeds.

Tarugi too, then Archbishop of Avignon, wrote to him very strongly to dissuade him from his design. He ends thus:—"Se posso consigliare, se posso pregare, se ho nel pensiero et [*sic*] animo di V.R. credito di saper discernere le tentazioni dalle buone ispirazioni, vi supplico, e vi scongiuro a deporre cotesto nuovo pensiero, et credere assolutissamente, che è tentazione, e tanto più gagliarda, quanto è coperta sotto colore di giustizia e di maggior perfezione."[56]

SECOND PAPER

SUMMARY

Genius of the Congregation.
Love the bond of the Oratory—humility and detachment from the world—Slowness in process a remarkable characteristic of St Philip's life.

Members.
S. Giovanni—Chiesa Nuova—Forlì—Bologna—Naples—Padua—Camerino—Fano—Brescia—Aquila—Casale.

Bulls.

Property.
Church, Abbey, vineyard; Royal offerings; Cures; Bequests; examples of Perugia, Fossombrone, Reggio, Florence, Forlì, Macerata, Lodi, Jesi, Cesena, Ripatransone, Fermo.

[55]"What have you done? May God forgive you. I trembled all over, as if at unexpected thunder when I read your letter. And so you would forget yourself and your brethren, and think of doing something which will imprint on you a mark of levity, and on us one of cruelty? . . . This is not the example which our Father left, to leave the camp and consult for yourself. He, an octogenarian, never lived for himself, but for the usefulness of all by day and by night up to the last hour . . . If you have any charity, any feelings of pity, I beg and entreat you, to console me by your letters, lest I break down altogether under too much sorrow. Again I say, we live, if you stand &c. [See p. 336.]

[56] I can advise if I may entreat, if I have any credit in the mind and soul of Your Reverence for being able to distinguish temptations from good inspirations, I beg and adjure you to put away this new thought, and to believe absolutely that it is a temptation, and all the more specious, in that it is covered with the colour of justice and of greater perfection. [See p. 336.]

Officials.

Constitutions.

St Philip draws up some *poche costituzioni*—rigid idea of obedience in the Annals—the Oratory like a *fil di seta*.

Novices.

The Four Associated Oratories.

Rome, Naples, S Severino, Lanciano; no idea of a distinct propagation of the Oratory in St Philip's mind. The Four Associated Oratories passed members from one to the other; they seem to have had their property in common.

Anomalies, Mistakes &c &c.

St Philip did not wish his Congregation to be a religion—no poverty or vows. The case of the Oratory at Camerino. Brescia and Lucca.

———

On the Santa Croce Papers in general, cf. above, pp. 135–8, and on this "Second Paper" in particular, cf. ib. pp. 136–7. "Notes on Oratorian History", where the significance of the last two sections of this paper (viz. The Four Associated Oratories, and Anomalies, Mistakes etc.) for the development of the English Oratory, is pointed out.

PAPER n

SUMMARY

Object.

Main object was to reform the state of Rome—St Philip reformed the clergy by making a new beginning of them as Lancfranc, St Anselm &c were a new beginning of the English clergy in the Middle Ages.

Means.

Sacrament, Preaching, Prayer. The Confessional. Plain and Simple preaching. Music. Spiritual Exercises.

Special Means: the Oratory.
  Instruments: A Set of priests answering in rank to members of the English Universities.
  Subjects: Youths; how far Women.
  The Small Oratory: Fratelli; Officials of the small Oratory.
  Propagation of the Oratory: More than 150 Oratories founded in the 17th cent—In St Philip's original idea, the existence of an Oratory except at Rome was impossible—He yields unwillingly to St Carlo—refuses Bologna, Florence, Fermo, Naples—Even when founded, the Naples house was at first only an extension of the Roman community— Instances of the foundation of Oratories—in various parts of Italy and Sicily.
  Calendar of the Oratory.

———

This "Paper n" should be compared with the Chapter Address of 20 January 1848, where the material collected here has been worked up into an Address. The question naturally arises in the reader's mind, whether Newman expected an analogous rapid and wide development of the Oratory in England. This question has been discussed above, pp. 102–4.

PAPER O

SUMMARY

Oratorii italici typus. . . .
  On the significance of this quotation from Brockie, *Codex Regularum* (1759), see above, pp. 107, 329, On Brockie see *Dict. d'Hist. et de Géog. Eccl,* X (1938), col. 800.

Vitae ratio in Congregatione Oratorii.
  This is a collection of passages culled by Newman from the original Latin text of the Rule of the Oratory, obviously in view of adapting it to England. He refers to this process in a letter of 22 January 1847 to Dalgairns:

"I am diligently analyzing St Philip's rule—and in the course of doing so yesterday and this morning this fact broke upon me—that the rule, though embodying the one idea we are contemplating, viz a body of priests labouring in the conversion of great towns, (yet with time for literary works), the rule, I say, was in almost all its parts perfectly unsuited to a country of heretics and Saxons. E.g. four sermons running every day, disciplining before or with a congregation, going in a troop from Church to Church, sitting down on the grass and singing, getting by heart a finished composition etc etc. Then again I found that the Pope had forbidden all alterations of St Philip's rule, and the appropriation of the name of St Philip by bodies making such alterations. This posed me . . ." *L.D.*, XII, p. 22.

The list of points culled by Newman from the Rule, in order to establish the framework of life in the Oratory is as follows:
The Daily Services in the Church
The Refectory and Recreation after meals
Confession and Chapter of Faults
The forms of election of the Provost and Deputati
List of offices in the community

———

See above, Chapter 9: "Newman's Oratorian Spirituality—Continuity of Principles" for a commentary on Newman's adaptation of the Italian Rule to English conditions.

There is one notable omission in these notes by Newman in this "Paper O", viz; the point incorporated in Decree LXX empowering the English Oratory to undertake University and school work. On this crucial point cf. above, p. 109.

THE PAPAL BRIEF
26 NOVEMBER 1847

INTRODUCTORY NOTE

This Foundation Brief of the English Oratory was an important document for Newman for several reasons. At the outset it gave him the papal sanction for founding the Oratory in England, such as he had outlined in his letter to Cardinal Fransoni of 18 February 1847, given above as Oratory Paper No. 2. It also provided the essential point of reference in the quarrel with the London House in 1855-6, on which Newman's most considered statement is to be found in his letter of 14 June 1856 to the Fathers of the Birmingham Oratory, *L.D.*, XVII, pp. 266–70. Furthermore, the phrase about the *ordo honestior* (the upper classes) as the scope of the Oratory's mission in England proved a serious source of tension in the development of the English Oratory (see above, Newman the Priest, chapter 6).

The style of the Brief, though couched in the usual Latin of official Roman documents, does nevertheless breathe a personal note of Pius IX's appreciation of Newman. The English translation has been prepared for the present work.

The Apostolic Brief of His Holiness Pope Pius IX, by which the Congregation of the Oratory of St Philip Neri is established in England.

POPE PIUS IX

A MEMORIAL FOREVER

It has always been our firm and joyful expectation, that the time would come when we could, with a view to spreading and consolidating the Catholic Religion in the powerful and thriving Kingdom of England, establish and authorise a society of men, outstanding in learning and holiness, who would themselves be Englishmen. It was our opinion that nothing could be imagined more suitable or better adapted for effecting so grand a purpose. We considered that from such a society a continual stream of gifted men would come, who would labour uninterruptedly and with zeal to fulfil the noble task set before them. While we were turning this over in our mind, and often praying to the almighty and good God that this plan for men's salvation might be realised, we rejoiced to find a way suddenly opened for its accomplishment. Among the many distinguished men who in recent years have abandoned ancient error and returned to the faith of the Catholic Church, John Henry Newman has, in the estimation of all, been pre-eminent on account of his learning and virtue in the University of Oxford, and he is thus the very person to carry into effect what we so ardently desire. For, with a number of others from the same university who have embraced the Catholic faith, he has come with eagerness to Rome, in order to prove his reverence for Us and for the Chair of St Peter. At Our Command, he and some of his companions were warmly welcomed in the College of Propaganda, where, after a happy stay of several months, and after receiving Minor and Sacred Orders and the Priesthood, he has petitioned us to approve of the foundation of the Congregation of the Oratory of St Philip Neri in England.

Sanctissimi domini nostri PII divina providentia Papae IX. Literae Apostolicae quibus Congregatio Oratorii Sancti Philippi Nerii in Anglia Instituitur.

PIUS PP. IX.

AD PERPETUAM REI MEMORIAM.

Magna Nobis semper animo spes, et plane jucunda expectatio fuit, eventurum, scilicet, aliquando, ut ad amplificandum, stabiliusque muniendum in florentissimo Angliae Regno Catholicae Religionis incrementum, societatem hominum doctrina, ac pietate praestantium, atque ad illam ipsam gentem pertinentium, instituere, et auctoritate Nostra firmare possemus. Nullum enim tali consilio ad tantum opus feliciter gerendum opportunius, nullum utilius excogitari posse jamdiu arbitrati sumus. Nam veluti perennem inde dimanaturam esse reputavimus excellentium virorum copiam, qui nunquam intermisso sibi invicem succedentium ordine, de praeclara illa re diligenter absolvenda studiose laborarent. Haec animo Nostro volventibus Nobis, atque ut eadem fieri revera possent, Deum Optimum Maximum saepenumero deprecantibus, pergrata repente oblata ratio est, qua ad salutare istud consilium implendum viam Nobis panditam esse laetati sumus. Etenim inter tot illos praeclaros viros, qui his annis, veteri errore relicto, ad Catholicae Ecclesiae fidem reversi sunt, communi omnium sermone, propter doctrinae, virtutisque laudem in Oxoniensi Universitate celebratus, Joannes Henricus Newmanius, ad hoc, quod valde cupiebamus, efficiendum, occasionem commodam suppeditavit. Nam is cum pluribus aliis ex eadem Universitate, catholicam fidem amplexus, Romam, ut suam erga Nos, et Divi Petri Cathedram venerationem profiteretur, alacri animo profectus, et jussu Nostro cum aliquibus suis in Collegio Urbano Sacri Consilii Christiano Nomini Propagando peramanter exceptus, ibique plures menses libenter commoratus, minoribus, sacrisque Ordinibus, et Presbyteratu suscepto, petiit deinde a Nobis, ut Congregatio Oratorii S. Philippi Nerii in Anglia, probantibus Nobis, institueretur. Quantopere Nobis hoc initum a Joanne Henrico Newmanio propositum

There is no need to say how pleased We were at this proposal, nor with what joy We learned as well that there were several other Englishmen, who had been stirred by his teaching and example to return to the Catholic Church after a careful study of the religious question, and who had decided to follow and imitate him also in setting up the English Congregation of the Oratory. Hence, in the full sight of Rome, at Our command a suitable residence has been prepared in the beautiful monastery of Santa Croce in Gerusalemme for Newman and his companions. There with the help of a devout priest[1] from the house of the Congregation of the Roman Oratory, Santa Maria in Vallicella, sent for the purpose, the above mentioned English churchmen are learning to live the Oratorian life, and being trained for the task of founding the Congregation in England. Although what we have said so far shows quite clearly Our intention of setting up the Congregation of the Oratory in England, that is not all it is customary for the Holy See to do in so important a matter. We know Our Brief must make it plain that the foundation of this Congregation has been done by Our authority, and how at the same time we must lay down whatever else is necessary for its success. Moreover, Newman himself and his companions have petitioned in writing not only for the foundation, but for various favours that will facilitate it. Taking everthing into consideration, therefore, and remembering the great benefits we hope from it for the promotion of religion in England: by Our Apostolic authority we establish and declare to be established, the Congregation of the Oratory of St Philip Neri in England, on the model of the Congregation of the Oratory in Rome. And so that this important work may be started as soon as possible, we approve, in the meantime, as Newman petitions in his letter, that a House of the Congregation of the Oratory be erected in the very centre of England, near the city of Birmingham, at Maryvale, which house is to form one family under the government of the same superior, with another house of the Congregation of the Oratory, to be erected later in the city of Birmingham

placuerit, quantoque gaudio praeterea acceperimus, una cum eo plures alios ex Anglia, qui post accuratam de Religione pertractationem, Newmanii ipsius monitis, exemploque com-moti, ad Catholicam Ecclesiam redierunt; eundem Newman-ium in Anglica Congregatione Oratorii constituenda sequi, et imitari statuisse; magis clara res est, quam ut eam oporteat verbis explicare. Etenim in media Urbis luce res a Nobis gesta est, et mandato Nostro in S. Crucis in Jerusalem pulcherrimo Coenobio, ipsi Newmanio, ceterisque ejus sociis, satis amplum domicilium comparatum fuit, in quo, operam dante uno ex pientissimis Romanae Congregationis Oratorii Presbyteris domus S. Mariae in Vallicella, a Nobis ad illud Coenobium accersito, memorati superius Angli Ecclesiastici viri, ad vitam secundum Oratorii Congregationis praescripta ducendam informentur, et ei congregationi in Anglia fundandae pares evadant. Verum etsi ista, quae hactenus commemoravimus, aperte evincant, mentem Nostram de instituenda in Angliae Regno Oratorii Congregatione omnino perspicuam esse; non sunt tamen ejusmodi ut ad tam grave negotium, ea, qua ab Apostolica Sede fieri solet ratione finiendum, a Nobis nihil aliud requirant. Intelligimus enim, literis a Nobis scriptis constare debere, illius Congregationis institutionem auctoritate Nostra factam esse, et ea simul a Nobis statui oportere, quae pro majori ejusdem bono servanda sunt. Accessit his, Newman-ium ipsum, ejusque socios supplici allato libello id a Nobis postulavisse, et praeter Congregationis institutionem, alia ad illam juvandam, ornandamque flagitasse. Itaque rei totius Nobis propositae ratione diligenter perpensa, habitaque prae oculis magna utilitate, quam ad quotidie latiorem obtinendam in Anglia Religionis propagationem, ex ea re profecturam esse speramus; Congregationem Oratorii S. Philippi Nerii in Anglia, ad instar Romanae Oratorii Congregationis, Apostolica Nostra auctoritate instituimus, et institutam esse declaramus. Atque ut praeclaro huic operi, quanto citius fieri poterit, rite sapien-terque exequendo manus sine mora imponantur, probamus interea, ut quemadmodum Newmanii supplici petitione con-tinetur, Domus Congregationis Oratorii in ipso Angliae Centro, prope urbem Birminghamiam, apud S. Mariam in Valle erigatur, quae Domus unam eamdemque familiam, unius,

itself. By Our authority we appoint John Henry Newman superior of this House of the Oratory at Maryvale and of the one to be erected in the city of Birmingham, and we give him the faculty of choosing this once the four priest deputies, without having to follow the usual method of election laid down in the Constitutions of the Congregation[2]. And at this point we think it right to state that we approve of each house or family of the Congregation of the Oratory set up in England following the law that holds good for every Congregation of the Oratory, and being ruled and governed separately from all the other houses.[3] We highly approve of the intention of Newman and his companions, who, while performing all the functions of the sacred ministry in England, have at the same time this specially in mind, to aim at doing whatever they think will best promote the cause of religion in the bigger cities, and among those in the higher ranks, the more learned and generally among the more educated.[4] Thus they will follow with great profit to the Church, the example of St Philip Neri, who did so much for religion in Rome, and who is renowned for having devoted his whole life to the salvation of souls, and by his labours and exertions for having been the father in Christ of countless persons. We further grant that the Congregation of the Oratory set up in England, while bound by the rules of the house of the Roman Oratory, may observe them as contained in the new edition of the said rules, or Constitutions of the Oratory, drawn up in this year 1847 at Rome for the government of the English Congregation.[5] Finally, since we desire to confer spiritual benefits on the English Congregation of the Oratory, a special rescript will be drawn up, containing the various privileges of this kind we shall judge suitable for the Congregation established in England.[6] These are the matters which, by these presents, we have thought it Our duty to put in to writing, in order to lay the foundations of the Congregation of the Oratory in England. But since we know for certain that neither he who plants nor he who waters is anything, but only God who gives the growth, we are confident

ejusdemque Superioris regimini subditam constituat cum alia
Congregationis Oratorii domo, quae in ipsa urbe Birminghamia
in posterum instituenda est. Ipsum vero Joannem Henricum
Newmanium istius Congregationis Oratorii Domus ad S.
Mariam in Valle, et in urbe Birminghamia statuendae Super-
iorem auctoritate Nostra constituimus, tributa simul ei facultate
ut quatuor Presbyteros deputatos, hac vice ipse eligat, quin
oporteat nunc Institutorum Congregationis praescripta hanc
electionem respicientia servare. Atque hoc quidem loco signifi-
candum esse censuimus, a Nobis probari, ut unaquaeque domus,
seu familia Congregationis Oratorii in Anglia deinde statuenda,
ad normam legis generatim in tota Oratorii Congregatione
obtinentis, separatim ab aliis ejusmodi domibus, regatur, et
gubernetur. Laudamus plurimum Newmanii, ejusque sociorum
propositum, ut dum sacri ministerii muneribus omnibus in
Anglia fungentur, illud simul animo defixum praecipue habeant,
et efficiendum curent, quod ad Religionem in amplioribus
praesertim urbibus, atque inter splendidioris, doctioris, et
honestioris ordinis hominum coetus, amplificandam perducere
posse putaverint. Nam ita, cum magna Ecclesiae utilitate D.
Philippi Nerii, de Religione ipsa in Romana potissimum Urbe
optime meriti, praeclara exempla sectabuntur, de quo memor-
iae proditum est, illum in animarum salute procuranda totum
fuisse, et laboribus suis, rebusque gestis, innumeros paene filios
Christo peperisse. Concedimus autem ut Oratorii Congregatio
in Anglia instituta, quantumvis secundum Romanae Oratorii
domus leges se gerere debeat, habita tamen locorum, temporum,
rerumque diversitatis ratione, eas servare possit prout in nova
earumdem legum, seu Congregationis Oratorii Institutorum
editione hoc ipso anno MDCCCXLVII pro Anglicae Congregationis regimine Romae facta continentur. Optantes denique
Anglicam Congregationem Oratorii spiritualibus beneficiis
ornare, speciali a Nobis tribuendo rescripto ostendetur, quali-
bus hujus generis beneficiis Congregationem ipsam in Anglia
institutam, donandam interea esse judicaverimus. Haec sunt,
quae in praesentiarum, ad jacienda quodammodo in Anglia
Congregationis Oratorii fundamenta, literis mandari debere
putavimus. Sed illud tamen certum esse scientes, non eum qui
plantat esse aliquid, neque qui rigat, sed qui incrementum dat

that God will consolidate these beginnings of a good work with His blessing, and confirm them with His Divine assistance so that it brings forth rich fruit for His Church in England.

Given at Rome, at St Mary Major, under the ring of the Fisherman, on the XXVI day of November 1847, in the second year of Our Pontificate.

A. Card. Lambruschini.

---

[1]Carlo Rossi (1802-83). See the biographical note on him in *L.D.*, XII, pp. 437, 438.

[2]Provision is made in Decree XXVII for the election of four deputies, priests who have been ten years in the Congregation, as the superior's council. *Instituta Congregationis Anglicae Oratorii S. Philippi Nerii.* Rome 1847, p. 18.

[3]On the interpretation of this point during the quarrel with the London Oratory in 1855-6 see *L.D.*, XVII, p. 124.

[4]On the crucial phrase, which was inserted by Pius IX, and its bearing on the scope of the English Oratory see above, *Newman the Priest,* Chapter 6,§ 'Birmingham, London and the "Ordo honestior".'

[5]On the *aggiornamento* of the Oratorian Rule to English conditions by Newman, see above, *Newman the Priest,* Chapter 6,§ 'Newman's *aggiornamento* of the Oratory', and see further Appendix 3.

[6]On this rescript and its role in the quarrel with the London House in 1855-6 see *L.D.*, XVII, pp. 126, 127.

Deus, confidimus futurum, ut Deus ipse benedictione sua haec boni operis initia confirmet, atque ad uberrimos in eo Regno fructus Ecclesiae percipiendos, iis quae a Nobis statuta sunt, Divini auxilii sui robur adjiciat.

Datum Romae apud Sanctam Mariam Majorem sub Annulo Piscatoris die XXVI. Novembris MDCCCXLVII. Pontificatus Nostri Anno Secundo.

A. CARD. LAMBRUSCHINI.

Appendix 3.

EXTRACTS CONCERNING THE ORATORIAN RULE AS ADAPTED BY NEWMAN FOR ENGLAND, ROME 1847

INTRODUCTORY NOTE

On Newman's *aggiornamento* of the Italian Oratory to English conditions see above pp. 90–3. The two following extracts from his memoranda on the subject provide the alternative plans he was going to submit to the Roman authorities for adapting the Rule. In the event, it was the second plan which he submitted and which was permitted. This hinged on the distinction between narrative and legislative matter in the Rule.

The Constitutions as printed for the English Congregation in Rome 1847, make the distinction clear by printing the Decrees in a smaller typeface. See above, p. 339.

EXTRACTS CONCERNING THE ORATORIAN RULE AS ADAPTED BY NEWMAN FOR ENGLAND. ROME 1847[1]

G.

This was the first idea for dividing the Rule, but was not given it [in].

1. Regula S. Philippi sponte sua in duas partes dividitur; quarum prima tria priora capita continet cum Appendice, secunda pars capita quae subsequuntur a quarto ad decimum inclusivè.

2. Prior spectat ad res Congregationi *externas*, seu ad speciales modos per quos Patres pastorali munere funguntur; altera ad relationes inter Patres intercedentes, seu ad ipsam Instituti

[1] *B. Or. Ar.* File 63, No. 67.

formam atque naturam:–i.e. prior ad *Oratorium* pertinet, altera ad *Congregationem.*

3. Capita quae ad Congregationem pertinent, 4–10, seu Pars altera Regulae orditur hoc titulo; "De Statu Congregationis Oratorii *perpetuo*", cui subsequuntur verba haec, *"Nunc* statum et formam Congregationis nostrae *penitus immutabilem* in promptu ponimus, duobus decretis expressam,"—quare ea quae antecesserat, i.e. de Oratorio ipso seu exercitiis in Oratorio et Ecclesia habitis, in perpetuum stabilita non fuerint.

4. Porro in initio Appendicis, i.e. sub partem secundam absolutam, statim haec legimus, quae sonant:—"De *ipsis* Constitutionibus haec habentur. Si quid ambiguum fuerit in nostris Constitutionibus, Praepositus et Deputati declarabunt, *nullo tamen modo possint eas immutare,* derogare, aut aliqua ex parte innovare vel novas condere." Quamvis autem ex his Constitutionibus ita immutabilibus capita tria priora disertis verbis non eximantur, Appendix ipse tamen excluditur, in qua⟨m⟩ praecipua vis eorum capitum jam reservata est.

5. Illud praeterea ipsum quod scilicet ea quae ad Oratorium pertinent in Appendicem conjecta sunt, pro argumento est, Oratorii consuetudines et observantias esse minutiora quam ut includantur in Constitutionibus iis, in quibus perpetuus Congregationis status definitur.

5.[6.] Accedit quòd, in ipso capiti primo, non obscurè innititur posse esse, ut Oratorii exercitia immutentur; nam quod Sto Philippo moris erat in S. Hieronymo et in S. Ioanne Florentino, id aliter statim factum est a Stâ Mariâ in Vallicellâ. "Verè, locum orationi destinatum Oratorium dicimus; nam familiaris in ipso *nata* divini verbi tractatio, posthaec tractanda, jam *adulta,* et in Ecclesiam nostram translata, nomen minus accomodate retinuit Oratorii &c."

7. Quare nemini mirum videatur, si nos hoc tempore, ipsâ formâ Congregationis severè conservatâ, (quae in capitibus septem posterioribus continetur,) ad utilitatem tamen patriae nostrae credimus esse cessuram, (retractatis tribus prioribus,) pristinam potius quam postea constitutam Oratorii conditionem, scilicet quemadmodum in S. Hieronymo de Caritate exstitit, quando praedicationes Patrum rariores erant, colloquia aut saltem breves sermones magis ordinarii; namque alia remedia

Italiae sunt idonea saeculo decimo sexto, alia Angliae nono-
decimo.

8. Verumtamen, hac licet ex parte a Regula Congregationis
de Urbe recedentes, summopere cautum judicamus, ne in
materie difficillima nova temere definiamus et elaboremus: nam,
si per totos triginta annos Regulae suae periculum fecerunt
primi Philippini, eximii viri, priusquam approbationem
Pontificiam ei impetrarunt, quam temere factum foret a nobis,
qui novum exercitiorum ordinem in Oratorio, nondum usu
tractatum, in perpetuum stabilitum et numine Ecclesiastico
munitum vellemus!

9. Quod cum evidentissimum sit, hanc regulam in immutando
nobis proposuimus:– in locum alicujus *exercitii* in Constitutionibus de Urbe occurrentis quod retractandum erit, non
unum aliud nudè et absolute supponere, sed liberum aperire
campum substituto hoc vel illo vel isto, prout usu exercitium
quoddam speciale optimum esse docebitur.

H.

This was the second idea of dividing the Rule, which was
laid before the Pope, as it stands in the paper that follows, and
was allowed.

Textum Regulae S. Philippi ex duobus constare elementis,
inter se a principiis usque ad finem perpetuo immixtis, mani-
festum erit inspicientibus:– ex *narrationibus* ⟨quasi historicis⟩, in
indicativo conceptis, vel *traditionibus consuetudinum* Congregationis Romanae, et ex certo *decretorum* vel *constitutionum* numero,
quos immutari vel abrogari nullo modo licitum est.

Quibus ex duobus, constitutiones illae seu decreta expedi-
tissimum habent usum in patria nostra; consuetudines autem
traditae observari vix possunt.

Quare hoc expetimus ex Sanctitate sua, ut textus Regulae
nullam subeat mutationem, sed, (exceptis duobus vel tribus
minutioribus rebus,) remaneat totus, uti nunc est;—hac tamen
conditione, ut *decreta* ipsa, quae in imperativo vel futuro promun-
tur, sint nobis obligativa, *consuetudines* non item, sed tamquam
monitus et suggestiones, quem proxime, mutatis mutandis,
prout nobis optime videbitur, obtemperentur. Prodeat itaque

in typis integra Regula S. Philippi; decretorum autem series, quae in ea identidem occurrit, grandioribus litteris exhibeatur, vocabulo "Decretum" in margine hic illic apposito.

Quo autem id quod volumus clarius exponatur, exemplar Regulae tibi, Vir Amplissime, transmisimus, linea ducta ad illos periodos, quos decreta vel consuetudines censemus, ut perpetuae observationi commendamus.

Caeterum tria ex his decretis, quae, upote nobis incommodiora, abrogata vel immutata volumus, occurunt pp. . . .

I

The few points referred to in the last sentence Paper H had relation to the length of recreation, the power of receiving Prelates into our House, and allowing boys to come into the Fathers' rooms[2]. These were granted us, as was whatever remains ungranted in the *list* of alterations sent in with the sketch of the Brief, and alluded to in its § 6. Such as these— (taken from the List).

—Ne Patribus incumbat, ut quotidie quatuor in Ecclesiâ sermones habeant; cum autem sermones fiunt, ea rationes licita sit praedicanti, quae idonea est auditoribus, vel a Catholicâ fide alienis vel inter alienos degentibus."

Against this Mgr Palma wrote, "Si potra dire invece, In Sermonibus habendis de iis maxime erit opportunum pertractare, quae rei catholicae in Angliâ augendae aut confirmandae utilia esse possunt." Which was inserted as a decree.

And this. "Ne sit absolute vetita Congregationi, pro praesenti statu rei Catholicae in Anglia, Seminariorum, Collegiorum, Universitatum tractatio—(Exemplum ejus rei habes ap. Bullarium continuat. t. 8 p. 40)"

---

[2]Newman later revoked this third point. See above, p. 376.

Appendix 4

MEMORANDUM

THE EARLY DAYS OF THE ENGLISH ORATORY [9 JUNE 1848]

INTRODUCTORY NOTE

This is an important account, written soon after the event, by Newman himself, of the process of the choice of the Oratory as a vocation for himself and his friends. He deals in turn with their examination of the Vincentians, the Redemptorists, and the project of a theological College in England. Then follow the choice of the Oratory, the Malta plan[1] and the beginning of their noviciate in the monastery of S. Croce (Rome).

This Memorandum should be completed by that of 10 May 1878 *On the choice of Vocation in Rome after Conversion* (Oratory Papers, No. 36, 10 May 1878). This was to rebut an assertion that Newman had applied to the Jesuits and had been refused admission. The long extract from the Decree Book (Oratory Papers, 25 January 1869, below, Appendix 6), takes up the thread at the foundation of the English Oratory on 1 February 1848 and brings the notices up to April 1, 1867.

Taken together these three Papers provide a fairly detailed chronology of Newman's Oratorian life for about twenty years from the beginnings of his vocation.

On the particular stage covered by the Paper of 9 June 1848, see above, pp. 75–82: 'Unrealized Projects of Vocation'.

THE EARLY DAYS OF THE ORATORY[2]

When St John and I left England, we were quite undecided about our vocation. Dr Whitty had spoken to us a good deal about the Lazarists, saying that they admitted of the union of

---

[1] See *L.D.*, XII, pp. 71–5.
[2] *B. Or. Ar*, File 63 No. 67.

reading with active life, and the one object of attraction we felt in Paris was their House and Church, where lies the body of St Vincent. The General being absent, we were not very well received there, and we seemed to feel that though a most important body of religious, they did not give to theology and literature that place in their system which we wished. We called on the Jesuits, and were much struck with them and their half empty House in the Rue des Postes.[3]

At Milan there were no orders established, and hardly congregations. We heard of the Barnabites as being almost in the hands of the (Austrian) Government; we went to see some of the Sunday Oratories, instituted in imitation of the Oratory of St Philip, and were much interested in them.[4]

At Genoa we received great kindness from the Jesuit Father Jourdan, and certainly felt drawn to the Society.[5]

When we had been some little time in Rome, St John said, 'We really ought to go to St Philip.' The idea of the Oratory had gone out of my head, and we had been occupied in going to the Seven Baslicas &c.

At this time our minds were going after two separate ideas. The one was that of becoming Redemptorists, seeing that it was a new Congregation, allowed of modification, (i.e. of being made to take in theology) better than an older one, and was founded by a Saint who had more to do than any one yet in changing the old system of theological teaching, so far as it was changed, (or could be changed). We had been in the company of one of them when F Marchi took us to the Catacombs on St Andrew's Day, and we saw him in the small Redemptorists' Church on January 9. 1847, he calling on us on the 12th, and promising his rule. He then left for Naples, and, before he returned, our thoughts were fixed in another direction.

The other idea was that of forming a theological school, under Propaganda, in England—a sort of English Propaganda College. I wrote to Dr Wiseman on this subject November 27th

[3] See *L.D.*, XI, p. 244.
[4] See *L.D.*, XI, pp. 248–66.
[5] See *L.D.*, XII, p. 4.

or December 16 more probably the latter[6]. His answer, highly approving of the idea, did not come to us till February 8, and meanwhile our thoughts had taken a very different turn. I had seemed to feel clearly, that it would not become me to take up theology as a professed object, much less teaching theology. The suspicions of Dr Grant[7] of the Scotch College about me, the criticisms in the schools upon my Essay on Development by F Passaglia[8], which F Mazio[9] seemed to defend, and perhaps the affair of St Isidore, seemed to force it on me that it could not be my line.

Meanwhile we had gained an introduction to the Chiesa Nuova, F Theiner had called on us, I suppose, in November; and on St Stephen's Day, he said Mass for our intention at St Philip's private altar and communicated us. On January 10 we went under F Theiner's guidance to the Sunday (musical) Oratory, which we did not think much of; some days later, we asked to borrow of him, the Annals of the Oratory, which he sent with the Pregi. On the 22nd St John called on him to ask him some questions about the Oratory, hinting to him that Dr Wiseman, before we started, had turned our thoughts towards it.

At this time I began a Novena to St Peter, going daily to the limina Apostolorum from January 17 ⟨Eve of Cath. S Petr. Rom.⟩ to January 25.

We had been to the Madre Makrena with Ld. Clifford on November 25 who had promised to pray for our vocation.

We had all along written to England (i.e. Maryvale) and Langres, about our thoughts and inquiries; viz. November 11.16.29, December 7.9.16.25.31. January 12.17. February 3.8.[10] And had had answers February 1.4.5.6.8.16.

At the end of January (29th) F Theiner asked us to dine at the Chiesa Nuova on the Feast of St Papias and Maurus, which St John was able to. He saw what an Oratorian dinner was, and went into the quire at High Mass or Vespers.

---

[6]See *L.D.*, XI, p. 307 for a reference to this.

[7]See *L.D.*, XII, p. 432.

[8]See *L.D.*, XII, p. 437.

[9]See *L.D.*, XII, p. 435.

[10]These dates do not seem to tally with those published in *L.D.*, XI and XII.

At this time we began to think definitely of introducing the Oratory into England, if we were allowed to do so. My reasons were such as these: that, whereas the tastes of all of us were very different, the Oratory allowed greater scope for them than any other Institution; again it seemed more adapted than any other for Oxford and Cambridge men.

We mentioned it to Mgr Brunelli, and I put into his hands a Paper which I had drawn up for Cardinal Fransoni[11] on the subject. This, I think was on February 14, and on Sunday the 21st Mgr Brunelli mentioned it to the Pope, who was pleased to approve of it.

He also wished me to send for the rest of our party, said he would give us a house, provide us with an Oratorian Father, instead of sending a Father to England (as I had proposed) and send us all home together at the year's end. In consequence I wrote home at once for the rest February 23.

Nothing seems to have occurred till March 14, when I find that St John, Coffin, (who had come to Rome but had not yet decided on the Oratory,) and I communicated at St Philip's Altar, F Theiner saying Mass.

On the Annunciation we dined with him at the Chiesa Nuova; and in the afternoon I went with him, Prince Hohenlohe, and a laybrother or aspirant, to the Ponte Molle.

Meanwhile the prospect rose of our being sent to Malta, in the following way:— Mgr Beccatini (Bettachini)[12] the Oratorian Bishop of Ceylon, (or a part of it,) had come to Rome, and in his way passed through Malta. There he found an Oratorian House with only one Father, an old man, remaining in it. Other bodies were naturally looking out for the property on his death: the property consisting not only of the House, but of a Church, well stored with vestments and a good library, and all of marble, and in a fine situation overlooking the sea, and near the quarter of the English soldiers and sailors. To this might be added that it was on English ground, in a most central situation, opening the way to the East, if we ever were able to strengthen or add to the Oratories there, and of special

---

[11]Latin text in *L.D.*, XII, pp. 36–40. See above *Or. P.* No. 2. pp. 151–6.

[12]See *L.D.*, XII, p. 111, note 4.

importance at the moment from Malta being the refuge of various apostate priests who had left Italy and set up a press there. As English we had a sort of claim to the property, and, as the sole tenant was old, no time was to be lost. Such was the representation made us by F. Theiner.

We made reply that we would do whatever the Pope wished—and, as not insensible to the advantage of the offer, yet not seeing how to reconcile it with the Pope's intentions about us, we wished to have no opinion about it. This we stated as clearly as possible to Mgr Brunelli, on F. Theiner pressing us to mention the subject to him, but it was impossible to do so at all without seeming to be asking for what we were but putting before him. On March 29, the day on which Penny and Stanton arrived in Rome, we were informed by Mgr Brunelli that the Pope had given us the House at Malta.

Nothing happened till after Easter. On the Thursday in Easter Week (April 8) St John and I went into retreat at St Eusebio—the day after we came out, April 18, F. Theiner took us to Cardinal Ostini, who had lately been Prefect of the Congregation of Bishops and Regulars, under which the Oratory (at least in Italy) is placed. Cardinal Ostini had already spoken to the Pope about us, and seemed to be taking the place of Mgr Brunelli, who on April 26 left Rome for Spain. This however put us into some difficulty, for in proportion as we got under the patronage of Cardinal Ostini, did we seem to be losing the patronage of Propaganda, to which we really belonged, and our friends at the Chiesa Nuova did not seem unwilling that we should lose its patronage.

For the moment, however, we could do nothing to hinder this effect; F. Theiner, on the other hand, with great zeal was hurrying us forward in his own direction. He wished us to present a memorial to the Pope or Propaganda praying for immediate ordinations &c. Meanwhile we had taken advice from friends at Propaganda, in consequence of which St John and I called upon Professor Palma, on April 30, hearing that he had more influence and got through more business than any one attached to Propaganda. The substance of our representation to him is contained, I believe in a memorandum of mine dated April 25, in which, after stating that the Pope had sent

for our friends, and promised us a house and Oratorian Father
in Rome, I go on to say that the Malta plan required that
there should be priests in Malta who were desirious of becoming
Oratorians and so would allow us soon to return to England.
—*were* there such there? 2. that we must go to Malta with a
brief from the Pope, or the old Oratorian Father would not
admit us—3. that we had no money to go there, and 4. that
Fr Theiner wished us to ask for the priesthood soon.

These requests were sufficient to show the great difficulty of
the Malta plan, tempting as it was; but another circumstance
had come to light [two] days before, on Dalgairns' and my calling
on Cardinal Ostini, which increased our suspicion of it[13].—It
was this; that the Pope wishing to keep us at Rome, yet wishing
at the same time to gratify us, (as he thought) in regard to
Malta, intended to divide into two parties, sending some of us
there, and keeping the rest at Rome.[14] This was so unpalatable
to all of us, that, with the wish of all, I presented a memorial
to the Pope to the effect, that, though we were quite at his
disposal, yet his original idea had been "formare in Roma un
corpo di novizii Filippini sotto la cura paterna" of his Holiness,
⟨and we were unwilling to lose the benefit of it⟩. This memorial
was graciously received; the Pope decided (May 2) that we
should remain all together in Rome, and the Malta scheme
was abandoned.

The kind zeal of F. Theiner now took a different turn; it was
to get us into the House at Rome where we were to perform
our noviciate, and to provide us with a novice master. Almost
as soon as the Pope heard of our acquiescence in his wish
that we should all come to Rome, he had pitched upon a house
for our reception. We were not told which it was, but Mgr
Brunelli said it was a bellissimo sito. Some of our friends
thought it was Sta Balbina, from the circumstance that the
Pope went unexpectedly there a day or two after he heard
about our wishes—but he had also been at the same time to
Sta Croce, and that was the place which he really destined for us.

[13]Marginal note by Newman. Dalgairns and Bowles arrived April 26, the day
of Mgr Brunelli's departure.

[14]Marginal note by Newman: On 28 April Dr Wilson (Bishop of Hobart) said
Mass for our intention and communicated us all at St Philip's altar.

30

In the first days of May it came out where we were to be, and on the 9th F. Theiner called on me, with the permission of Cardinal Ostini backed by a letter from the abbot of Sta Croce, urging us to go and see the rooms with a view to taking possession. We settled to go there with him on the 11th; but thinking better of it, and not having heard any thing from the Pope, who was to send us there, we determined to defer it, and wrote to F. Theiner to this effect. In about a week, however, for some reason or other we made an appointment with him to go to Sta Croce; and then I believe in consequence of Palma's advice, we put it off.

On the 26th, St Philip's day, St John and I received the Subdiaconate, which, as well as the orders which followed, was owing to F. Theiner's urgency with Cardinal Ostini.

In the meantime, F. Theiner had found for us an Oratorian Father to teach us the costumi and exercises of the Oratory. The Pope's intention was to have got us a Father from Fermo or Recanati: but when the Malta plan was in agitation, he (i.e. F. Theiner) mentioned F. Rossi of the Chiesa Nuova as a suitable person to go with us. He now mentioned him again; and at his instance I mentioned him to Palma, and wrote a Supplicat to the Pope petitioning for him to be sent to Sta Croce with us, which the Pope granted. This must have been at the beginning of June, though I have a letter of F. Rossi's at [sic] early as May 22.

Before this, however, on May 27, while we were in retreat at Propaganda, between our ordinations, a letter came to me from F. Theiner, pressing me to go to Sta Croce, saying that the Abbot had been expecting us a fortnight since, and that it would have a bad appearance, if I did not. Directly that our ordinations were over May 30, I wrote to the abbot, apologizing for the delay, and proposing to visit him at once, for which we had now Palma's leave.

We called accordingly at Sta Croce with Father Rossi the next day May 31—and inspected the rooms. Propaganda, under the Pope's directions, was to supply us with furniture, and we were to get together there by the end of June.

I have already noticed incidentally the arrival of the rest of our party. Penny and Stanton had arrived on Monday in

Holy Week (March 29) and Dalgairns and Bowles on April 26. All four went, immediately on their arrival, to the Passionist House on Monte Celio; where Coffin joined them, I suppose the beginning [sic] of April, having made up his mind to be an Oratorian, in his retreat at St Eusebio which ended March 31.

The Rooms at Sta Croce were ready by June 21, on which day Penny and Stanton took up their residence there: Bowles and Coffin followed on the 23rd; Dalgairns on the 24th; St John on the 26th, and I on 28th. Father Rossi joined us on July 2.

There we resided till November or December,[15] leaving in the following order:—Dalgairns and Stanton left November 12; Coffin on November 27; Penny on Dec 4; St John and I on December 6; Bowles stayed behind and went into Propaganda, where he remained till the Spring of 1848, when he left for England, arriving at Maryvale May 16. Fr Rossi left Sta Croce Nov. 27, which was the day our Brief came to us.

We went out of Rome during our residence there for the following times altogether, reckoning from the beginning of June:—I for 23 days; Penny for 1 day; St John for 25 days; Dalgairns for 6 days; Coffin for 12 days, Bowles for 7 days; and Stanton, I think, for 14 days. F. Rossi was absent for 48 days.

The Ordinations were as follows: St John, Dalgairns and I came up to Sta Croce priests; Coffin was tonsured July 17, and received minor orders July 18. Coffin, Bowles, and Stanton the Subdiaconate August 1. Stanton the Diaconate on the 8th. Stanton the Priesthood, Aug 15. [Penny?] the subdiaconate Sept 18; Penny and Coffin the Diaconate Oct 24; and the Priesthood Oct 31. Bowles was ordained deacon and Priest after we left in the Spring of 1848.

Our time at Sta Croce was spent, first in learning the exercises &c of the Oratory, and next in transacting business at Propagands with reference to our Brief ⟨our Rule⟩ the ordinations, and the privileges which we hoped to gain from Propaganda.

On July 5 we assumed the Oratorian cassock, and began the Exercises.

---

[15]Marginal note by Newman: Dr Wiseman induced the Pope to curtail the time of our residence in Rome, which originally was to have been a year.

On the 9th of August the Pope paid us a visit, going up stairs into Father Rossi's room, and inspecting our rooms above and below. Cardinal Ostini called on us 4 times, Cardinal Fransoni once, as also did Cardinals Maii [sic] and Lambruschini. Dr Wiseman dined with us Aug. 1.

On August 4 I left with Palma my sketch for our Brief[16], the Pope having committed it to him for the sake of despatch. On Sept 8 the Brief was finished, having been already read to the Pope and received his corrections. (It had been drawn up from his instructions.) [17] and was read to us by Mgr Palma. It was not put into our hands till Nov 27.

We had some difficulty about the Rule, part of it being inapplicable to England, yet it being impossible to say how much. My first idea was to separate it into what was external and what was internal to the Congregation;[18] the latter admitting of an exact fulfilment, while the former would be but partially observed. But on second thoughts I thought it better to divide it into the Decrees, and what was narrative in it or historical[19]; the Decrees being with very slight alterations observable, and[20] on the other hand the narrative or traditionary portion being in great measure inexpedient. On Mgr Palma's mentioning this to the Pope, he acceded; and he ordered us to print the Rule at the Propaganda Press, after the Chiesa Nova [sic] copy with the two or three alterations in the Decrees which we requested, with the understanding that we were only bound in strictness to observe the Decrees.

As to the privileges of Propaganda, the Pope granted them to us on June 6. On July 11, he granted us permission to make our Exercises for Orders in our own House, as the Philippini at Rome, and when we left Rome ⟨he gave us the body of S. Valentinus, and a daily plenary indulgence for our altar at Maryvale, and⟩ we received 600 scudi from Propaganda for our expences.

[16]Marginal note by Newman: vid appendix E.
[17]Marginal note by Newman (the first ten words deleted by him): We had some difficulty in finding the brief did not vid. appendix F.
[18]Marginal note by Newman: vid appendix G.
[19]Marginal note by Newman: vid appendix H.
[20]Marginal note by Newman: vid Appendix I. [The Appendices G, H and I are to be found above pp. 430–3].

During the time we were at Rome we were presented to the Pope, as follows:—Nov. 22. 1846 St John and I on our arrival; —April[;] Penny, Coffin, and Stanton on their arrival; June 20. St John and I on our ordination; Nov 11. Dalgairns to kiss hands; Nov 28, Penny, St John, Bowles, Knox and I with F Rossi to take leave. Dec 3. in the morning St John and I when we went to present our (printed) Brief.

On leaving Sta Croce, where the Abbot and Monks had treated us with the greatest kindness, we presented them with a Benedictine Missal[21].

[21]Marginal note by Newman: vid. Appendix K. [This contained the inscription in the missal, printed in *L.D.*, XII, p. 142, note 3.]

Appendix 5.

ALTERNATIVE VERSIONS OF LETTER V

INTRODUCTORY NOTE

These earlier versions of letter V. of the *Remarks on the Oratorian Vocation* are reproduced here on account of the fuller treatment they offer on the subject of obedience in the Oratory. See above, Introductory Note to Paper No. 24, p. 299.

REMARKS ON THE ORATORIAN VOCATION: ALTERNATIVE VERSION OF LETTER V

February 28. 1856

So far as the Oratory adds any thing to the perfection of its subjects, beyond their perfection as secular priests, this perfection does not 'ie in any counsel of fasting, or of poverty, or of renunciation of the domestic affections, or of external inconveniences; nor again of vow. The question follows, after considering what its perfection does not consist in, has it any perfection above that of the secular priest, and if so what.

The question is this—whereas, as I have said, perfection consists in the exact, ready, pleasant performance of the precepts of the New Law, and the avoidance of known venial sin in performing them; and whereas it is not to be expected that any one will succeed in this exact fulfilment who aims at nothing more, or can possess the spirit to obey exactly, who has not the spirit to obey heartily and generously, and since such generous obedience is in other words the obedience which embraces counsels as well as precepts, and in this way the observance of some or other counsels are [sic] necessary for perfection, and whereas chastity and the vow of it are the great counsels which every priest has embraced, is there any other counsel over and above this, and parallel to this, which the Fathers of the Oratory take upon them on entering the Oratory, as their special instrument of going on to perfection.

Of course there is one, and that both from the nature of the case, and from the express appointment of St Philip and the declaration of his first disciples, and that is *obedience,* though not the vow of it. ⟨This is expressed in the apophthegm which is found in the Pregi "Vita communis, mortificatio maxima."⟩

I might consider this obedience in three points of view: as obedience to the *community,* obedience to its *Superiors,* and obedience to the *Rule.* And much might be said under the two latter heads of Superiors and Rule, as bringing out what I mean by the perfection of a Father of the Oratory: but they would draw me aside from the direct line of these remarks, and therefore I shall pass them by. Superiors could not properly exist without a Rule, and there was no Rule at the beginning of the Oratory. What always was from the first was Community; this was its very idea. In other religious institutions obedience is directed to a Rule or to a vow, and the community is obeyed on that account; here obedience is paid to the community as a first principle; and hence it is both necessary to the Oratory from the nature of the case, and its peculiarity as distinguished from other Congregations. I shall consider then obedience to the Community as our special means of perfection.

Among regulars the vow is the elementary principle of religious society; they obey because they have solemnly promised to do so. It is otherwise with us, we obey for the sake of obedience; we obey because we choose to obey, and for nothing ·else. Obedience then is our elementary principle, and thus we differ from others who live in community. And again, I say that obedience is not only special to us, but necessary from the nature of the case; for without this obedience for obedience for obedience [sic] sake, though we lived in one house, we should fall back into the state of secular priests. Thus we are kept out of that state, or rather elevated into something more than that state by the faculty of living together: since we are not obliged to do so, it is a matter of counsel. It is the counsel peculiar to us as members of the Oratory, and the means of our sanctification.

It is not every one who has the gift of living in community; not every holy soul, not every good secular priest, can live in community. Great as is the privilege, supposing he has the power and will, few have the opportunity, and fewer still the gift. Very few have the gift; for you will observe I have already refused to ascribe it to the Regular. The members of a religious order often are not members of a given community at all; today they are here, tomorrow there, ⟨sent about from place to place.⟩ They are under Superiors, they are under Rules; but not under a Community. Again, supposing them bonâ fide to live and die in a community: still they cannot help it; they do not do so, because they can do it, but, because whether they could do it or no, their vow compels them. They have great merit of course, the less they really have the gift of bearing community life; I only say that not because they happen to live together, have they that gift. It is a gift, which is rare, if the experience of life is to be our guide.

It is more than rare, it scarcely exists, as an abstract principle, and without the assistance of association, habit, and attachment. It would not have been possible for St Philip, without a continual miracle, to have formed a community, depending for its union on nothing but the resolution of its members to be united. A liking for each other is of course the support and sustenance and reward of the union I am speaking of; but, even granting such mutual attachment, how rare is the gift of enduring domestic union without a vow! Though woman is inferior to man and depends on him, though marriage does not take place without mutual liking, and deliberate purpose, though the pledge of children is added, yet all this is not enough for the security of the union without a vow. Can there be a great[er] proof of the rarity of the gift of obedience as the elementary bond of community life? Difficult as it is for man and wife to live together, much more difficult is the domestic association of man with man. Even when they like and respect each other, it is most rare for men to live together and to persevere in doing so. Accordingly we pray in the devotions of the Oratory continually for perseverance. Hence it is that this gift deserves to be our peculiarity, and the instrument of our perfection. It *is* truly a great counsel of perfection, and equal to many others. Hence it is that, when a Father of the Chiesa Nuova, on St Philip's death, thought of passing to a stricter religion, FF. Baronius and Tarugi both were earnest, or even tragic in dissuading him. "Quid fecisti?" said the former "parcat tibi Deus."[1] "I conjure you" said the latter "to put aside the temptation." For they felt that to remain firm in a good purpose without vow was as fine and acceptable an offering to the Most High as could well be offered, as sure to draw a blessing upon the offerer, and as sure a human means, as could be selected, for raising the general standard of his obedience, and for leading him to that exactness in fulfilling the precepts of the New Law which is the substance of charity and the ⟨sure⟩ way to heaven.

Febr 29. 1856

I have said that the Perfection of the Oratory lies in Community Life, and I have defined Community Life to mean obedience or conformity to a Community for the sake of that obedience, in opposition to obedience on account of a vow. Further, I have said that human affection, so far from being excluded in the Oratory, is the animating principle of that obedience, not to the exclusion indeed of supernatural charity, far from it—but as the vehicle and instrument of that charity. In consequence the vocation to the Oratory, or what the Rule means, by men being "idonei"[2] and as it were "born for the Oratory", lies in the desire and capacity of this obedience or conformity to a Community, that is, not to a Community in the abstract, but to a given community; it is the will and power to live a community life, ⟨as a Priest,⟩ with certain other given Priests.

There is something very peculiar and special in this; and now I shall consider 1. what that conformity is. 2. what the human affection 3. the mode of forming an Oratory—and 4. the mode of adding members to it, or continuing it.

A community[3] is more than a lodging house—it is more than a number of priests living in one house. It is a home and family; it is a number of Priests living as one family; and hence the Superior is, in the Oratory, called simply "Father"—and the rest are called by their Christian names. A community is a

---

[1] i.e. 'What have you done'? 'May God forgive you.' [See p. 417.]

[2] Fit, suitable or proper persons.

[3] This paragraph has 1. before these two words; it was cancelled by Newman, nor does he follow out the numbering 1–4, as given in the preceding paragraph.

whole or unity; it has one spirit, one mind, one view of things, one action; and the obedience which it exacts from its members, in which lies their perfection, is acquiescence, concurrence in this one spirit, view and action, as an act of loyal and dutiful submission.

March 1. 1856

For perfection some observance of counsels is necessary. In the perfection of Regulars, the three great counsels and the vows attached to them have been assigned. A Father of the Oratory, as being a Priest, is under one of these three, that of chastity—but not as belonging to the Oratory. The Counsel of Perfection which belongs to us is that of *community life*;—according to the Filippine maxim, Vita communis mortificatio maxima.

It is tempered to us by the permission, or rather the injunction, of having and cherishing a personal affection for the members of the community. It is this personal feeling which draws us to the Community, and keeps us in it; heightened of course and perfected by that supernatural charity, which enables us to retain and strenghten an affection, year after year, which, if left simply human, would surely die away. Perseverance in that affection is the work of grace.

Now then, when, having said as much as this, I come to the third and fourth point, which I wished to urge, how to make and how to keep up an Oratory, I can only consider them truly, by keeping strictly in view the first and second, viz that the vocation of the Oratory consists in community life animated by personal affection. The Oratory, as such, is this and nothing else; an Oratory is a community of priests who love each other; to make an Oratory is to get together a number of priests ⟨and ecclesiastics⟩ who love each other; and to continue it is to add to it a succession of others who love its members and love each other.

We start then with supposing Priests probatæ vitæ⁴— serious, religious men, who wish to fulfil their mission, and save their souls; who do not seek their ease or comfort, but feel

---

⁴i.e. 'of approved life'.

that it is not easy to please God, that it is not satisfactory to have heavy responsibilities, that it is very desirable to live to their Lord's glory, and who wish helps for doing all this.

Can these good Priests live together? they may be able—they may not be able. Let them try. I consider that the proof of their vocation lies in this.

Accordingly in founding a new Oratory, it does not seem to me enough for given individuals to have passed a time of probation at any existing one. The question is, whether, when they come together by themselves, they can continue together. Without a nucleus of this sort, from the nature of the problem, no Oratory can begin.

Two persons may be able to live with a third who cannot live with each other. One pair may live together, another pair may live together—and all four may not live together. Every thing which is to last must have a basis or formation. The formation or element of an Oratory lies in this—good and serious priests who can live together without vows.

Time alone can tell when men can live together. One, two, three years is the least trial to be satisfactory.

And, when this is passed well, when once we get a few priests who can live together, and who wish to live (by the terms of the problem) after St Philip's pattern, an Oratory is forthwith formed. I do not see any thing more that is wanted for the vocation of the individuals, for the formation of the body.

This quite agrees with what we were told at Rome, when we first went there, and with the Pope's conduct towards us. The first question which I was asked by the Jesuits at Propaganda was, Can you all live together? When it was found that we already knew each other, and had lived together as Protestants, the work was thought half done. And so again at Santa Croce, there was no need of a long noviciate—there was nothing which any Father of the Chiesa Nuova could teach us. There was no particular training necessary—the simple question was, Could we live together? It was not necessary to be in Rome, it was not necessary to be at the Chiesa Nuova to determine this; it must be determined by the past and the future.

If this be not so, we had a very insufficient time[5] at Rome—if

[5]Erased original text: noviciate.

all was done that was necessary, then the Oratorian has very little, as such, to learn—he has not so much to be trained as to be tried.

Such being the foundation and the formation of an Oratory, we come next to its continuation and increase, and how subjects are to be added to it. And here I begin with a caution, lest I be misunderstood. It will commonly happen that the first comers are young—it is common and expedient—because the minds of the young are more easily formed. But if they are young, they have to undergo a double discipline, first for the Priesthood, second for the Oratory; they are in a sort of seminary as well as in a noviciate. Let us separate the two ideas. I am not speaking of these new comers as under training for the Priesthood—I am not asking how they are to get the knowledge and the spirit of good Priests. I am viewing them simply as candidates for the Oratory, that is, as those, who being Priests, are to live happily in community, and that from love of the body and its individual members.

This then being taken into account, I say the process is the same. The simple object of the noviciate, so to call it, is to ascertain whether they can live comfortably in the body they have joined, and can take obedience to it as that mortification which is to lead them to the perfection of a secular Priest. They are not properly novices; the Rule calls them "tyrones"; the custom of Italy "giovani"; Van Espen, in his Canon Law, calls them "probationers." They are being tried, not formed, considered as candidates for the Oratory. This principle applies, I consider, in its fulness to those who come to the Oratory already Priests. We have only one thing to do to them; to make out whether, being good Priests and desiring to be better, they can live in community.

Returning then to my original formation, two, three, four, or more priests, who have already found they can live together, I suppose them to increase their numbers by a series of trials of individual candidates to live with these three or four. And here, by the way, you see how it is, that Oratories differ so much in spirit; for these original three or four are likely to perpetuate the spirit with which they start, for those will join them who love them and are drawn to them and others will not—or, if others do, they will not stay—or if they stay, they will tend to the disorganization of the body.

Here we see too, how it is, that any Oratory, which is to grow well, must grow very slowly. It cannot take up many members well and also quickly. There must be a process of digestion by assimilation, like that in the animal economy, and any Oratory, which is premature in growth, is likely to be premature in dissolution.

. . . if I am asked what are the direct duties of a Father of the Oratory, I say they are those of public instruction, and the sacraments. These are the duties of all, though of one more than another.

Next to these, I think the Father of the Oratory may do, and have to do, according to his powers and openings, every thing which a secular priest can do, except the care of temporals; though an exception must be made even here, in the case of the curate or missioner, if the Oratory have a Parish. But the general rule is laid down in a maxim of the Blessed Sebastian, which I have quoted already. 'As far as possible, without omission of community acts, we must aid our neighbour and serve all persons.' It is his duty to make his Oratory as useful as he can.

Appendix 6.

FROM THE DECREE BOOK OF THE BIRMING-HAM ORATORY 25 JANUARY 1869

INTRODUCTORY NOTE

This important analysis of the history of the Birmingham Oratory, 1848–1869, was first detected as Newman's work by the present editor, and has been confirmed as such by C. S. Dessain, from internal evidence of style, although only the opening entry is in Newman's hand. Newman liked symbolic dates, and '25 January', the feast of St Paul's conversion, pinpoints as nearly as is humanly possible, his decision on the Oratory in 1847 in Rome (see above, p. 90, and Oratory Papers, Memorandum, p. 434, 9 June 1848).

The Decree Book contains the formal decrees of events of major interest to the community; it is not a Diary or Community Annals. This accounts for the formal, almost legal, phraseology.

When read in conjunction with *Trevor* I and II (up to 1869), this Index provides an invaluable summary of this complicated series of events, as seen from Newman's standpoint.

FROM THE DECREE BOOK OF THE BIRMING-HAM ORATORY

p. 133
1869
C.D. Jany 25
417

Resolved to allow Father Superior to insert into this book an Index, which he is preparing, of its contents during the foregoing twenty one years of the Congregation.

[*This entry in Newman's handwriting.* Ed.]

pp. 136–152
First Head   Historical Notices

The references are to the numbers of the Decrees as marked in the Register. [*This is in the text.* Ed.]

I. Historical Notices of the Congregation
1848

1848 Feb 1.	The English Congregation of the Oratory established for Maryvale and Birmingham, as the Mother House, at Maryvale, on the
Foundation of the English Oratory	first Vespers of the Purification. Preface Form used on the occasion ibid Foundation Members, seven:– F. F. Newman; Penny, St John, Dalgairns, Bowles, Coffin, and Stanton, of whom F. Bowles, being still at Rome, was not admitted till May 25 following. There was one Probationer (Novice) Thomas F. Knox. Three Lay Brothers ibid Creation of Decennials ibid
Feb. 2.	Nomination of Deputati 1
Letters	Formal Letters to Ecclesiastical Authorities announcing the establishment' of the Congregation 2 Filling up of Offices ibid (no mention of Confessor. Our missioner at Maryvale was F. A. St John)
Feb. 4	Association of Masses with the English secular Priesthood 3
11 St Wilfrid's Fathers	Reception of St Wilfrid's Community into our Congregation; five, viz F. W. Faber, W. A. Hutchinson, H. A. Mills, F. A. Wells, N. Darnell. 5
11 Rambler	Relations entered into with the Rambler Magazine 6
25 St Valentine	Reception of St Valentine's Body, the gift of the Holy Father, and as it were, the foundation of our prospective Church 10
March 2 Brief	Formal transmission of our Brief to the Ecclesiastical Authorities in Great Britain and Ireland. 11

Ap. 18.	Acceptance of our Bishop's offer of ground for House, Oratory and Church at Derret End, Birmingham, on the condition that we found it practicable soon to commence building 18
June 20 Bayswater	Negotiation with the Revd Mr O'Neale of London about the House and Land at Bayswater offered by him to the Congregation; the present site of St Mary of the Angels
July 22	The Father who had been pro tempore Novice Master resigns it to Fr Faber. 23
Aug. 28 Plan for Bayswater House	Purchase of additional land at Bayswater contemplated and provided for, and a plan of House and Chapel obtained from Mr Hansom. 27 & 76
Septr 29 Derrit End	Acceptance for three years of our Bishop's offer to provide us with a Mission House near Derrit End, under the hope of our forming a Fund in that time for the erection of a Church and Oratory on the grounds which he offered to us in April last. 30 (There was a question, in consequence of an offer made us, whether we should not go to Nottingham instead of Birmingham)
Leaving Maryvale for St Wilfrid's	In prospect of this removal into Birmingham, the relinquishment of Maryvale is agreed upon, and the removal to St Wilfrid's of that portion of the Congregation, which is not engaged in Birmingham. 30, 31
Octr. 5	Additions made to St Wilfrid's (to fit it to the purpose of our Community) 32 During this year, there is a gradual development of the body internally by advancing the members in the ecclesiastical and Oratorian course, i.e. presenting for Orders, and dispensing with the triennium and decennium. Fr Wilfrid Faber also is made Novice-Master. 14.19.22.23.36 &c

1849

1849 Feb. 1	Fr Superior, with the Deputati, F. F. St John, Dalgairns, (who with the Father are considered to represent the Congregatio
Alcester Street	Deputata) and with Fr Bowles take possession of premises (not at Derrit End or provided by the Bishop, but) in Alcester Street, for House and Chapel, the solemn opening of the latter being on the 2nd. · 46
St Wilfrid's	Also leave of absence at St Wilfrid's (for want of room in Alcester Street) being given to Fr Coffin, as Rector of the House, F. F. Penny, Stanton and Faber, Hutchison and Mills, triennials, all the Probationers (or novices) 6 in number, and some Lay-brothers. ibid
Feb 24 Birmingham Mission	In compliance with the Bishop's wish, though he cannot provide a Mission House (vid. 30) the Congregation undertakes a Mission in Birmingham for the present, without binding themselves to do so, when possessed of an Oratorian House and Church. 49
Feb. 28	Our missioner at Birmingham is Fr Bernard Dalgairns. 50
May 28 Mission in London King William Street	Resolution to send subjects of the Congregation to London (to King William Street, Strand.) with the view of establishing ultimately a separate House there; viz. two of the Deputies. F. F. Coffin and Stanton, Fr Faber as Rector of the new Community, two other Wilfridians, F. F. Hutchison and Wells, Fr Knox, two Probationers (Philip Gordon and John Edward Bowden) and sundry Lay-Brothers. The other members who are at St Wilfrid's recalled to Birmingham, viz. F. F. Penny, Mills, Darnell, Joseph Gordon, with two

Probationers, (Robert Whitty and Stanislas
Flanagan) to join the Father Superior, F. F.
St John Dalgairns and Bowles   ibid

Dec 31   The Congregation begins to receive subjects
for membership with the contemplated
London House   63
In the course of this year the internal development of the Oratorian body has proceeded,
as during 1848, and so on to Jan. 16, 1854.
vid 208

1850

1850
Janry 13   St Wilfrid's being still on our hands, it is
St Wilfrid's   determined to place two Fathers there, one
a Mission   from Birmingham, one from the London
and a College   House, with the provision that each of the
other Fathers should be bound to reside
there as much as a month each year. Moreover, that in addition to the Mission, a
College should be established there, the age of
the youths received being for the present
undertermined. Fr Nicholas Darnell was
chosen to carry out this Decree with leave of
absence for a year (vid. 72) (and Fr Coffin
went as his companion from the London
House.)   64

Febr 2   Resolved that the Fathers in London shall
Fathers in   resign their their offices in the Congregation;
London   henceforth, to the end of the three years, the
Deputies are F. F. Penny, Bowles, Mills and
Gordon, and Fr St John Confessor. For the
Auditors one Father is taken from Birming-
ham, one from London.   67

Joint Tenancy   At the same time a Trust is made for our
Property, the Trustees (Joint Tenants) being
the Father, F. F. St John, Gordon and
Darnell.   ibid

Febr 8 Donation	A large donation made to the Congregation at Birmingham by Mr E. Caswall. 70
March 2	A debt of £800 for current and sacristy expenses shared equally between the two communities. 78
March 11 Edgbaston	Purchase of land for House and Church &c at Edgbaston. 80
April 20 May 22 Church at Edgbaston	Exchange of it for our present site. 89.94 Resolution to build a House and to collect money for a Church. 95
June 3	The London House so far separated from us as to be allowed to note down its own occurrences and appointments. 96
Octr 9 Foundation of London House	After raising all the London Fathers, down to Fr Philip Gordon to the rank and privileges of Decennials, we formally released them from their allegiance to the Birmingham House, in order to their forming a London Congregation of the Oratory, viz. F. F. Dalgairns, Coffin, Stanton, Faber, Hutchison, Knox, Wells, and Gordon; with the Probationers, John Bowden, Bagshaw and Rowe. 102
Giving up St Wilfrid's	And we formally made over to them St Wilfrid's, saving the private claims upon it of F. Austin Mills. ibid
Nov 11 House at Edgbaston	It was resolved to commence building our House at Edgbaston (which took place on the following Decr 13.) 105
Nov 18 Father John Cooke's death	Incidental notice here of Fr John Cook's death (which took place on the preceding Novr 12)
Dec 31 The Discipline	The question of the Discipline, deferred Febry 5. 1848 (5), was this day decided in favour of its immediate introduction. 114

1851

Janry 9
Donation

The year opens with another munificent donation to the Congregation from an Anonymous Benefactor.   115

30
Fr
William
Penny

Another event, at this time, of a grave nature, has reference to one of our seven foundation members, Fr Penny. It is the deliberate expression of our unanimous sentiment, that from his indifference to community life, and of his neglect of the great Oratorian principle "He who wishes to live in his own way is not good for the Congregation", he is unsuitable for us, in spite of his unusual gifts, his most exemplary correctness of moral deportment and high aspirations after Sanctity. It is considered that, having been made with the rest a decennial from the first, he has by this time only fulfilled the usual period of probation, which is so necessary to determine a vocation; and therefore there is nothing wonderful that a fact should have come out at the end of three years, which it would have been wrong to anticipate, on our first coming from Rome. On this being put before him, he requested permission to retire from the Congregation; and we "with real sorrow at the loss of so highly endowed a Father, yet from love of him, as well as from loyalty to St Philip, with the special advice of our Father whom the Sovereign Pontiff has by Brief charged with the establishment of the Oratory in England, accede to his request.   117

Marh. 17.18.
House at
Edgbaston

The expense of building our House turns out to be greater than we expected, and we look for the debt incurred being paid off gradually by the profits resulting from taking pupils or in some other way. The top story [sic] (back) is especially pointed out as suitable to this purpose. 126

April 14
Leeds

A prospect of an Oratory at Leeds is opened on us (in consequence of our having received into the Church the Anglican community there of St Saviour's) 133

The Editorship of the Lives of the Saints, (an undertaking of Fr Faber's previously to his joining our body,) and accepted by us after he had joined it (41) is now given back to him, the Houses being distinct. ibid

Septr 24
Achilli matter

(The Achilli proceedings having commenced) F. F. Darnell and Gordon are sent to Italy, to collect information in the Father's behalf, as also for the health of Fr Gordon. 147

1852

1852
April 1
Title Deeds

The current expenses of the Achilli matter being considerable, the Congregation allows the Father to deposit the title deeds of the Edgbaston ground with his Bankers, as security for a loan of £3000. 163

Ap. 26
Habit worn
out of doors

By an entry here, it is implied that we wore out of doors our cassock &c (This was left off shortly afterwards.)

Irish
University

Permission given to the Father to accept the appointment of President of the contemplated Catholic University of Ireland. 165

1853

1853
March 4
Fr Joseph
Gordon's death

Notice is incidentally made of Fr Joseph Gordon's death (on the preceeding Febry 13) 183

March 7

Alcester Street House and Chapel not yet off our hands, (though we had moved up to our new House on Low Sunday, 1852.) 186

April 18
Donation
Octr 23

Fr Bernard
Dalgairns

Fr. Bernard
Dalgairns

A large donation to the Father for the Oratory   189
The Father having, in consequence of the deaths of F. F. Cooke and Gordon, asked the London Fathers (who were still partially under him) to grant to our Congregation, Fr Bernard Dalgairns, one of its first Fathers and acting members, and at an earlier period the intimate friend and associate of himself and others in it (moved moreover to this request by Fr Dalgairns himself who had taken the initiative by privately suggesting it to him) they consented in a Letter in which they expressed their sense of the greatness of the favour, and the Congregation in consequence admits Fr Dalgairns to his original place and rank among its members, and, in gratitude to the London Fathers decrees that Michaelmas Day shall henceforth be kept as one of its Festivals, with high Mass and Vespers, and that each Father shall on that day say Mass for the spiritual and temporal welfare of the London House.   196

1854

1854
January 16
The last
curtailment of
the Decennium
August 22
The Father at
Dublin

Septr 25
Beginning of
the School

F. F. Bittleston and Caswall being created Decennial Fathers, by dispensation, it is decreed that they are the last Fathers whose full term of years is to be dispensed with   208
The Father is to have the power to name his representative in the Congregation (Rector) during his absence in Dublin (vid. 165.) up to next Feby 2, 1855. (This leave is renewed for an additional year Feby 2, 1855, vid. 237)   222
At this time certain boys are incidentally mentioned as being under our care in our house, (as in Alcester Street in 1851 vid. 133)   223

1855

June 2nd
Enlargement of
Church

Consequent enlargement of our Chapel into a Church, by raising the Nave 10 feet, adding an aisle, throwing the two small sacristies into the large Sacristy (in order to make it St Philip's chapel) and covering the adjacent court with glass and throwing into it the room beyond by way of providing a new Sacristy, (such as it remains at this date 1869.) [and still today 1968! Editor.]   293

1859

1859
March 14
The Rambler

The Father allowed to undertake the Rambler Magazine up to the ensuing Christmas, vid. Feb 11. 1848 (6)   301

1860

1860
Febry 2
F Robert
Tillotson

Formal acts of releasing Fr Robert Tillotson from his association with us, who, while on leave of absence in New York, had offered himself to a religious body there, and wrote to us to say that he had left this House for ever.   313

Ap 9 and May 14

Commendatore
April 9
Form of
accepting
property

Negotiations with the Commendatore at Naples (for the establishment of a trust for educating at our Oratory Italian youths)
A form appointed as the necessary condition and mode of the Congregation's accepting for itself donations of whatever sort.   317
[On the Commendatore see *L.D.* XVIII, p. 54.]

May 28
School
Buildings
Second
Enlargement of
Church

New buildings contemplated for the Oratory School, and a further enlargement of the Church (viz. the transept made in which is the Altar of the Sacred Heart, and the Sanctuary thrown back, and a new and larger apse made.)   321

1861
Feb 1
Elementary
Duties of a
Father
Feb 18
School
Buildings

(Difficulties having arisen as to the strictness of the tie binding our subjects to the Congregation) A special Decree drawn up on the subject.   332
Considering that the excess of expenditure in building our House had led to our raising loans from the Fathers, which, as involving the payment to them of interest has been set against their pensions and occasioned serious deficits in our annual Domus account, and considering that such expenditure was allowed in contemplation of our receiving boys as pupils in our upper (back) story [sic], who might repay us, (126) it was resolved to provide sleeping accomodations in our house for the boys of our new school, provided it can be done first without expense to the Congregation, second without sacrificing our own room, third without interfering with our own privacy, fourth "with the ulterior plan of building in front of the Church"(?)
                                           335

The School
formally
undertaken by
the Oratory

Also, at this time the Congregation takes upon itself the whole liabilities of the School (which till this time were upon Fr Nicholas Darnell, as those of the later Orphanage are now (A.D. 1869) on Fr Austin Mills) having had from London Mr Riley, the accountant, to ascertain them (in fulfilment of 330) taking the receipts and payments out of Fr. N. Darnell's hands and making Fr. Superior our cashier (or Treasurer 341(2))   ibid

April 1

Also (with the view of bringing the whole School under one roof) the Congregation takes a Lease of Fr Ambrose St John's adjacent houses (Nos 67, 68 Hagley Road) for seven years.   336

April 22 School Buildings	On the expectation that the profits of the School will allow it, it is proposed to build to the amount of £3.000, the Duchess of Norfolk's gift of £500 being available for our immediate interest of that sum, and obviating any infringement of the first condition laid down in 335. 337
May 6	Accordingly it is determined to fit up the upper back block of our house as a dormitory, and to build a School-room, play-room, and head-master's rooms. 339
Septr 1	Under a (false) idea that there was at this time a balance in the School account in our favour, of £118, we abstract this sum from the School purse. 341(2)

1862

1862 January 13 Fr Nicholas Darnell	F. Nicholas Darnell for special reasons allowed six months leave of absence from this day. 349
April 15 Fr Stanislas Flanagan	Fr Stanislas Flanagan allowed to be three months at our Mission House at Smethwick on the ground that at present community duties would as he conceives, be a most serious injury to his mind and body. . 353
July 18 Fr. N.D. released Fr Ambrose St John Prefect of School	Fr Nicholas Darnell, at the end of six months, repeating his application for release from the Congregation, it is granted, F. Ambrose St John taking his place in the School as the Father's representative vid 292. 354
July 21	Fr Stanislas Flanagan's leave of absence continued till Septr 29.
Aug 17 Fr S. F released	At the urgent request of Fr. Stanislas Flanagan (who would brook no delay) his release from the Congregation is granted to him. 357

Appendix 7.

EXTRACT FROM NEWMAN'S PRIVATE DIARY FOR 1853

The Private Diary, Commencing January 1853 contains a note on p. 110 on possible topics for Chapter Addresses, which must have occurred to Newman during that year. No trace remains in the Birmingham Oratory Archives of these Addresses, even supposing that Newman did in fact compose them. The note is included here for the light it throws on what Newman felt to be matters of concern for the community in 1853. The subject of the first is dealt with equivalently in *Or. P.* N°s 8, 22 and 23. The second is treated of in *Or. P.* N° 24, while the third is mentioned implicitly in *Or. P.* N° 33.

Chapters.[1]

on *internal* confidence in each other.
on not going from home.
on studying moral theology
on thinking oneself wrong at first sight
(and with what limitations)

---

[1] *B. Or. Ar., The Private Diaries.*

INDEX

GENERAL INDEX

32

Obedience, one of the three bonds of community, 109 n.14; Newman's distinction between 'voluntary' and 'vowed', 113–4; the backbone of community life, 113; idea of total obedience in St Philip, 114; relative merits of vowed and unvowed obedience according to Newman, 115; religious obedience produces a different ethos to that achieved by the Oratory, 115; Newman exacts the full measure of, without basing it on a vow, 116; Newman wishes obedience to be the immediate result of charity, 116

O Faolain, Seán, 101

Old Catholics as recruits for the Oratory, 71

Oratory in England, rapid initial growth, 6; ethos of, differences between Newman and Faber, 7; Newman had worked out the idea of before Faber had even donned the Oratorian cassock, 7; process of Newman's choice of, provides an insight into his whole idea of priestly spirituality, 9; that candidates for should have had the education of a gentleman before entering, was a constant principle with Newman, 10; as a means of Christian perfection for its own members, 10; Newman's moulding of, a true development of the existing Oratorian tradition, 10; resembles an Oxford College, 23; Old Catholics and Irish recruits for, 71; Newman deprecates any assumption of a superiority complex by members of,

INDEX TO THE ORATORY PAPERS

NOTE

The purpose of this separate Index to the Oratory Papers is to facilitate reference to Newman's own words on the main points of Oratorian spirituality.
For the identification of the persons mentioned in the Papers (St Philip's own circle, as also the list of Oratorian writers from the sixteenth to the nineteenth century, and Newman's own contemporaries), recourse has been had to Trevor, *Apostle of Rome* (and occasionally to Bacci as translated by F.I. Antrobus), to Marchese di Villarosa, *Memorie* (see above, p. 197 n.5), and finally to the Indexes in vols. XI–XVIII of *The Letters and Diaries*.
I am indebted to Miss N. Bergin for considerable help in preparing this Index for the press.

Breinigsville, PA USA
29 December 2010
252387BV00004B/56/P